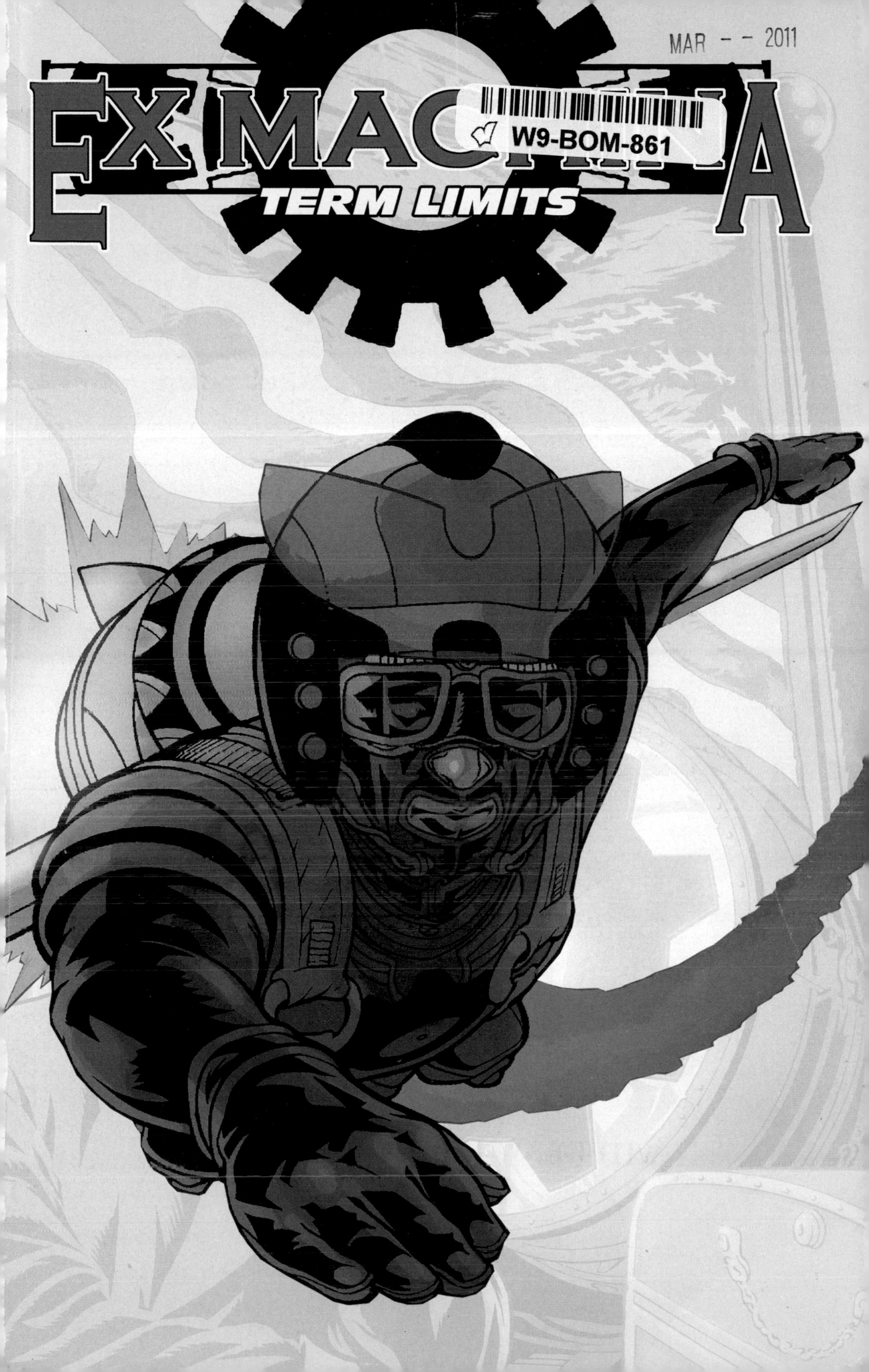
TERM LIMITS

CREDITS

BRIAN K. VAUGHAN: WRITER
TONY HARRIS: ARTIST
JD METTLER: COLORS
JARED K. FLETCHER: LETTERS

Ex Machina created by Vaughan and Harris
Collected Edition Cover by Harris and Mettler
Original Series Covers by Harris

Ben Abernathy	Editor, Original Series
Kristy Quinn	Assistant Editor, Original Series
Kristy Quinn	Editor
Larry Berry	Art Director
Trisha Allex	Designer
Diane Nelson	President
Dan DiDio and Jim Lee	Co-Publishers
Geoff Johns	Chief Creative Officer
John Rood	Executive Vice President–Sales, Marketing and Business Development
Patrick Caldon	Executive Vice President–Finance and Administration
Amy Genkins	Senior VP–Business and Legal Affairs
Steve Rotterdam	Senior VP–Sales and Marketing
John Cunningham	VP–Marketing
Terri Cunningham	VP–Managing Editor
Alison Gill	VP–Manufacturing
David Hyde	VP–Publicity
Hank Kanalz	VP–General Manager, WildStorm
Sue Pohja	VP–Book Trade Sales
Alysse Soll	VP–Advertising and Custom Publishing
Bob Wayne	VP–Sales
Mark Chiarello	Art Director

EX MACHINA: TERM LIMITS. Published by WildStorm Productions, an imprint of DC Comics. 888 Prospect St. #240, La Jolla, CA 92037. Cover and compilation Copyright © 2011 Brian K. Vaughan and Tony Harris. All Rights Reserved. EX MACHINA is ™ Brian K. Vaughan and Tony Harris. Originally published in single magazine form as EX MACHINA #45-50 © 2009-2010 Brian K. Vaughan and Tony Harris.

WildStorm and logo are trademarks of DC Comics. The stories, characters, and incidents mentioned in this magazine are entirely fictional. Printed on recyclable paper. WildStorm does not read or accept unsolicited submissions of ideas, stories or artwork. Printed in the United States.

DC Comics, a Warner Bros. Entertainment Company.

ISBN: 978-1-4012-2836-1

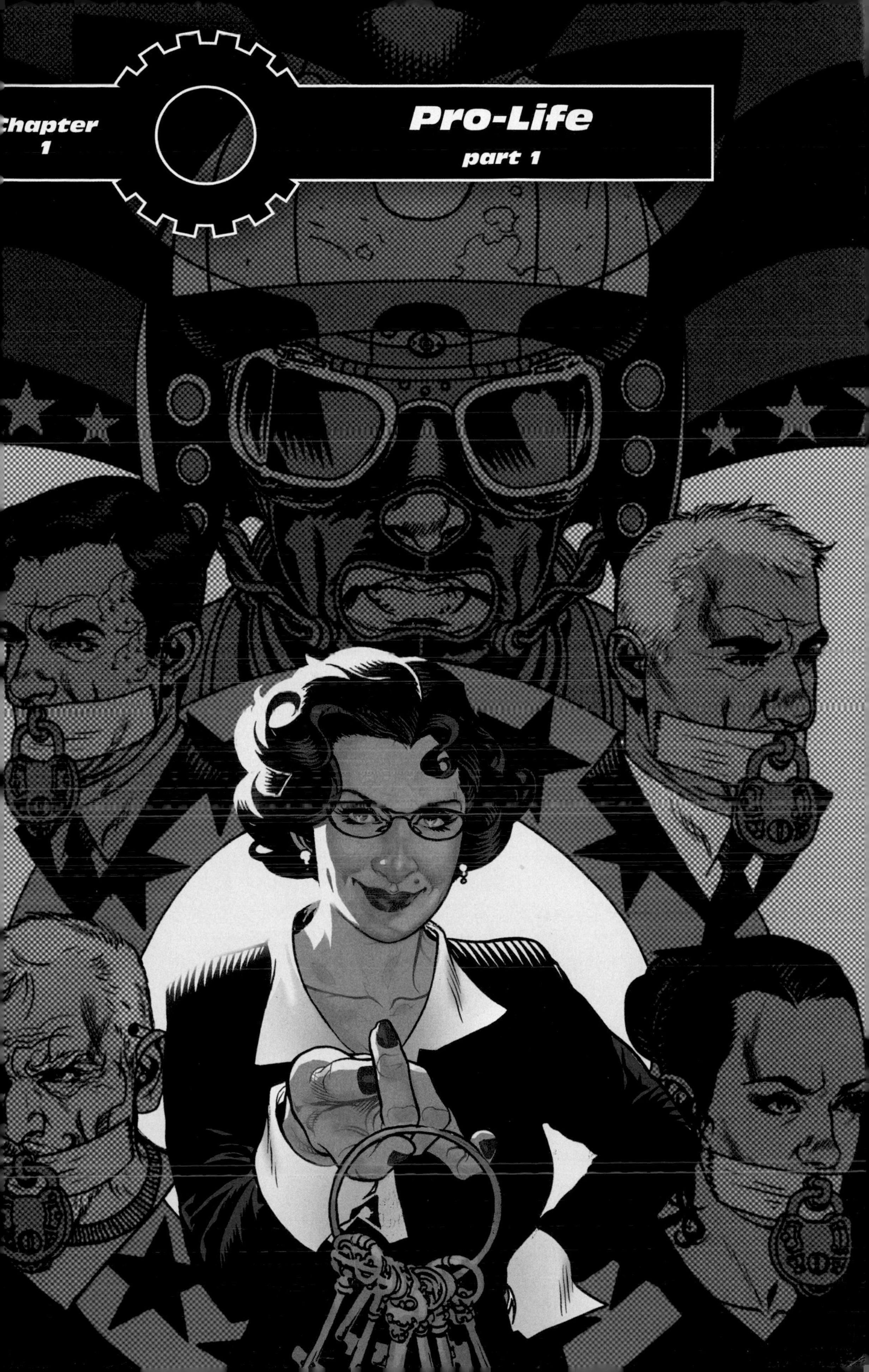
Chapter 1
Pro-Life
part 1

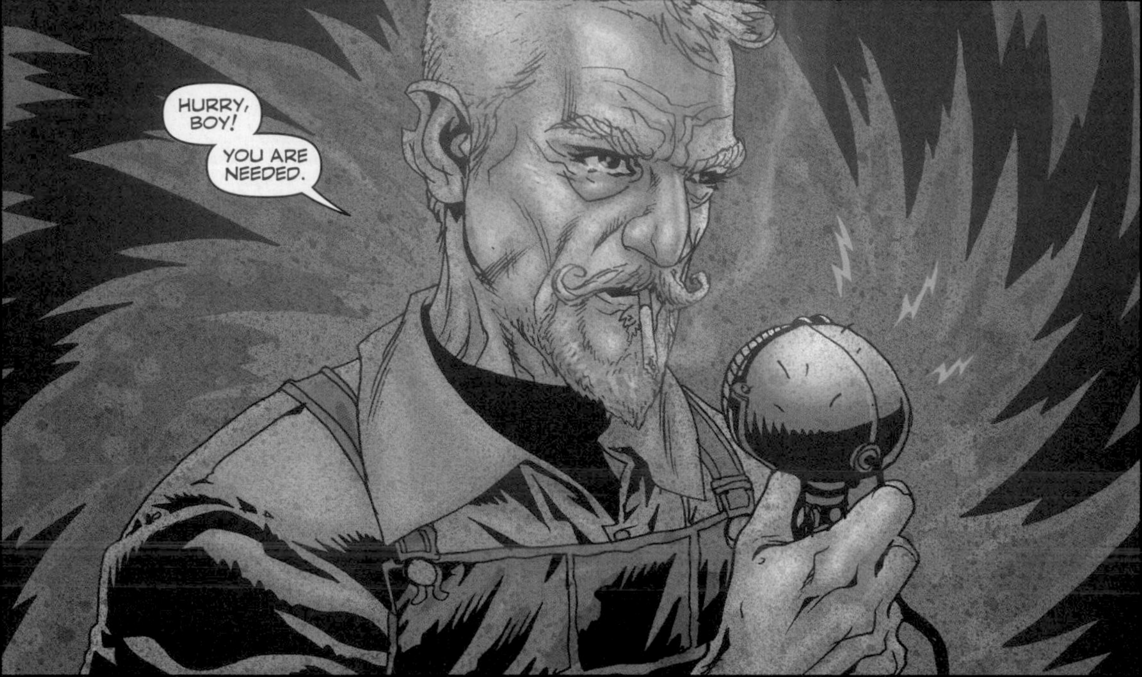
HURRY, BOY!
YOU ARE NEEDED.

TUESDAY, DECEMBER 5, 2000

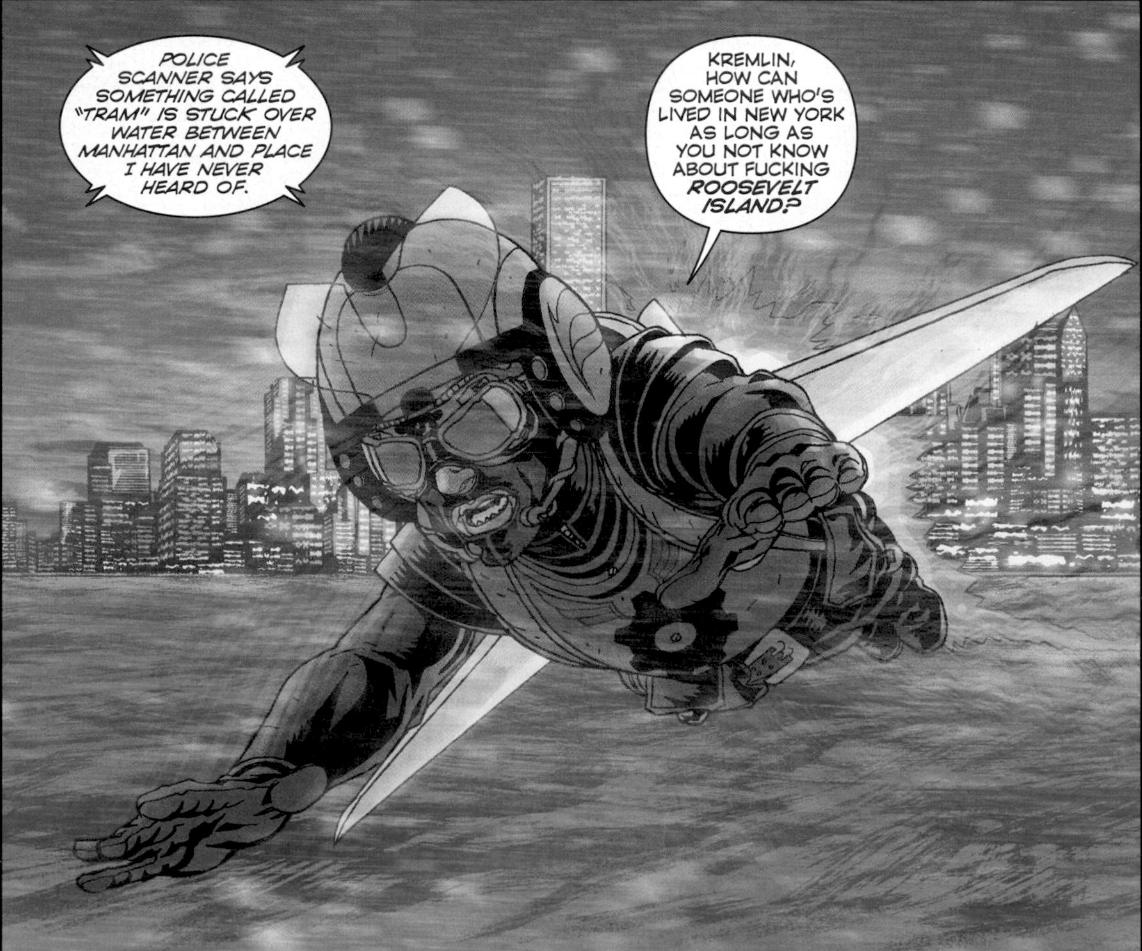
POLICE SCANNER SAYS SOMETHING CALLED "TRAM" IS STUCK OVER WATER BETWEEN MANHATTAN AND PLACE I HAVE NEVER HEARD OF.
KREMLIN, HOW CAN SOMEONE WHO'S LIVED IN NEW YORK AS LONG AS YOU NOT KNOW ABOUT FUCKING ROOSEVELT ISLAND?

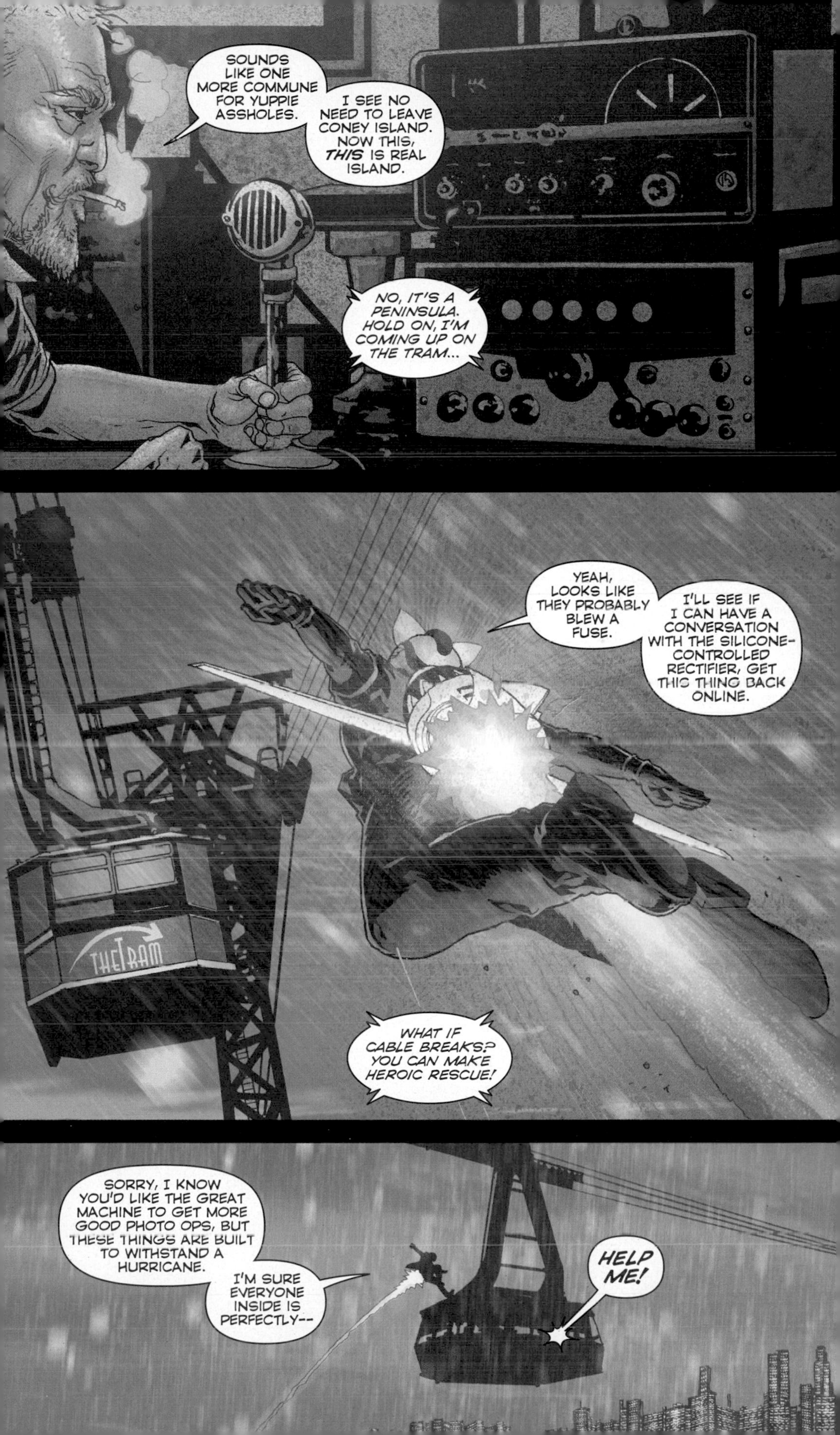
SOUNDS LIKE ONE MORE COMMUNE FOR YUPPIE ASSHOLES.
I SEE NO NEED TO LEAVE CONEY ISLAND. NOW THIS, *THIS* IS REAL ISLAND.
NO, IT'S A PENINSULA. HOLD ON, I'M COMING UP ON THE TRAM...
YEAH, LOOKS LIKE THEY PROBABLY BLEW A FUSE.
I'LL SEE IF I CAN HAVE A CONVERSATION WITH THE SILICONE-CONTROLLED RECTIFIER, GET THIS THING BACK ONLINE.
THE TRAM
WHAT IF CABLE BREAKS? YOU CAN MAKE HEROIC RESCUE!
SORRY, I KNOW YOU'D LIKE THE GREAT MACHINE TO GET MORE GOOD PHOTO OPS, BUT THESE THINGS ARE BUILT TO WITHSTAND A HURRICANE.
I'M SURE EVERYONE INSIDE IS PERFECTLY--
HELP ME!

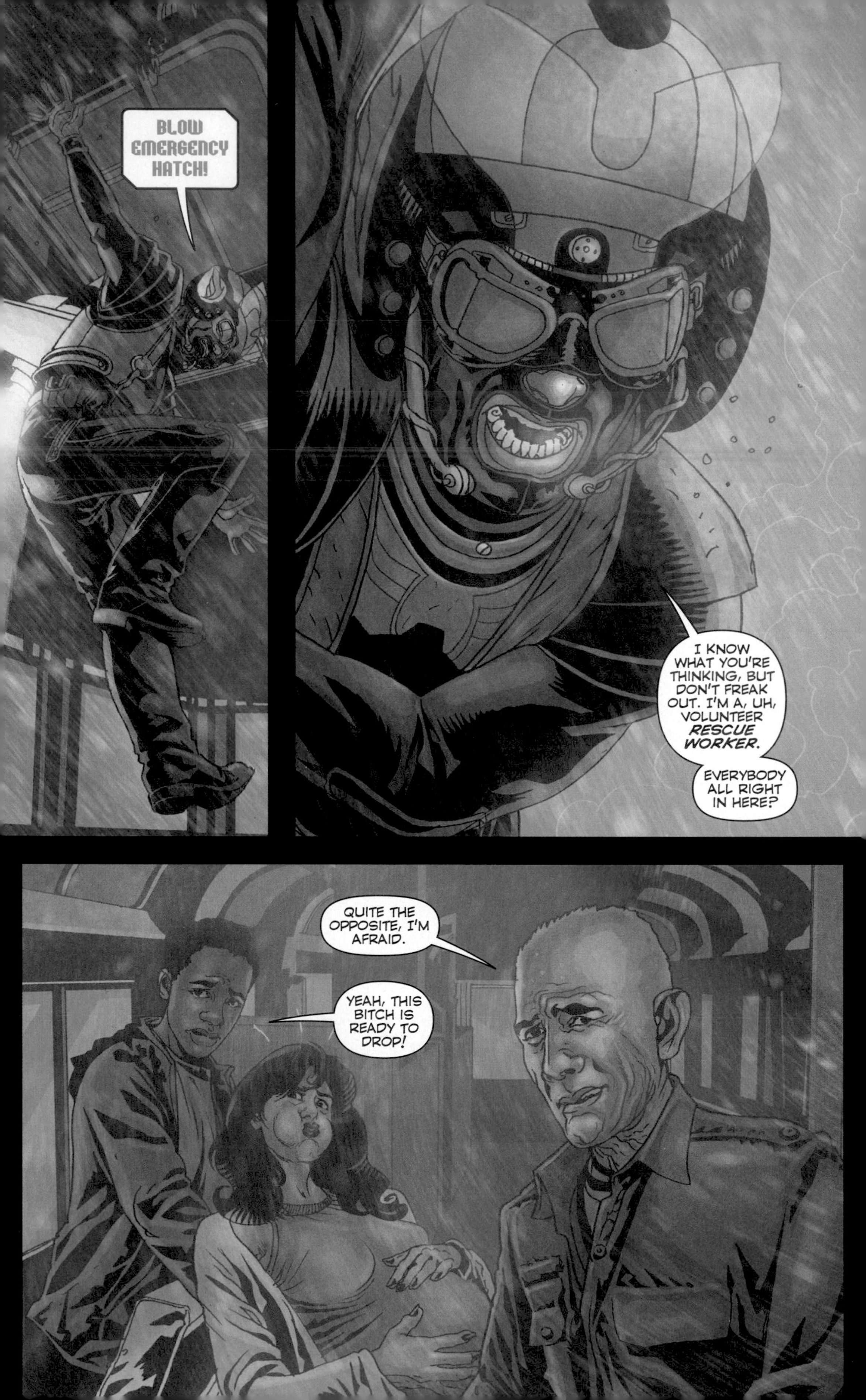

BLOW EMERGENCY HATCH!
I KNOW WHAT YOU'RE THINKING, BUT DON'T FREAK OUT. I'M A, UH, VOLUNTEER *RESCUE WORKER.*
EVERYBODY ALL RIGHT IN HERE?
QUITE THE OPPOSITE, I'M AFRAID.
YEAH, THIS BITCH IS READY TO *DROP!*

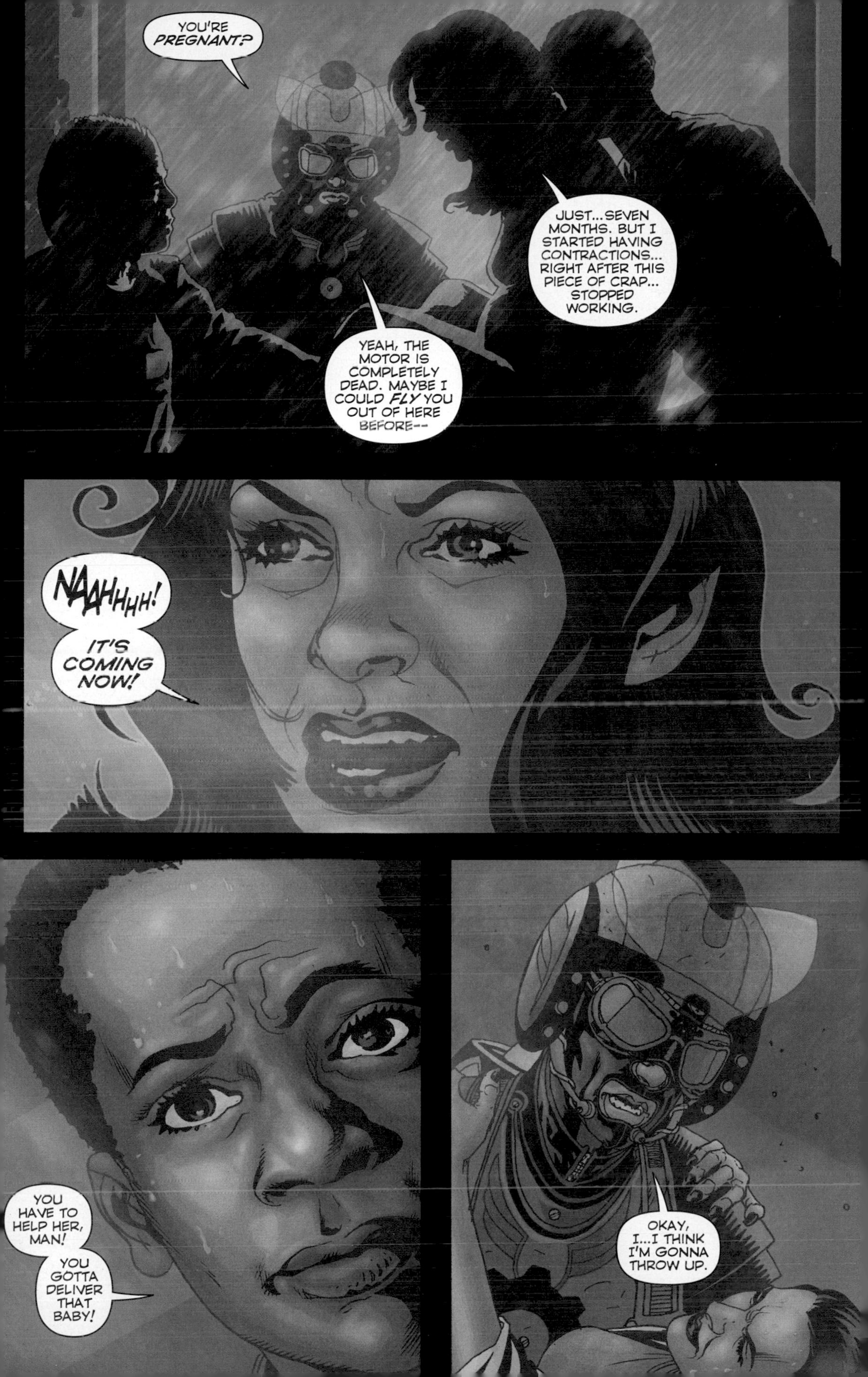
YOU'RE PREGNANT?
JUST...SEVEN MONTHS. BUT I STARTED HAVING CONTRACTIONS... RIGHT AFTER THIS PIECE OF CRAP... STOPPED WORKING.
YEAH, THE MOTOR IS COMPLETELY DEAD. MAYBE I COULD FLY YOU OUT OF HERE BEFORE--
NAAHHHH!
IT'S COMING NOW!
YOU HAVE TO HELP HER, MAN!
YOU GOTTA DELIVER THAT BABY!
OKAY, I...I THINK I'M GONNA THROW UP.

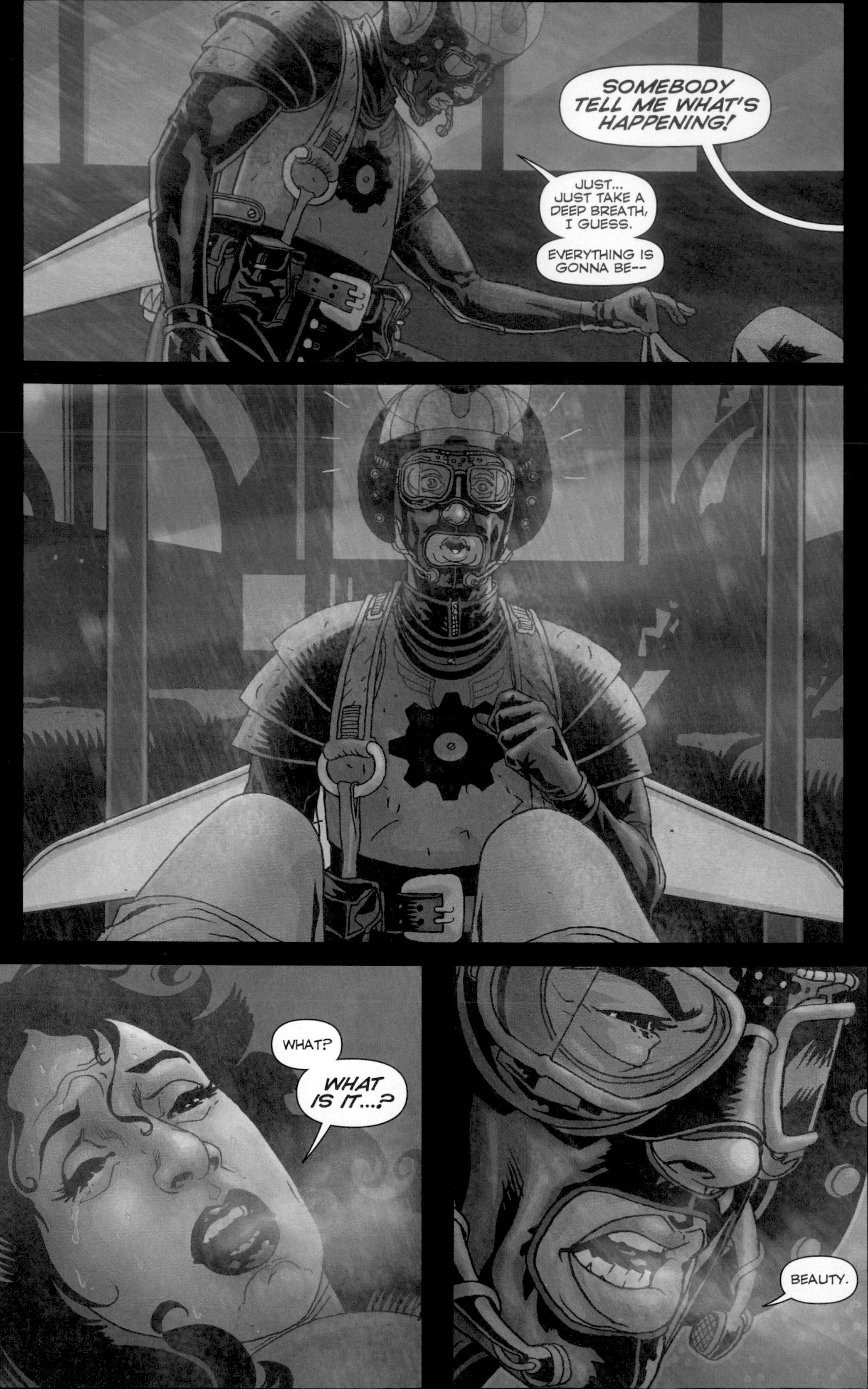
SOMEBODY TELL ME WHAT'S HAPPENING!
JUST... JUST TAKE A DEEP BREATH, I GUESS.
EVERYTHING IS GONNA BE--
WHAT?
WHAT IS IT...?
BEAUTY.

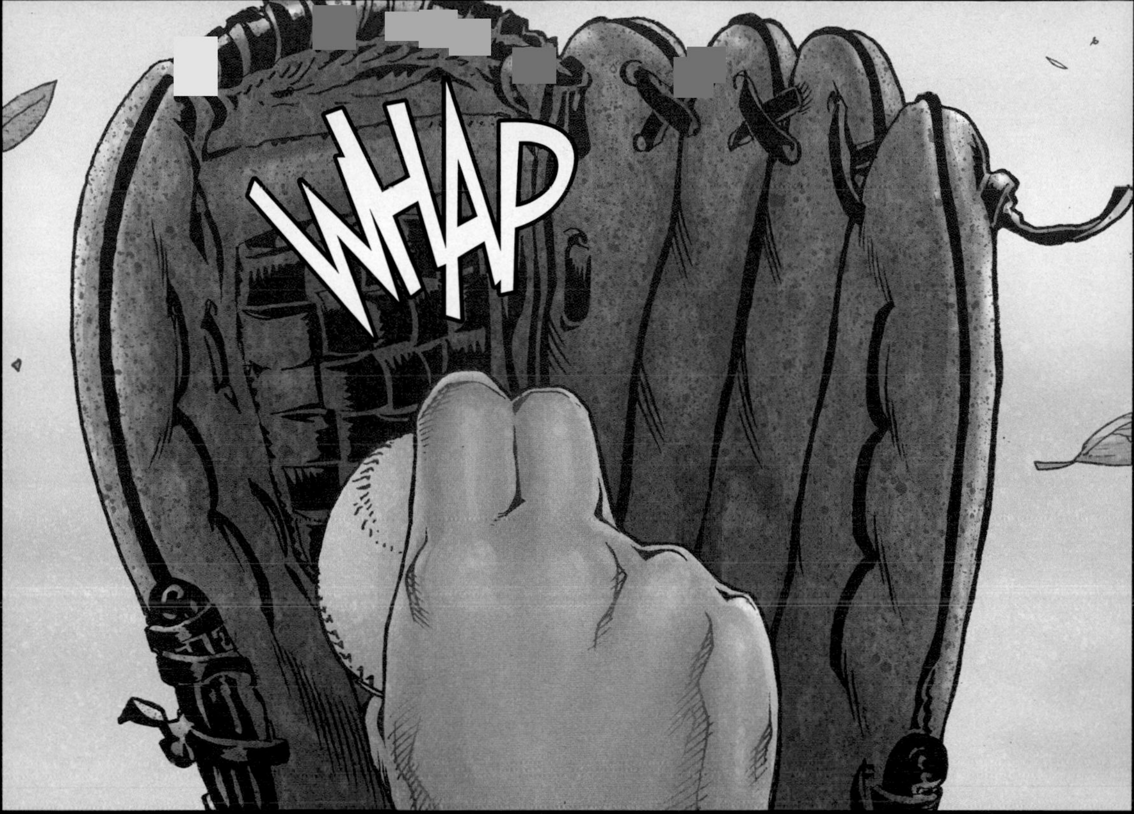
WHAP

SATURDAY, APRIL 2, 2005

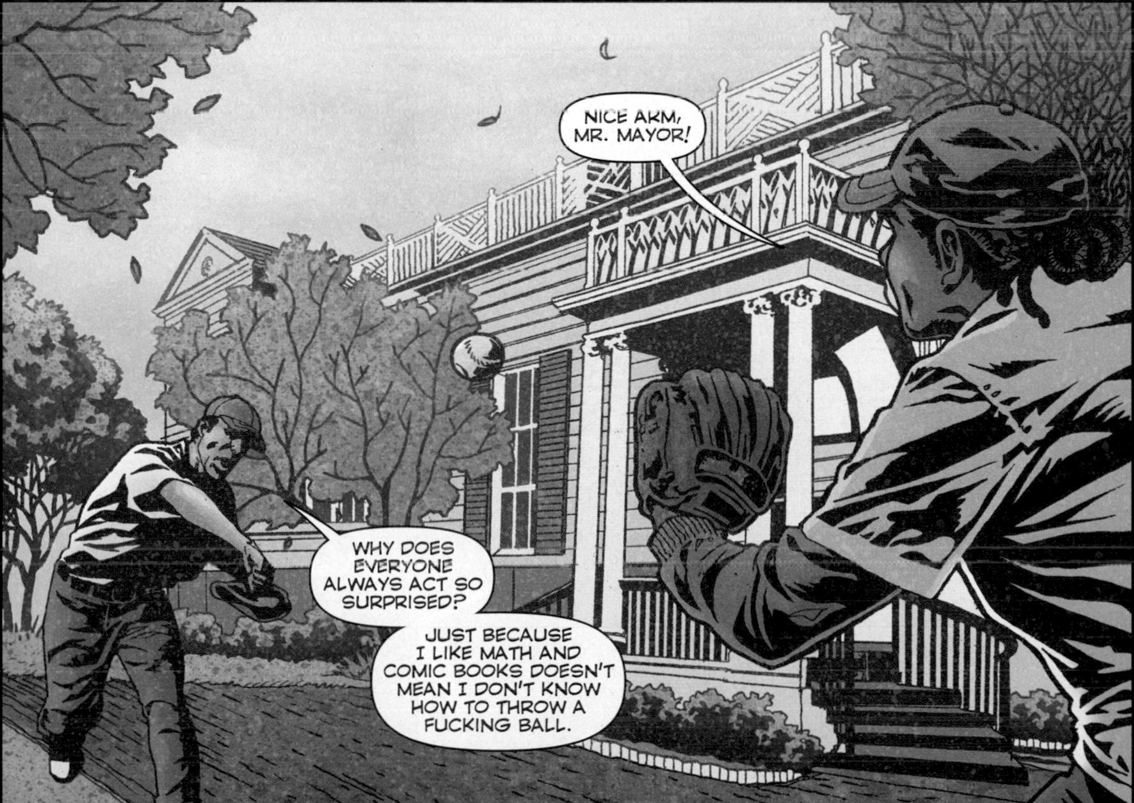
NICE ARM, MR. MAYOR!
WHY DOES EVERYONE ALWAYS ACT SO SURPRISED?
JUST BECAUSE I LIKE MATH AND COMIC BOOKS DOESN'T MEAN I DON'T KNOW HOW TO THROW A FUCKING BALL.

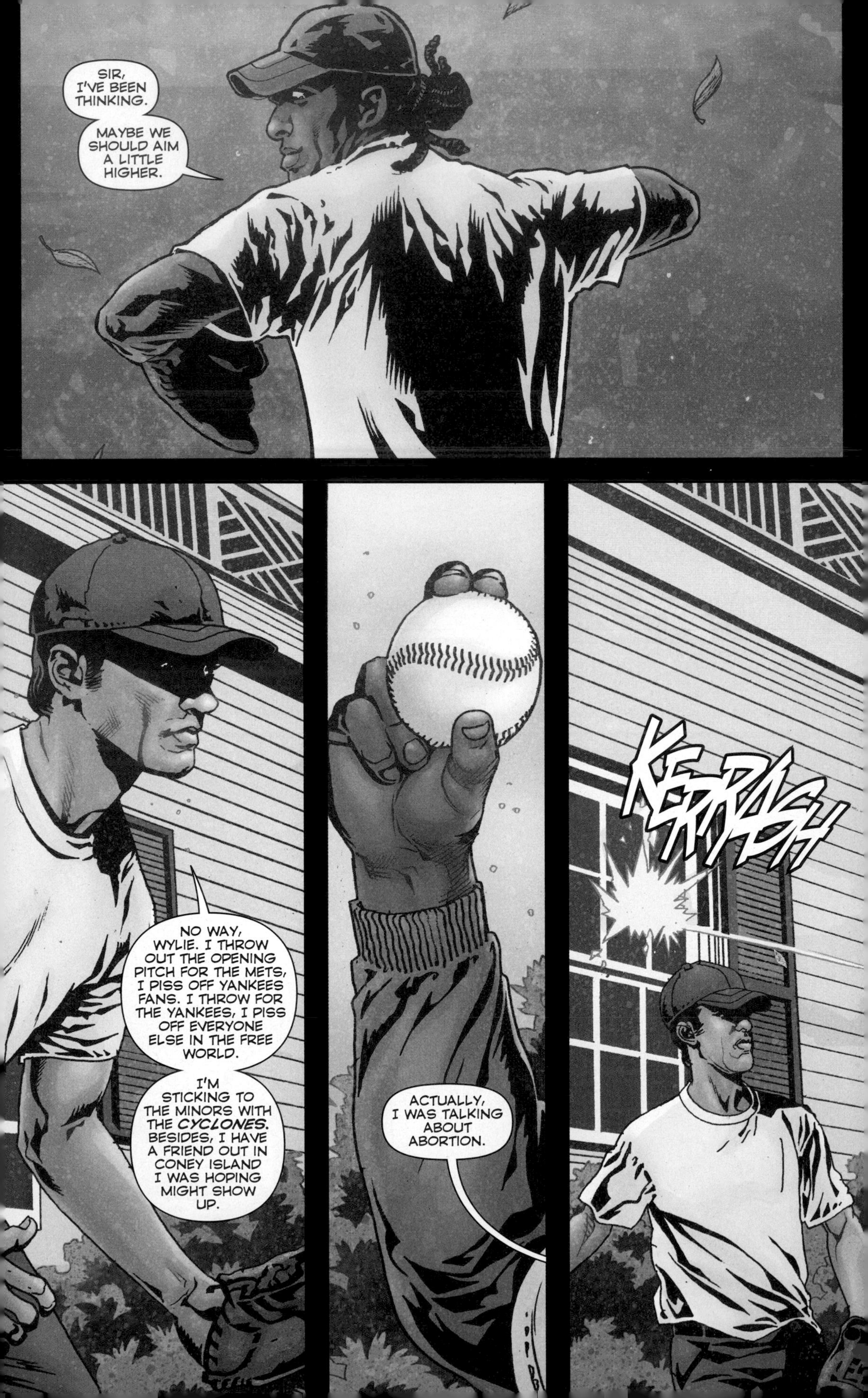
SIR, I'VE BEEN THINKING.
MAYBE WE SHOULD AIM A LITTLE HIGHER.
NO WAY, WYLIE. I THROW OUT THE OPENING PITCH FOR THE METS, I PISS OFF YANKEES FANS. I THROW FOR THE YANKEES, I PISS OFF EVERYONE ELSE IN THE FREE WORLD.
I'M STICKING TO THE MINORS WITH THE *CYCLONES*. BESIDES, I HAVE A FRIEND OUT IN CONEY ISLAND I WAS HOPING MIGHT SHOW UP.
ACTUALLY, I WAS TALKING ABOUT ABORTION.
KERRASH

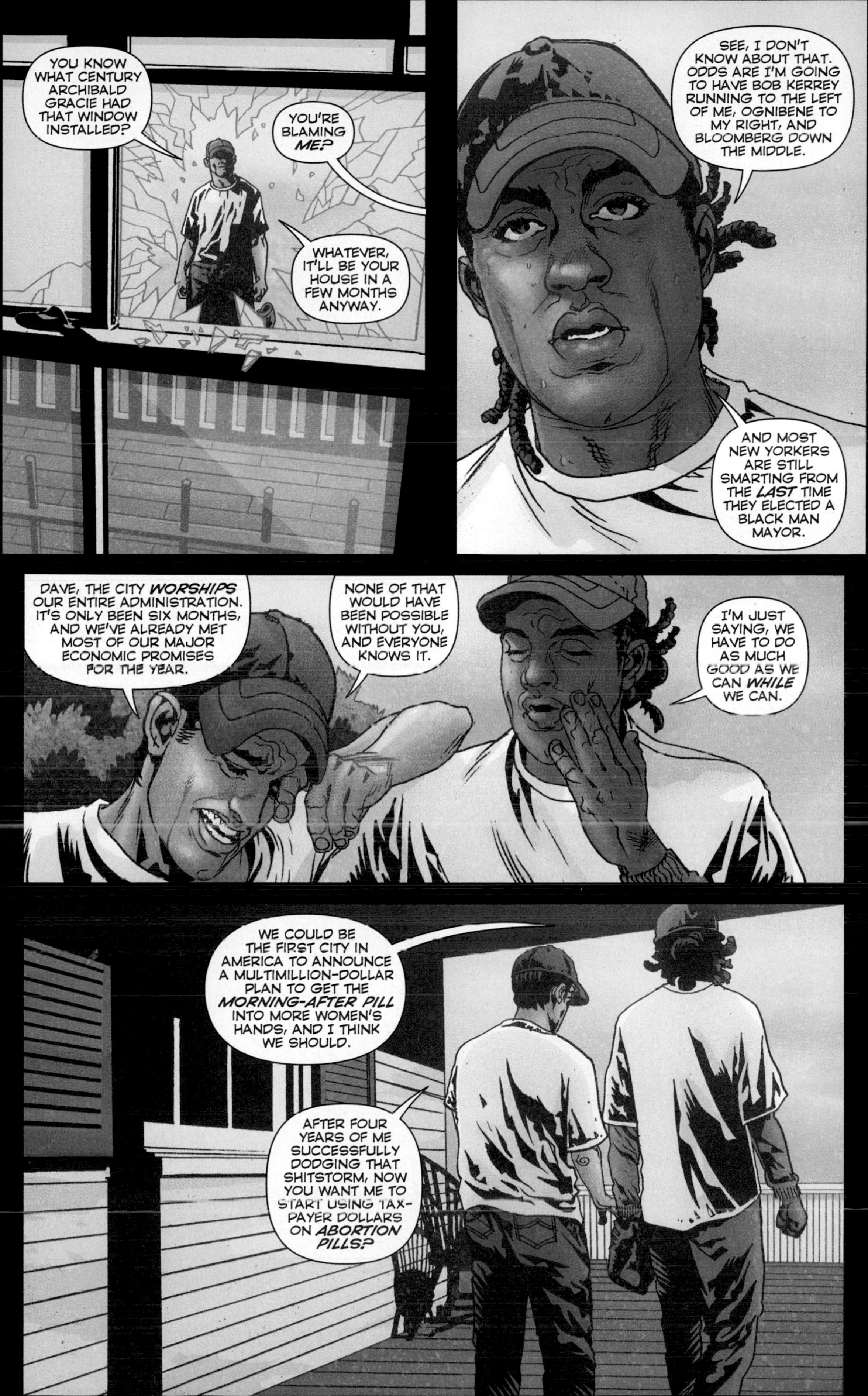
YOU KNOW WHAT CENTURY ARCHIBALD GRACIE HAD THAT WINDOW INSTALLED?
YOU'RE BLAMING *ME?*
WHATEVER, IT'LL BE YOUR HOUSE IN A FEW MONTHS ANYWAY.
SEE, I DON'T KNOW ABOUT THAT. ODDS ARE I'M GOING TO HAVE BOB KERREY RUNNING TO THE LEFT OF ME, OGNIBENE TO MY RIGHT, AND BLOOMBERG DOWN THE MIDDLE.
AND MOST NEW YORKERS ARE STILL SMARTING FROM THE *LAST* TIME THEY ELECTED A BLACK MAN MAYOR.
DAVE, THE CITY *WORSHIPS* OUR ENTIRE ADMINISTRATION. IT'S ONLY BEEN SIX MONTHS, AND WE'VE ALREADY MET MOST OF OUR MAJOR ECONOMIC PROMISES FOR THE YEAR.
NONE OF THAT WOULD HAVE BEEN POSSIBLE WITHOUT YOU, AND EVERYONE KNOWS IT.
I'M JUST SAYING, WE HAVE TO DO AS MUCH GOOD AS WE CAN *WHILE* WE CAN.
WE COULD BE THE FIRST CITY IN AMERICA TO ANNOUNCE A MULTIMILLION-DOLLAR PLAN TO GET THE *MORNING-AFTER PILL* INTO MORE WOMEN'S HANDS, AND I THINK WE SHOULD.
AFTER FOUR YEARS OF ME SUCCESSFULLY DODGING THAT SHITSTORM, NOW YOU WANT ME TO START USING TAX-PAYER DOLLARS ON *ABORTION PILLS?*

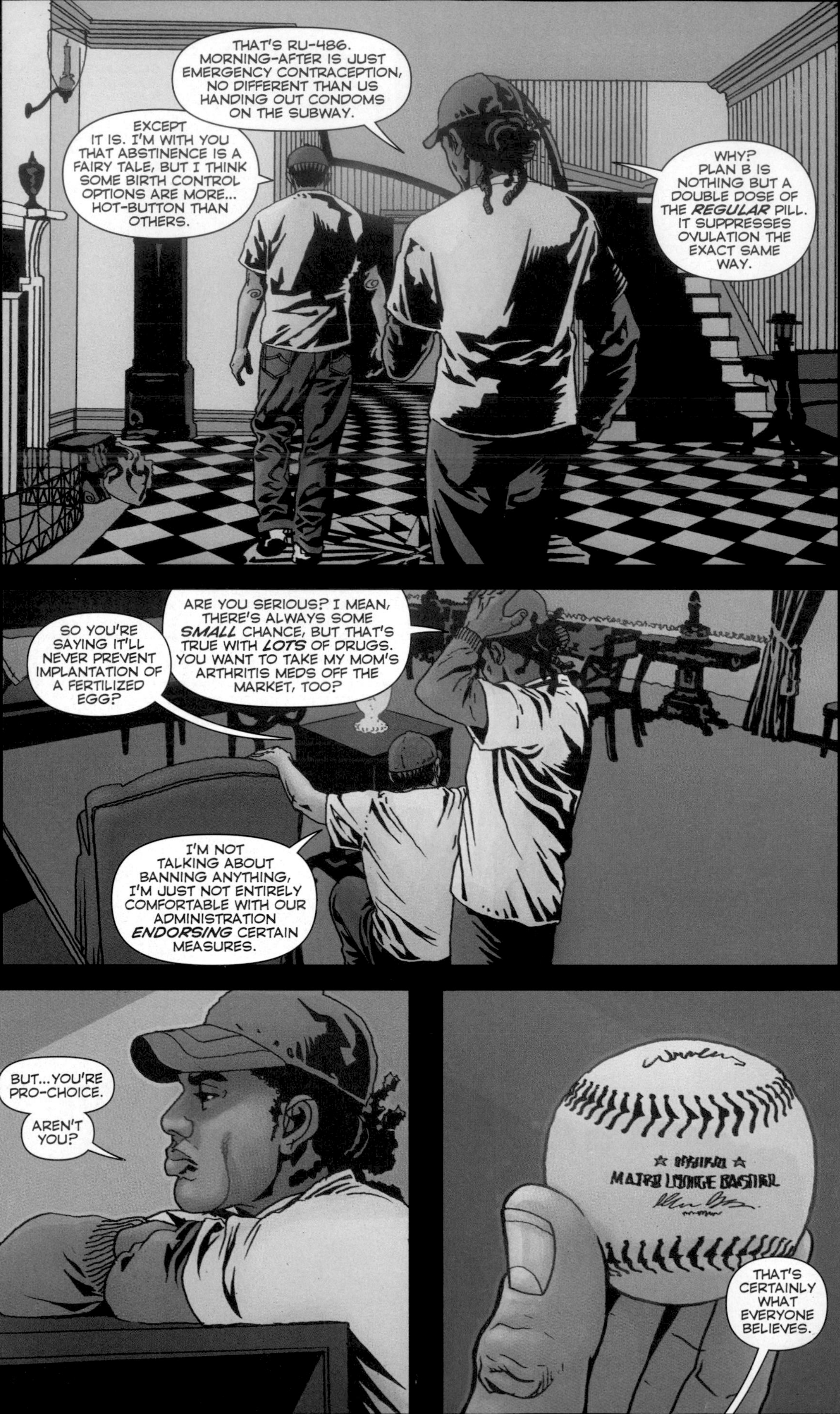

THAT'S RU-486. MORNING-AFTER IS JUST EMERGENCY CONTRACEPTION, NO DIFFERENT THAN US HANDING OUT CONDOMS ON THE SUBWAY.
EXCEPT IT IS. I'M WITH YOU THAT ABSTINENCE IS A FAIRY TALE, BUT I THINK SOME BIRTH CONTROL OPTIONS ARE MORE... HOT-BUTTON THAN OTHERS.
WHY? PLAN B IS NOTHING BUT A DOUBLE DOSE OF THE *REGULAR* PILL. IT SUPPRESSES OVULATION THE EXACT SAME WAY.
SO YOU'RE SAYING IT'LL NEVER PREVENT IMPLANTATION OF A FERTILIZED EGG?
ARE YOU SERIOUS? I MEAN, THERE'S ALWAYS SOME *SMALL* CHANCE, BUT THAT'S TRUE WITH *LOTS* OF DRUGS. YOU WANT TO TAKE MY MOM'S ARTHRITIS MEDS OFF THE MARKET, TOO?
I'M NOT TALKING ABOUT BANNING ANYTHING, I'M JUST NOT ENTIRELY COMFORTABLE WITH OUR ADMINISTRATION *ENDORSING* CERTAIN MEASURES.
BUT... YOU'RE PRO-CHOICE.
AREN'T YOU?
THAT'S CERTAINLY WHAT EVERYONE BELIEVES.

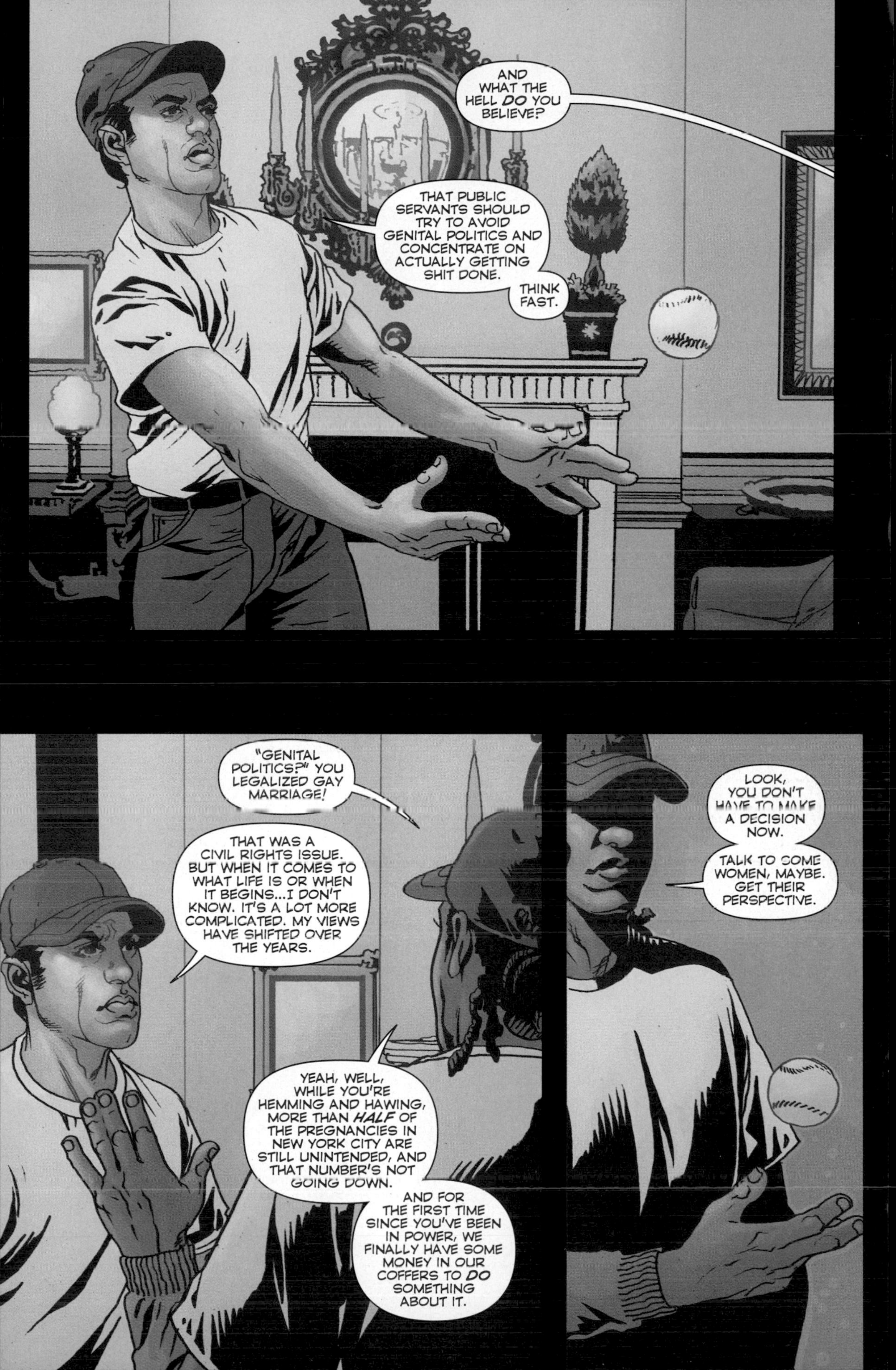
AND WHAT THE HELL DO YOU BELIEVE?
THAT PUBLIC SERVANTS SHOULD TRY TO AVOID GENITAL POLITICS AND CONCENTRATE ON ACTUALLY GETTING SHIT DONE.
THINK FAST.
"GENITAL POLITICS?" YOU LEGALIZED GAY MARRIAGE!
THAT WAS A CIVIL RIGHTS ISSUE. BUT WHEN IT COMES TO WHAT LIFE IS OR WHEN IT BEGINS...I DON'T KNOW. IT'S A LOT MORE COMPLICATED. MY VIEWS HAVE SHIFTED OVER THE YEARS.
YEAH, WELL, WHILE YOU'RE HEMMING AND HAWING, MORE THAN HALF OF THE PREGNANCIES IN NEW YORK CITY ARE STILL UNINTENDED, AND THAT NUMBER'S NOT GOING DOWN.
AND FOR THE FIRST TIME SINCE YOU'VE BEEN IN POWER, WE FINALLY HAVE SOME MONEY IN OUR COFFERS TO DO SOMETHING ABOUT IT.
LOOK, YOU DON'T HAVE TO MAKE A DECISION NOW.
TALK TO SOME WOMEN, MAYBE. GET THEIR PERSPECTIVE.

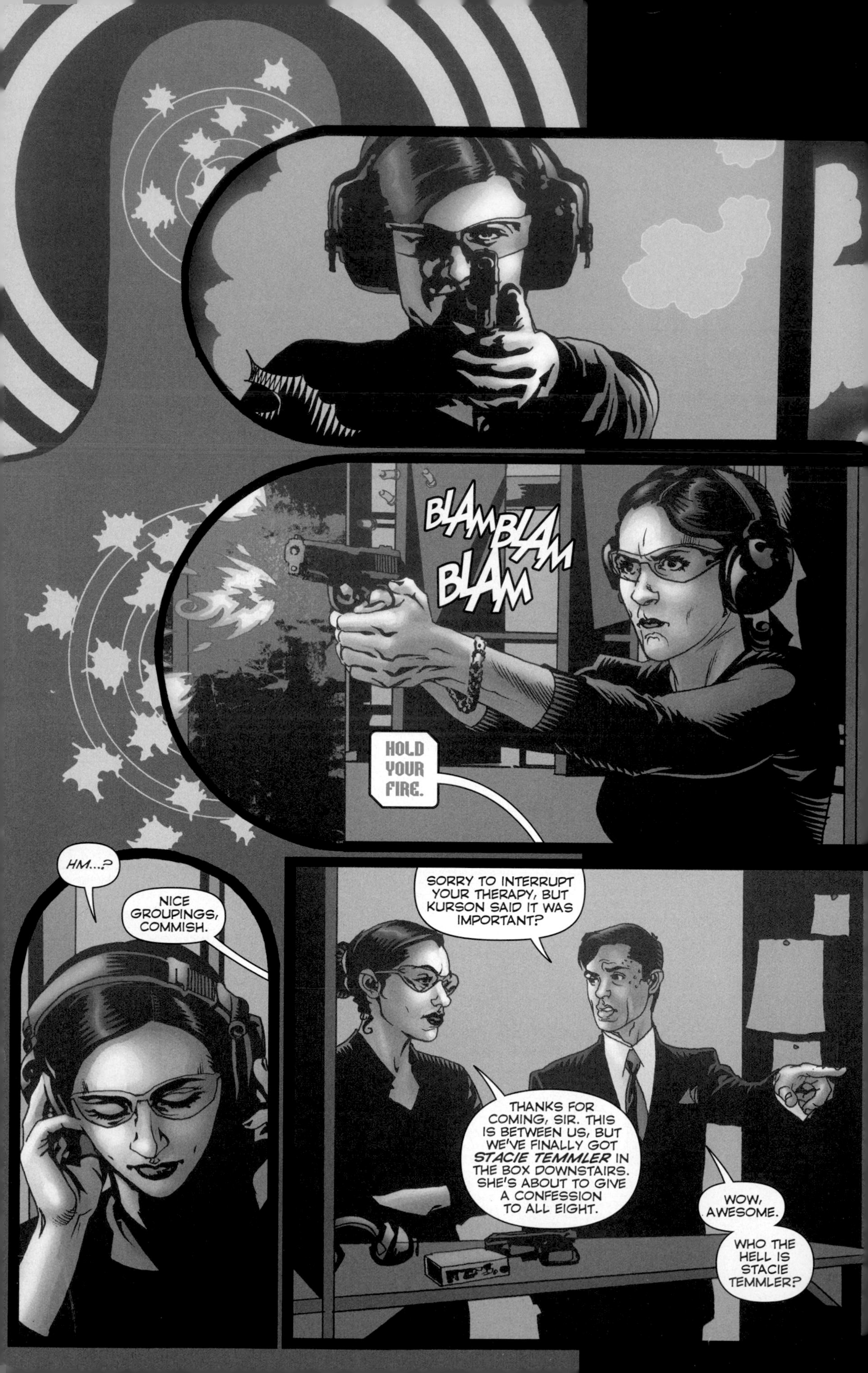
BLAM BLAM
BLAM
HOLD YOUR FIRE.
HM...?
NICE GROUPINGS, COMMISH.
SORRY TO INTERRUPT YOUR THERAPY, BUT KURSON SAID IT WAS IMPORTANT?
THANKS FOR COMING, SIR. THIS IS BETWEEN US, BUT WE'VE FINALLY GOT STACIE TEMMLER IN THE BOX DOWNSTAIRS. SHE'S ABOUT TO GIVE A CONFESSION TO ALL EIGHT.
WOW, AWESOME.
WHO THE HELL IS STACIE TEMMLER?

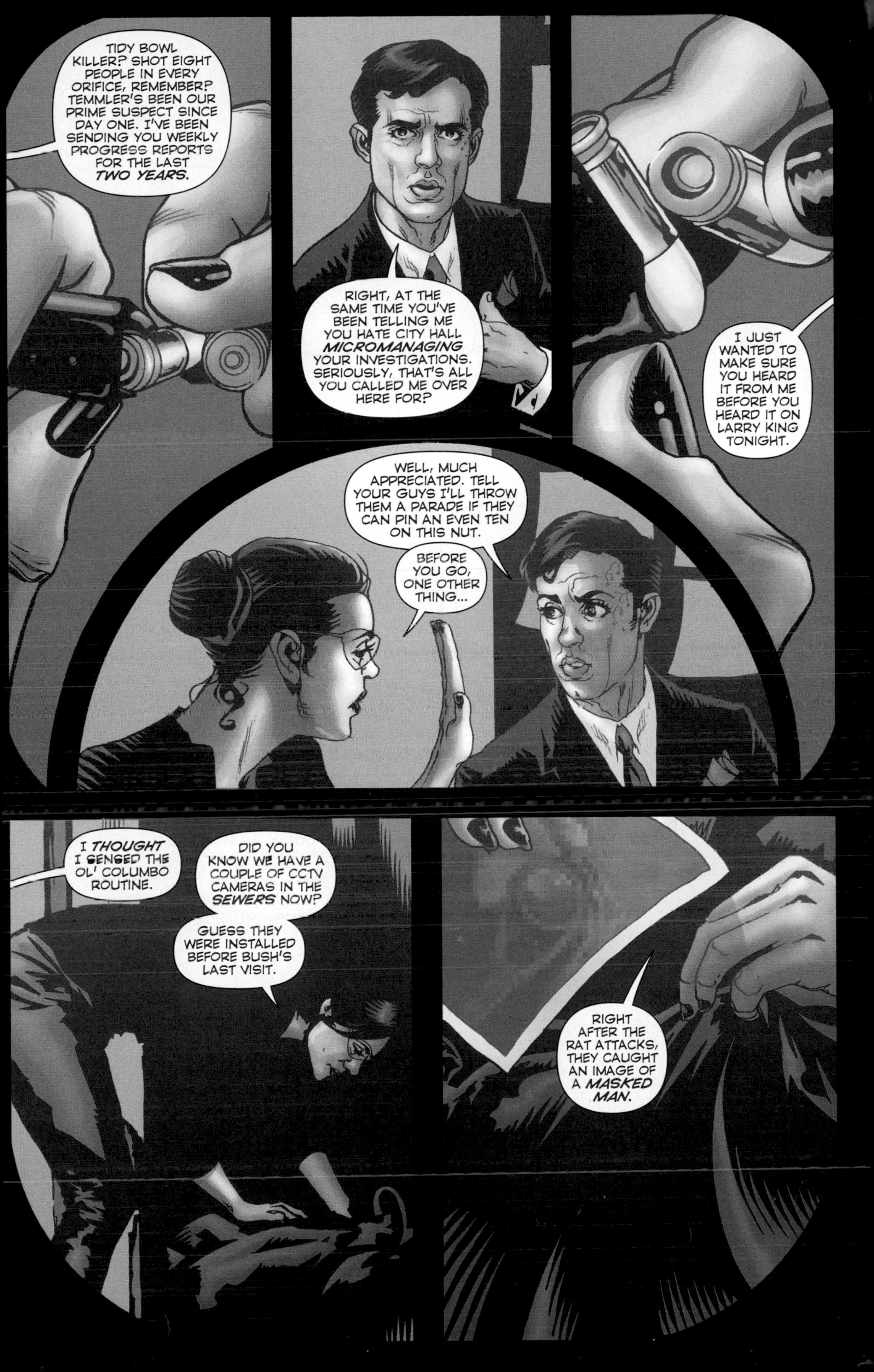
TIDY BOWL KILLER? SHOT EIGHT PEOPLE IN EVERY ORIFICE, REMEMBER? TEMMLER'S BEEN OUR PRIME SUSPECT SINCE DAY ONE. I'VE BEEN SENDING YOU WEEKLY PROGRESS REPORTS FOR THE LAST *TWO YEARS*.
RIGHT, AT THE SAME TIME YOU'VE BEEN TELLING ME YOU HATE CITY HALL *MICROMANAGING* YOUR INVESTIGATIONS. SERIOUSLY, THAT'S ALL YOU CALLED ME OVER HERE FOR?
I JUST WANTED TO MAKE SURE YOU HEARD IT FROM ME BEFORE YOU HEARD IT ON LARRY KING TONIGHT.
WELL, MUCH APPRECIATED. TELL YOUR GUYS I'LL THROW THEM A PARADE IF THEY CAN PIN AN EVEN TEN ON THIS NUT.
BEFORE YOU GO, ONE OTHER THING...
I *THOUGHT* I SENSED THE OL' COLUMBO ROUTINE.
DID YOU KNOW WE HAVE A COUPLE OF CCTV CAMERAS IN THE *SEWERS* NOW?
GUESS THEY WERE INSTALLED BEFORE BUSH'S LAST VISIT.
RIGHT AFTER THE RAT ATTACKS, THEY CAUGHT AN IMAGE OF A *MASKED MAN*.

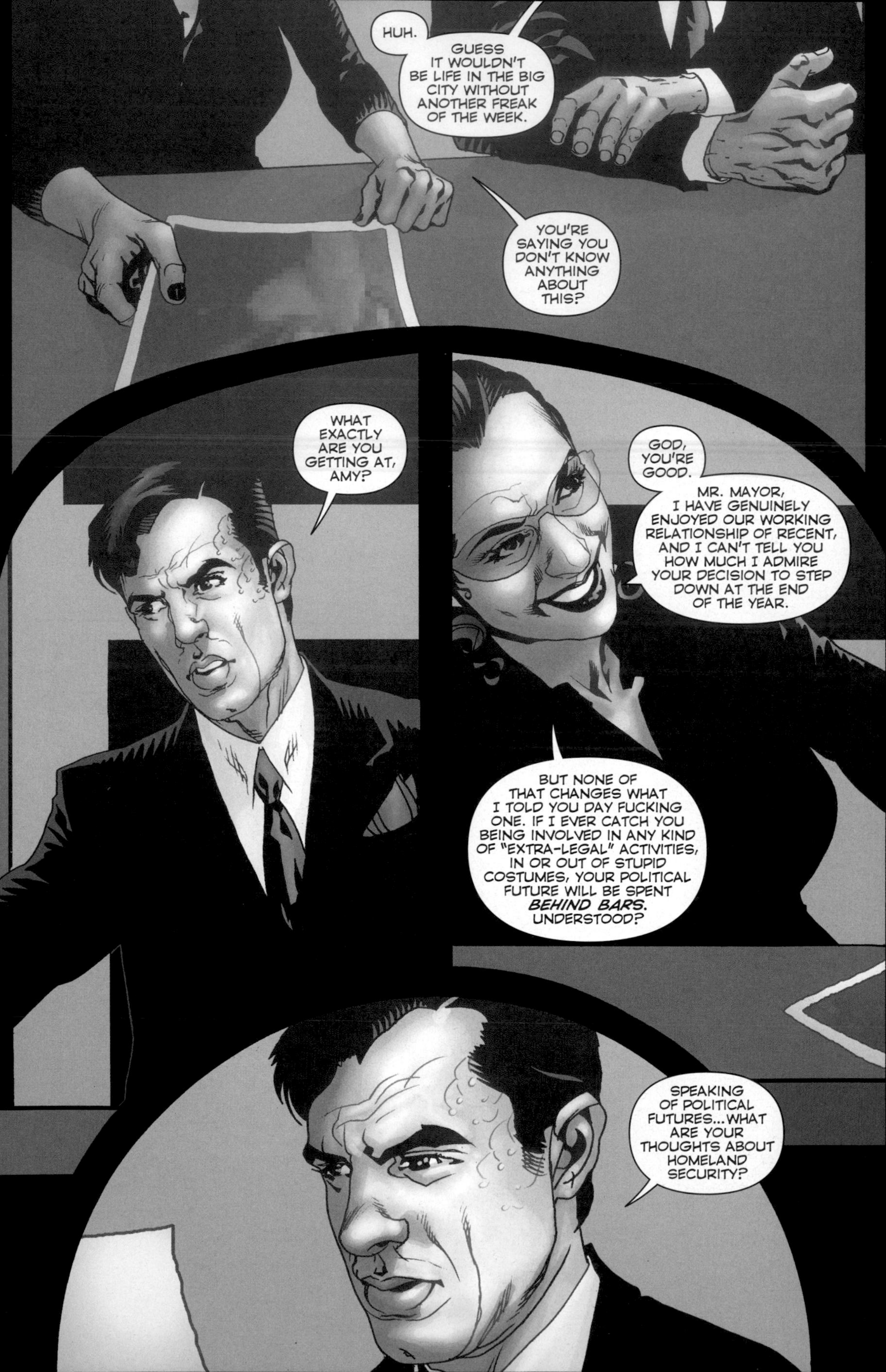
HUH.
GUESS IT WOULDN'T BE LIFE IN THE BIG CITY WITHOUT ANOTHER FREAK OF THE WEEK.
YOU'RE SAYING YOU DON'T KNOW ANYTHING ABOUT THIS?
WHAT EXACTLY ARE YOU GETTING AT, AMY?
GOD, YOU'RE GOOD.
MR. MAYOR, I HAVE GENUINELY ENJOYED OUR WORKING RELATIONSHIP OF RECENT, AND I CAN'T TELL YOU HOW MUCH I ADMIRE YOUR DECISION TO STEP DOWN AT THE END OF THE YEAR.
BUT NONE OF THAT CHANGES WHAT I TOLD YOU DAY FUCKING ONE. IF I EVER CATCH YOU BEING INVOLVED IN ANY KIND OF "EXTRA-LEGAL" ACTIVITIES, IN OR OUT OF STUPID COSTUMES, YOUR POLITICAL FUTURE WILL BE SPENT ***BEHIND BARS***. UNDERSTOOD?
SPEAKING OF POLITICAL FUTURES...WHAT ARE YOUR THOUGHTS ABOUT HOMELAND SECURITY?

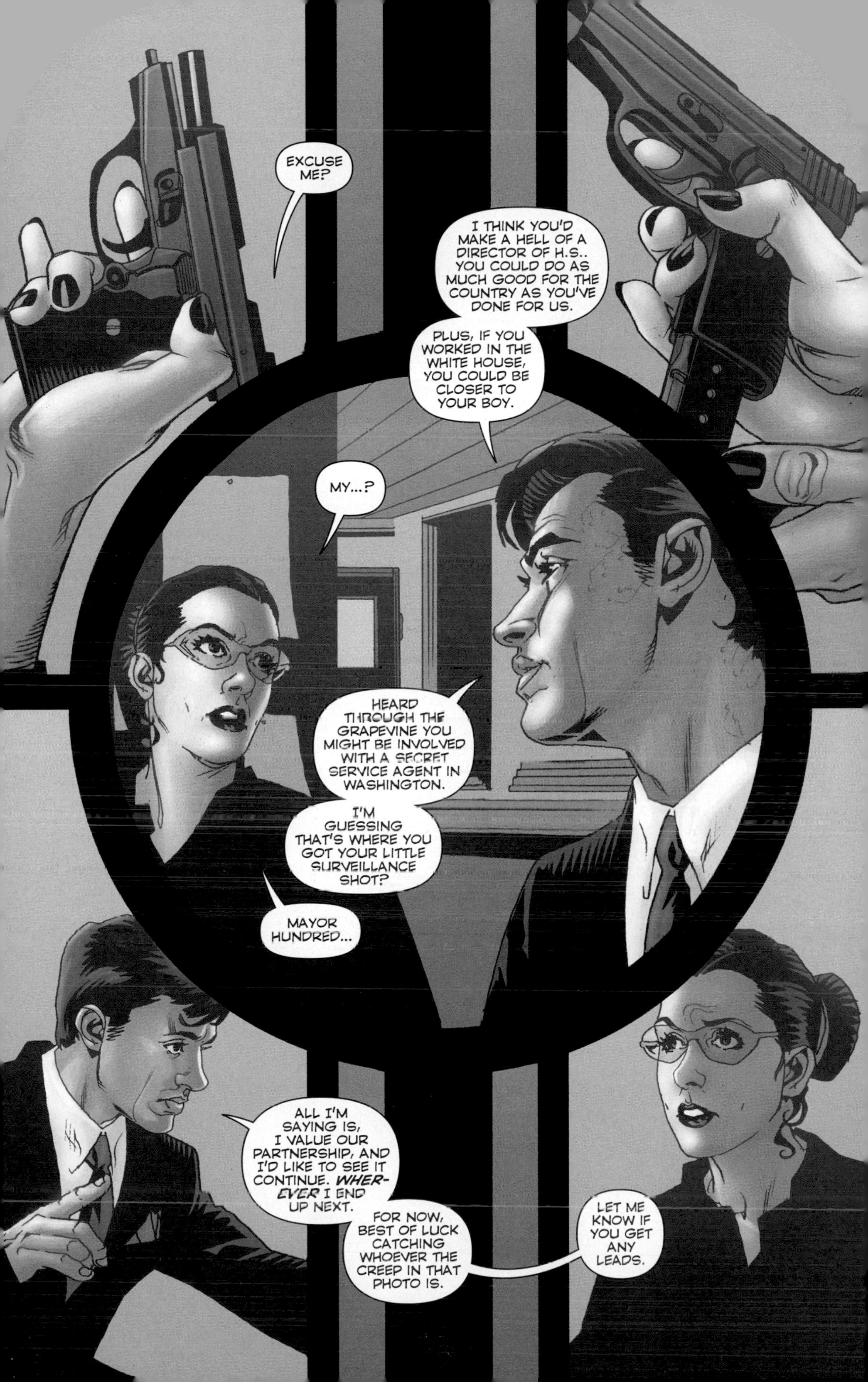
EXCUSE ME?
I THINK YOU'D MAKE A HELL OF A DIRECTOR OF H.S.. YOU COULD DO AS MUCH GOOD FOR THE COUNTRY AS YOU'VE DONE FOR US.
PLUS, IF YOU WORKED IN THE WHITE HOUSE, YOU COULD BE CLOSER TO YOUR BOY.
MY...?
HEARD THROUGH THE GRAPEVINE YOU MIGHT BE INVOLVED WITH A SECRET SERVICE AGENT IN WASHINGTON.
I'M GUESSING THAT'S WHERE YOU GOT YOUR LITTLE SURVEILLANCE SHOT?
MAYOR HUNDRED...
ALL I'M SAYING IS, I VALUE OUR PARTNERSHIP, AND I'D LIKE TO SEE IT CONTINUE. *WHER-EVER* I END UP NEXT.
FOR NOW, BEST OF LUCK CATCHING WHOEVER THE CREEP IN THAT PHOTO IS.
LET ME KNOW IF YOU GET ANY LEADS.

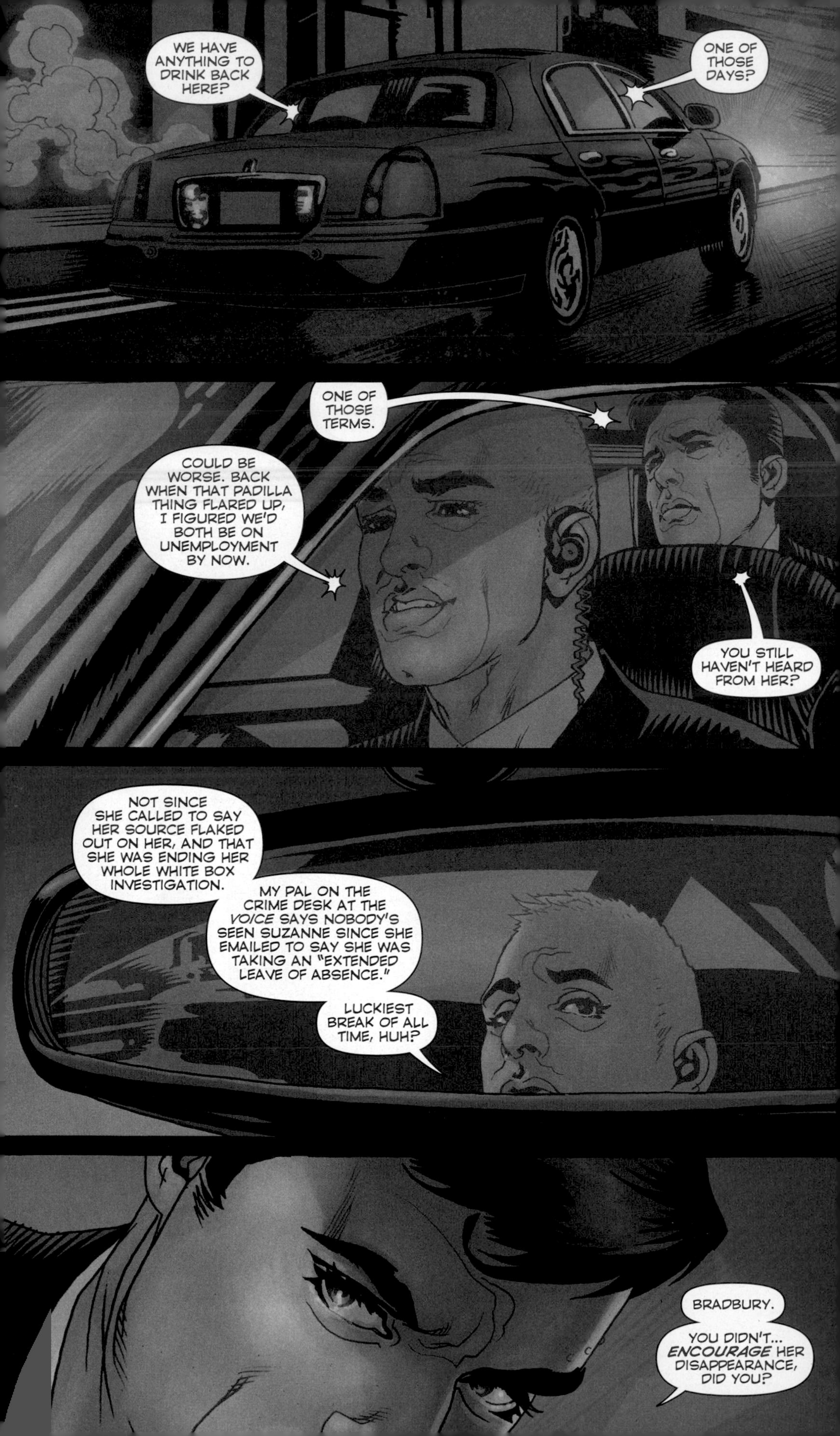
WE HAVE ANYTHING TO DRINK BACK HERE?
ONE OF THOSE DAYS?
ONE OF THOSE TERMS.
COULD BE WORSE. BACK WHEN THAT PADILLA THING FLARED UP, I FIGURED WE'D BOTH BE ON UNEMPLOYMENT BY NOW.
YOU STILL HAVEN'T HEARD FROM HER?
NOT SINCE SHE CALLED TO SAY HER SOURCE FLAKED OUT ON HER, AND THAT SHE WAS ENDING HER WHOLE WHITE BOX INVESTIGATION.
MY PAL ON THE CRIME DESK AT THE *VOICE* SAYS NOBODY'S SEEN SUZANNE SINCE SHE EMAILED TO SAY SHE WAS TAKING AN "EXTENDED LEAVE OF ABSENCE."
LUCKIEST BREAK OF ALL TIME, HUH?
BRADBURY.
YOU DIDN'T... ***ENCOURAGE*** HER DISAPPEARANCE, DID YOU?

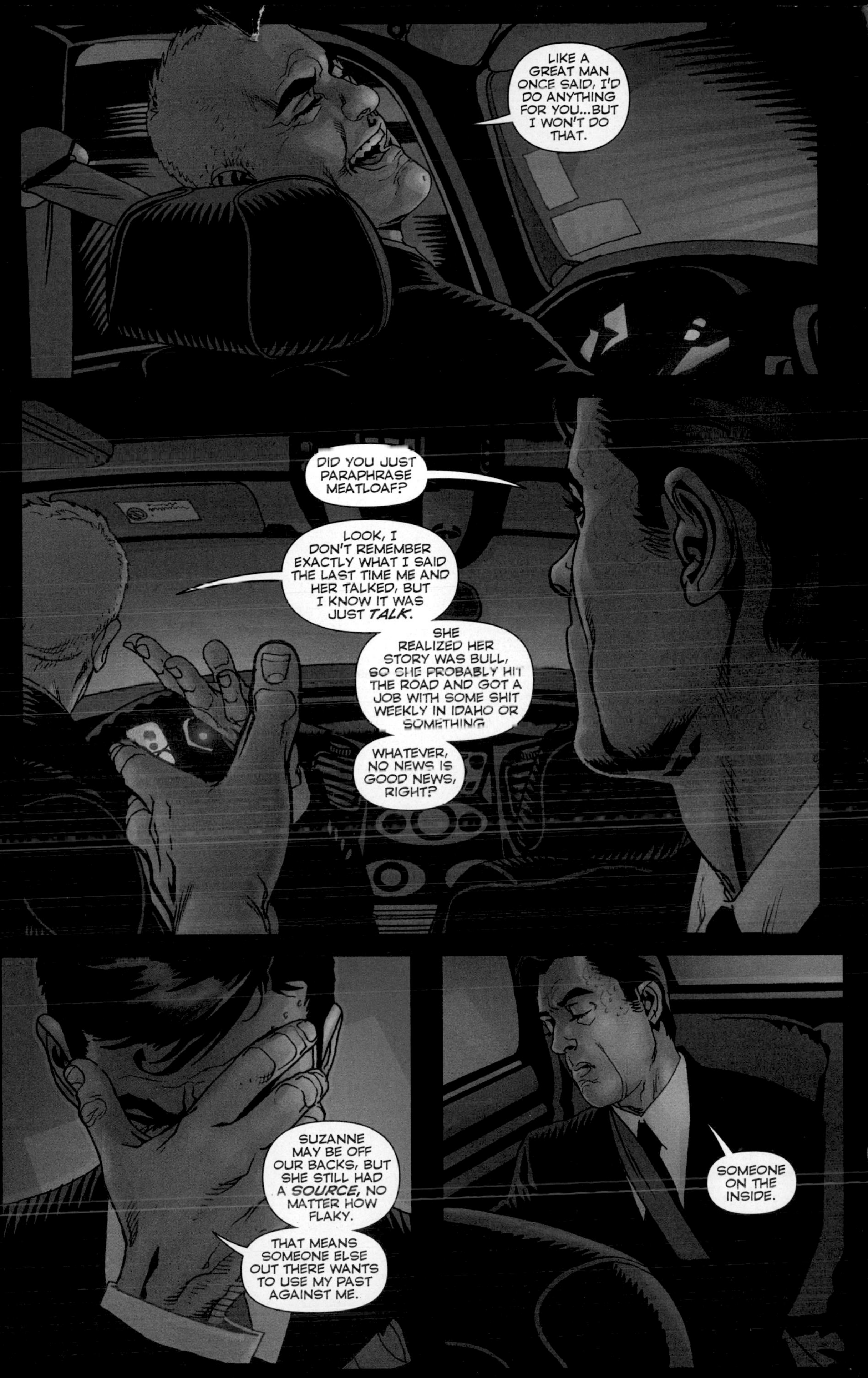
LIKE A GREAT MAN ONCE SAID, I'D DO ANYTHING FOR YOU...BUT I WON'T DO THAT.
DID YOU JUST PARAPHRASE MEATLOAF?
LOOK, I DON'T REMEMBER EXACTLY WHAT I SAID THE LAST TIME ME AND HER TALKED, BUT I KNOW IT WAS JUST TALK.
SHE REALIZED HER STORY WAS BULL, SO SHE PROBABLY HIT THE ROAD AND GOT A JOB WITH SOME SHIT WEEKLY IN IDAHO OR SOMETHING.
WHATEVER, NO NEWS IS GOOD NEWS, RIGHT?
SUZANNE MAY BE OFF OUR BACKS, BUT SHE STILL HAD A SOURCE, NO MATTER HOW FLAKY.
THAT MEANS SOMEONE ELSE OUT THERE WANTS TO USE MY PAST AGAINST ME.
SOMEONE ON THE INSIDE.

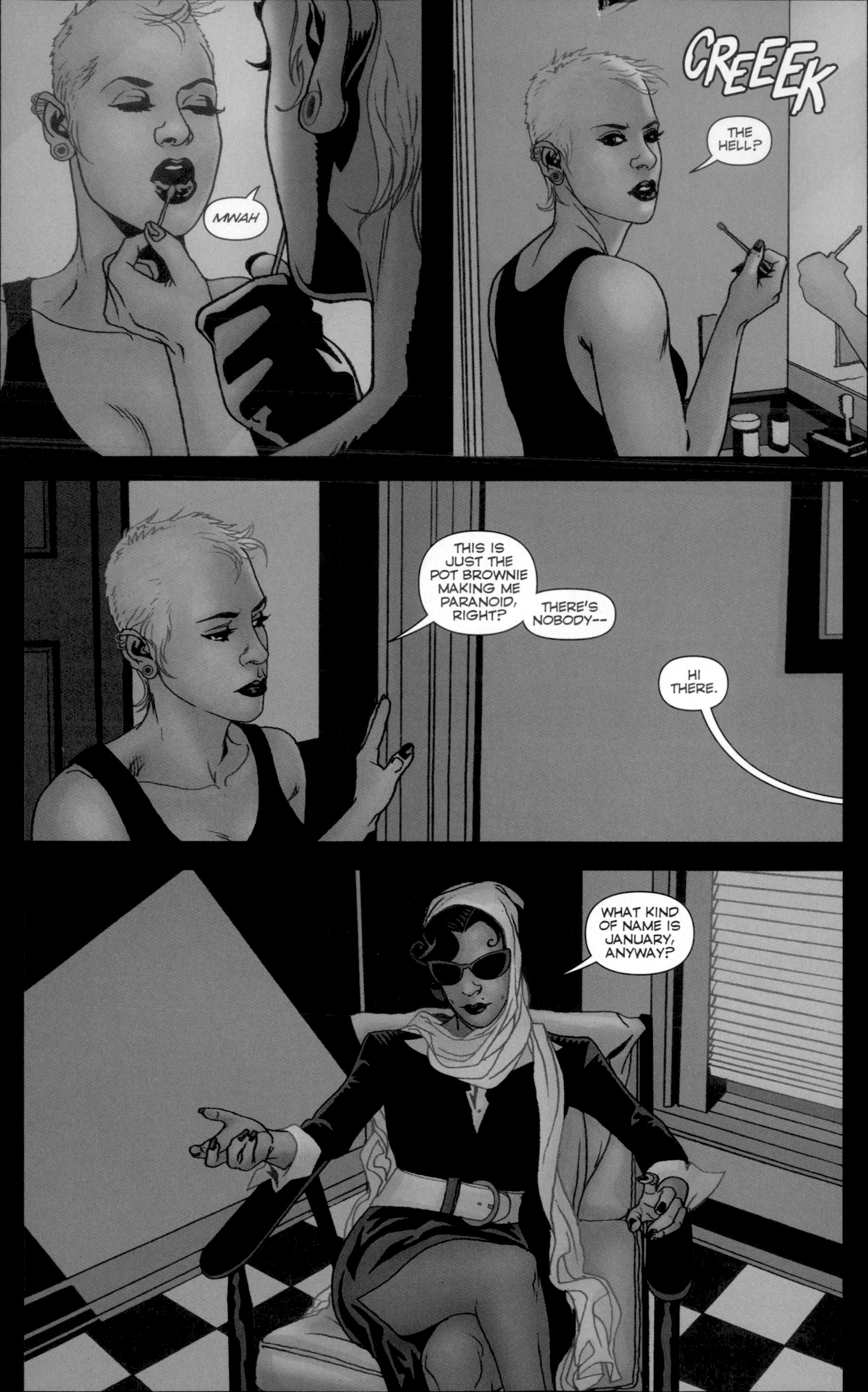
MWAH
CREEEK
THE HELL?
THIS IS JUST THE POT BROWNIE MAKING ME PARANOID, RIGHT?
THERE'S NOBODY--
HI THERE.
WHAT KIND OF NAME IS JANUARY, ANYWAY?

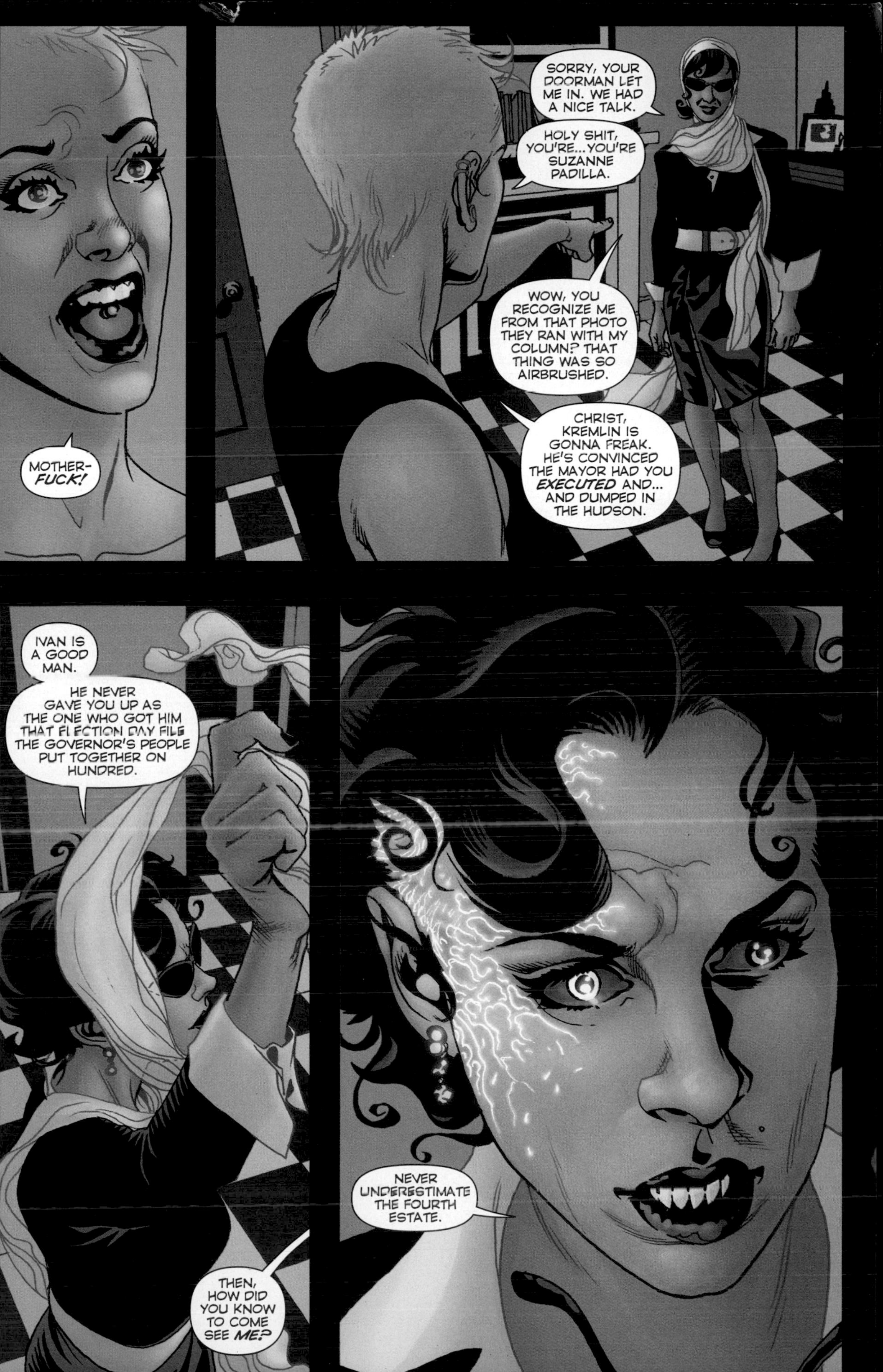
MOTHER-FUCK!
SORRY, YOUR DOORMAN LET ME IN. WE HAD A NICE TALK.
HOLY SHIT, YOU'RE...YOU'RE SUZANNE PADILLA.
WOW, YOU RECOGNIZE ME FROM THAT PHOTO THEY RAN WITH MY COLUMN? THAT THING WAS SO AIRBRUSHED.
CHRIST, KREMLIN IS GONNA FREAK. HE'S CONVINCED THE MAYOR HAD YOU EXECUTED AND... AND DUMPED IN THE HUDSON.
IVAN IS A GOOD MAN.
HE NEVER GAVE YOU UP AS THE ONE WHO GOT HIM THAT ELECTION DAY FILE THE GOVERNOR'S PEOPLE PUT TOGETHER ON HUNDRED.
THEN, HOW DID YOU KNOW TO COME SEE ME?
NEVER UNDERESTIMATE THE FOURTH ESTATE.

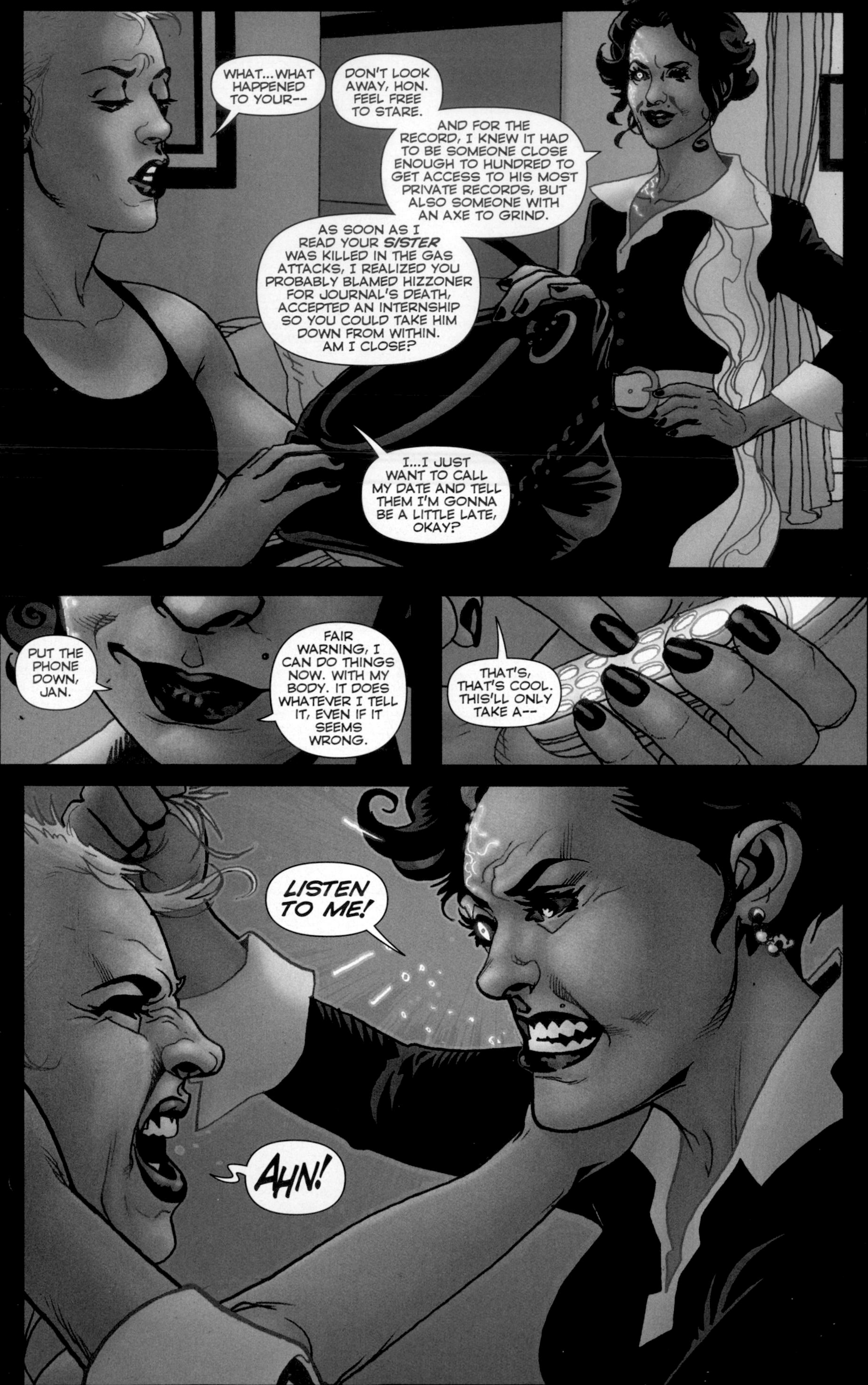
WHAT...WHAT HAPPENED TO YOUR--
DON'T LOOK AWAY, HON. FEEL FREE TO STARE.
AND FOR THE RECORD, I KNEW IT HAD TO BE SOMEONE CLOSE ENOUGH TO HUNDRED TO GET ACCESS TO HIS MOST PRIVATE RECORDS, BUT ALSO SOMEONE WITH AN AXE TO GRIND.
AS SOON AS I READ YOUR *SISTER* WAS KILLED IN THE GAS ATTACKS, I REALIZED YOU PROBABLY BLAMED HIZZONER FOR JOURNAL'S DEATH, ACCEPTED AN INTERNSHIP SO YOU COULD TAKE HIM DOWN FROM WITHIN. AM I CLOSE?
I...I JUST WANT TO CALL MY DATE AND TELL THEM I'M GONNA BE A LITTLE LATE, OKAY?
PUT THE PHONE DOWN, JAN.
FAIR WARNING, I CAN DO THINGS NOW. WITH MY BODY. IT DOES WHATEVER I TELL IT, EVEN IF IT SEEMS WRONG.
THAT'S, THAT'S COOL. THIS'LL ONLY TAKE A--
LISTEN TO ME!
AHN!

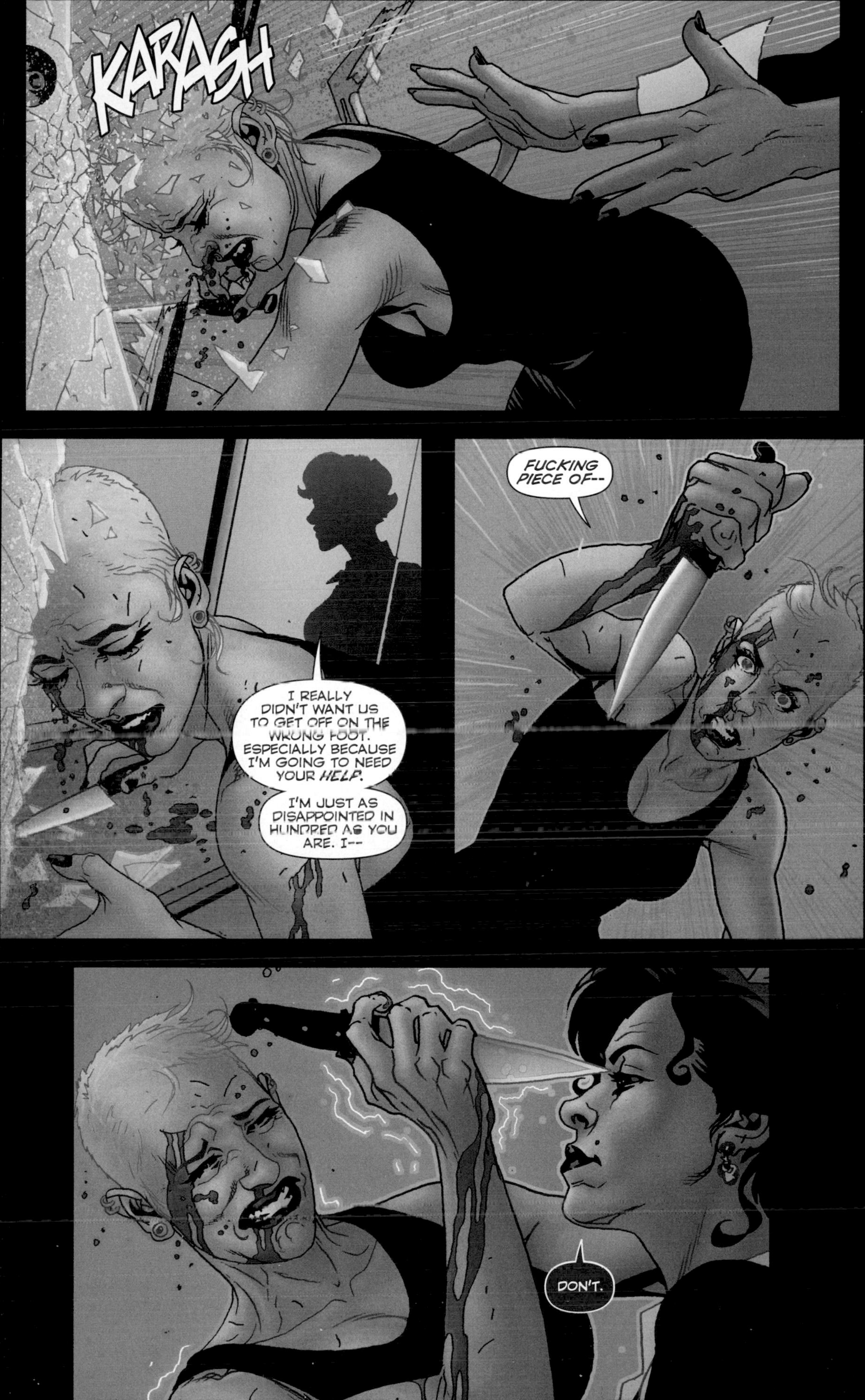
KARASH
I REALLY DIDN'T WANT US TO GET OFF ON THE WRONG FOOT. ESPECIALLY BECAUSE I'M GOING TO NEED YOUR HELP.
I'M JUST AS DISAPPOINTED IN HUNDRED AS YOU ARE. I--
FUCKING PIECE OF--
DON'T.

HOW...?

PUT IT DOWN.

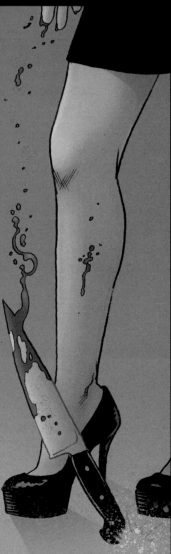

THE MAYOR.

YOU'RE... YOU'RE GONNA *KILL* HIM, AREN'T YOU?

YOU SWEET GIRL.

DON'T BE RIDICULOUS.

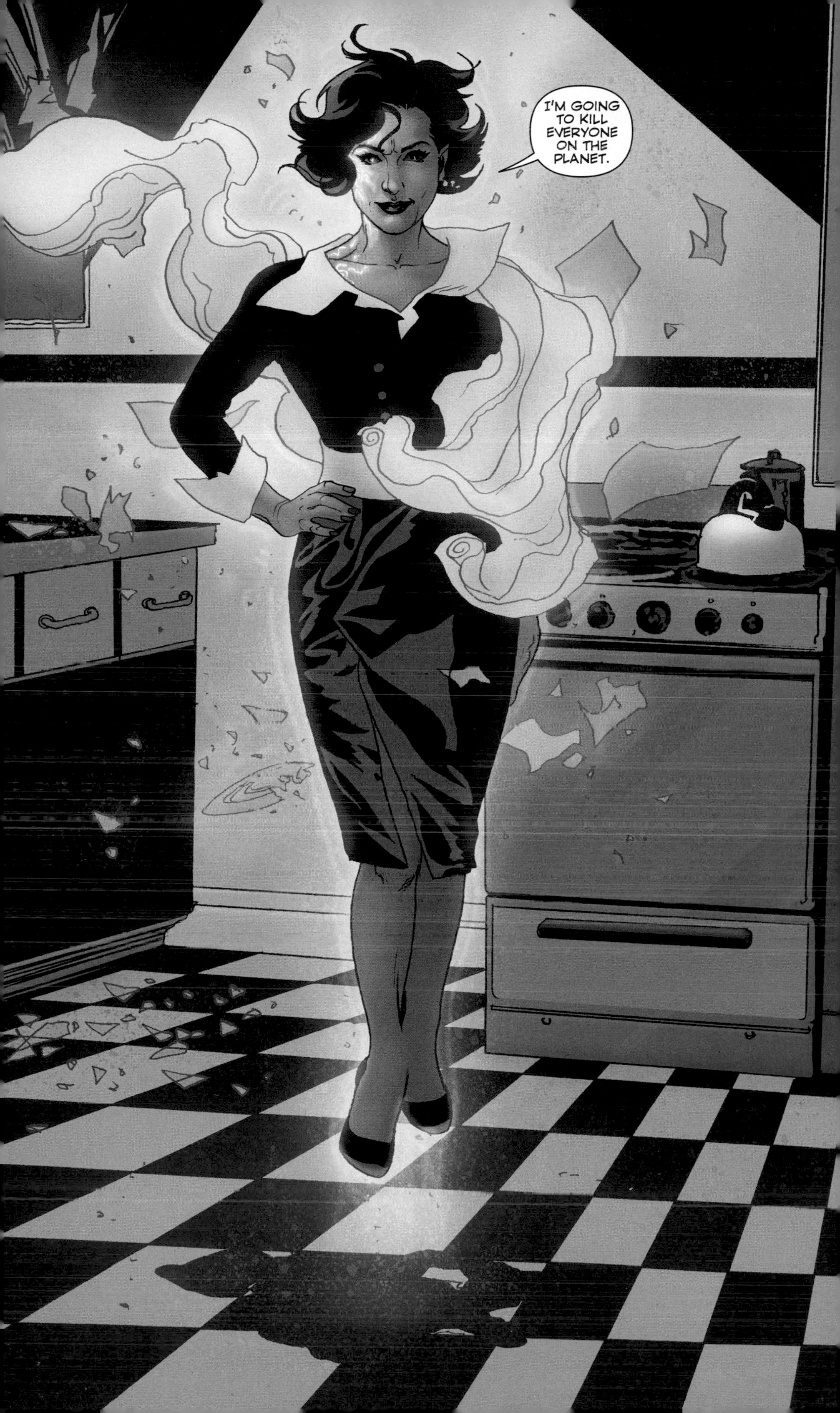
I'M GOING TO KILL EVERYONE ON THE PLANET.

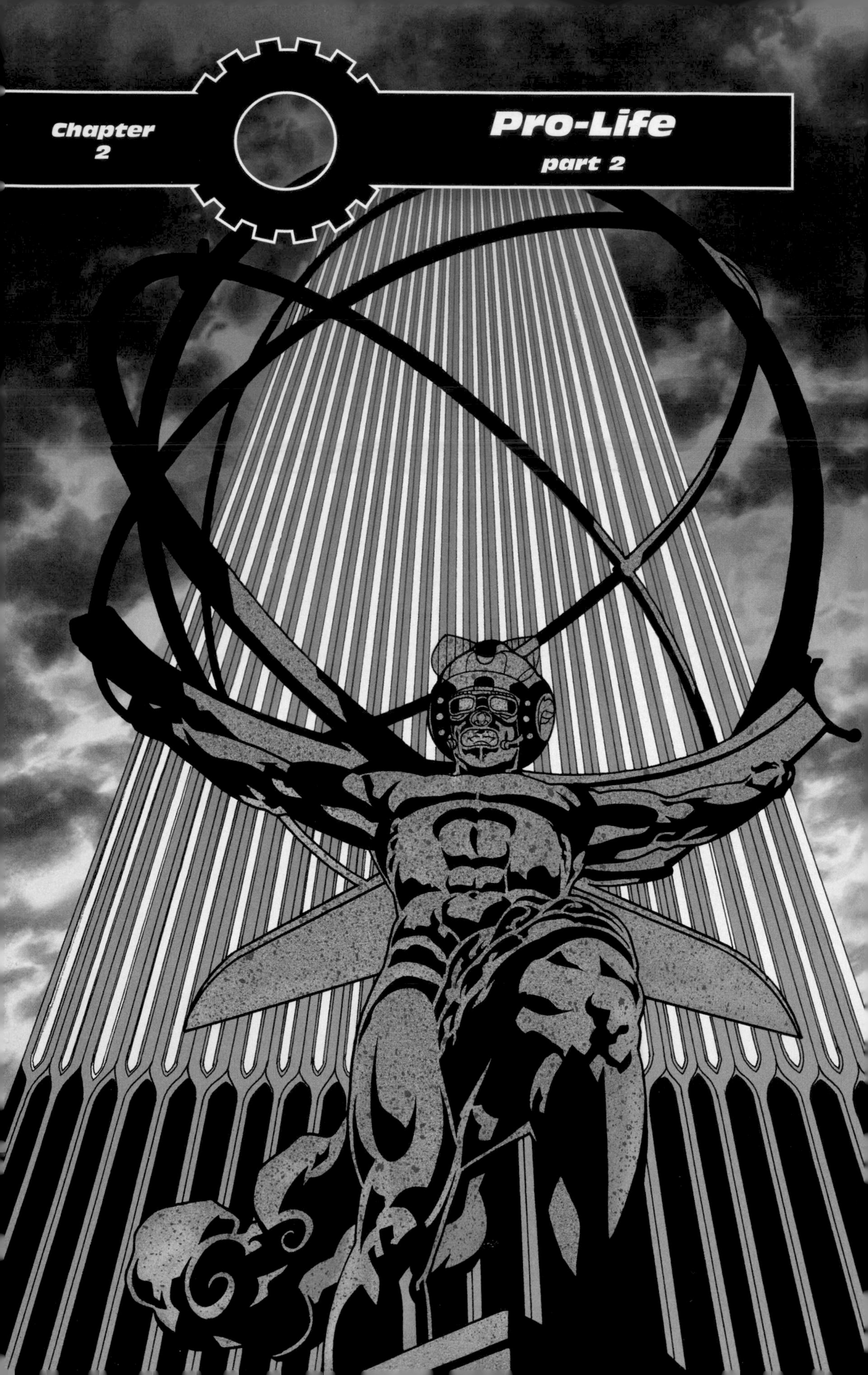
Chapter 2
Pro-Life
part 2

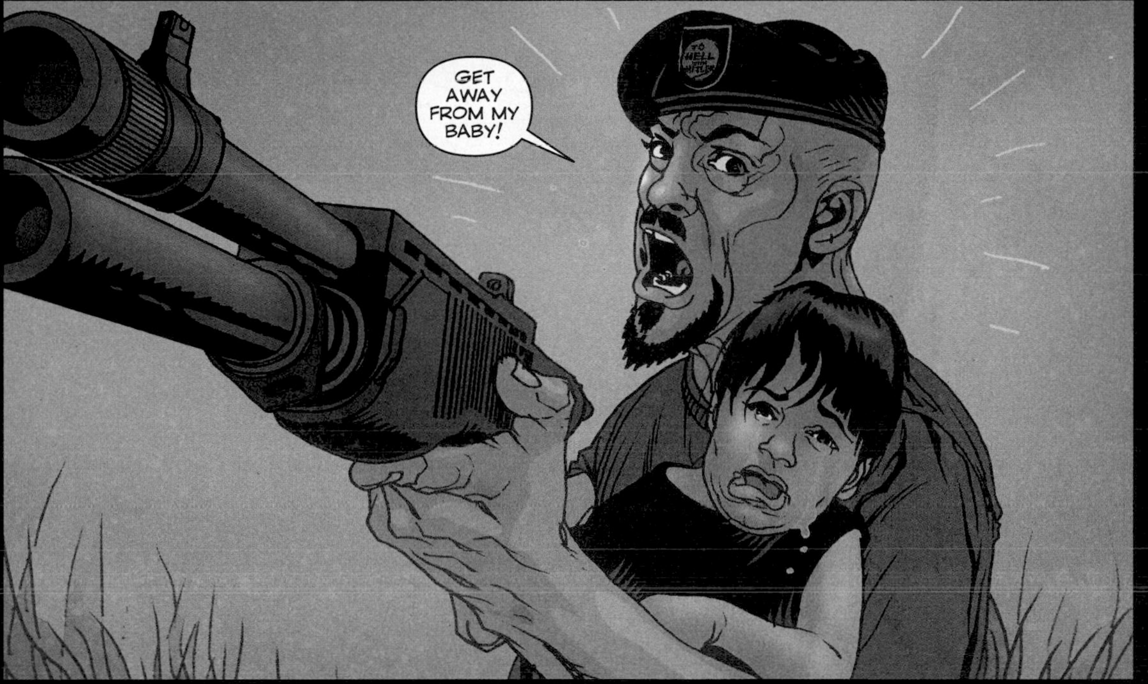
GET AWAY FROM MY BABY!

SATURDAY, MARCH 10, 2001

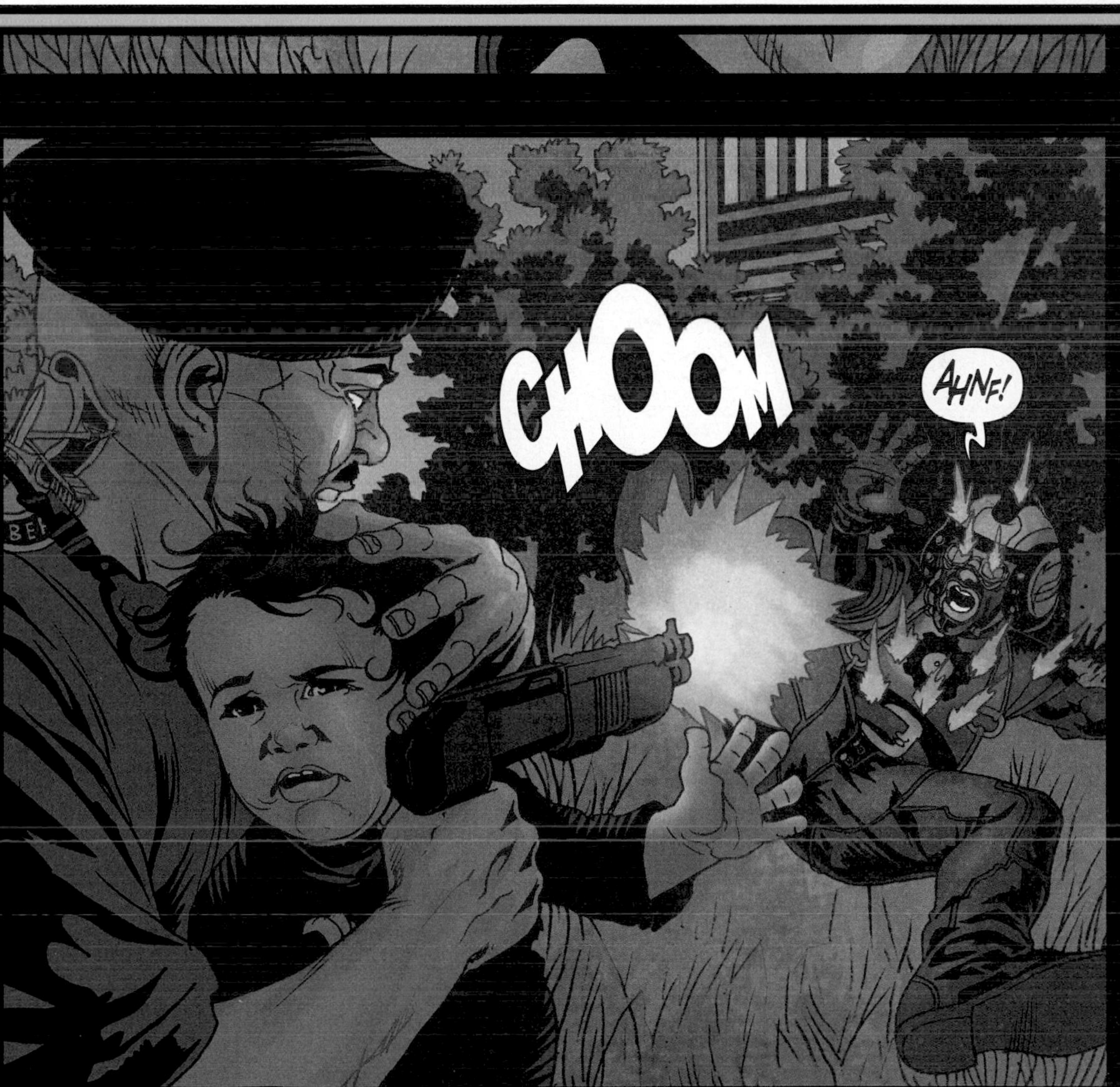
CHOOM
AHNF!

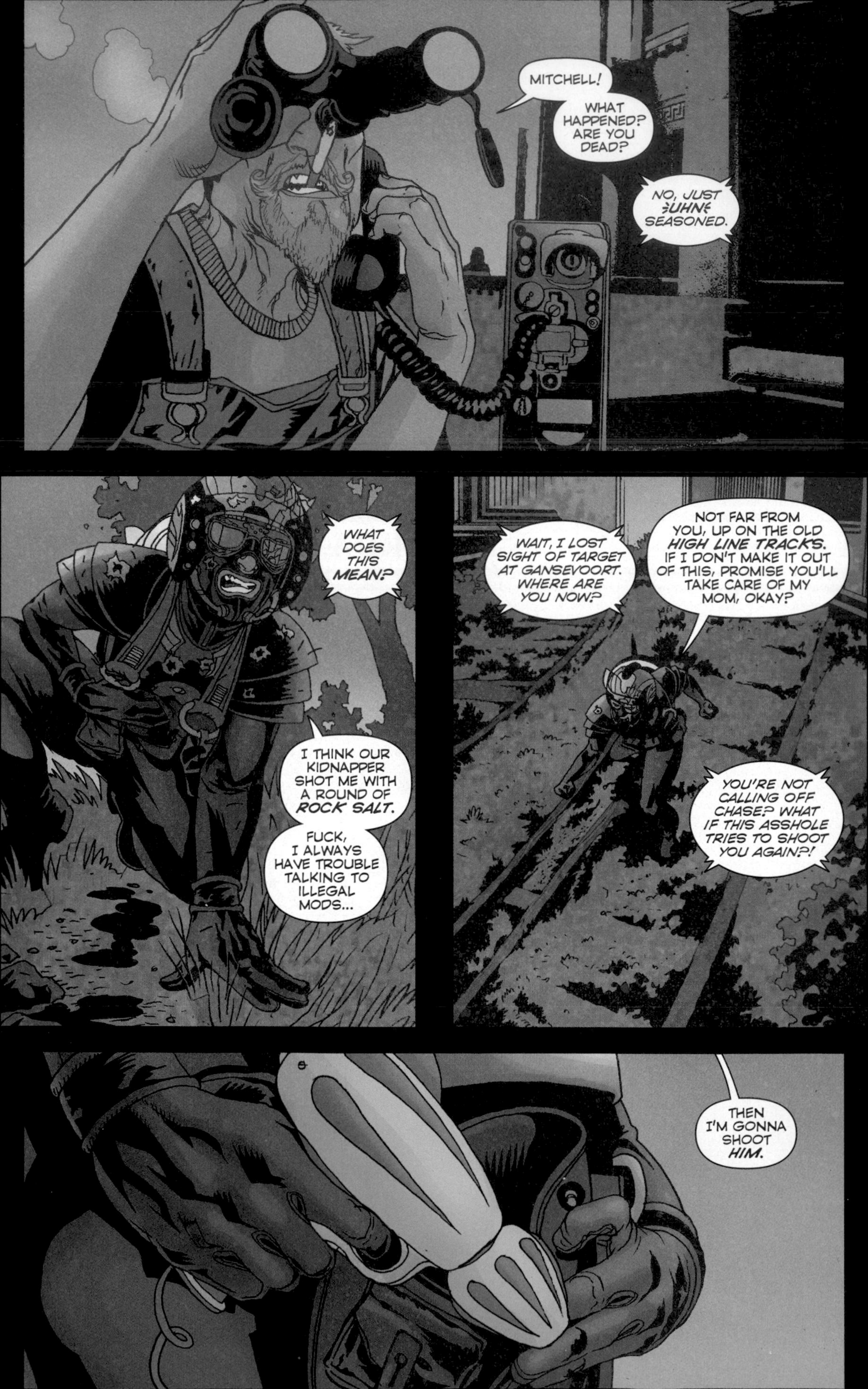
MITCHELL!
WHAT HAPPENED? ARE YOU DEAD?
NO, JUST *UHN* SEASONED.
WHAT DOES THIS MEAN?
I THINK OUR KIDNAPPER SHOT ME WITH A ROUND OF ROCK SALT.
FUCK, I ALWAYS HAVE TROUBLE TALKING TO ILLEGAL MODS...
WAIT, I LOST SIGHT OF TARGET AT GANSEVOORT. WHERE ARE YOU NOW?
NOT FAR FROM YOU, UP ON THE OLD HIGH LINE TRACKS. IF I DON'T MAKE IT OUT OF THIS, PROMISE YOU'LL TAKE CARE OF MY MOM, OKAY?
YOU'RE NOT CALLING OFF CHASE? WHAT IF THIS ASSHOLE TRIES TO SHOOT YOU AGAIN?!
THEN I'M GONNA SHOOT HIM.

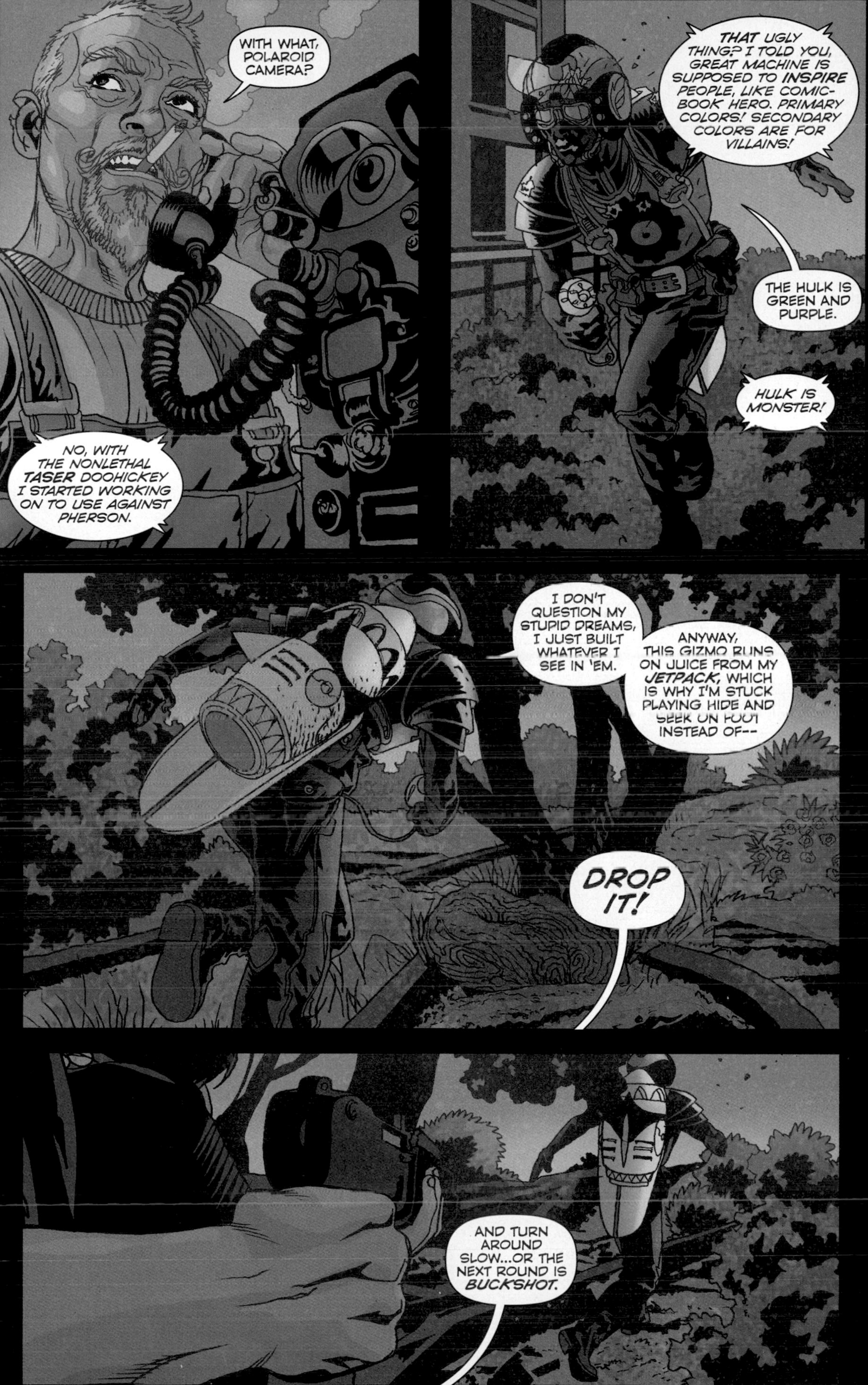
WITH WHAT, POLAROID CAMERA?
NO, WITH THE NONLETHAL TASER DOOHICKEY I STARTED WORKING ON TO USE AGAINST PHERSON.
THAT UGLY THING? I TOLD YOU, GREAT MACHINE IS SUPPOSED TO INSPIRE PEOPLE, LIKE COMIC-BOOK HERO. PRIMARY COLORS! SECONDARY COLORS ARE FOR VILLAINS!
THE HULK IS GREEN AND PURPLE.
HULK IS MONSTER!
I DON'T QUESTION MY STUPID DREAMS, I JUST BUILT WHATEVER I SEE IN 'EM.
ANYWAY, THIS GIZMO RUNS ON JUICE FROM MY JETPACK, WHICH IS WHY I'M STUCK PLAYING HIDE AND SEEK ON FOOT INSTEAD OF--
DROP IT!
AND TURN AROUND SLOW...OR THE NEXT ROUND IS BUCKSHOT.

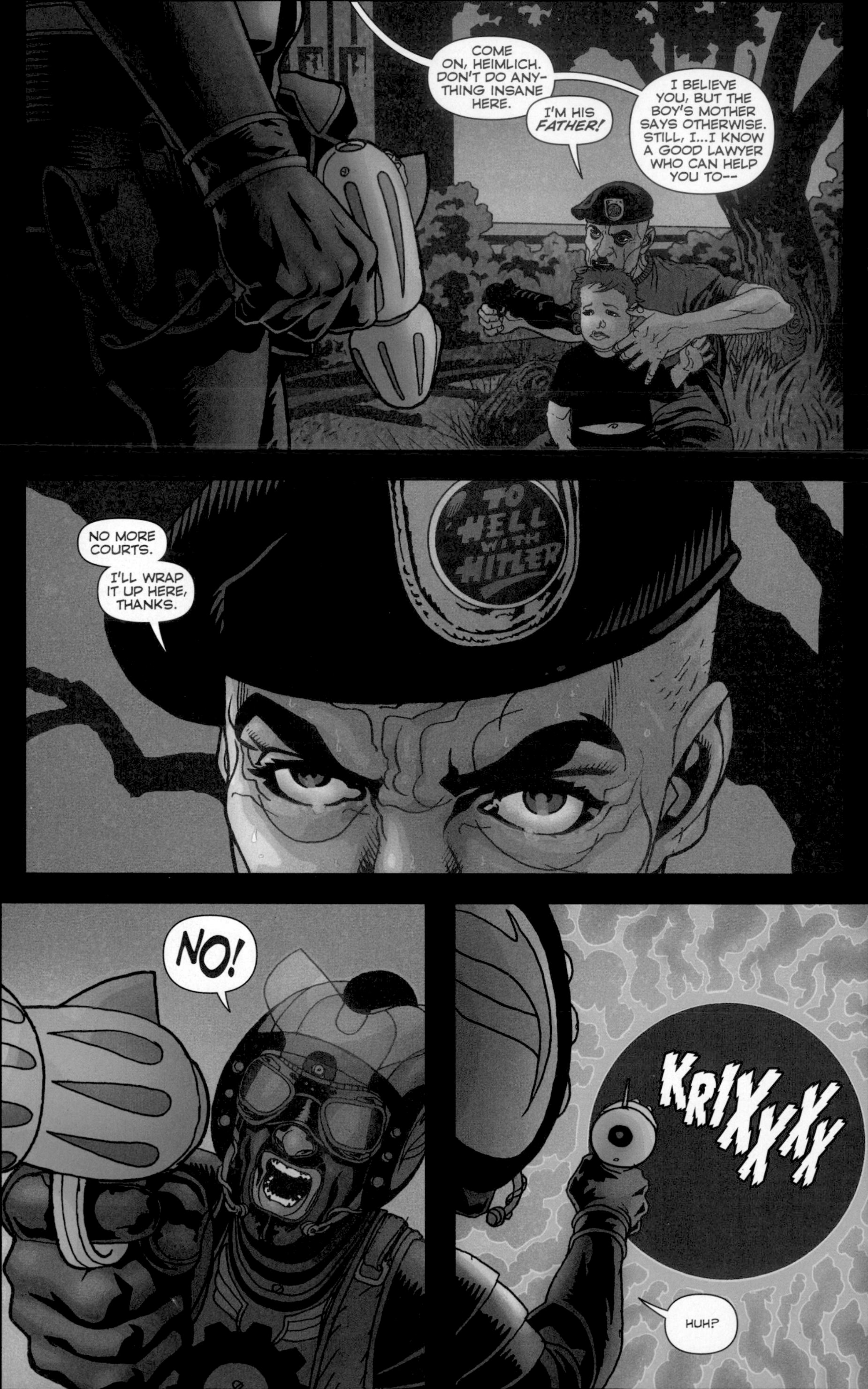
COME ON, HEIMLICH. DON'T DO ANYTHING INSANE HERE.
I'M HIS *FATHER!*
I BELIEVE YOU, BUT THE BOY'S MOTHER SAYS OTHERWISE. STILL, I...I KNOW A GOOD LAWYER WHO CAN HELP YOU TO--
NO MORE COURTS.
I'LL WRAP IT UP HERE, THANKS.
TO HELL WITH HITLER
NO!
KRIXXXX
HUH?

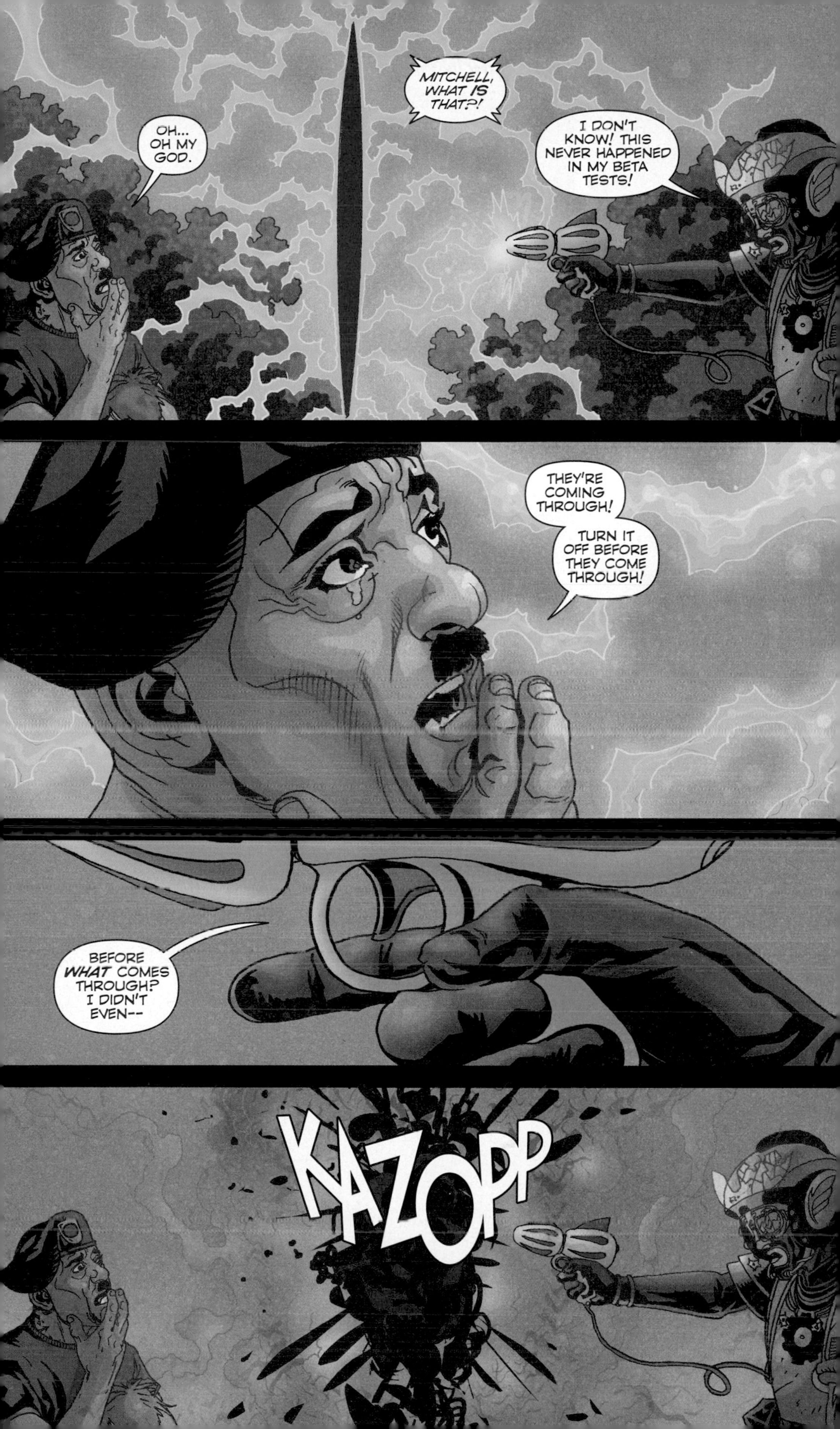
OH... OH MY GOD.
MITCHELL, WHAT IS THAT?!
I DON'T KNOW! THIS NEVER HAPPENED IN MY BETA TESTS!
THEY'RE COMING THROUGH!
TURN IT OFF BEFORE THEY COME THROUGH!
BEFORE WHAT COMES THROUGH? I DIDN'T EVEN--
KAZOPP

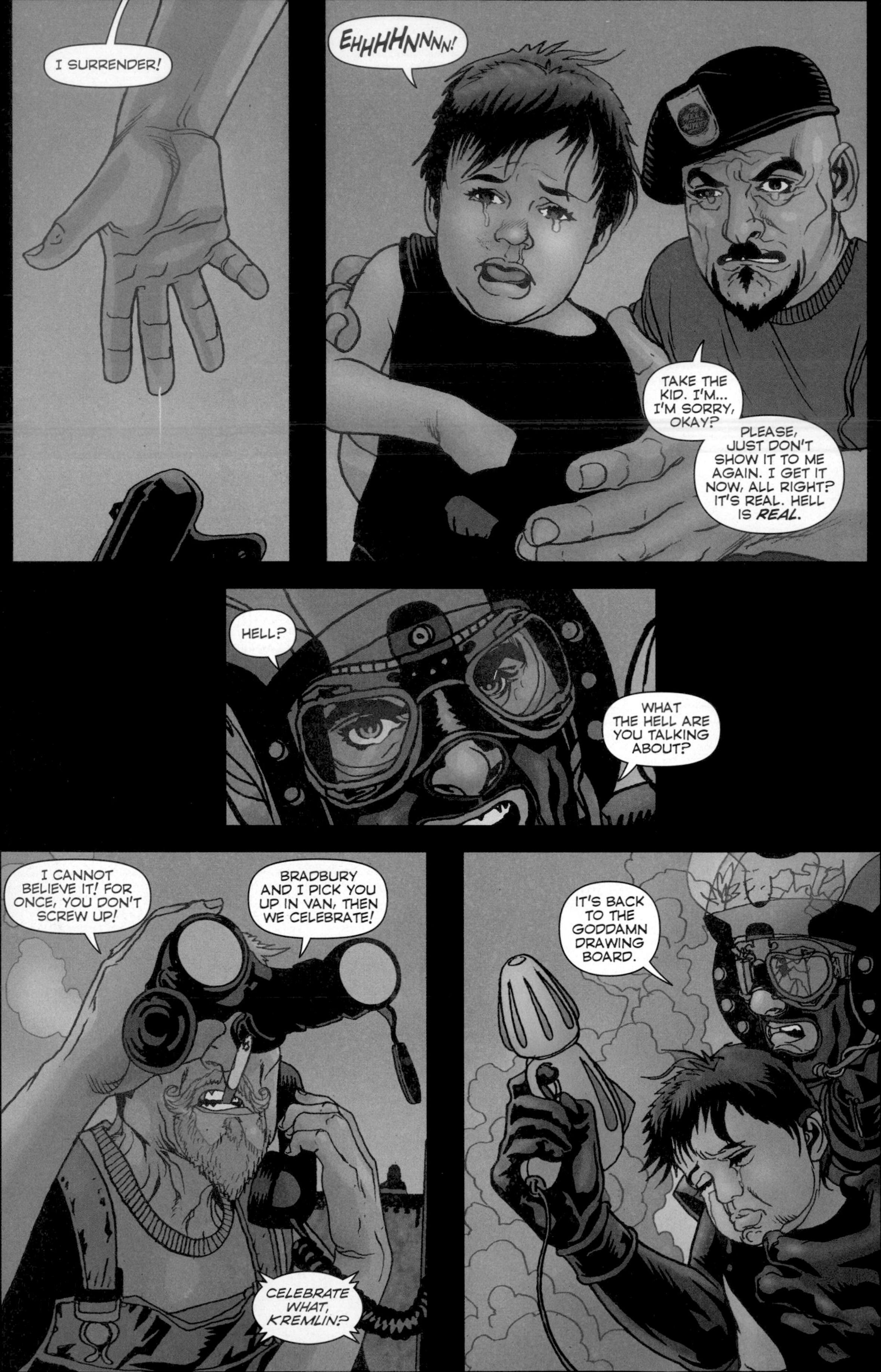
I SURRENDER!
EHHHHNNNN!
TAKE THE KID. I'M... I'M SORRY, OKAY?
PLEASE, JUST DON'T SHOW IT TO ME AGAIN. I GET IT NOW, ALL RIGHT? IT'S REAL. HELL IS *REAL*.
HELL?
WHAT THE HELL ARE YOU TALKING ABOUT?
I CANNOT BELIEVE IT! FOR ONCE, YOU DON'T SCREW UP!
BRADBURY AND I PICK YOU UP IN VAN, THEN WE CELEBRATE!
CELEBRATE WHAT, KREMLIN?
IT'S BACK TO THE GODDAMN DRAWING BOARD.

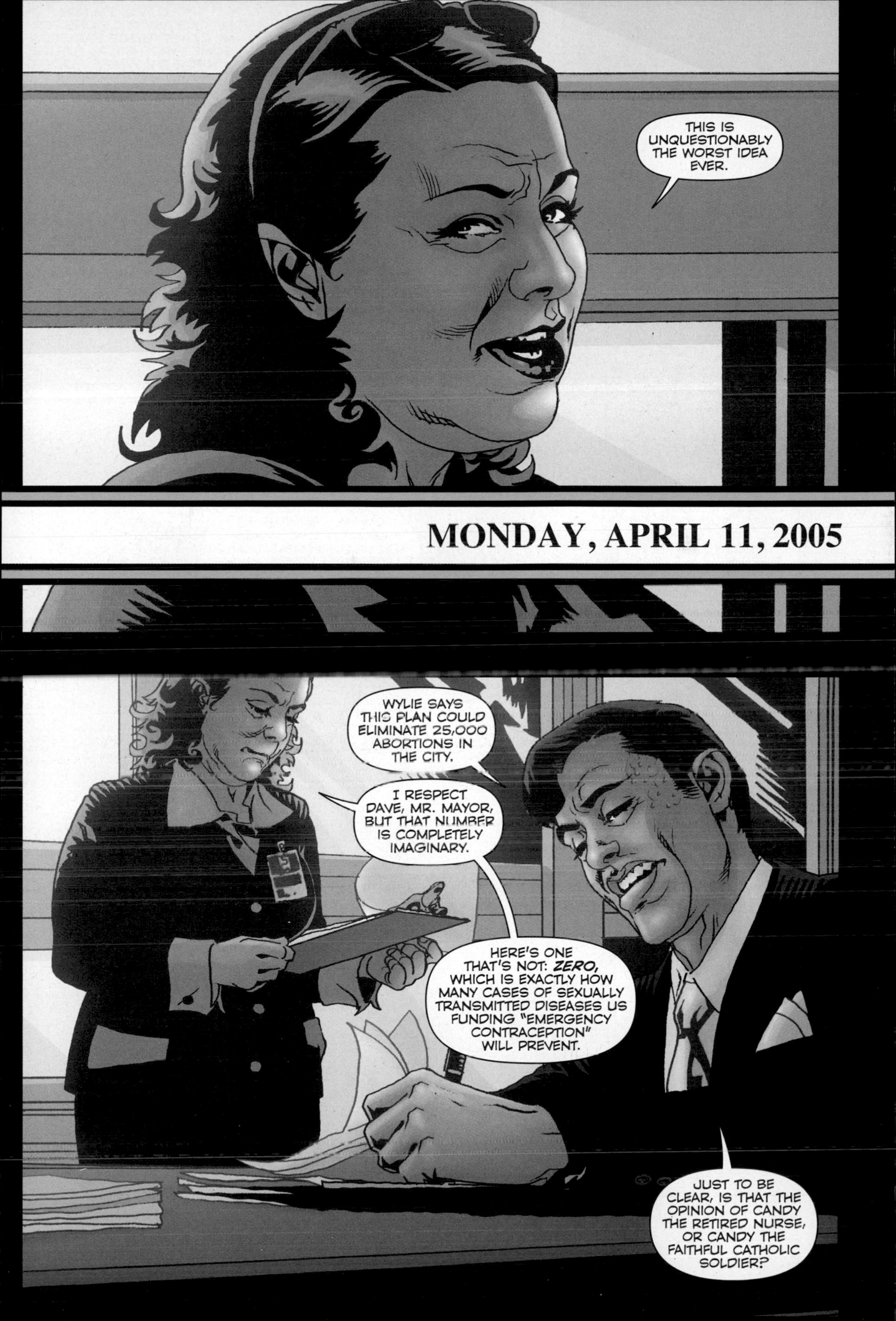
THIS IS UNQUESTIONABLY THE WORST IDEA EVER.
MONDAY, APRIL 11, 2005
WYLIE SAYS THIS PLAN COULD ELIMINATE 25,000 ABORTIONS IN THE CITY.
I RESPECT DAVE, MR. MAYOR, BUT THAT NUMBER IS COMPLETELY IMAGINARY.
HERE'S ONE THAT'S NOT: *ZERO,* WHICH IS EXACTLY HOW MANY CASES OF SEXUALLY TRANSMITTED DISEASES US FUNDING "EMERGENCY CONTRACEPTION" WILL PREVENT.
JUST TO BE CLEAR, IS THAT THE OPINION OF CANDY THE RETIRED NURSE, OR CANDY THE FAITHFUL CATHOLIC SOLDIER?

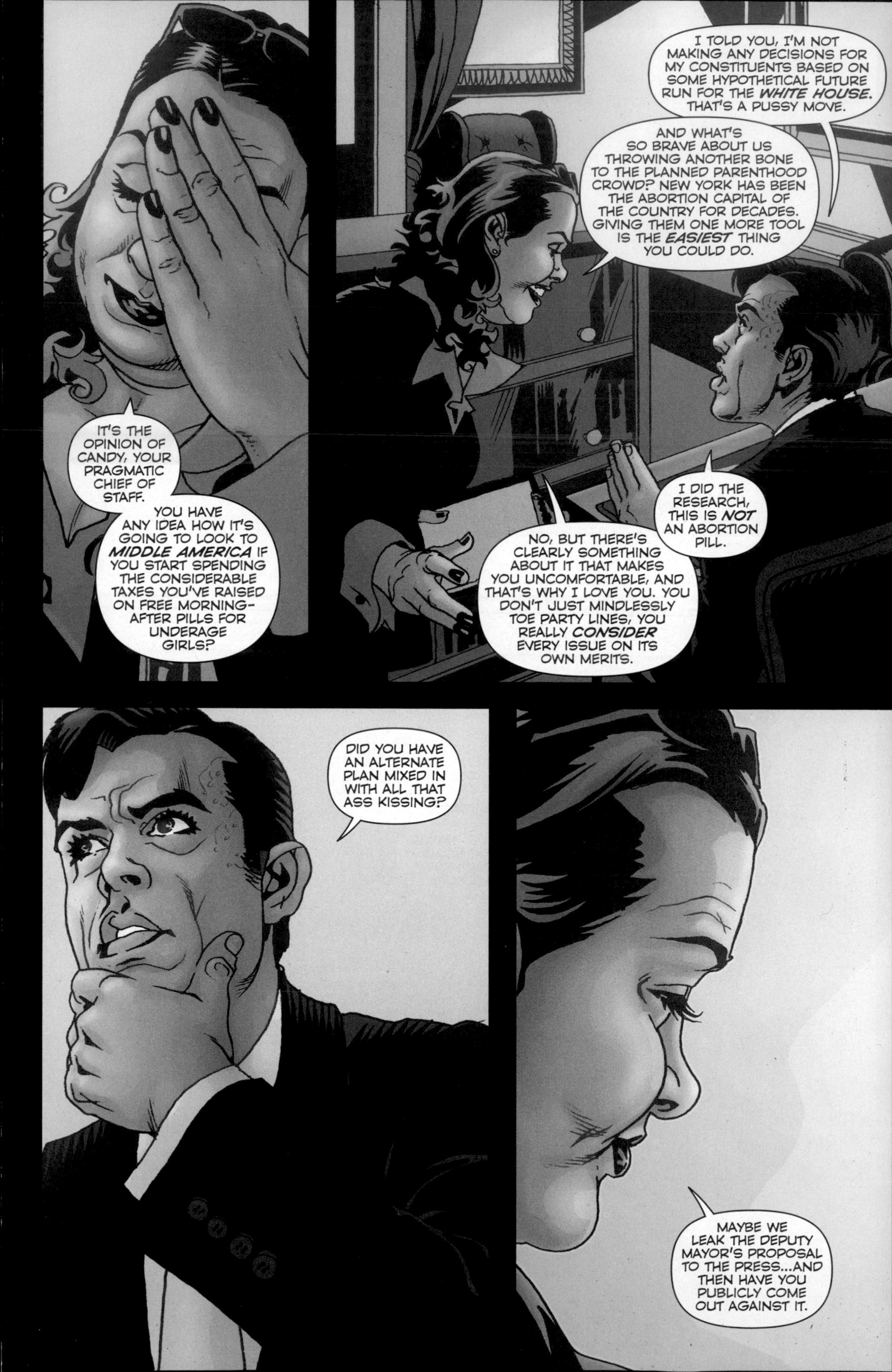
IT'S THE OPINION OF CANDY, YOUR PRAGMATIC CHIEF OF STAFF.
YOU HAVE ANY IDEA HOW IT'S GOING TO LOOK TO MIDDLE AMERICA IF YOU START SPENDING THE CONSIDERABLE TAXES YOU'VE RAISED ON FREE MORNING-AFTER PILLS FOR UNDERAGE GIRLS?
I TOLD YOU, I'M NOT MAKING ANY DECISIONS FOR MY CONSTITUENTS BASED ON SOME HYPOTHETICAL FUTURE RUN FOR THE WHITE HOUSE. THAT'S A PUSSY MOVE.
AND WHAT'S SO BRAVE ABOUT US THROWING ANOTHER BONE TO THE PLANNED PARENTHOOD CROWD? NEW YORK HAS BEEN THE ABORTION CAPITAL OF THE COUNTRY FOR DECADES. GIVING THEM ONE MORE TOOL IS THE EASIEST THING YOU COULD DO.
I DID THE RESEARCH, THIS IS NOT AN ABORTION PILL.
NO, BUT THERE'S CLEARLY SOMETHING ABOUT IT THAT MAKES YOU UNCOMFORTABLE, AND THAT'S WHY I LOVE YOU. YOU DON'T JUST MINDLESSLY TOE PARTY LINES, YOU REALLY CONSIDER EVERY ISSUE ON ITS OWN MERITS.
DID YOU HAVE AN ALTERNATE PLAN MIXED IN WITH ALL THAT ASS KISSING?
MAYBE WE LEAK THE DEPUTY MAYOR'S PROPOSAL TO THE PRESS...AND THEN HAVE YOU PUBLICLY COME OUT AGAINST IT.

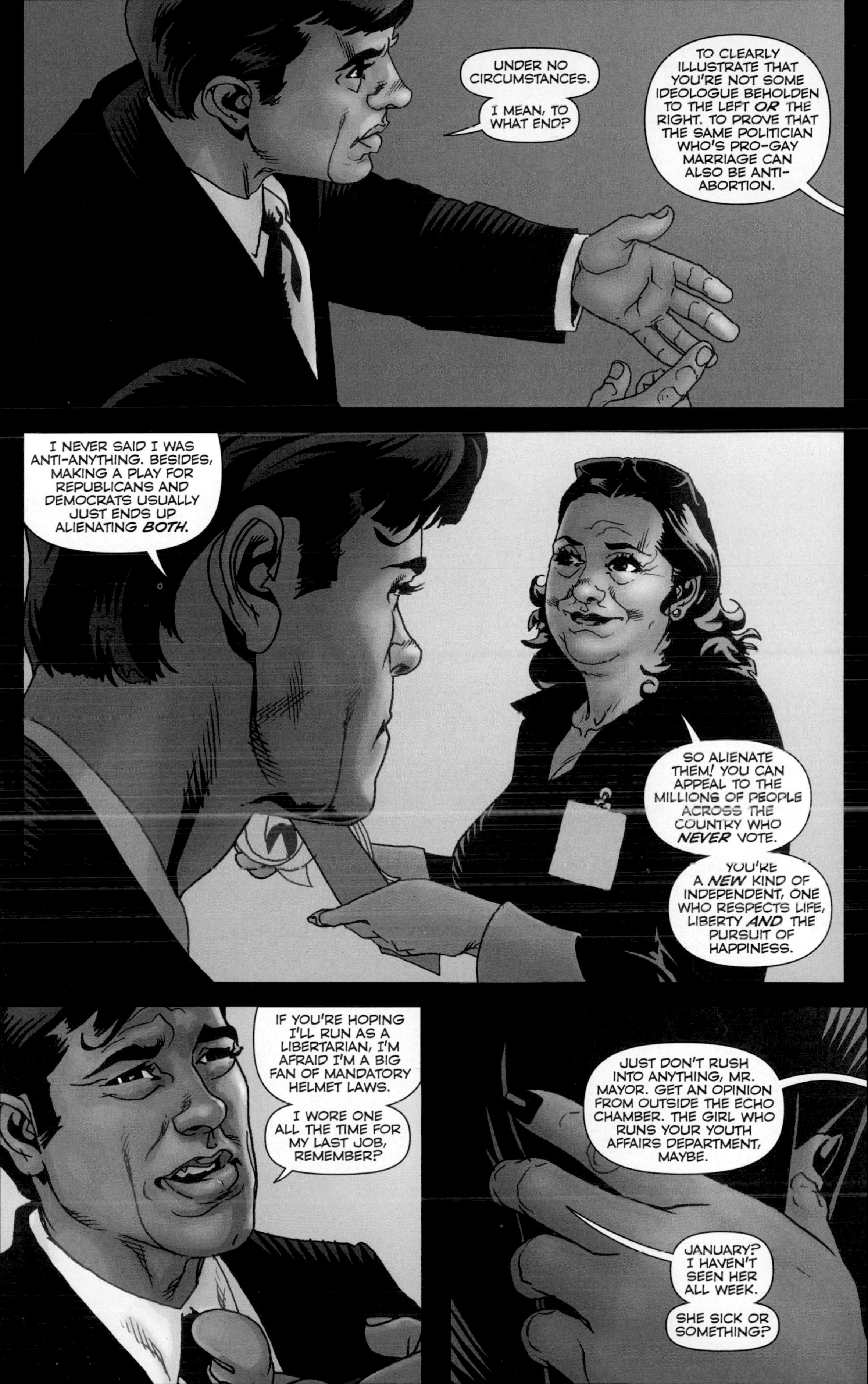
UNDER NO CIRCUMSTANCES.
I MEAN, TO WHAT END?
TO CLEARLY ILLUSTRATE THAT YOU'RE NOT SOME IDEOLOGUE BEHOLDEN TO THE LEFT *OR* THE RIGHT. TO PROVE THAT THE SAME POLITICIAN WHO'S PRO-GAY MARRIAGE CAN ALSO BE ANTI-ABORTION.
I NEVER SAID I WAS ANTI-ANYTHING. BESIDES, MAKING A PLAY FOR REPUBLICANS AND DEMOCRATS USUALLY JUST ENDS UP ALIENATING *BOTH*.
SO ALIENATE THEM! YOU CAN APPEAL TO THE MILLIONS OF PEOPLE ACROSS THE COUNTRY WHO *NEVER* VOTE.
YOU'RE A *NEW* KIND OF INDEPENDENT, ONE WHO RESPECTS LIFE, LIBERTY *AND* THE PURSUIT OF HAPPINESS.
IF YOU'RE HOPING I'LL RUN AS A LIBERTARIAN, I'M AFRAID I'M A BIG FAN OF MANDATORY HELMET LAWS.
I WORE ONE ALL THE TIME FOR MY LAST JOB, REMEMBER?
JUST DON'T RUSH INTO ANYTHING, MR. MAYOR. GET AN OPINION FROM OUTSIDE THE ECHO CHAMBER. THE GIRL WHO RUNS YOUR YOUTH AFFAIRS DEPARTMENT, MAYBE.
JANUARY? I HAVEN'T SEEN HER ALL WEEK.
SHE SICK OR SOMETHING?

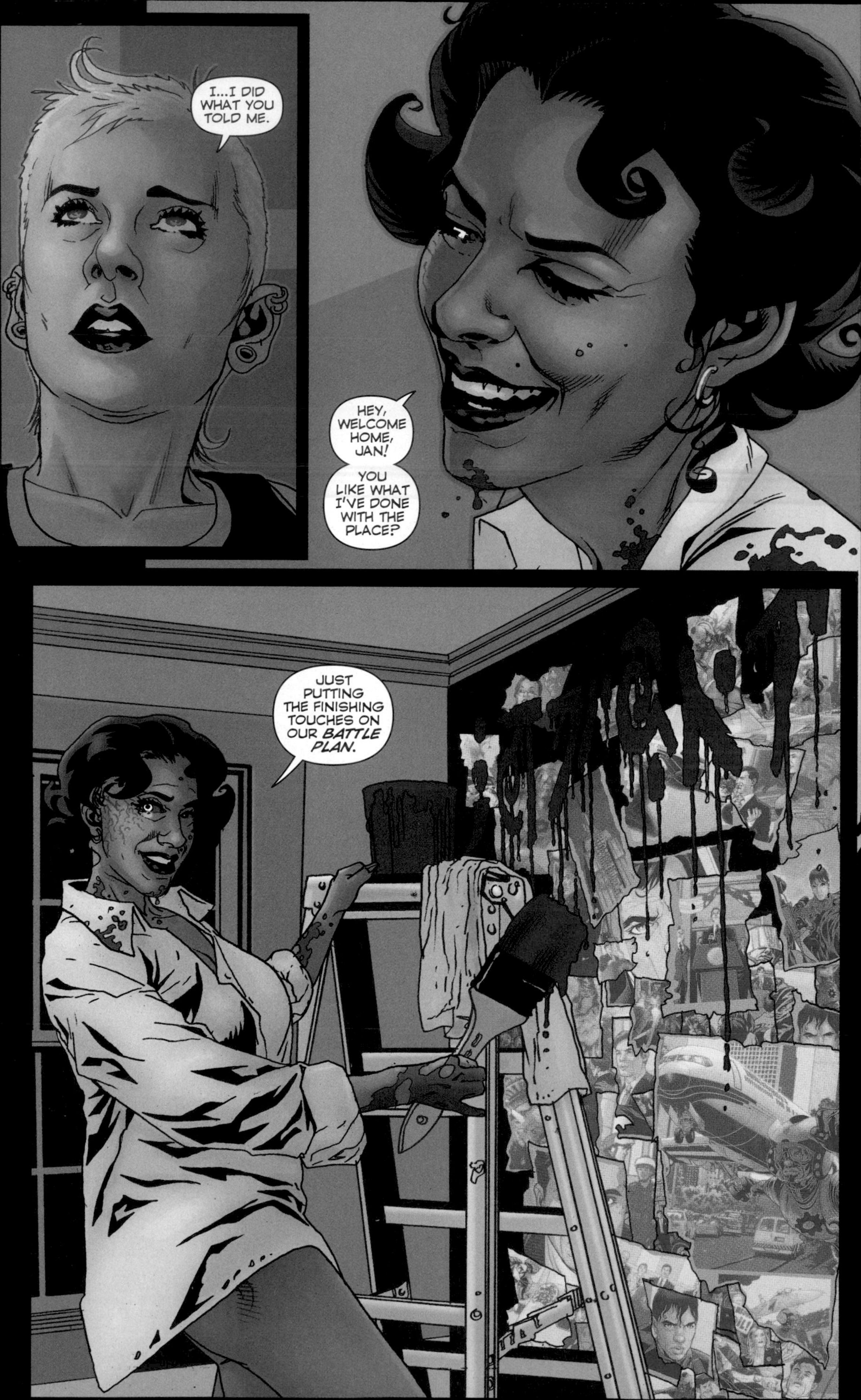

I...I DID WHAT YOU TOLD ME.
HEY, WELCOME HOME, JAN!
YOU LIKE WHAT I'VE DONE WITH THE PLACE?
JUST PUTTING THE FINISHING TOUCHES ON OUR *BATTLE PLAN*.

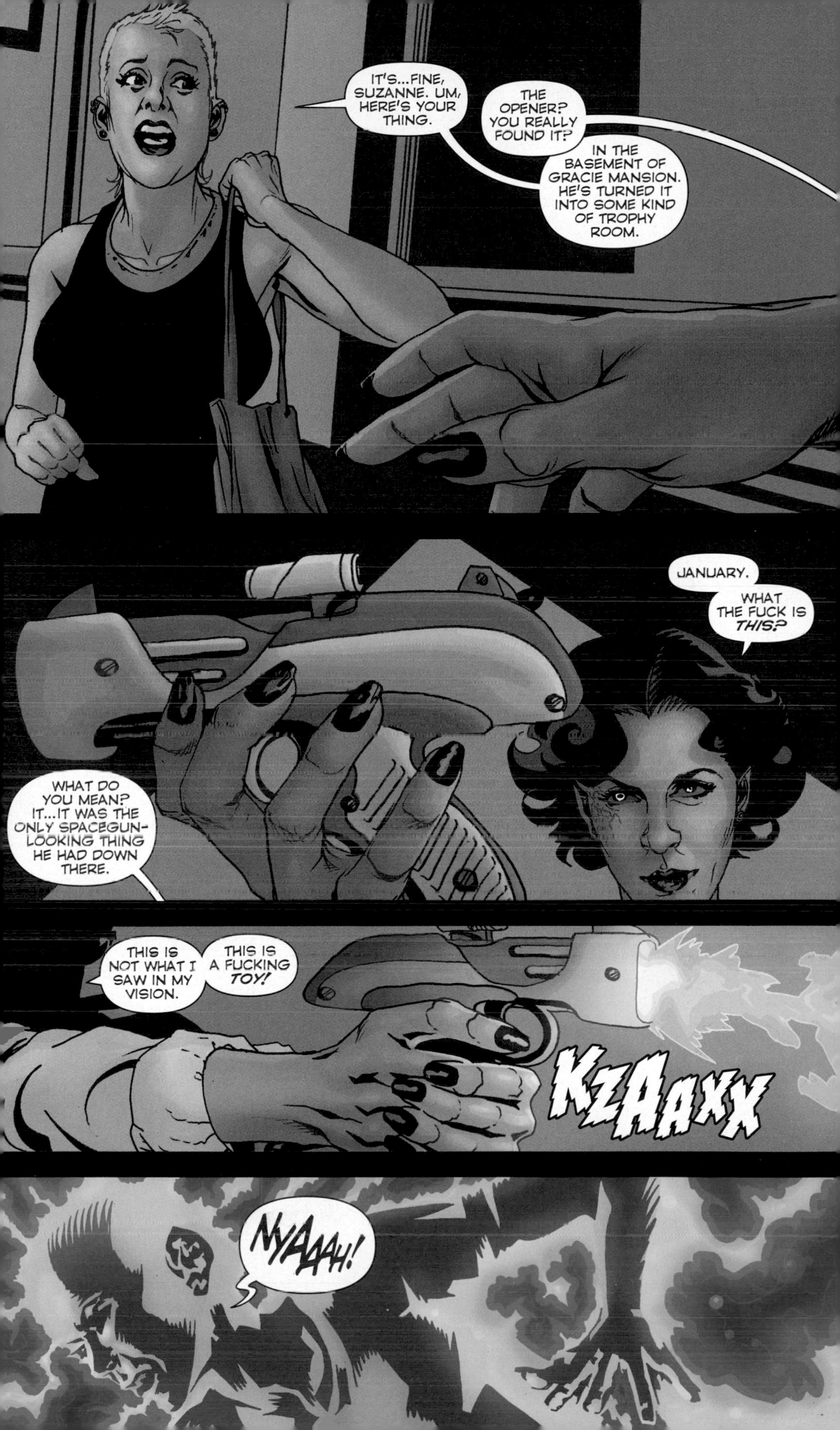

IT'S...FINE, SUZANNE. UM, HERE'S YOUR THING.
THE OPENER? YOU REALLY FOUND IT?
IN THE BASEMENT OF GRACIE MANSION. HE'S TURNED IT INTO SOME KIND OF TROPHY ROOM.
JANUARY.
WHAT THE FUCK IS *THIS?*
WHAT DO YOU MEAN? IT...IT WAS THE ONLY SPACEGUN-LOOKING THING HE HAD DOWN THERE.
THIS IS NOT WHAT I SAW IN MY VISION.
THIS IS A FUCKING *TOY!*
KZAAXX
NYAAAH!

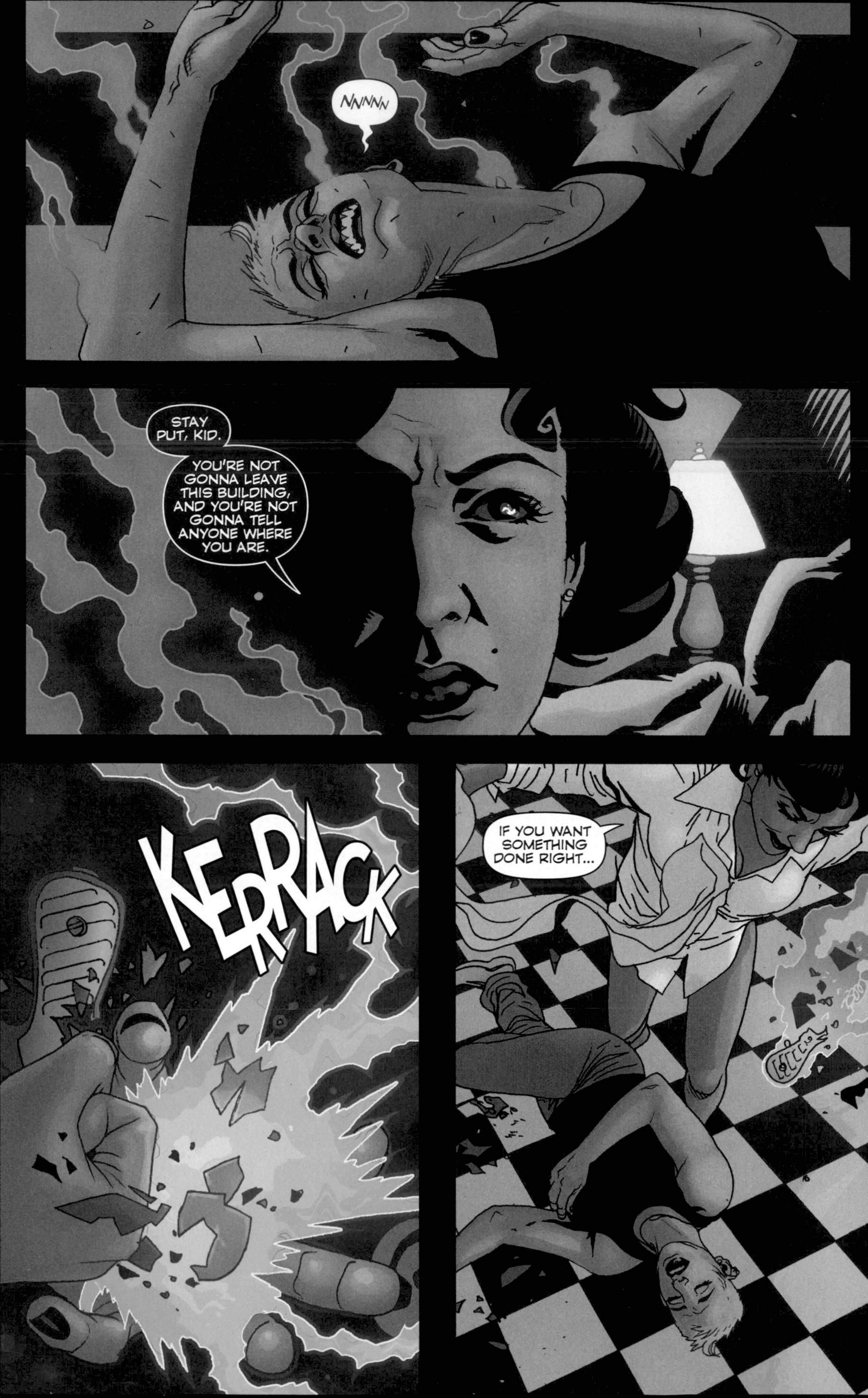
NNNNN
STAY PUT, KID.
YOU'RE NOT GONNA LEAVE THIS BUILDING, AND YOU'RE NOT GONNA TELL ANYONE WHERE YOU ARE.
KERRACK
IF YOU WANT SOMETHING DONE RIGHT...

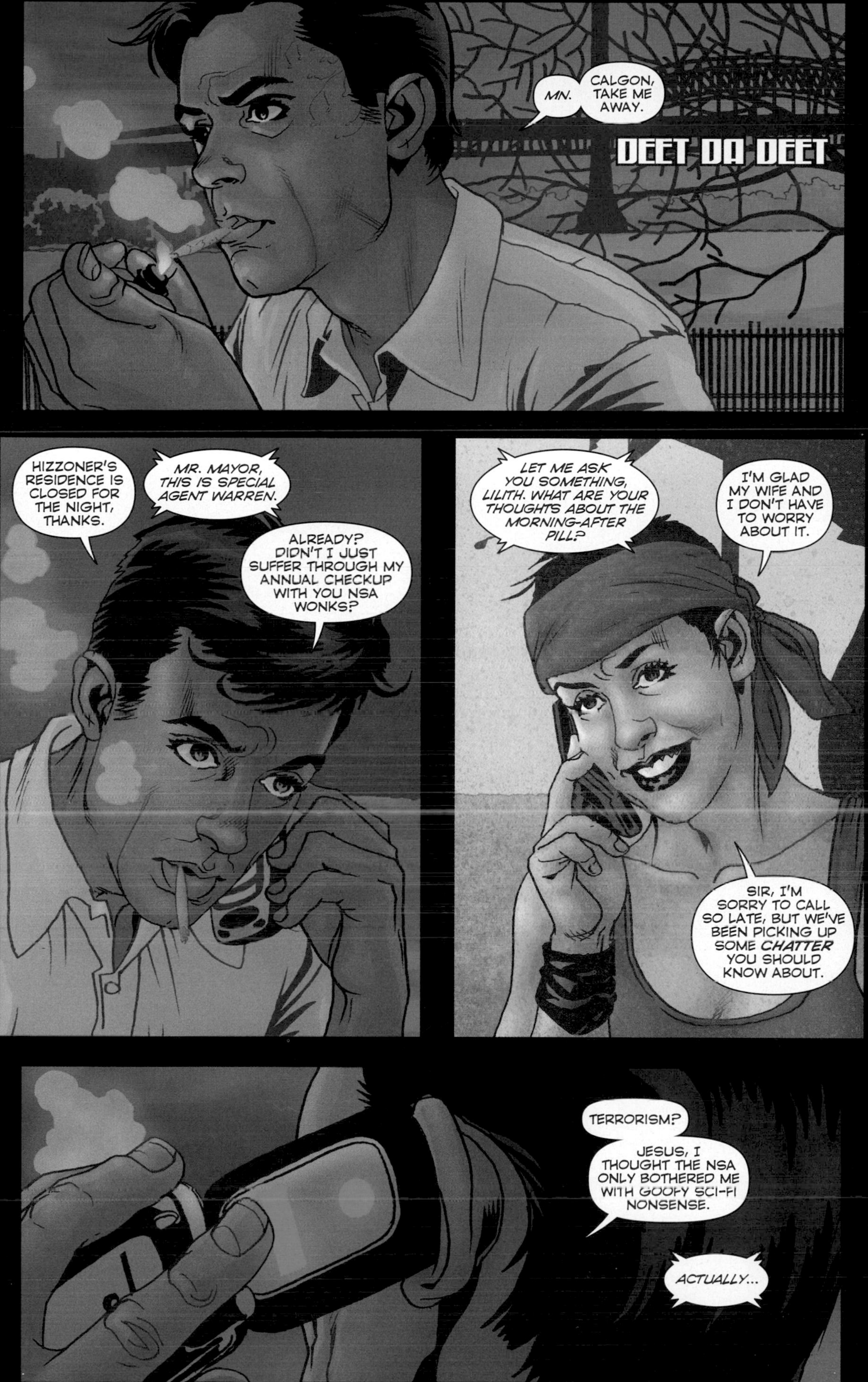
MN.
CALGON, TAKE ME AWAY.
DEET DA DEET
HIZZONER'S RESIDENCE IS CLOSED FOR THE NIGHT, THANKS.
MR. MAYOR, THIS IS SPECIAL AGENT WARREN.
ALREADY? DIDN'T I JUST SUFFER THROUGH MY ANNUAL CHECKUP WITH YOU NSA WONKS?
LET ME ASK YOU SOMETHING, LILITH. WHAT ARE YOUR THOUGHTS ABOUT THE MORNING-AFTER PILL?
I'M GLAD MY WIFE AND I DON'T HAVE TO WORRY ABOUT IT.
SIR, I'M SORRY TO CALL SO LATE, BUT WE'VE BEEN PICKING UP SOME *CHATTER* YOU SHOULD KNOW ABOUT.
TERRORISM?
JESUS, I THOUGHT THE NSA ONLY BOTHERED ME WITH GOOFY SCI-FI NONSENSE.
ACTUALLY...

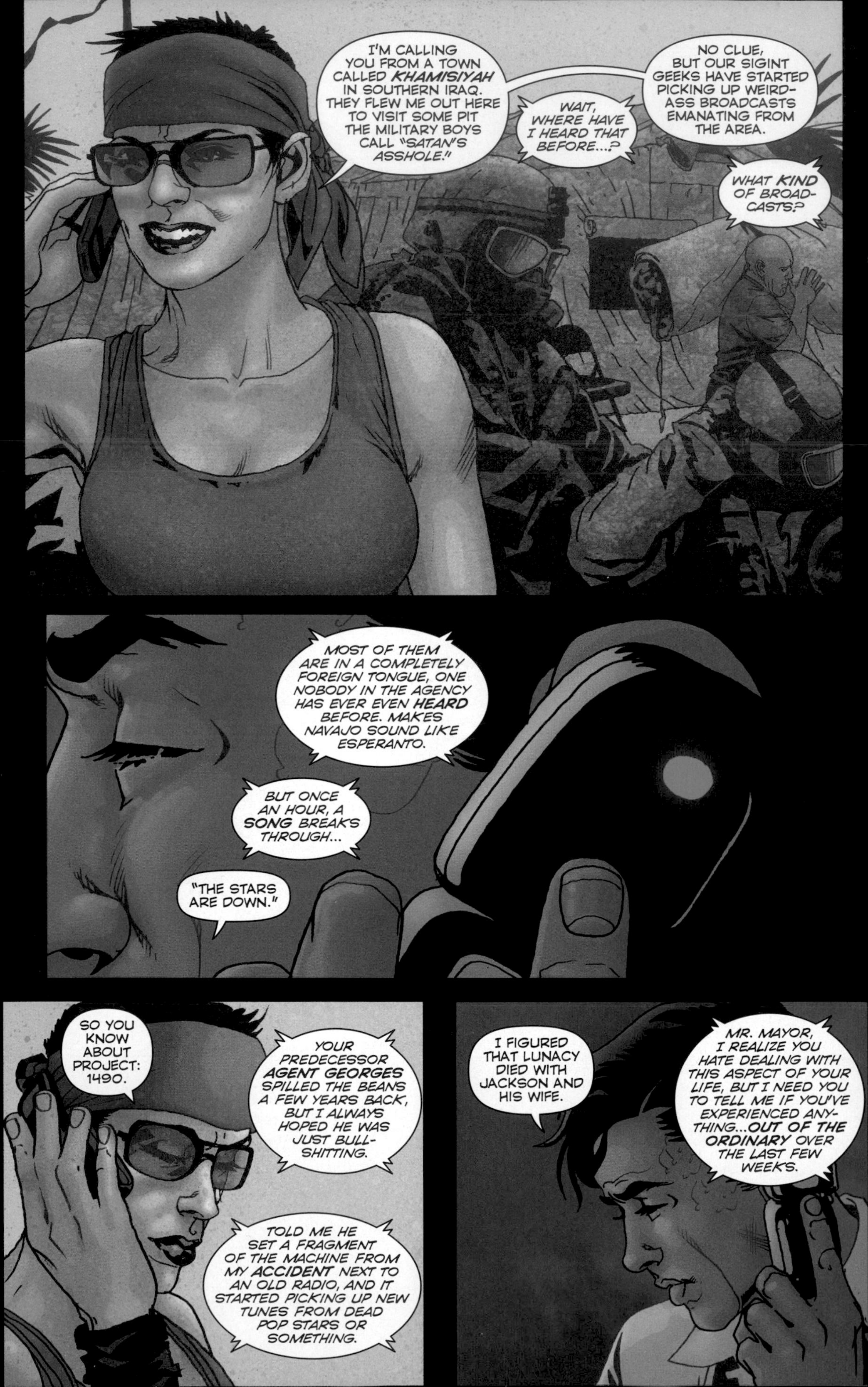
I'M CALLING YOU FROM A TOWN CALLED KHAMISIYAH IN SOUTHERN IRAQ. THEY FLEW ME OUT HERE TO VISIT SOME PIT THE MILITARY BOYS CALL "SATAN'S ASSHOLE."
WAIT, WHERE HAVE I HEARD THAT BEFORE...?
NO CLUE, BUT OUR SIGINT GEEKS HAVE STARTED PICKING UP WEIRD-ASS BROADCASTS EMANATING FROM THE AREA.
WHAT KIND OF BROAD-CASTS?
MOST OF THEM ARE IN A COMPLETELY FOREIGN TONGUE, ONE NOBODY IN THE AGENCY HAS EVER EVEN HEARD BEFORE. MAKES NAVAJO SOUND LIKE ESPERANTO.
BUT ONCE AN HOUR, A SONG BREAKS THROUGH...
"THE STARS ARE DOWN."
SO YOU KNOW ABOUT PROJECT: 1490.
YOUR PREDECESSOR AGENT GEORGES SPILLED THE BEANS A FEW YEARS BACK, BUT I ALWAYS HOPED HE WAS JUST BULL-SHITTING.
TOLD ME HE SET A FRAGMENT OF THE MACHINE FROM MY ACCIDENT NEXT TO AN OLD RADIO, AND IT STARTED PICKING UP NEW TUNES FROM DEAD POP STARS OR SOMETHING.
I FIGURED THAT LUNACY DIED WITH JACKSON AND HIS WIFE.
MR. MAYOR, I REALIZE YOU HATE DEALING WITH THIS ASPECT OF YOUR LIFE, BUT I NEED YOU TO TELL ME IF YOU'VE EXPERIENCED ANY-THING...OUT OF THE ORDINARY OVER THE LAST FEW WEEKS.

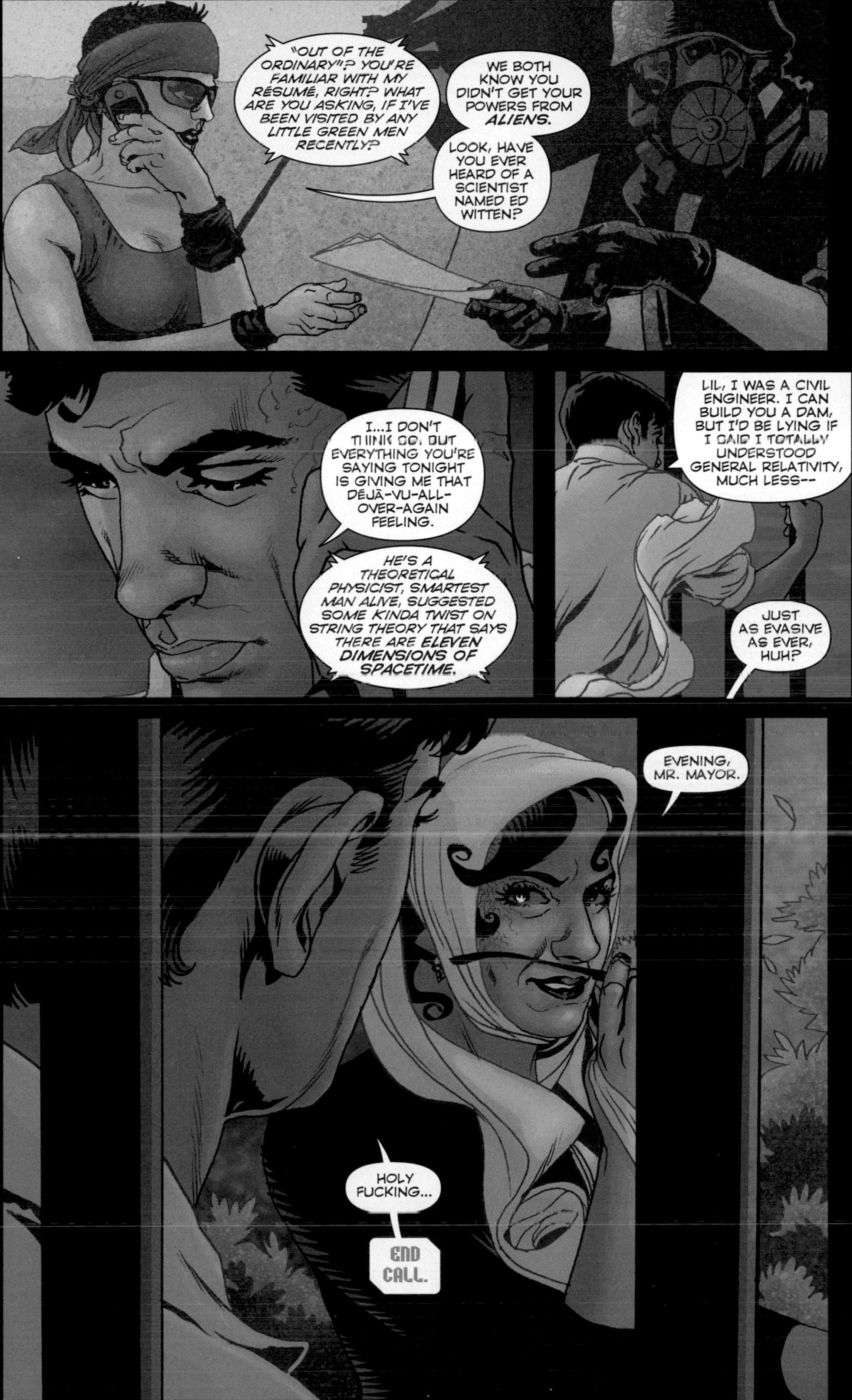
"OUT OF THE ORDINARY"? YOU'RE FAMILIAR WITH MY RÉSUMÉ, RIGHT? WHAT ARE YOU ASKING, IF I'VE BEEN VISITED BY ANY LITTLE GREEN MEN RECENTLY?
WE BOTH KNOW YOU DIDN'T GET YOUR POWERS FROM ALIENS.
LOOK, HAVE YOU EVER HEARD OF A SCIENTIST NAMED ED WITTEN?
I...I DON'T THINK SO. BUT EVERYTHING YOU'RE SAYING TONIGHT IS GIVING ME THAT DÉJÀ-VU-ALL-OVER-AGAIN FEELING.
HE'S A THEORETICAL PHYSICIST, SMARTEST MAN ALIVE, SUGGESTED SOME KINDA TWIST ON STRING THEORY THAT SAYS THERE ARE ELEVEN DIMENSIONS OF SPACETIME.
LIL, I WAS A CIVIL ENGINEER. I CAN BUILD YOU A DAM, BUT I'D BE LYING IF I SAID I TOTALLY UNDERSTOOD GENERAL RELATIVITY, MUCH LESS--
JUST AS EVASIVE AS EVER, HUH?
EVENING, MR. MAYOR.
HOLY FUCKING...
END CALL.

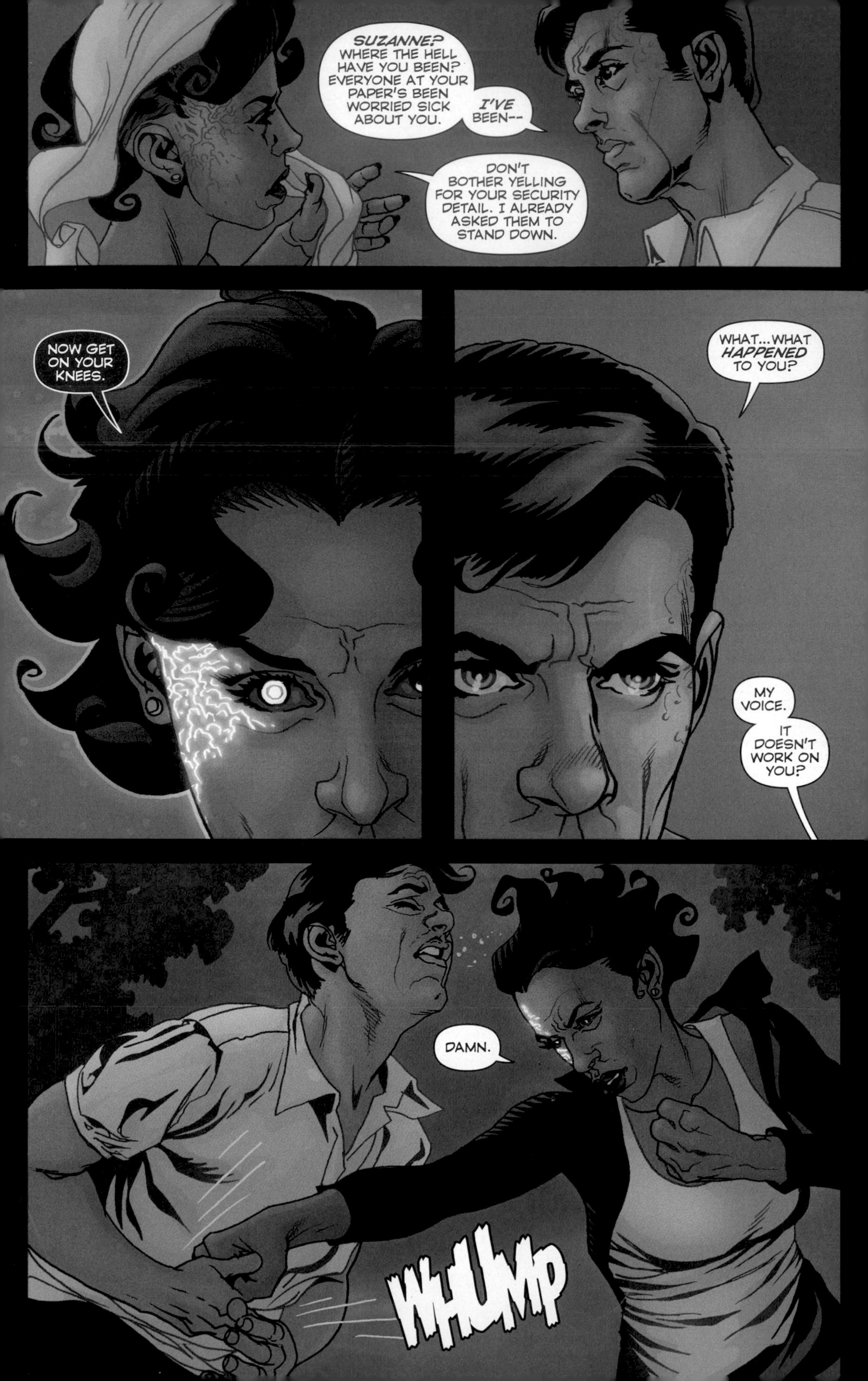
SUZANNE? WHERE THE HELL HAVE YOU BEEN? EVERYONE AT YOUR PAPER'S BEEN WORRIED SICK ABOUT YOU.
I'VE BEEN--
DON'T BOTHER YELLING FOR YOUR SECURITY DETAIL. I ALREADY ASKED THEM TO STAND DOWN.
NOW GET ON YOUR KNEES.
WHAT...WHAT HAPPENED TO YOU?
MY VOICE.
IT DOESN'T WORK ON YOU?
DAMN.
WHUMP

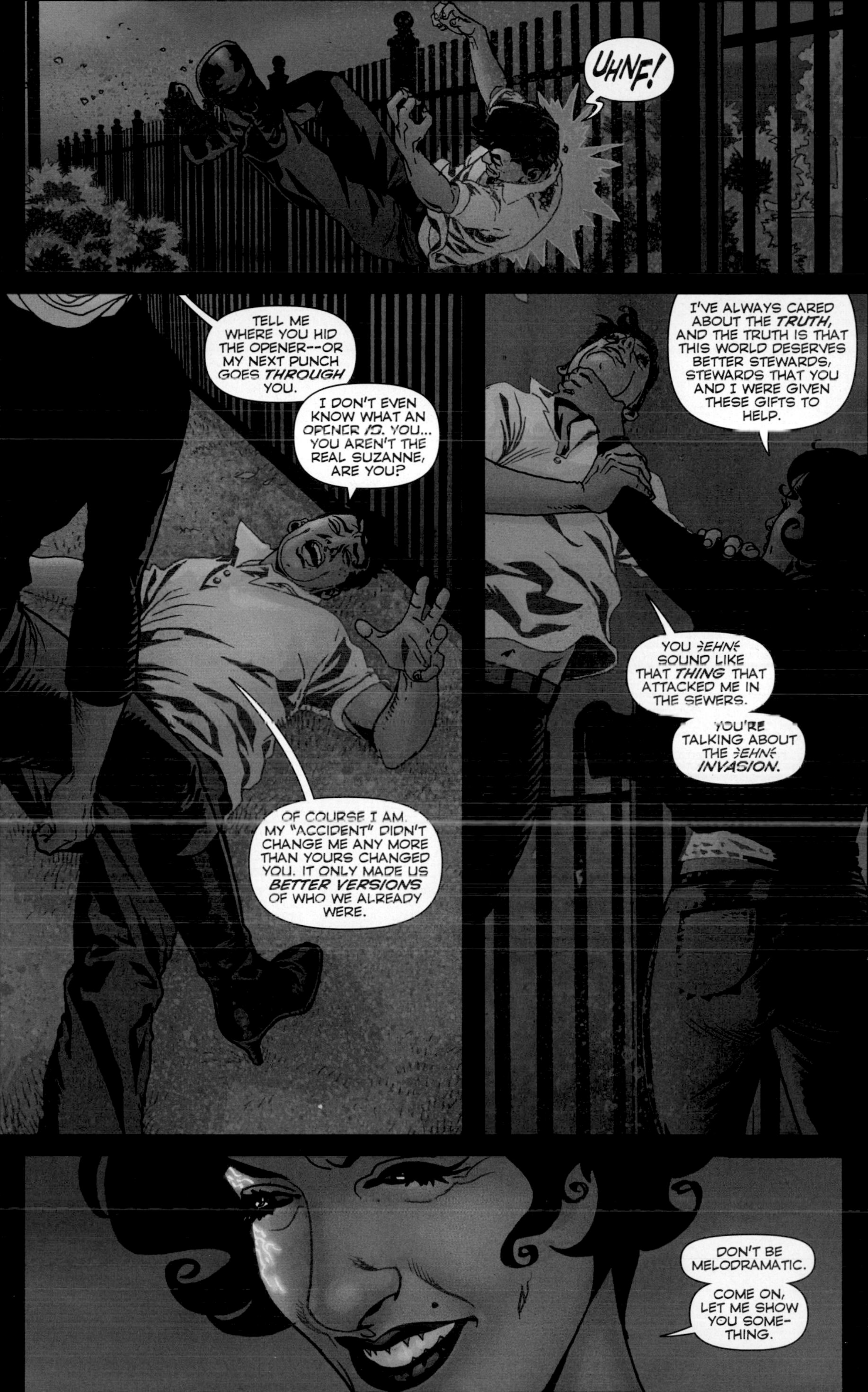
UHNF!
TELL ME WHERE YOU HID THE OPENER--OR MY NEXT PUNCH GOES *THROUGH* YOU.
I DON'T EVEN KNOW WHAT AN OPENER *IS*. YOU... YOU AREN'T THE REAL SUZANNE, ARE YOU?
OF COURSE I AM. MY "ACCIDENT" DIDN'T CHANGE ME ANY MORE THAN YOURS CHANGED YOU. IT ONLY MADE US *BETTER VERSIONS* OF WHO WE ALREADY WERE.
I'VE ALWAYS CARED ABOUT THE *TRUTH,* AND THE TRUTH IS THAT THIS WORLD DESERVES BETTER STEWARDS, STEWARDS THAT YOU AND I WERE GIVEN THESE GIFTS TO HELP.
YOU ⋺EHN⋹ SOUND LIKE THAT *THING* THAT ATTACKED ME IN THE SEWERS.
YOU'RE TALKING ABOUT THE ⋺EHN⋹ *INVASION*.
DON'T BE MELODRAMATIC.
COME ON, LET ME SHOW YOU SOME-THING.

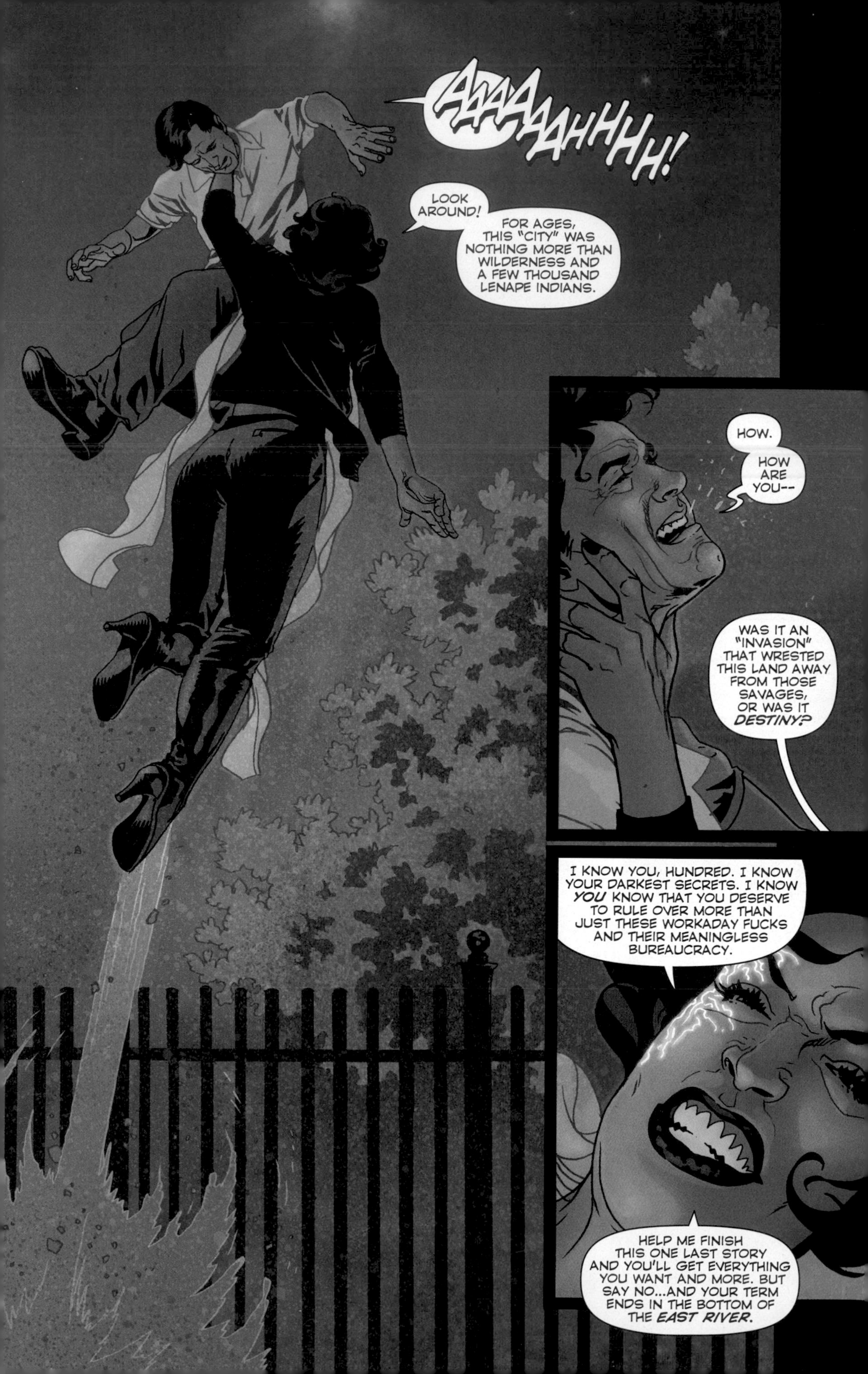
AAAAAAHHHHH!
LOOK AROUND!
FOR AGES, THIS "CITY" WAS NOTHING MORE THAN WILDERNESS AND A FEW THOUSAND LENAPE INDIANS.
HOW.
HOW ARE YOU--
WAS IT AN "INVASION" THAT WRESTED THIS LAND AWAY FROM THOSE SAVAGES, OR WAS IT *DESTINY?*
I KNOW YOU, HUNDRED. I KNOW YOUR DARKEST SECRETS. I KNOW *YOU* KNOW THAT YOU DESERVE TO RULE OVER MORE THAN JUST THESE WORKADAY FUCKS AND THEIR MEANINGLESS BUREAUCRACY.
HELP ME FINISH THIS ONE LAST STORY AND YOU'LL GET EVERYTHING YOU WANT AND MORE. BUT SAY NO...AND YOUR TERM ENDS IN THE BOTTOM OF THE *EAST RIVER.*

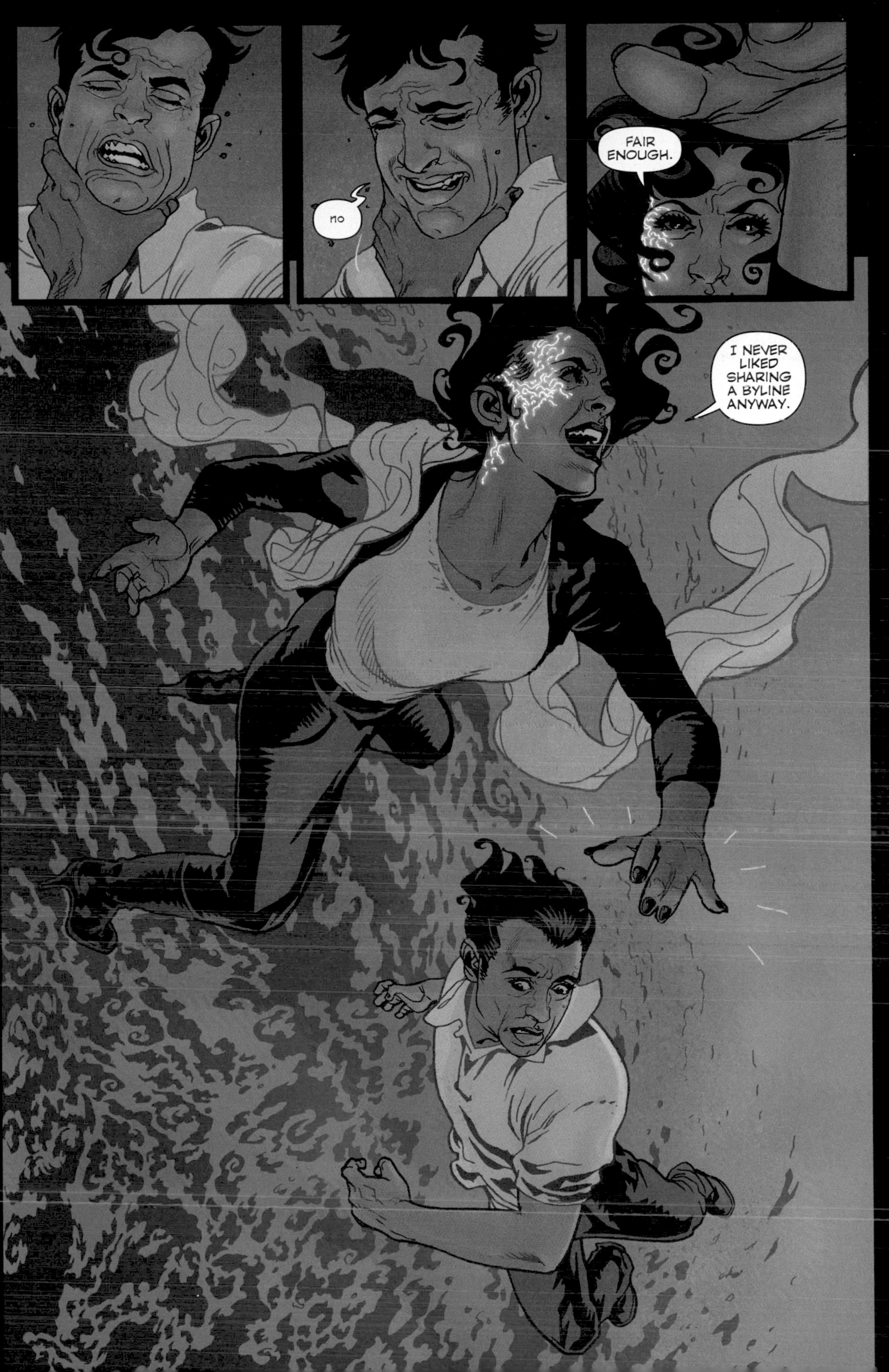
no
FAIR ENOUGH.
I NEVER LIKED SHARING A BYLINE ANYWAY.

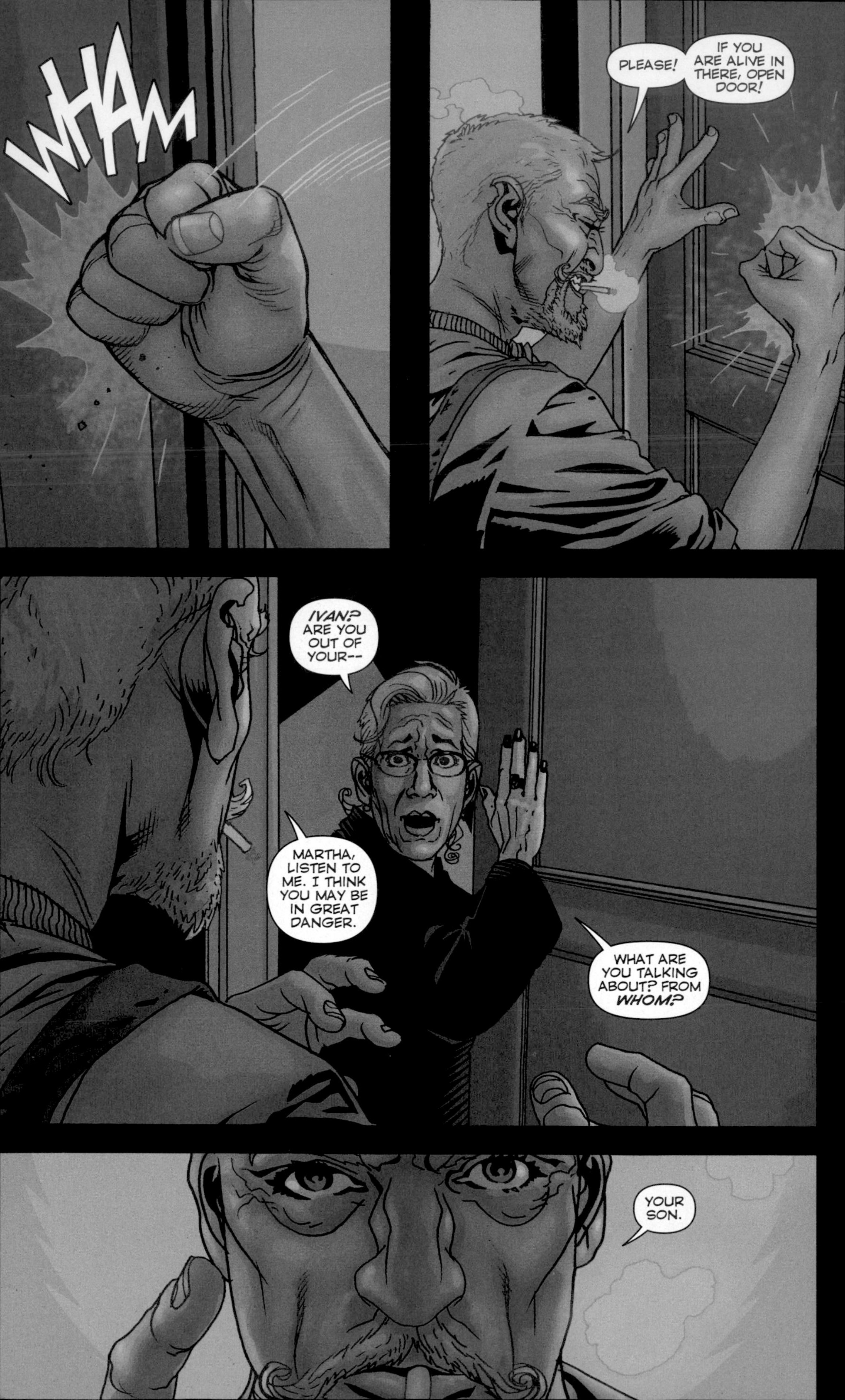
WHAM
PLEASE!
IF YOU ARE ALIVE IN THERE, OPEN DOOR!
IVAN? ARE YOU OUT OF YOUR--
MARTHA, LISTEN TO ME. I THINK YOU MAY BE IN GREAT DANGER.
WHAT ARE YOU TALKING ABOUT? FROM WHOM?
YOUR SON.

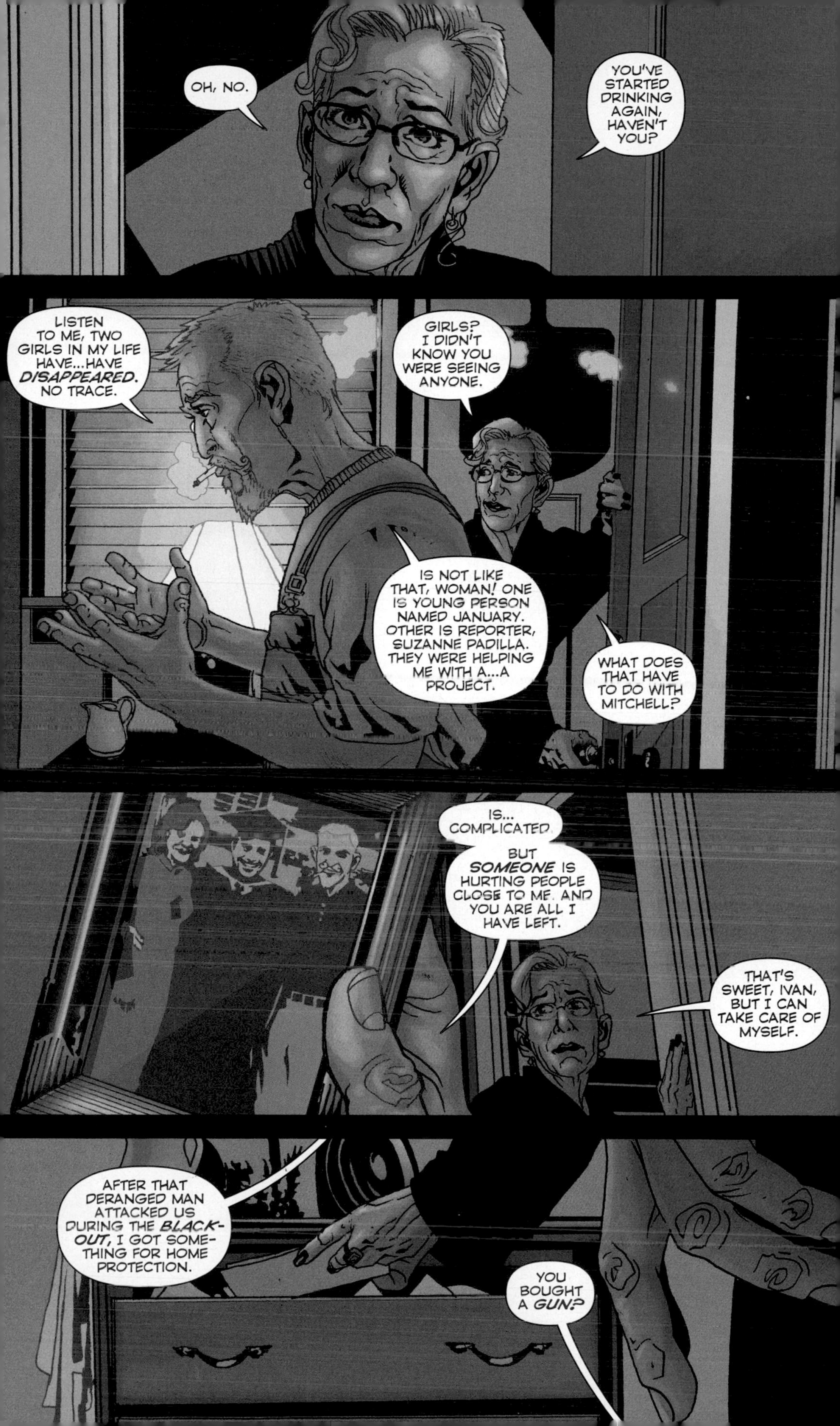
OH, NO.
YOU'VE STARTED DRINKING AGAIN, HAVEN'T YOU?
LISTEN TO ME, TWO GIRLS IN MY LIFE HAVE...HAVE *DISAPPEARED.* NO TRACE.
GIRLS? I DIDN'T KNOW YOU WERE SEEING ANYONE.
IS NOT LIKE THAT, WOMAN! ONE IS YOUNG PERSON NAMED JANUARY. OTHER IS REPORTER, SUZANNE PADILLA. THEY WERE HELPING ME WITH A...A PROJECT.
WHAT DOES THAT HAVE TO DO WITH MITCHELL?
IS... COMPLICATED.
BUT *SOMEONE* IS HURTING PEOPLE CLOSE TO ME. AND YOU ARE ALL I HAVE LEFT.
THAT'S SWEET, IVAN, BUT I CAN TAKE CARE OF MYSELF.
AFTER THAT DERANGED MAN ATTACKED US DURING THE *BLACK-OUT,* I GOT SOME-THING FOR HOME PROTECTION.
YOU BOUGHT A *GUN?*

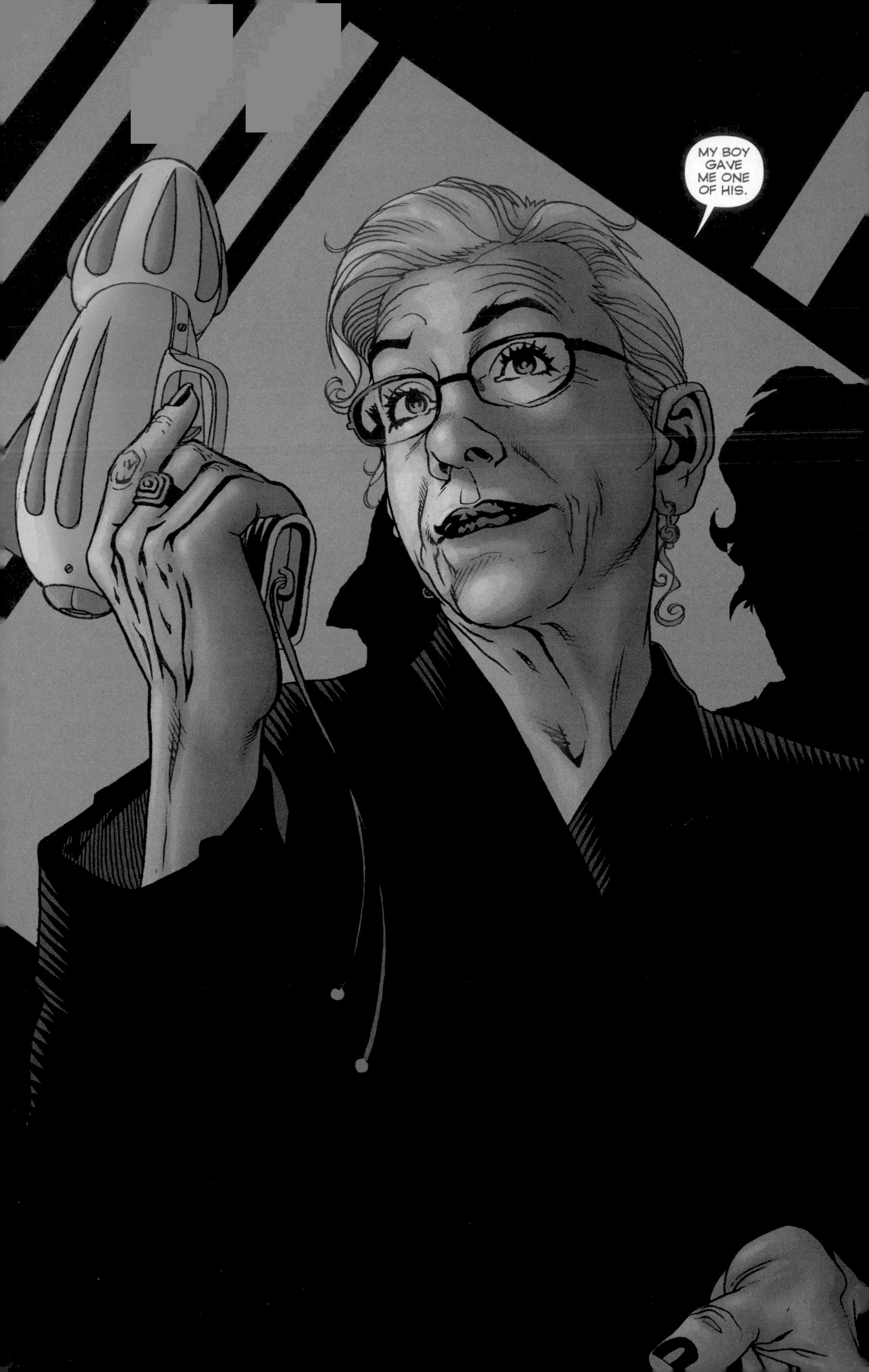
MY BOY GAVE ME ONE OF HIS.

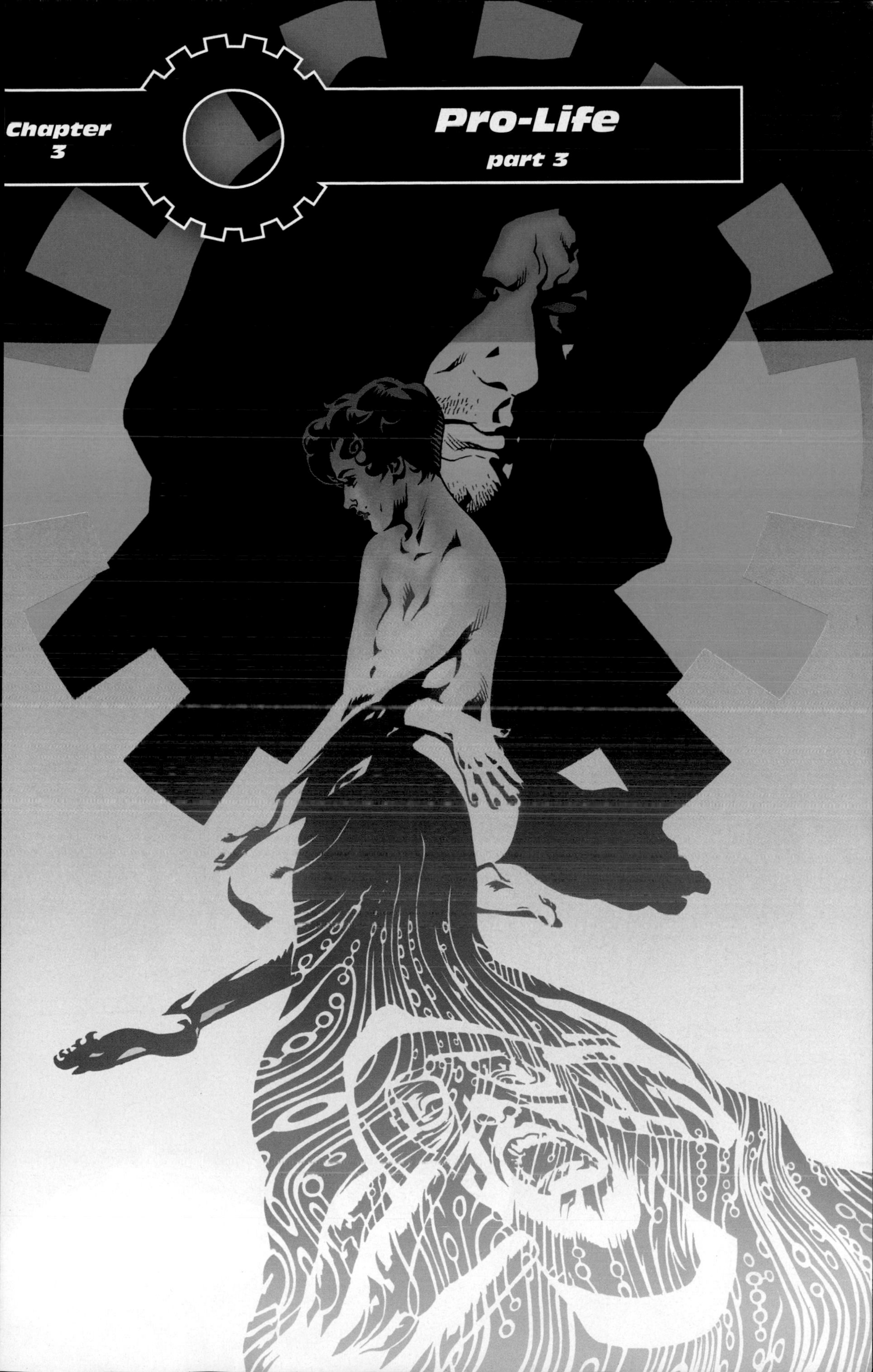
Chapter 3
Pro-Life
part 3

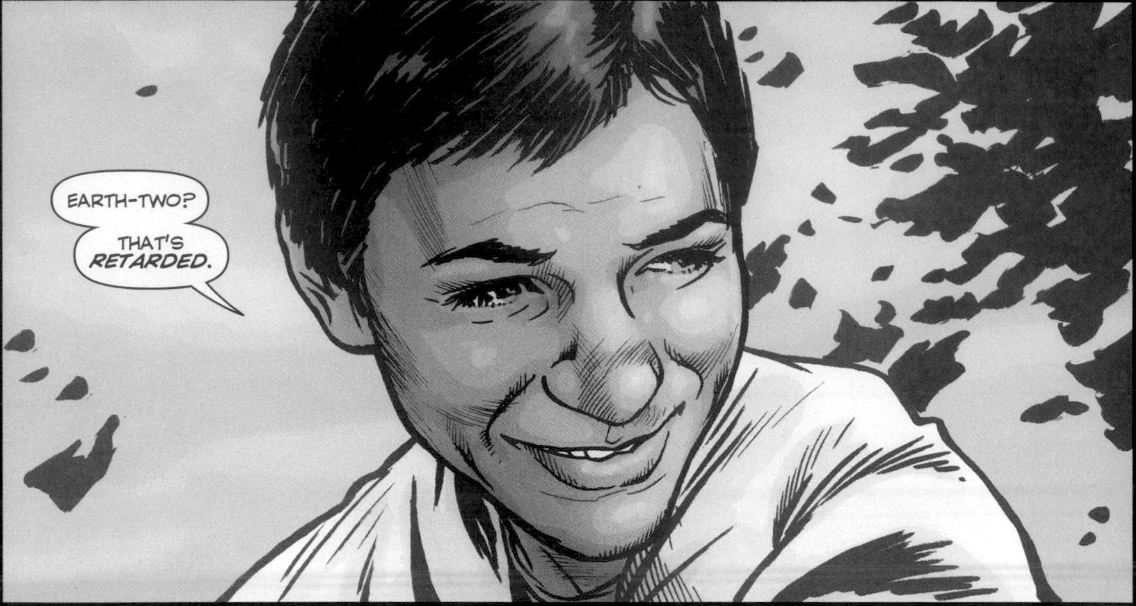
EARTH-TWO?
THAT'S *RETARDED*.

MONDAY, MARCH 10, 1980

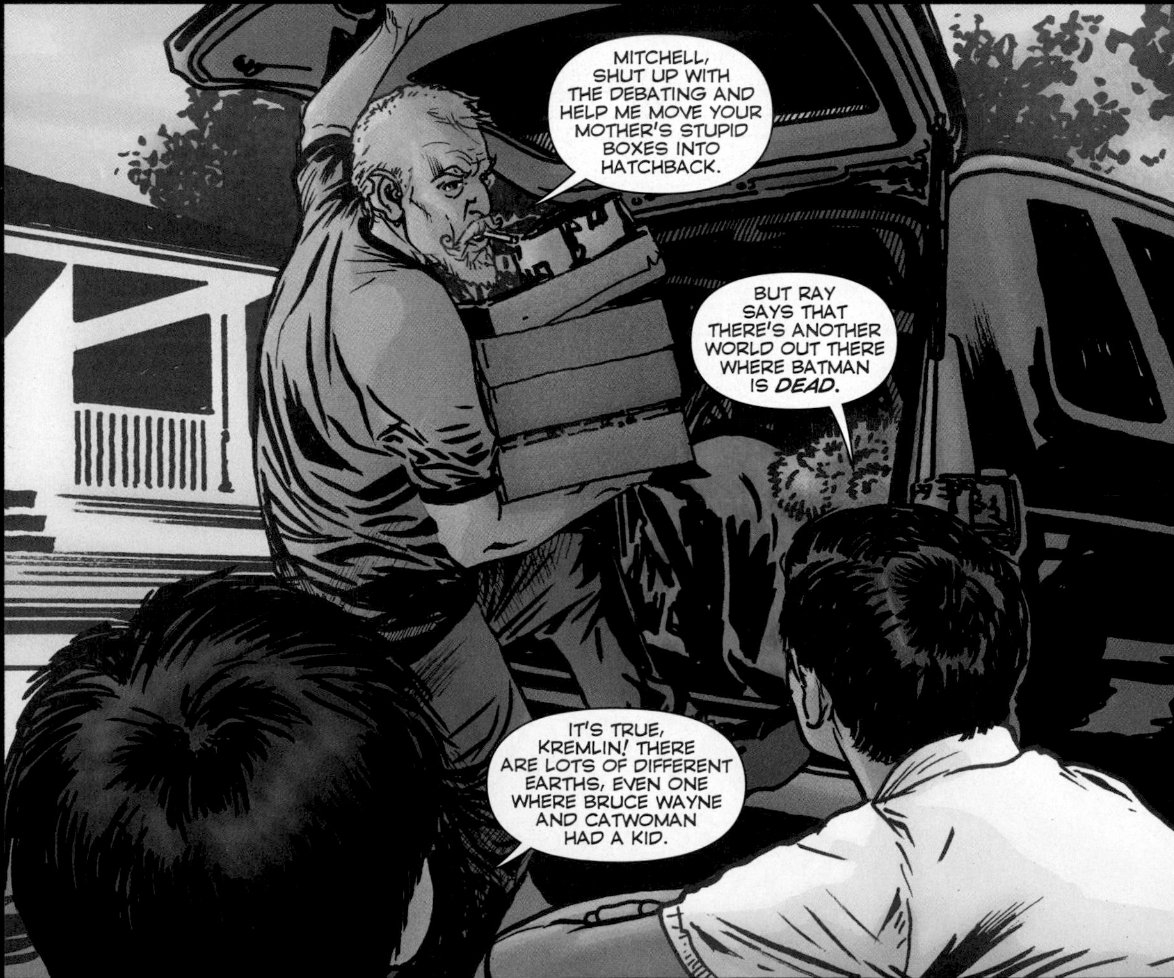
MITCHELL, SHUT UP WITH THE DEBATING AND HELP ME MOVE YOUR MOTHER'S STUPID BOXES INTO HATCHBACK.
BUT RAY SAYS THAT THERE'S ANOTHER WORLD OUT THERE WHERE BATMAN IS *DEAD*.
IT'S TRUE, KREMLIN! THERE ARE LOTS OF DIFFERENT EARTHS, EVEN ONE WHERE BRUCE WAYNE AND CATWOMAN HAD A KID.

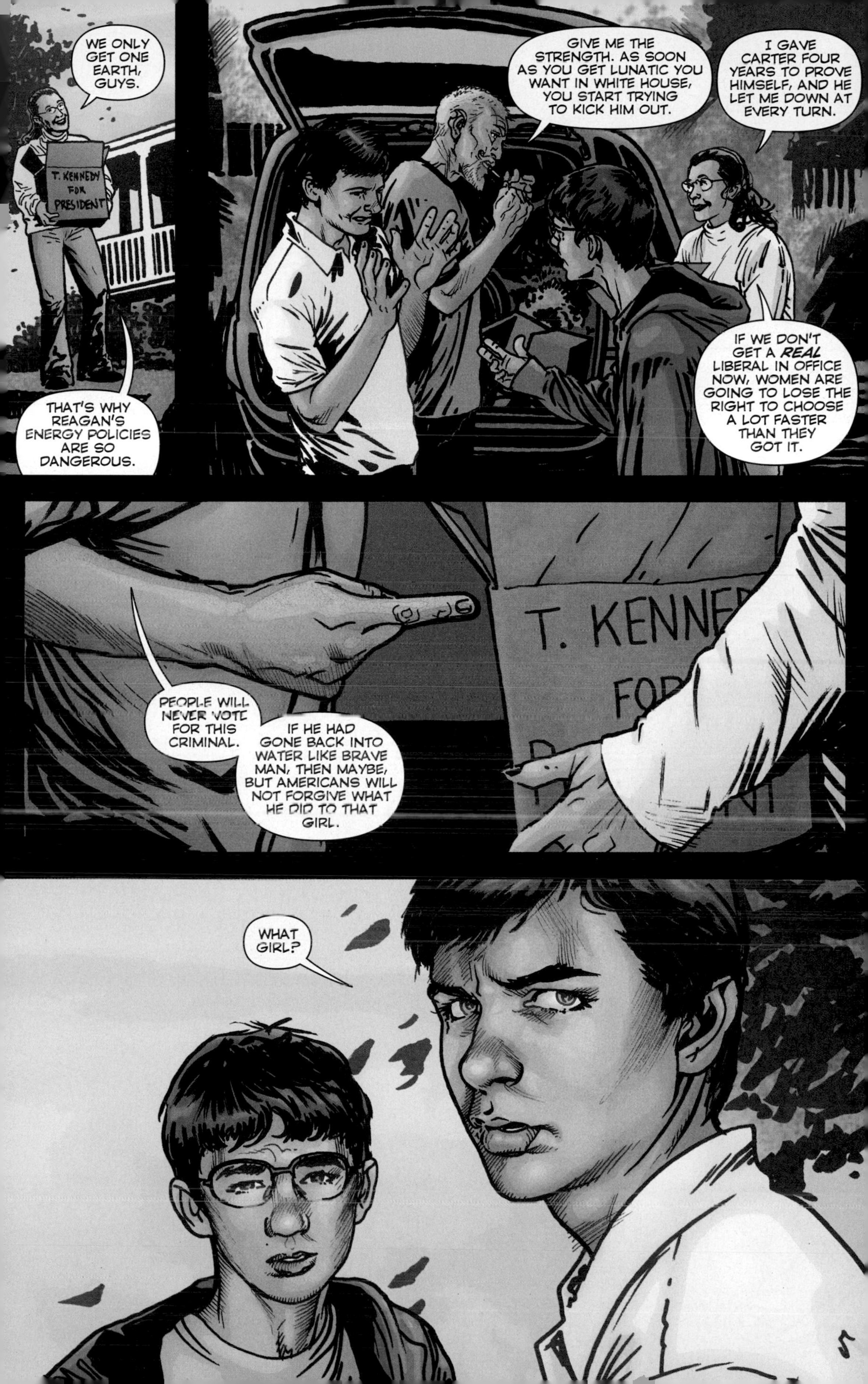
WE ONLY GET ONE EARTH, GUYS.
T. KENNEDY FOR PRESIDENT
THAT'S WHY REAGAN'S ENERGY POLICIES ARE SO DANGEROUS.
GIVE ME THE STRENGTH. AS SOON AS YOU GET LUNATIC YOU WANT IN WHITE HOUSE, YOU START TRYING TO KICK HIM OUT.
I GAVE CARTER FOUR YEARS TO PROVE HIMSELF, AND HE LET ME DOWN AT EVERY TURN.
IF WE DON'T GET A *REAL* LIBERAL IN OFFICE NOW, WOMEN ARE GOING TO LOSE THE RIGHT TO CHOOSE A LOT FASTER THAN THEY GOT IT.
T. KENNE
PEOPLE WILL NEVER VOTE FOR THIS CRIMINAL.
IF HE HAD GONE BACK INTO WATER LIKE BRAVE MAN, THEN MAYBE, BUT AMERICANS WILL NOT FORGIVE WHAT HE DID TO THAT GIRL.
WHAT GIRL?

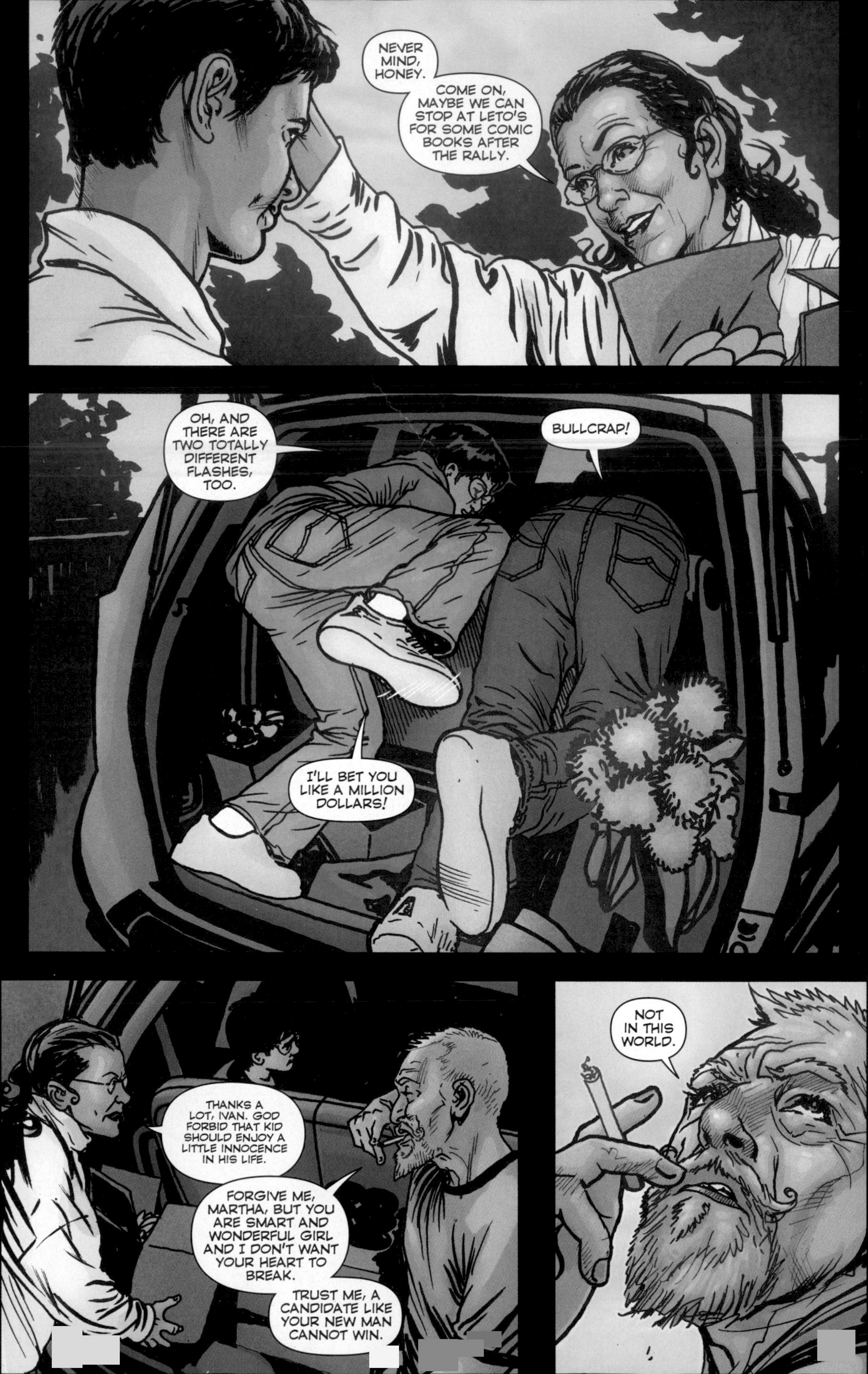

NEVER MIND, HONEY.
COME ON, MAYBE WE CAN STOP AT LETO'S FOR SOME COMIC BOOKS AFTER THE RALLY.
OH, AND THERE ARE TWO TOTALLY DIFFERENT FLASHES, TOO.
BULLCRAP!
I'LL BET YOU LIKE A MILLION DOLLARS!
THANKS A LOT, IVAN. GOD FORBID THAT KID SHOULD ENJOY A LITTLE INNOCENCE IN HIS LIFE.
FORGIVE ME, MARTHA, BUT YOU ARE SMART AND WONDERFUL GIRL AND I DON'T WANT YOUR HEART TO BREAK.
TRUST ME, A CANDIDATE LIKE YOUR NEW MAN CANNOT WIN.
NOT IN THIS WORLD.

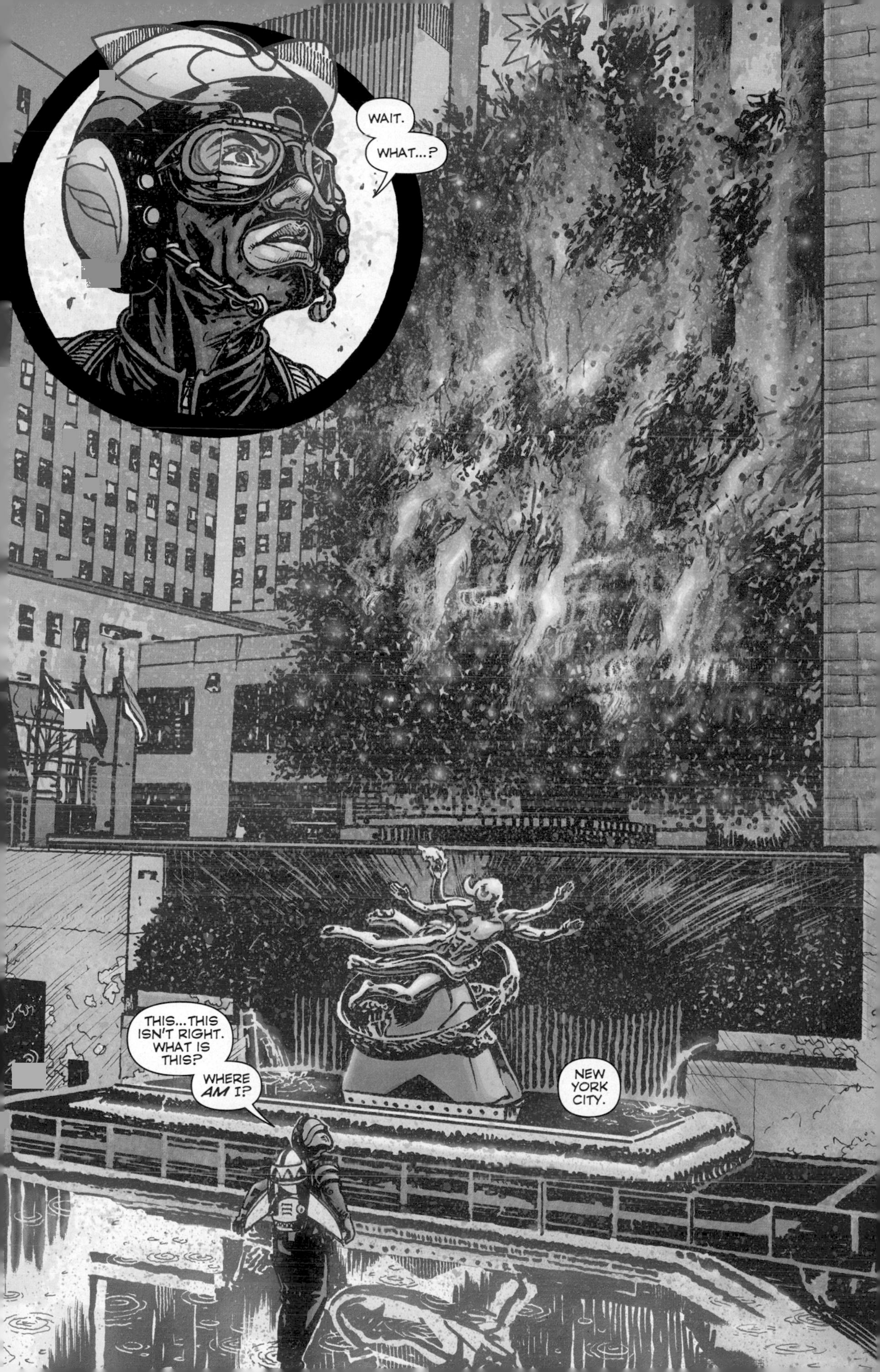
WAIT.
WHAT...?
THIS...THIS ISN'T RIGHT. WHAT IS THIS?
WHERE AM I?
NEW YORK CITY.

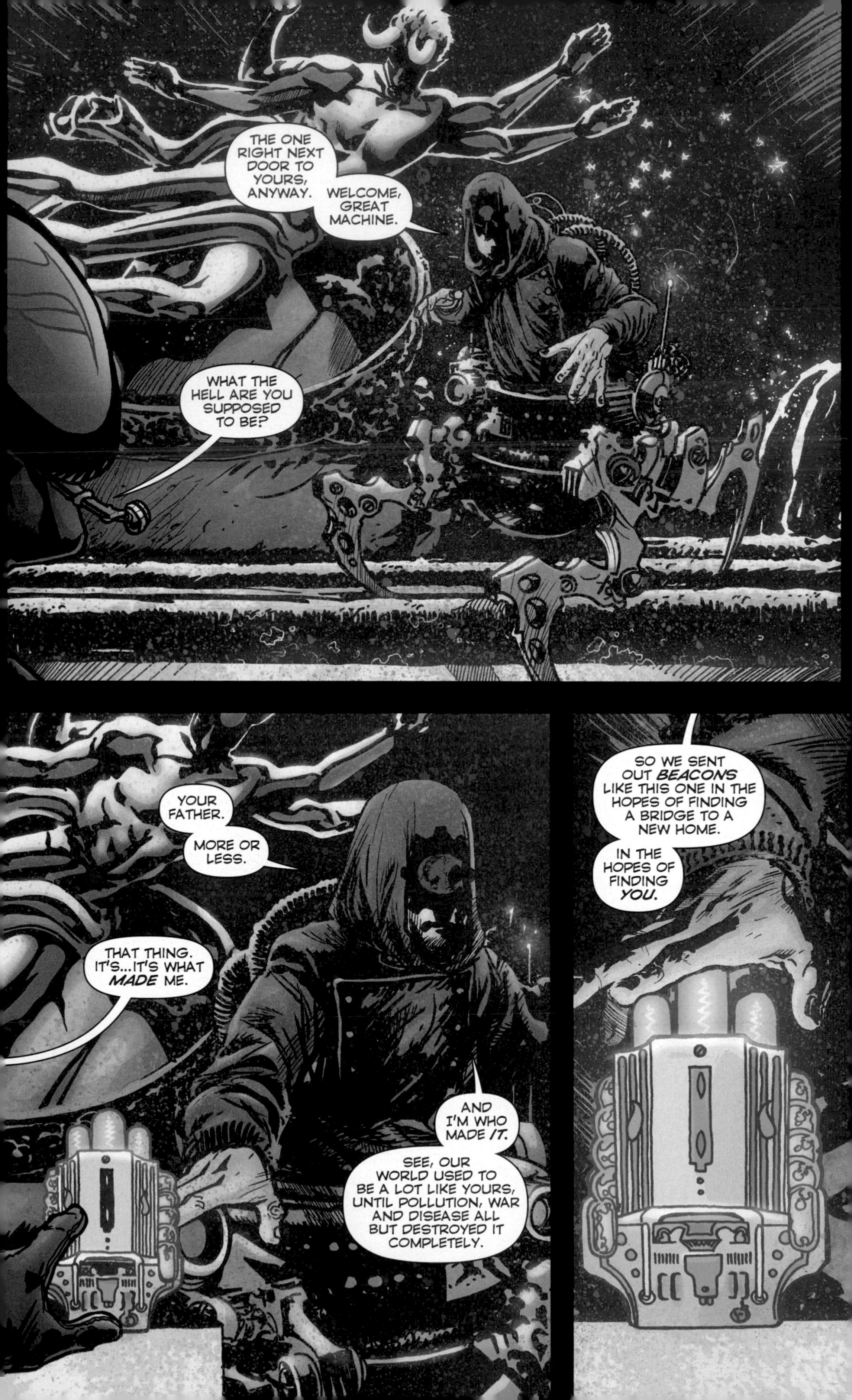
THE ONE RIGHT NEXT DOOR TO YOURS, ANYWAY.
WELCOME, GREAT MACHINE.
WHAT THE HELL ARE YOU SUPPOSED TO BE?
YOUR FATHER.
MORE OR LESS.
THAT THING. IT'S...IT'S WHAT *MADE* ME.
AND I'M WHO MADE *IT*.
SEE, OUR WORLD USED TO BE A LOT LIKE YOURS, UNTIL POLLUTION, WAR AND DISEASE ALL BUT DESTROYED IT COMPLETELY.
SO WE SENT OUT *BEACONS* LIKE THIS ONE IN THE HOPES OF FINDING A BRIDGE TO A NEW HOME.
IN THE HOPES OF FINDING *YOU*.

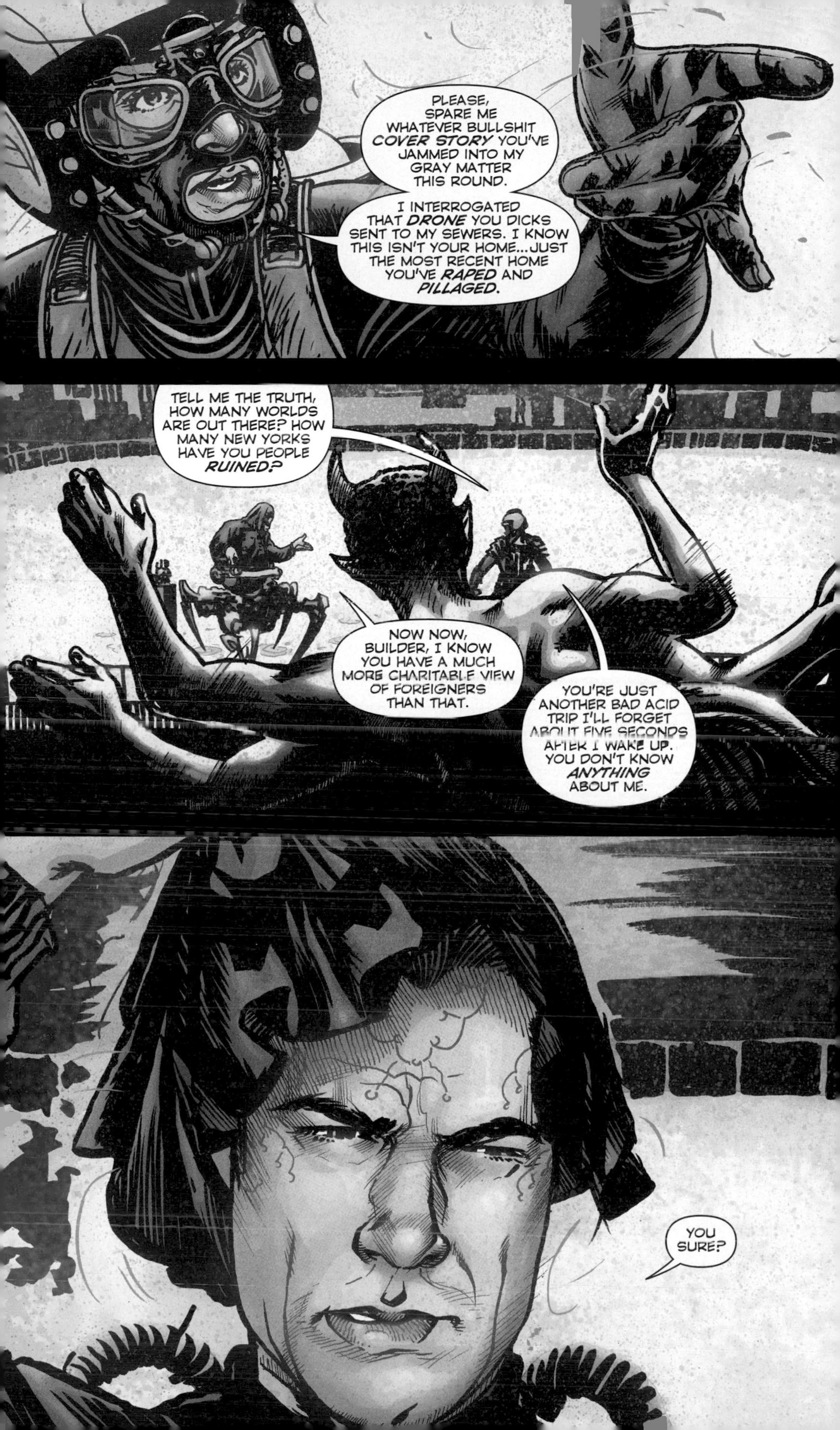
PLEASE, SPARE ME WHATEVER BULLSHIT COVER STORY YOU'VE JAMMED INTO MY GRAY MATTER THIS ROUND.
I INTERROGATED THAT DRONE YOU DICKS SENT TO MY SEWERS. I KNOW THIS ISN'T YOUR HOME...JUST THE MOST RECENT HOME YOU'VE RAPED AND PILLAGED.
TELL ME THE TRUTH, HOW MANY WORLDS ARE OUT THERE? HOW MANY NEW YORKS HAVE YOU PEOPLE RUINED?
NOW NOW, BUILDER, I KNOW YOU HAVE A MUCH MORE CHARITABLE VIEW OF FOREIGNERS THAN THAT.
YOU'RE JUST ANOTHER BAD ACID TRIP I'LL FORGET ABOUT FIVE SECONDS AFTER I WAKE UP. YOU DON'T KNOW ANYTHING ABOUT ME.
YOU SURE?

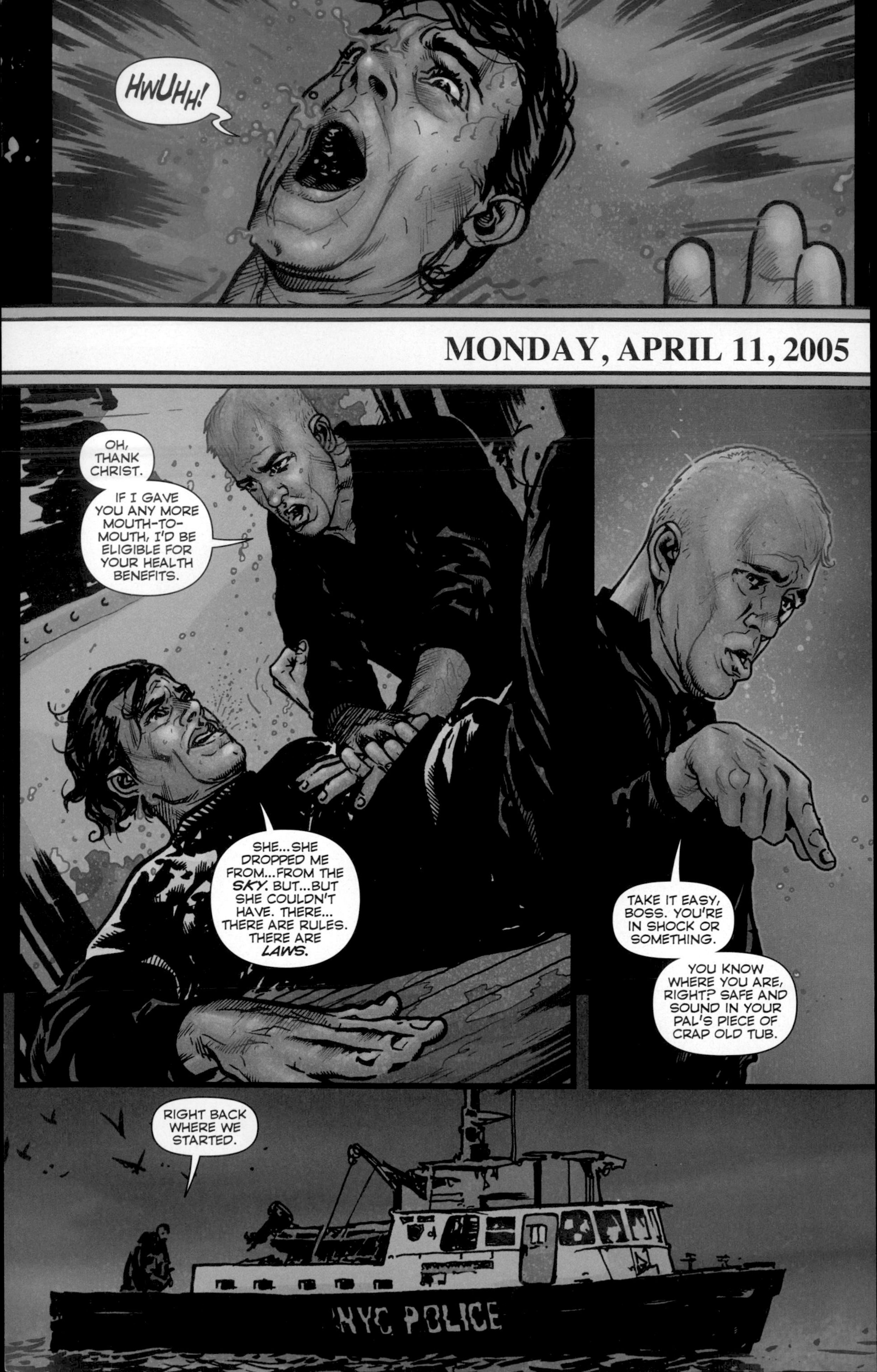
HWUHH!
MONDAY, APRIL 11, 2005
OH, THANK CHRIST.
IF I GAVE YOU ANY MORE MOUTH-TO-MOUTH, I'D BE ELIGIBLE FOR YOUR HEALTH BENEFITS.
SHE...SHE DROPPED ME FROM...FROM THE SKY. BUT...BUT SHE COULDN'T HAVE. THERE... THERE ARE RULES. THERE ARE LAWS.
TAKE IT EASY, BOSS. YOU'RE IN SHOCK OR SOMETHING.
YOU KNOW WHERE YOU ARE, RIGHT? SAFE AND SOUND IN YOUR PAL'S PIECE OF CRAP OLD TUB.
RIGHT BACK WHERE WE STARTED.
NYC POLICE

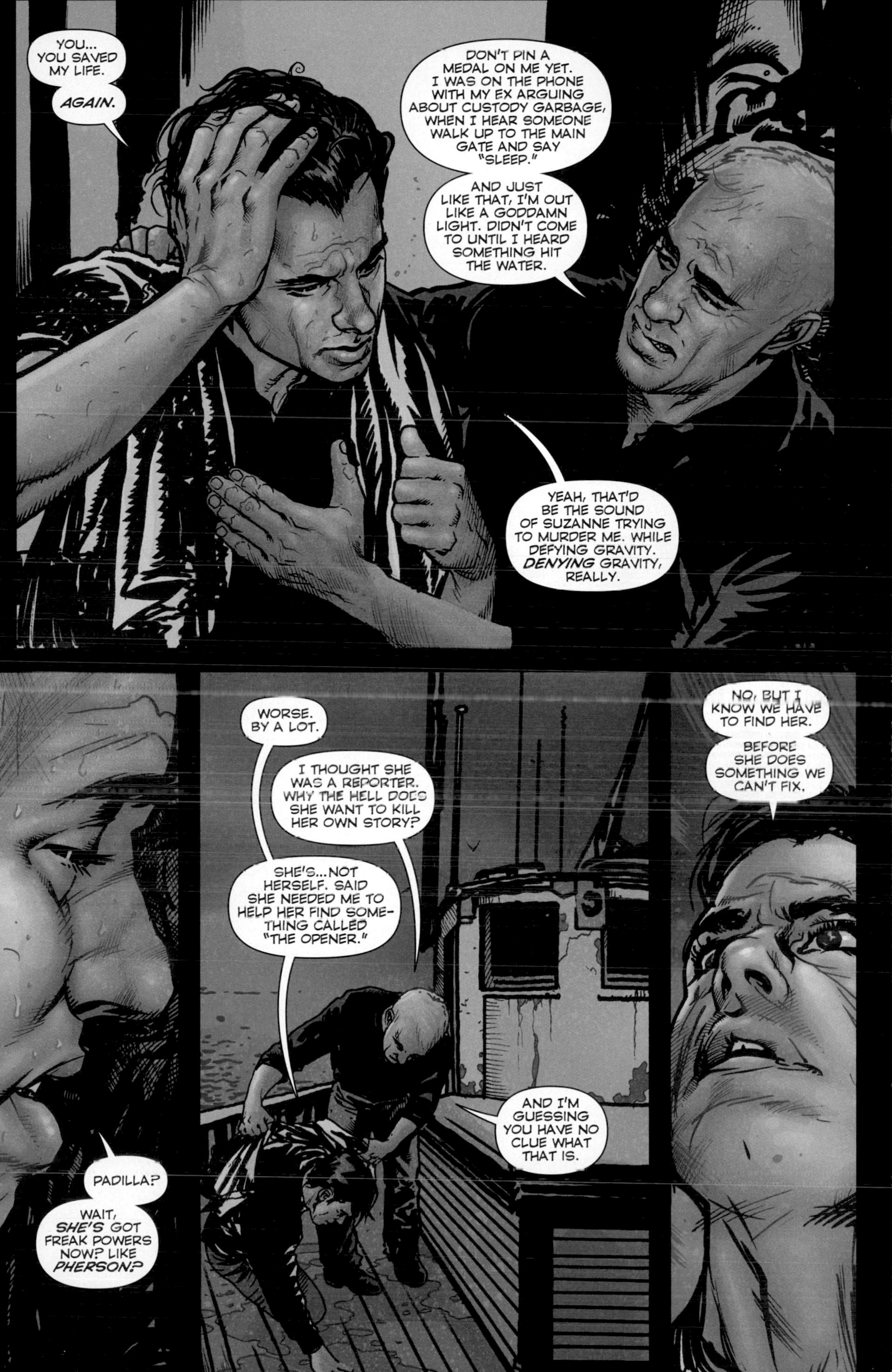
YOU... YOU SAVED MY LIFE.
AGAIN.
DON'T PIN A MEDAL ON ME YET. I WAS ON THE PHONE WITH MY EX ARGUING ABOUT CUSTODY GARBAGE, WHEN I HEAR SOMEONE WALK UP TO THE MAIN GATE AND SAY "SLEEP."
AND JUST LIKE THAT, I'M OUT LIKE A GODDAMN LIGHT. DIDN'T COME TO UNTIL I HEARD SOMETHING HIT THE WATER.
YEAH, THAT'D BE THE SOUND OF SUZANNE TRYING TO MURDER ME. WHILE DEFYING GRAVITY. DENYING GRAVITY, REALLY.
PADILLA?
WAIT, SHE'S GOT FREAK POWERS NOW? LIKE PHERSON?
WORSE. BY A LOT.
I THOUGHT SHE WAS A REPORTER. WHY THE HELL DOES SHE WANT TO KILL HER OWN STORY?
SHE'S...NOT HERSELF. SAID SHE NEEDED ME TO HELP HER FIND SOMETHING CALLED "THE OPENER."
AND I'M GUESSING YOU HAVE NO CLUE WHAT THAT IS.
NO, BUT I KNOW WE HAVE TO FIND HER.
BEFORE SHE DOES SOMETHING WE CAN'T FIX.

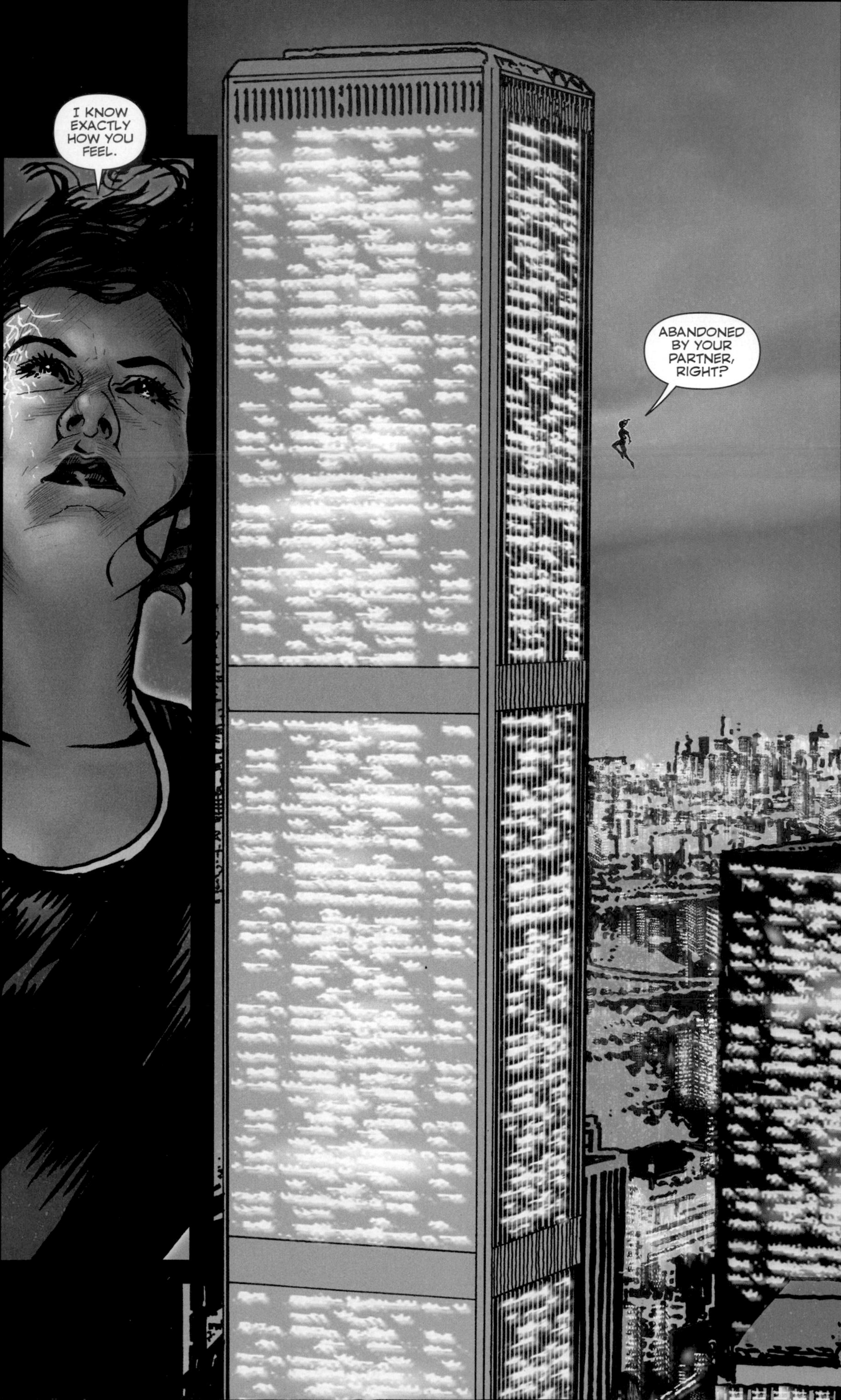
I KNOW EXACTLY HOW YOU FEEL.
ABANDONED BY YOUR PARTNER, RIGHT?

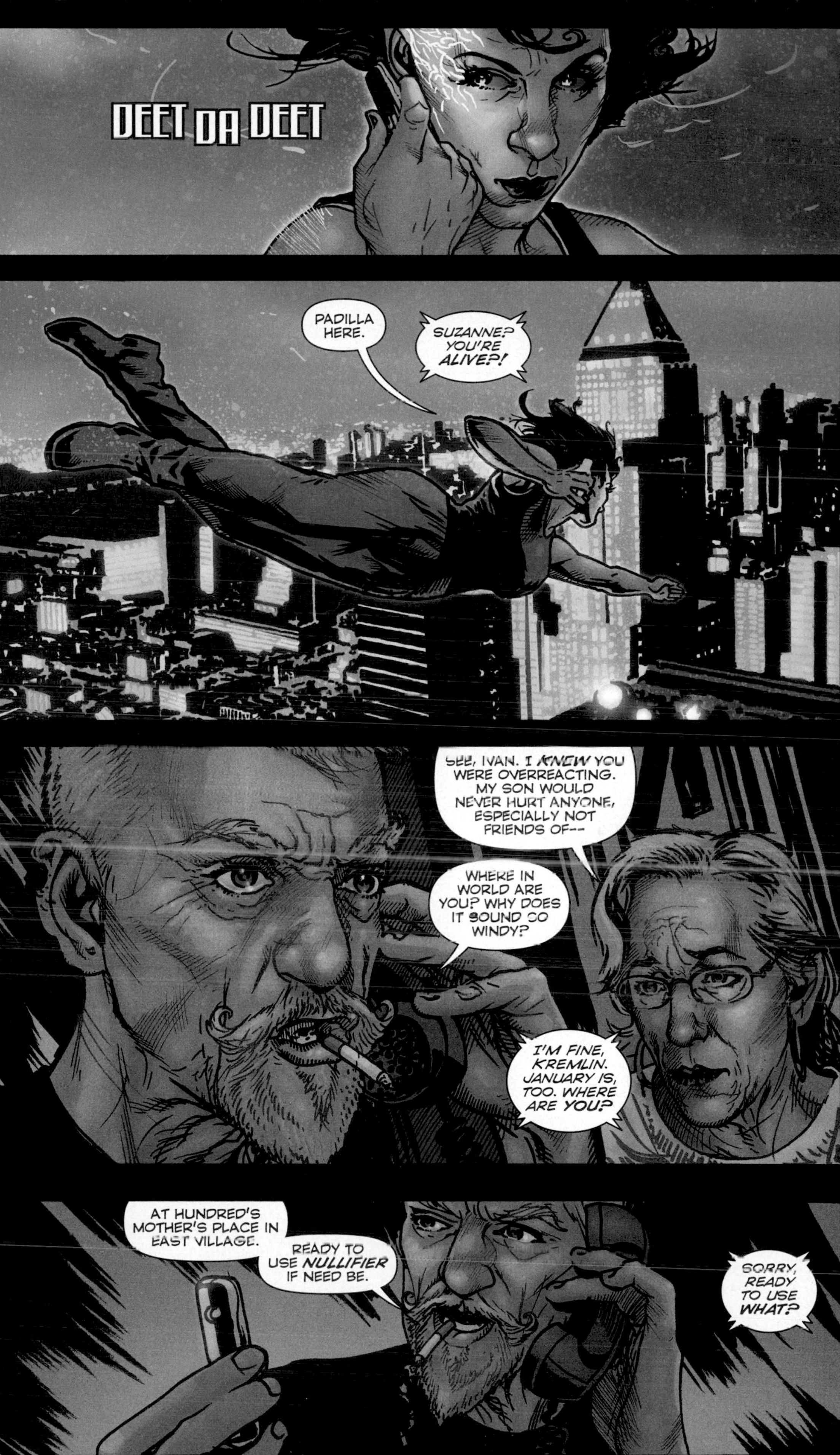
DEET DA DEET
PADILLA HERE.
SUZANNE? YOU'RE ALIVE?!
SEE, IVAN. I KNEW YOU WERE OVERREACTING. MY SON WOULD NEVER HURT ANYONE, ESPECIALLY NOT FRIENDS OF--
WHERE IN WORLD ARE YOU? WHY DOES IT SOUND SO WINDY?
I'M FINE, KREMLIN. JANUARY IS, TOO. WHERE ARE YOU?
AT HUNDRED'S MOTHER'S PLACE IN EAST VILLAGE.
READY TO USE NULLIFIER IF NEED BE.
SORRY, READY TO USE WHAT?

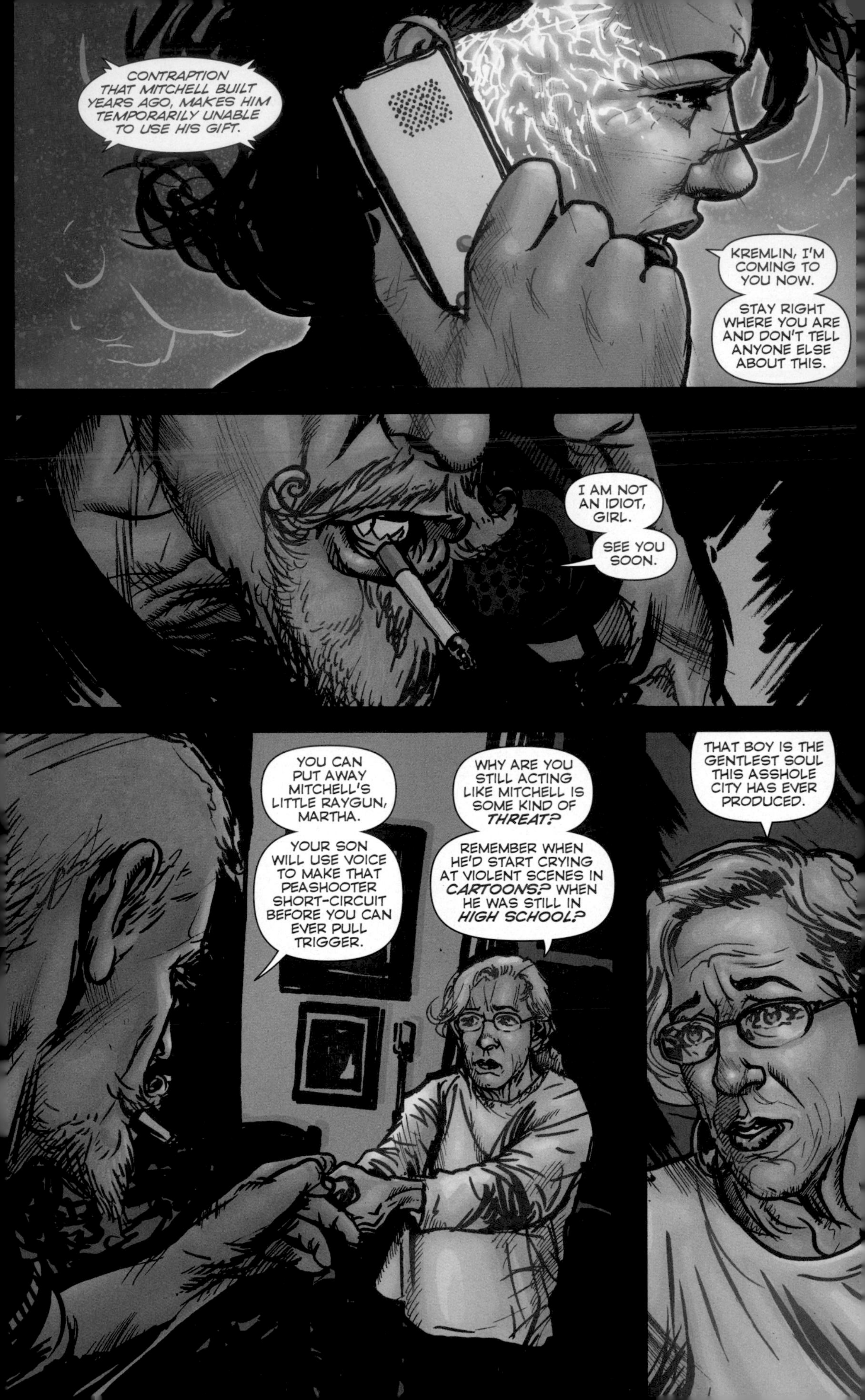

CONTRAPTION THAT MITCHELL BUILT YEARS AGO, MAKES HIM TEMPORARILY UNABLE TO USE HIS GIFT.
KREMLIN, I'M COMING TO YOU NOW.
STAY RIGHT WHERE YOU ARE AND DON'T TELL ANYONE ELSE ABOUT THIS.
I AM NOT AN IDIOT, GIRL.
SEE YOU SOON.
YOU CAN PUT AWAY MITCHELL'S LITTLE RAYGUN, MARTHA.
YOUR SON WILL USE VOICE TO MAKE THAT PEASHOOTER SHORT-CIRCUIT BEFORE YOU CAN EVER PULL TRIGGER.
WHY ARE YOU STILL ACTING LIKE MITCHELL IS SOME KIND OF *THREAT?*
REMEMBER WHEN HE'D START CRYING AT VIOLENT SCENES IN *CARTOONS?* WHEN HE WAS STILL IN *HIGH SCHOOL?*
THAT BOY IS THE GENTLEST SOUL THIS ASSHOLE CITY HAS EVER PRODUCED.

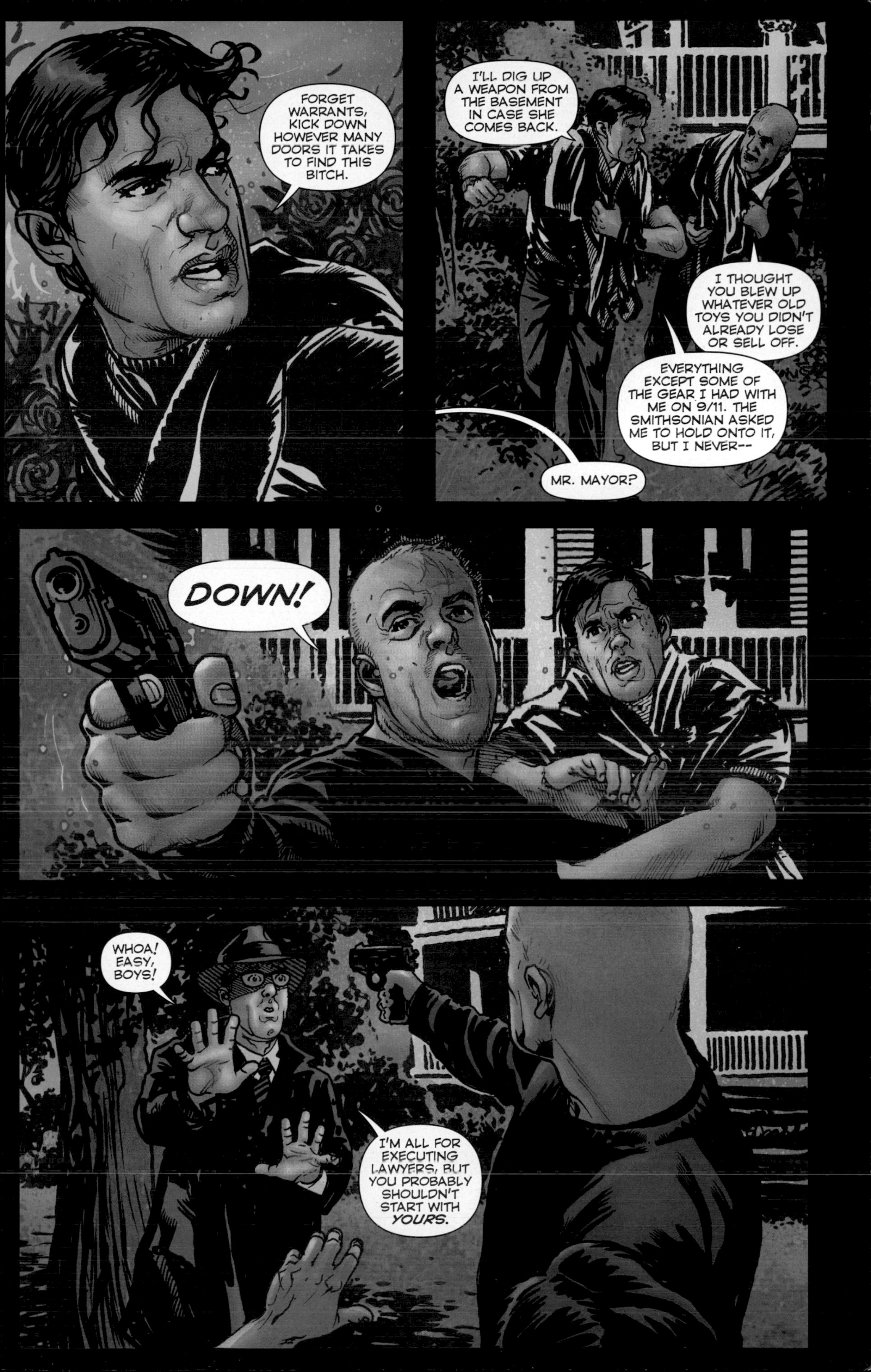
FORGET WARRANTS, KICK DOWN HOWEVER MANY DOORS IT TAKES TO FIND THIS BITCH.
I'LL DIG UP A WEAPON FROM THE BASEMENT IN CASE SHE COMES BACK.
I THOUGHT YOU BLEW UP WHATEVER OLD TOYS YOU DIDN'T ALREADY LOSE OR SELL OFF.
EVERYTHING EXCEPT SOME OF THE GEAR I HAD WITH ME ON 9/11. THE SMITHSONIAN ASKED ME TO HOLD ONTO IT, BUT I NEVER--
MR. MAYOR?
DOWN!
WHOA! EASY, BOYS!
I'M ALL FOR EXECUTING LAWYERS, BUT YOU PROBABLY SHOULDN'T START WITH *YOURS*.

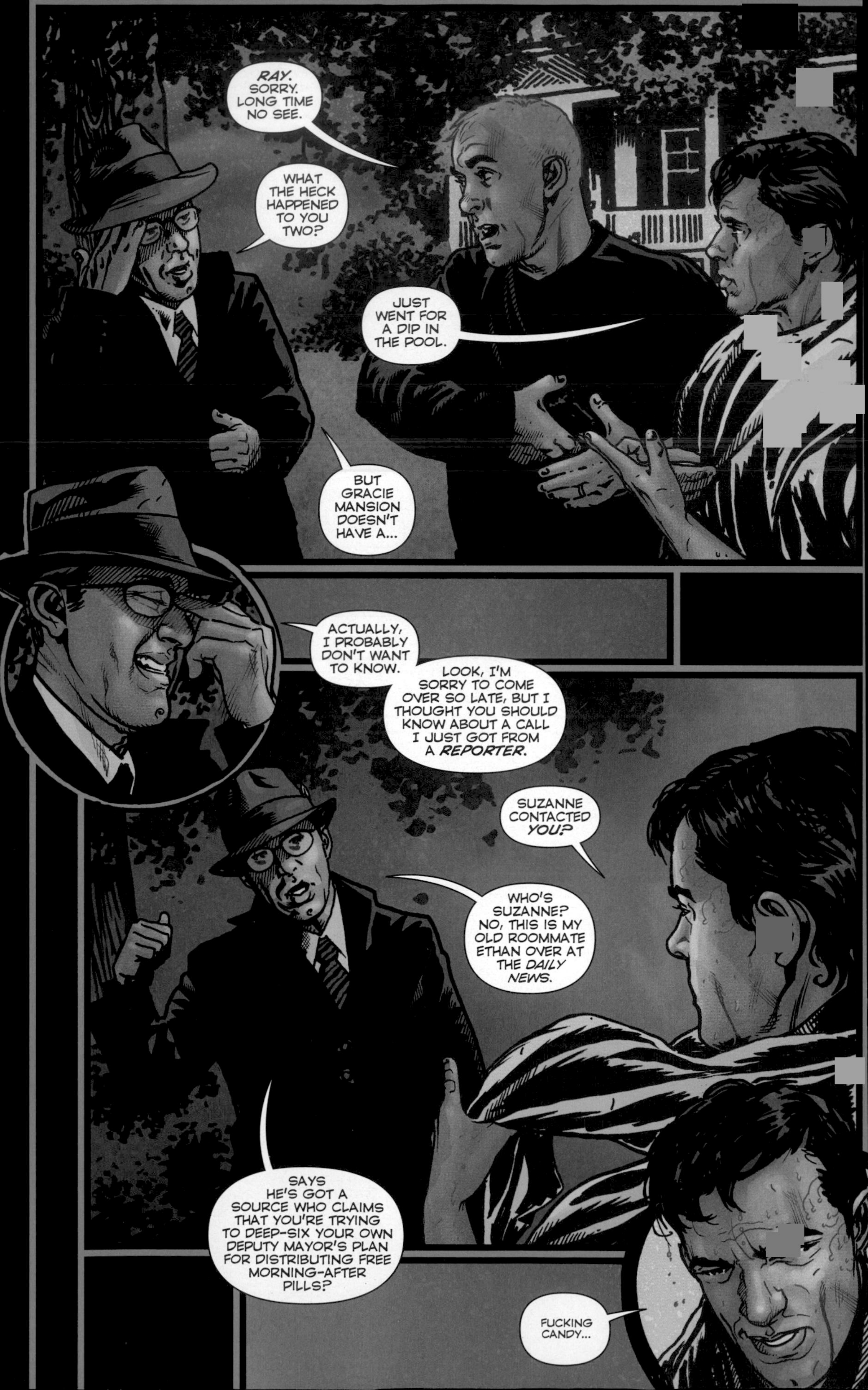
RAY. SORRY. LONG TIME NO SEE.
WHAT THE HECK HAPPENED TO YOU TWO?
JUST WENT FOR A DIP IN THE POOL.
BUT GRACIE MANSION DOESN'T HAVE A...
ACTUALLY, I PROBABLY DON'T WANT TO KNOW.
LOOK, I'M SORRY TO COME OVER SO LATE, BUT I THOUGHT YOU SHOULD KNOW ABOUT A CALL I JUST GOT FROM A REPORTER.
SUZANNE CONTACTED YOU?
WHO'S SUZANNE? NO, THIS IS MY OLD ROOMMATE ETHAN OVER AT THE DAILY NEWS.
SAYS HE'S GOT A SOURCE WHO CLAIMS THAT YOU'RE TRYING TO DEEP-SIX YOUR OWN DEPUTY MAYOR'S PLAN FOR DISTRIBUTING FREE MORNING-AFTER PILLS?
FUCKING CANDY...

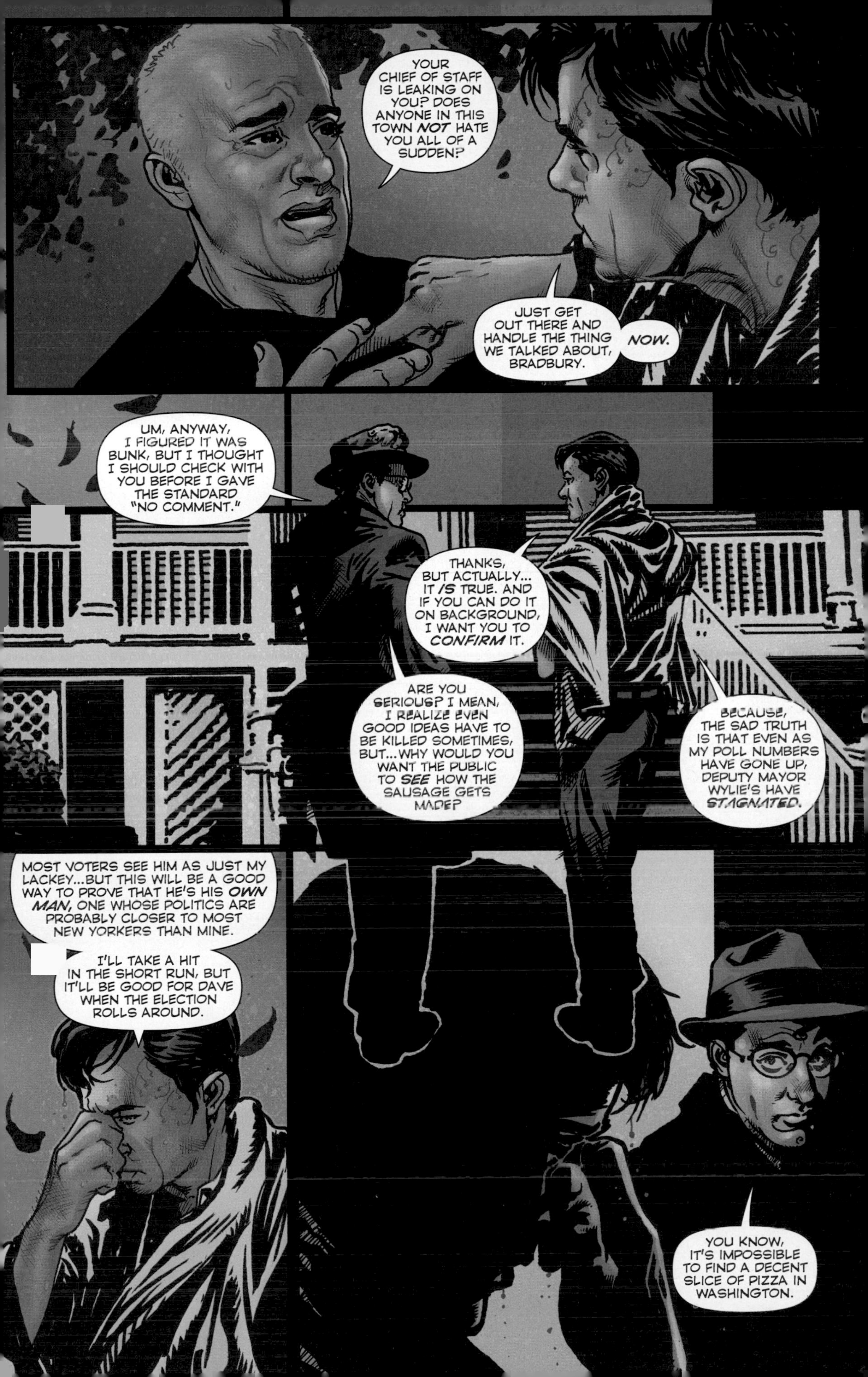
YOUR CHIEF OF STAFF IS LEAKING ON YOU? DOES ANYONE IN THIS TOWN NOT HATE YOU ALL OF A SUDDEN?
JUST GET OUT THERE AND HANDLE THE THING WE TALKED ABOUT, BRADBURY.
NOW.
UM, ANYWAY, I FIGURED IT WAS BUNK, BUT I THOUGHT I SHOULD CHECK WITH YOU BEFORE I GAVE THE STANDARD "NO COMMENT."
THANKS, BUT ACTUALLY... IT IS TRUE. AND IF YOU CAN DO IT ON BACKGROUND, I WANT YOU TO CONFIRM IT.
ARE YOU SERIOUS? I MEAN, I REALIZE EVEN GOOD IDEAS HAVE TO BE KILLED SOMETIMES, BUT...WHY WOULD YOU WANT THE PUBLIC TO SEE HOW THE SAUSAGE GETS MADE?
BECAUSE, THE SAD TRUTH IS THAT EVEN AS MY POLL NUMBERS HAVE GONE UP, DEPUTY MAYOR WYLIE'S HAVE STAGNATED.
MOST VOTERS SEE HIM AS JUST MY LACKEY...BUT THIS WILL BE A GOOD WAY TO PROVE THAT HE'S HIS OWN MAN, ONE WHOSE POLITICS ARE PROBABLY CLOSER TO MOST NEW YORKERS THAN MINE.
I'LL TAKE A HIT IN THE SHORT RUN, BUT IT'LL BE GOOD FOR DAVE WHEN THE ELECTION ROLLS AROUND.
YOU KNOW, IT'S IMPOSSIBLE TO FIND A DECENT SLICE OF PIZZA IN WASHINGTON.

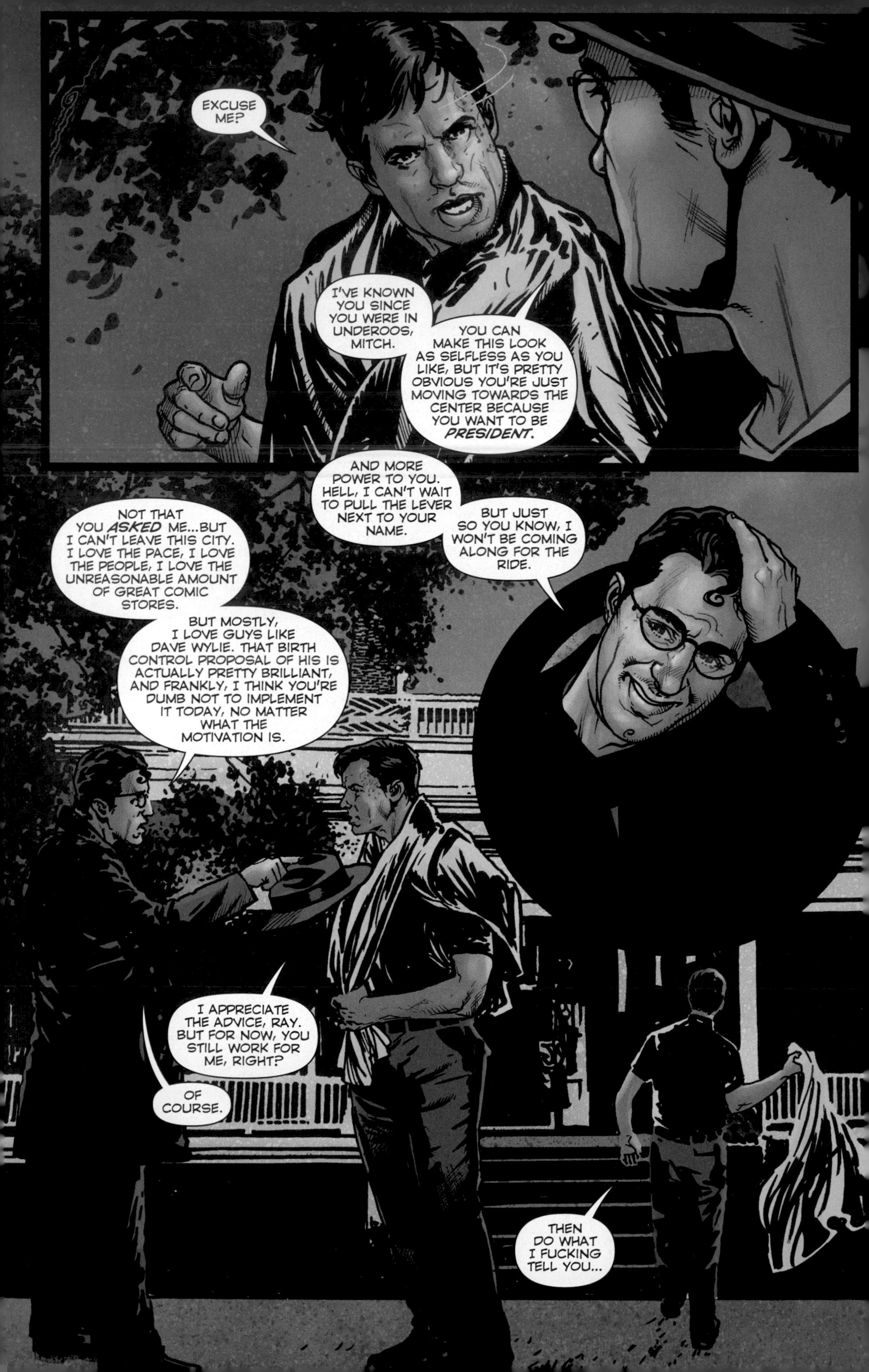
EXCUSE ME?
I'VE KNOWN YOU SINCE YOU WERE IN UNDEROOS, MITCH.
YOU CAN MAKE THIS LOOK AS SELFLESS AS YOU LIKE, BUT IT'S PRETTY OBVIOUS YOU'RE JUST MOVING TOWARDS THE CENTER BECAUSE YOU WANT TO BE ***PRESIDENT***.
AND MORE POWER TO YOU. HELL, I CAN'T WAIT TO PULL THE LEVER NEXT TO YOUR NAME.
BUT JUST SO YOU KNOW, I WON'T BE COMING ALONG FOR THE RIDE.
NOT THAT YOU ***ASKED*** ME...BUT I CAN'T LEAVE THIS CITY. I LOVE THE PACE, I LOVE THE PEOPLE, I LOVE THE UNREASONABLE AMOUNT OF GREAT COMIC STORES.
BUT MOSTLY, I LOVE GUYS LIKE DAVE WYLIE. THAT BIRTH CONTROL PROPOSAL OF HIS IS ACTUALLY PRETTY BRILLIANT, AND FRANKLY, I THINK YOU'RE DUMB NOT TO IMPLEMENT IT TODAY, NO MATTER WHAT THE MOTIVATION IS.
I APPRECIATE THE ADVICE, RAY. BUT FOR NOW, YOU STILL WORK FOR ME, RIGHT?
OF COURSE.
THEN DO WHAT I FUCKING TELL YOU...

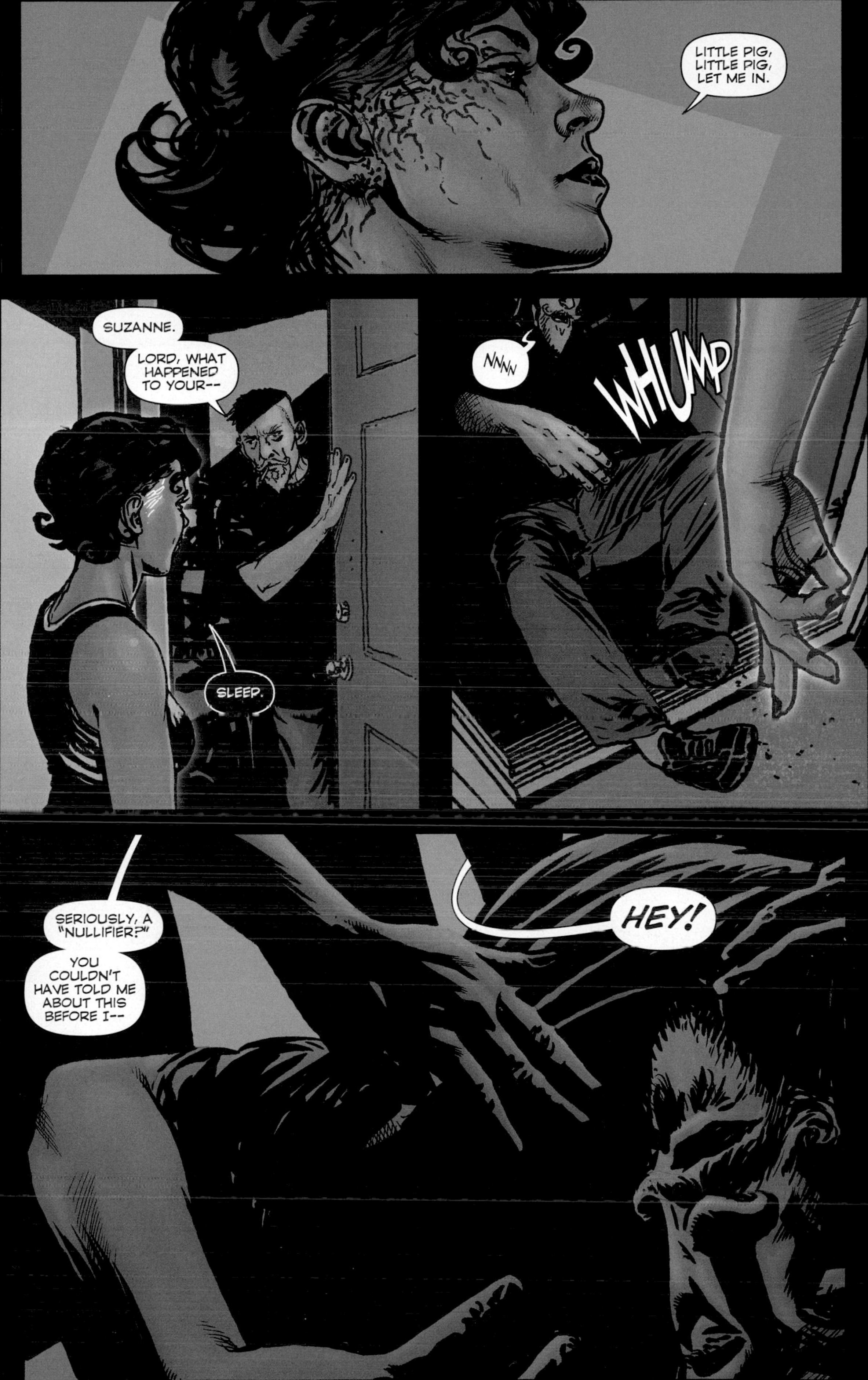
LITTLE PIG, LITTLE PIG, LET ME IN.
SUZANNE.
LORD, WHAT HAPPENED TO YOUR--
SLEEP.
NNNN
WHUMP
SERIOUSLY, A "NULLIFIER?"
YOU COULDN'T HAVE TOLD ME ABOUT THIS BEFORE I--
HEY!

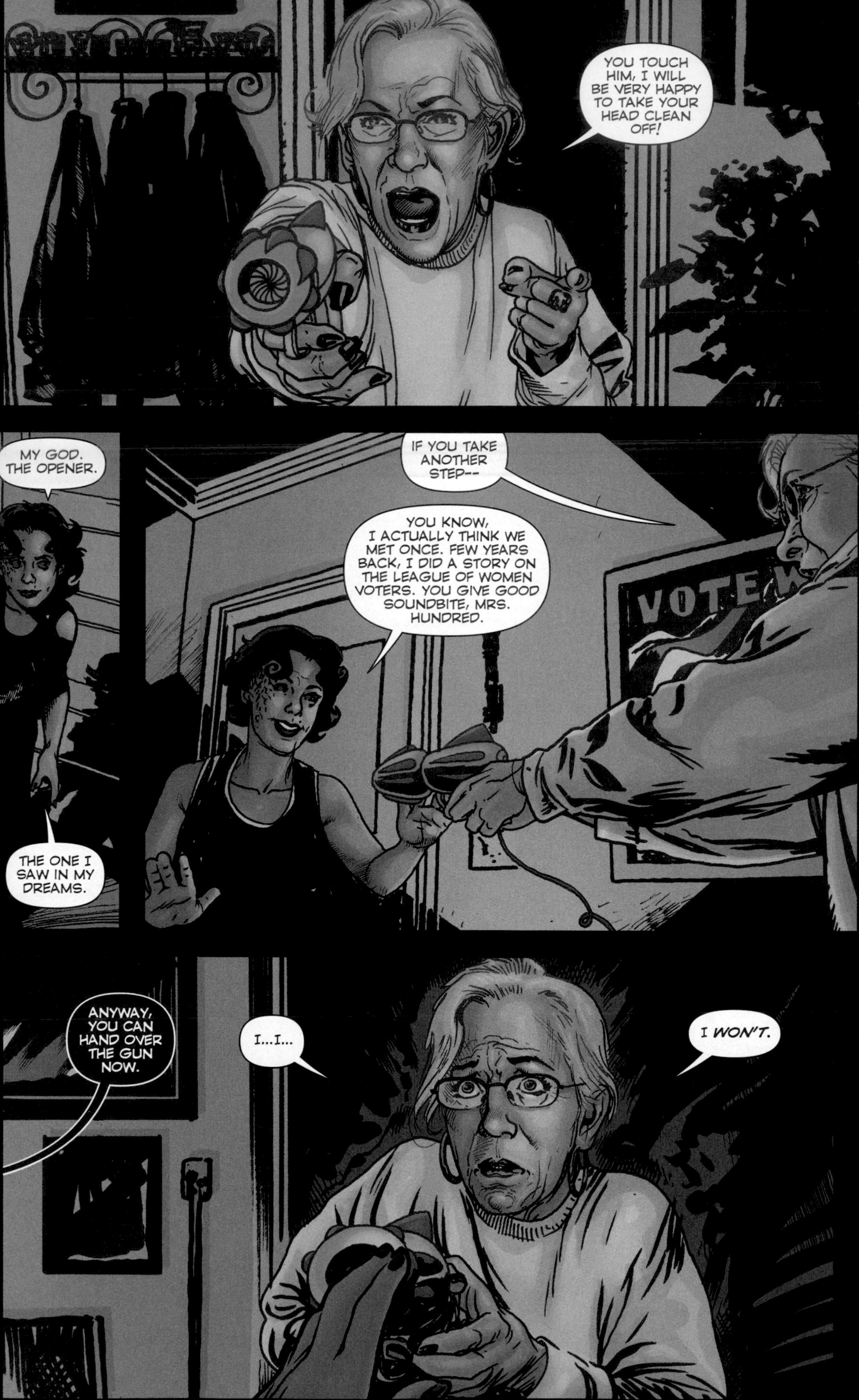
YOU TOUCH HIM, I WILL BE VERY HAPPY TO TAKE YOUR HEAD CLEAN OFF!
MY GOD. THE OPENER.
THE ONE I SAW IN MY DREAMS.
IF YOU TAKE ANOTHER STEP--
YOU KNOW, I ACTUALLY THINK WE MET ONCE. FEW YEARS BACK, I DID A STORY ON THE LEAGUE OF WOMEN VOTERS. YOU GIVE GOOD SOUNDBITE, MRS. HUNDRED.
VOTE
ANYWAY, YOU CAN HAND OVER THE GUN NOW.
I...I...
I WON'T.

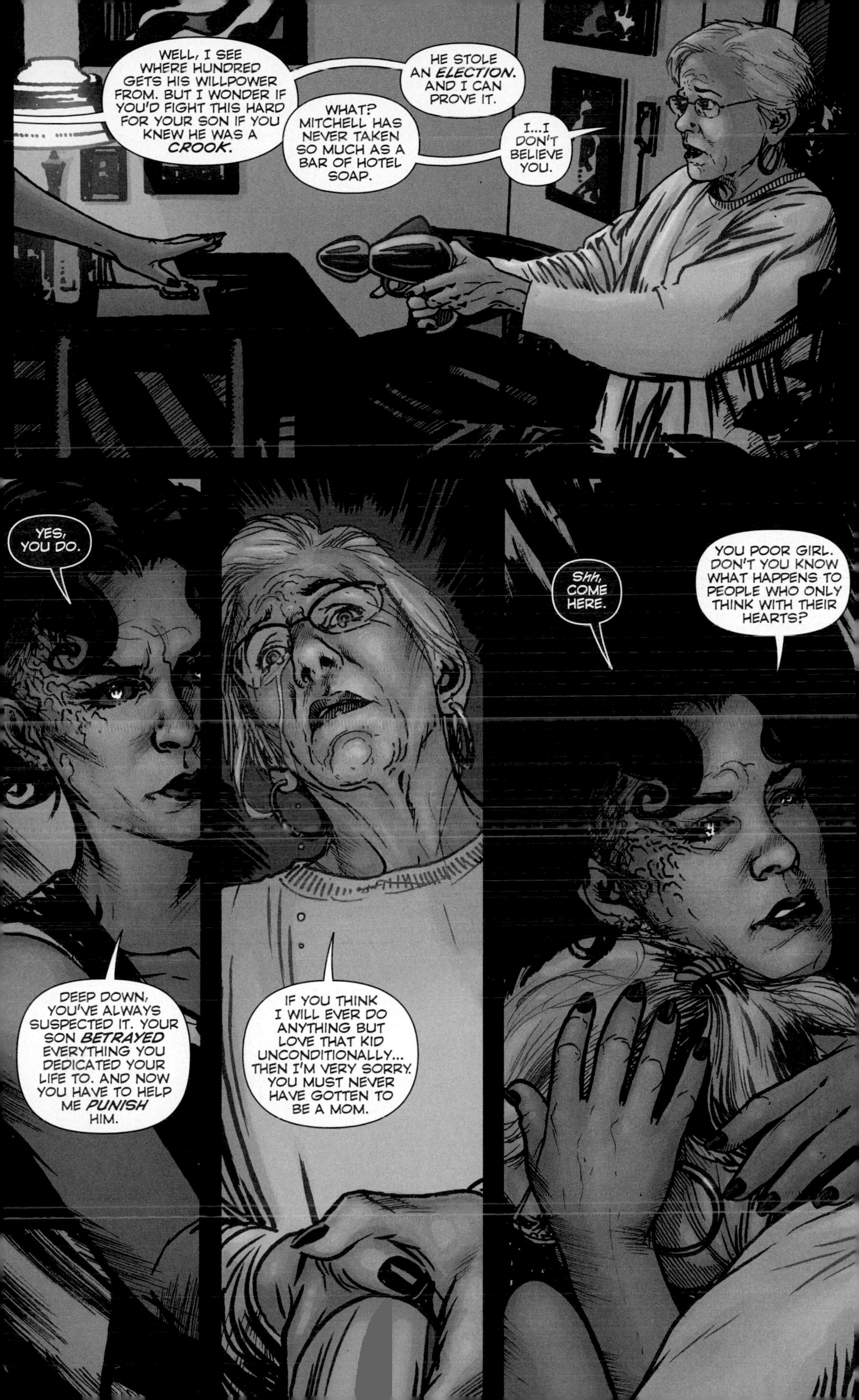
WELL, I SEE WHERE HUNDRED GETS HIS WILLPOWER FROM. BUT I WONDER IF YOU'D FIGHT THIS HARD FOR YOUR SON IF YOU KNEW HE WAS A *CROOK*.
WHAT? MITCHELL HAS NEVER TAKEN SO MUCH AS A BAR OF HOTEL SOAP.
HE STOLE AN *ELECTION*. AND I CAN PROVE IT.
I...I DON'T BELIEVE YOU.
YES, YOU DO.
DEEP DOWN, YOU'VE ALWAYS SUSPECTED IT. YOUR SON *BETRAYED* EVERYTHING YOU DEDICATED YOUR LIFE TO. AND NOW YOU HAVE TO HELP ME *PUNISH* HIM.
IF YOU THINK I WILL EVER DO ANYTHING BUT LOVE THAT KID UNCONDITIONALLY... THEN I'M VERY SORRY. YOU MUST NEVER HAVE GOTTEN TO BE A MOM.
Shh, COME HERE.
YOU POOR GIRL. DON'T YOU KNOW WHAT HAPPENS TO PEOPLE WHO ONLY THINK WITH THEIR HEARTS?

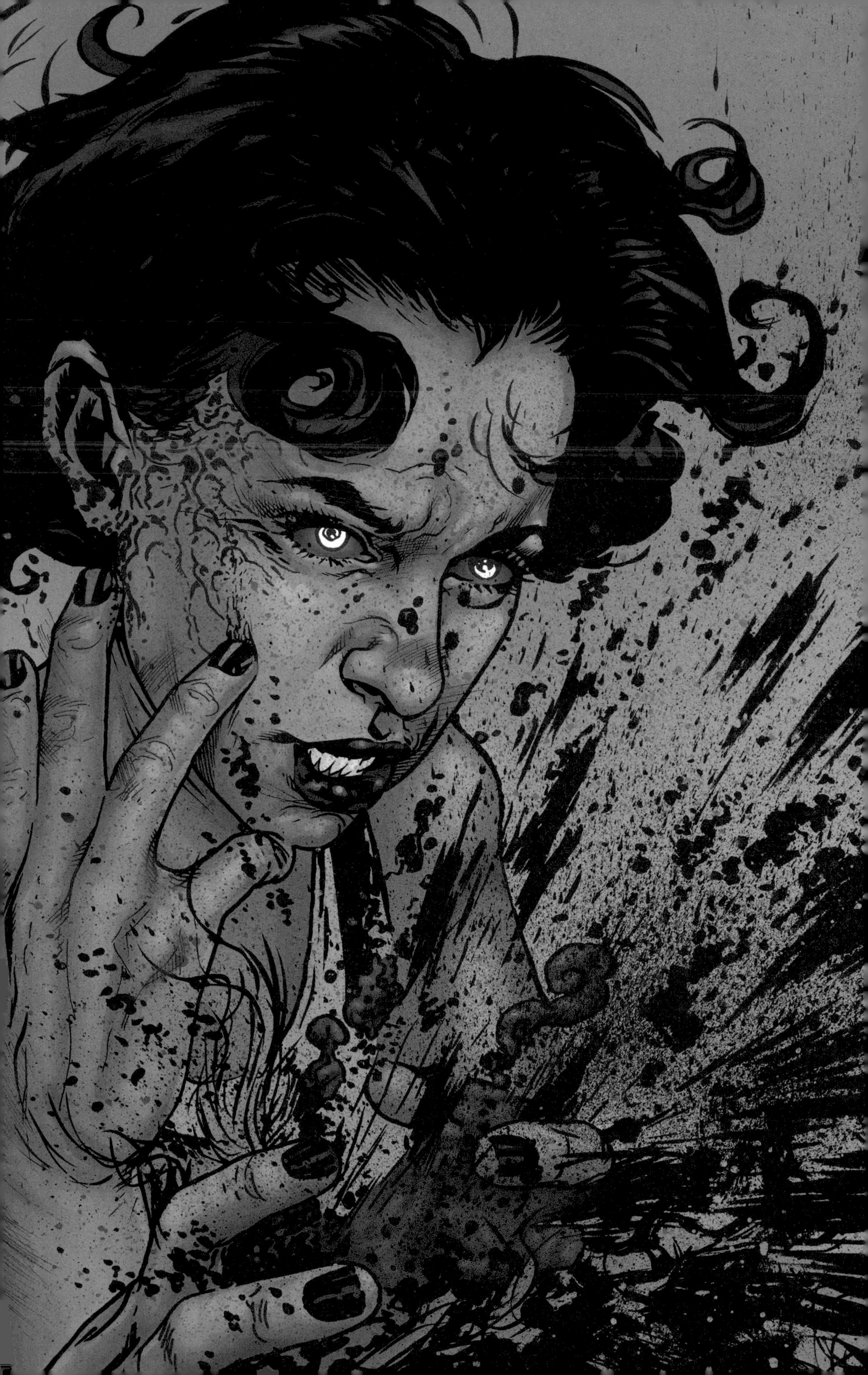

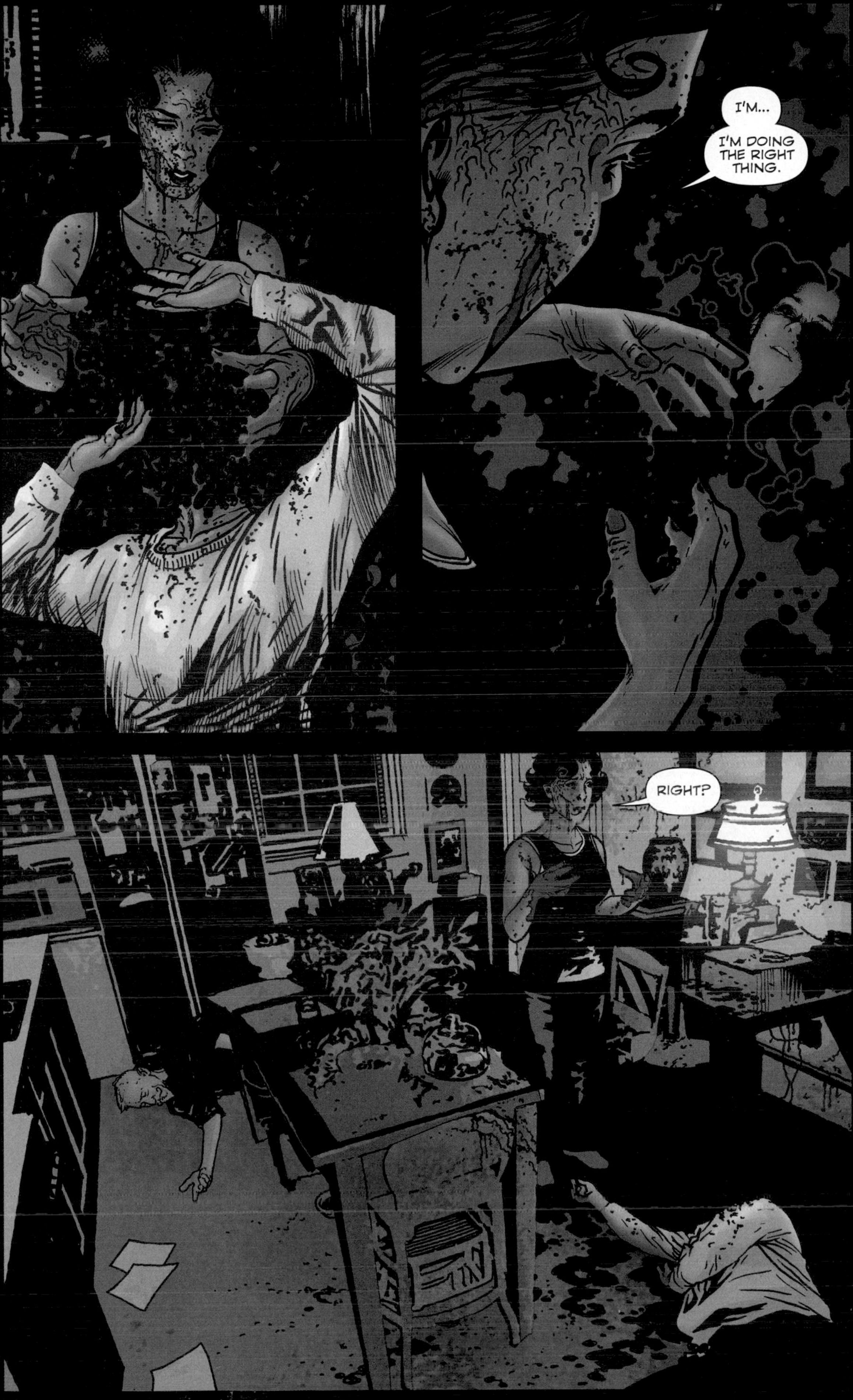
I'M...
I'M DOING THE RIGHT THING.
RIGHT?

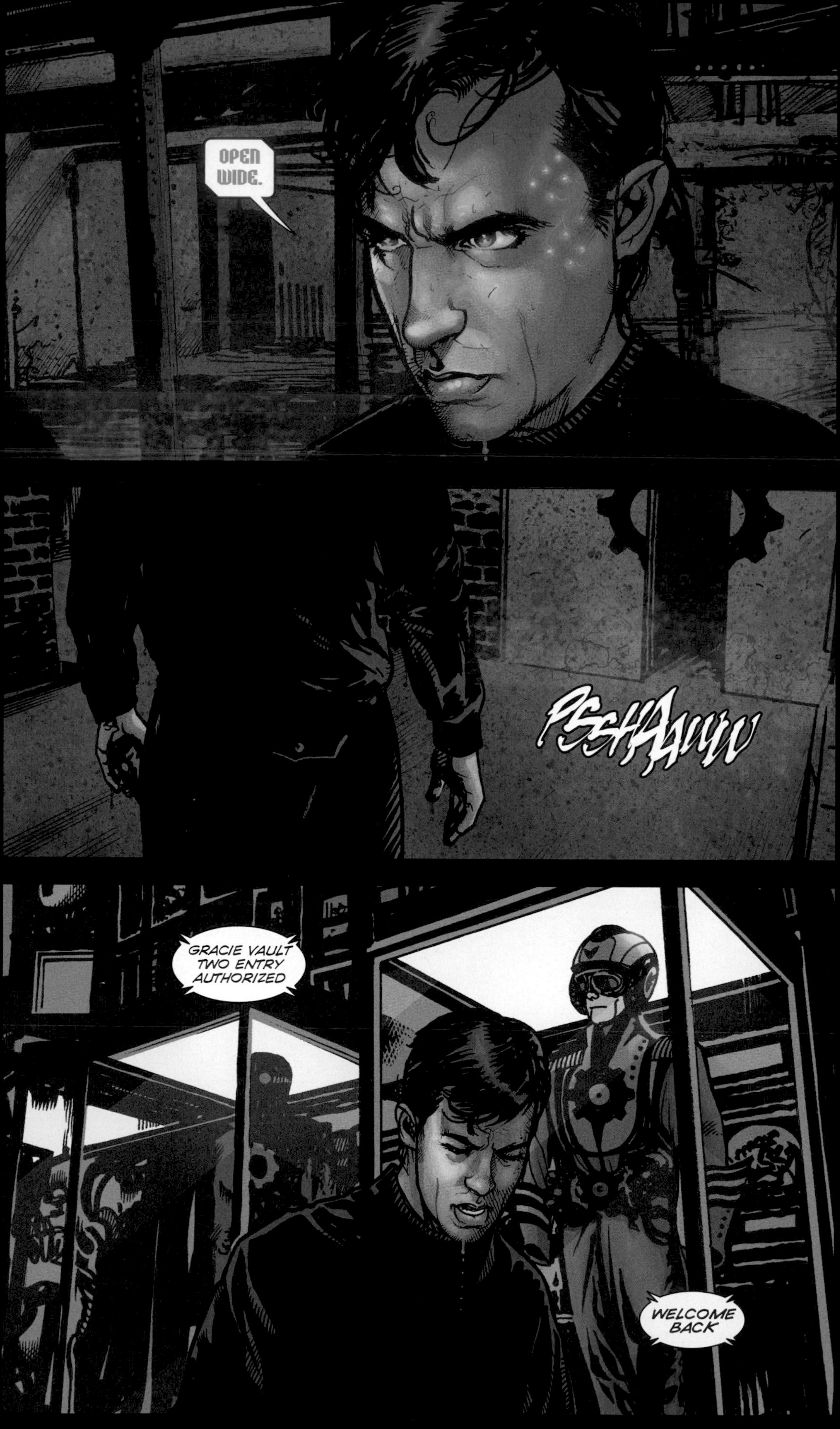
OPEN WIDE.
PSSHAAWW
GRACIE VAULT TWO ENTRY AUTHORIZED
WELCOME BACK

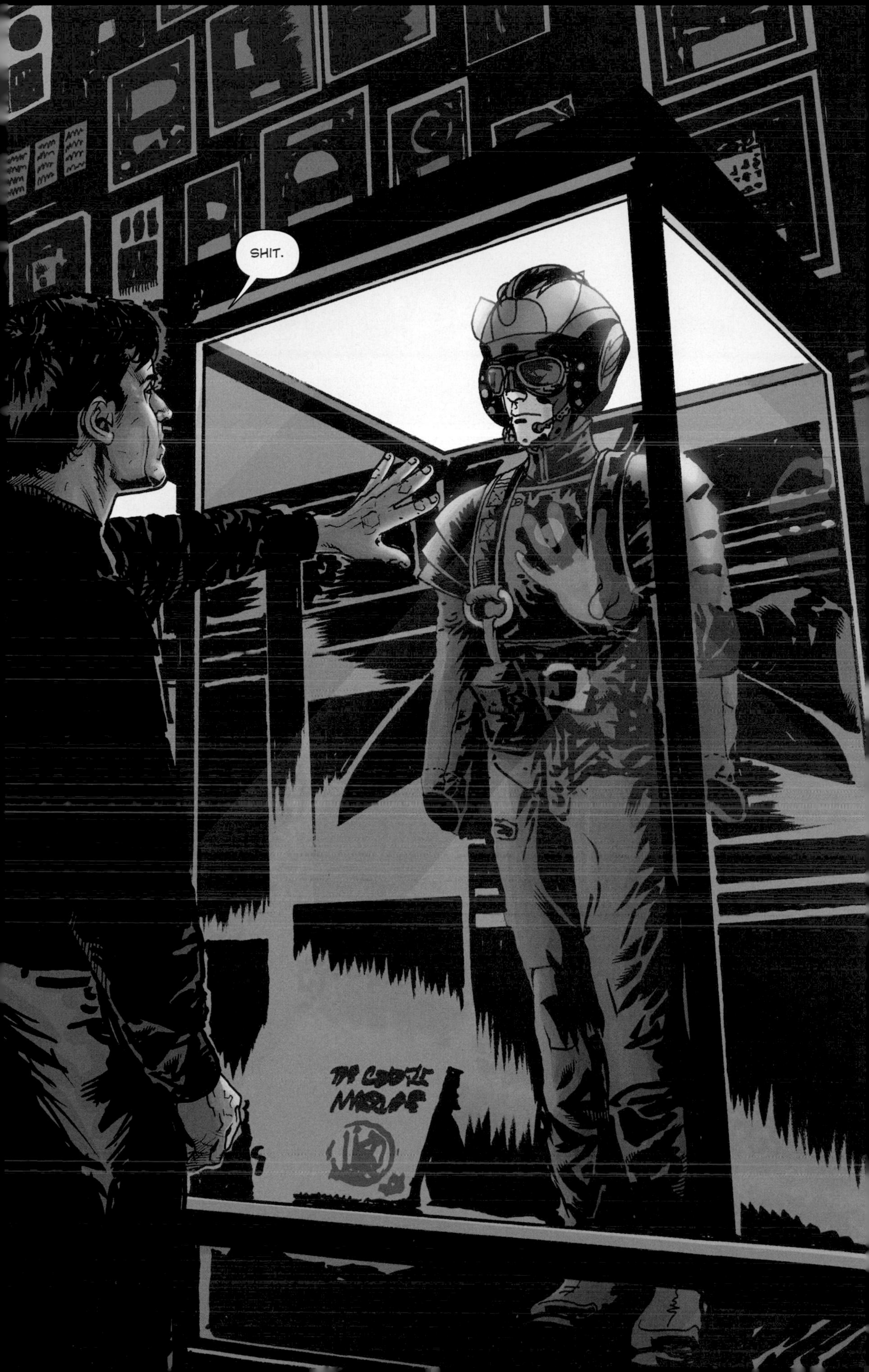
SHIT.

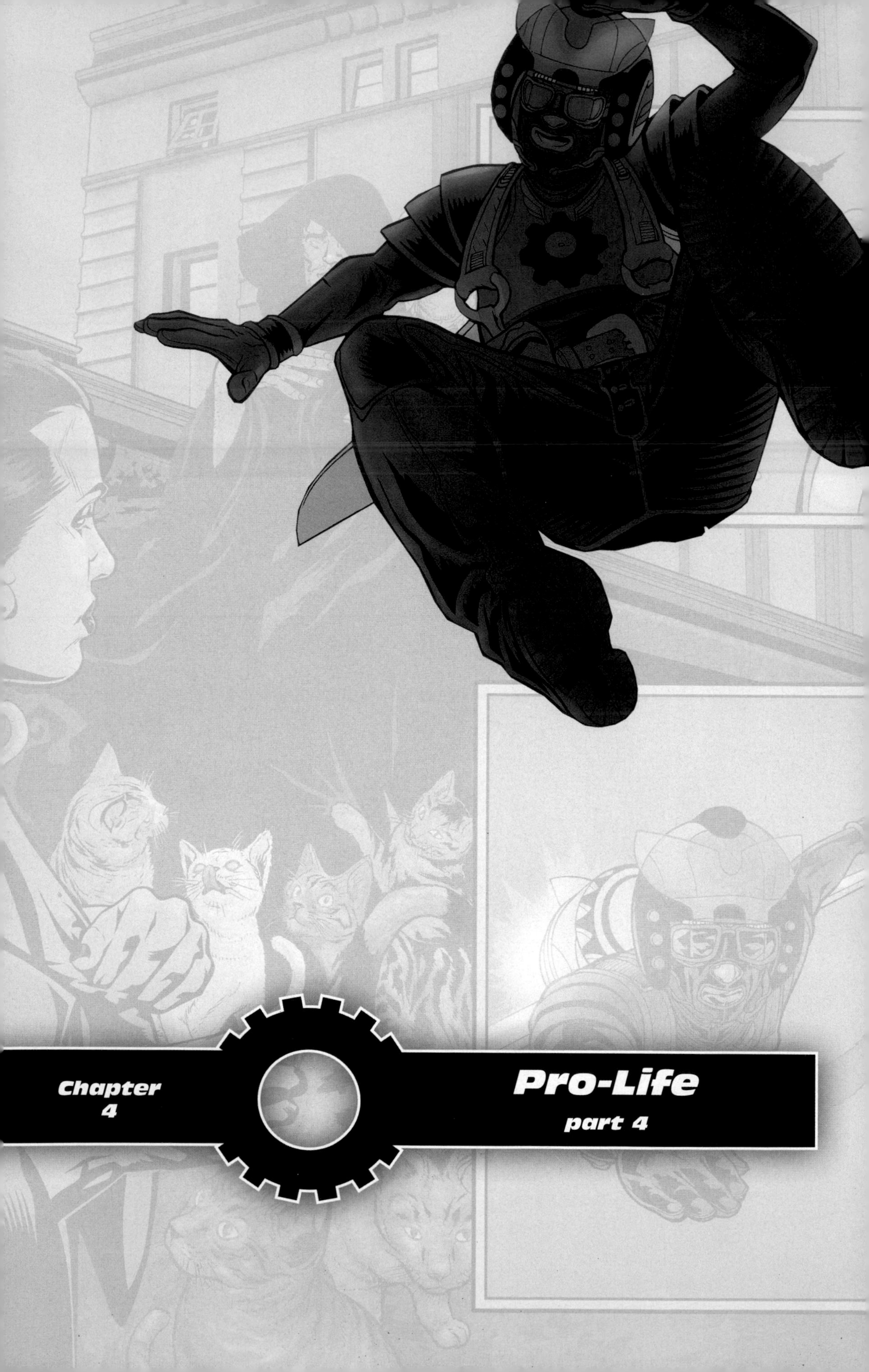
Chapter 4
Pro-Life
part 4

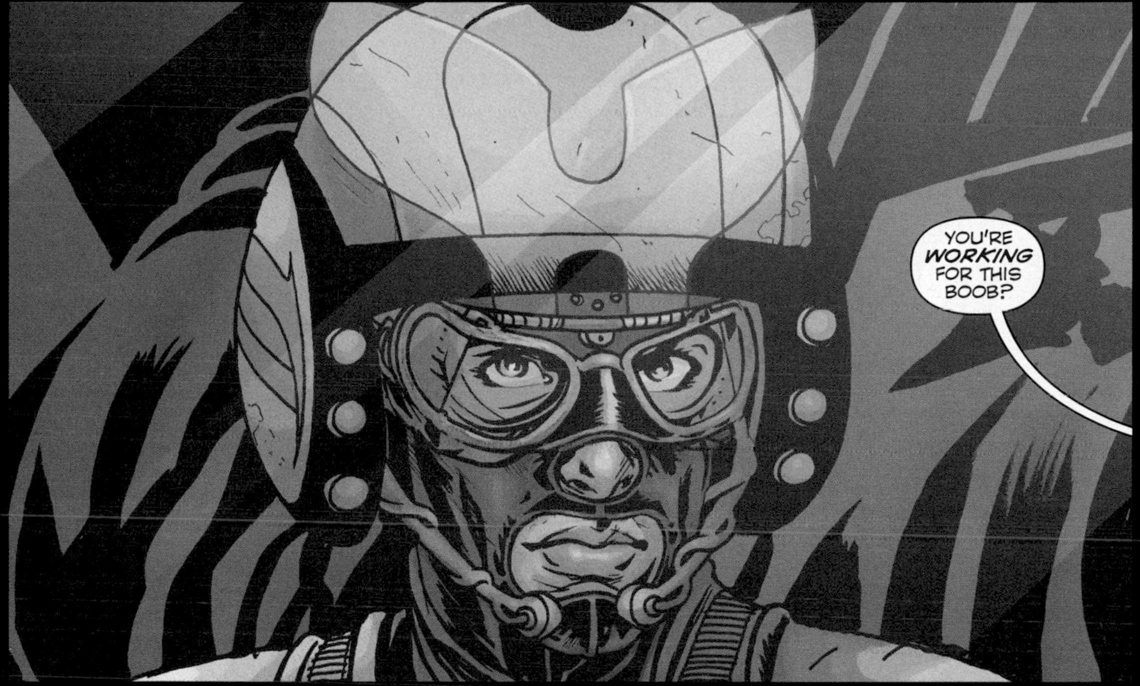
YOU'RE *WORKING* FOR THIS BOOB?

MONDAY, JANUARY 5, 2002

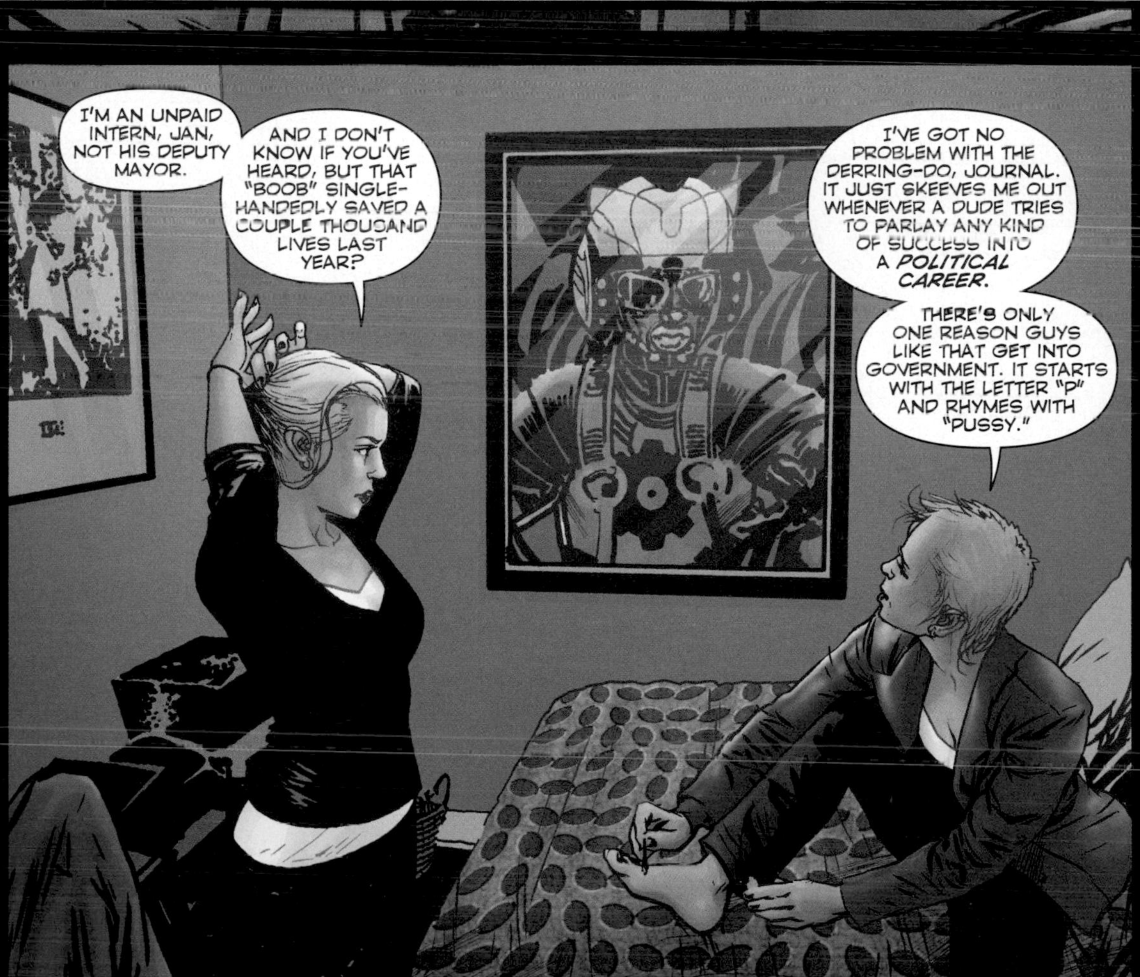
I'M AN UNPAID INTERN, JAN, NOT HIS DEPUTY MAYOR.
AND I DON'T KNOW IF YOU'VE HEARD, BUT THAT "BOOB" SINGLE-HANDEDLY SAVED A COUPLE THOUSAND LIVES LAST YEAR?
I'VE GOT NO PROBLEM WITH THE DERRING-DO, JOURNAL. IT JUST SKEEVES ME OUT WHENEVER A DUDE TRIES TO PARLAY ANY KIND OF SUCCESS INTO A *POLITICAL CAREER.*
THERE'S ONLY ONE REASON GUYS LIKE THAT GET INTO GOVERNMENT. IT STARTS WITH THE LETTER "P" AND RHYMES WITH "PUSSY."

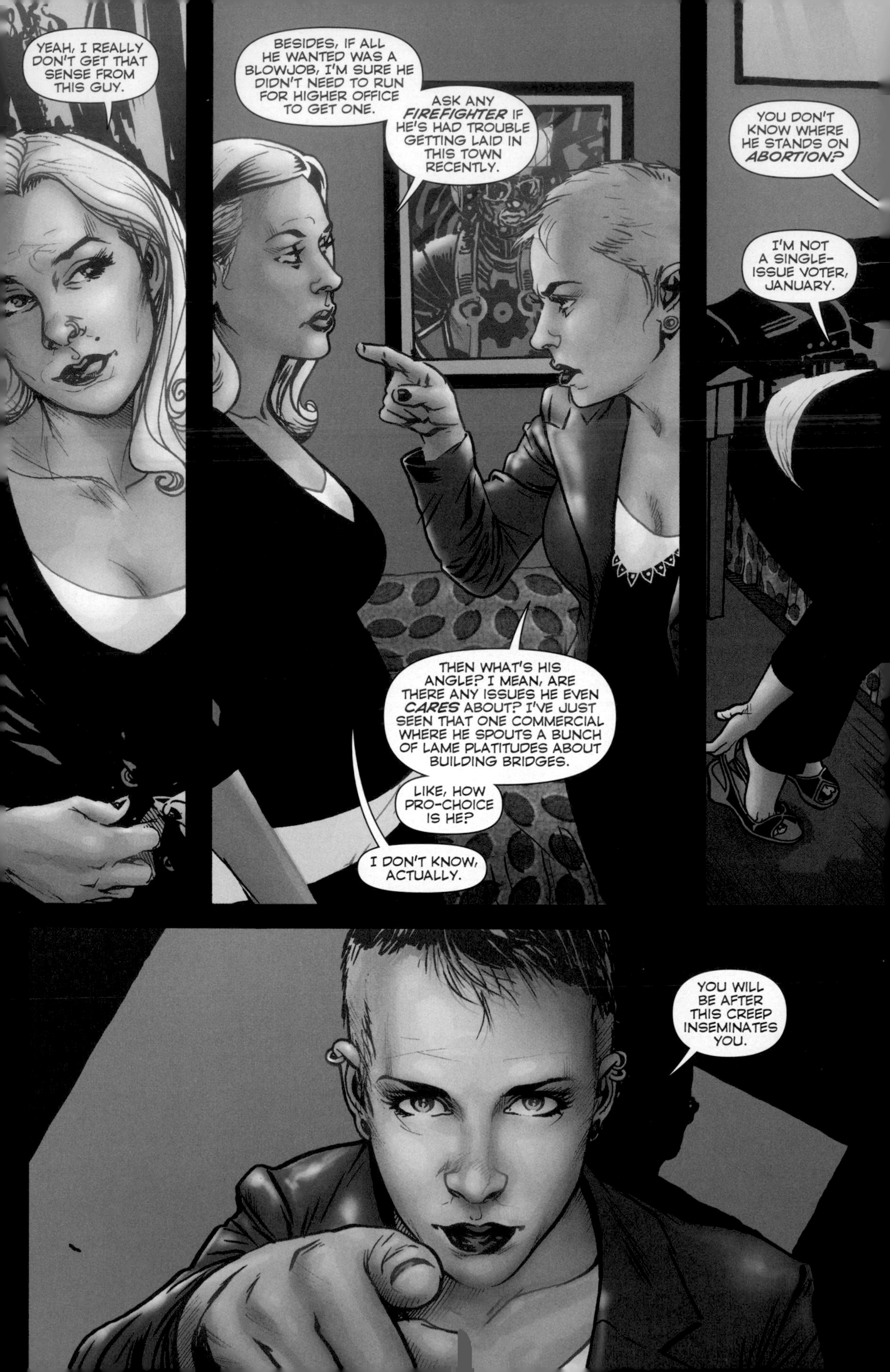
YEAH, I REALLY DON'T GET THAT SENSE FROM THIS GUY.
BESIDES, IF ALL HE WANTED WAS A BLOWJOB, I'M SURE HE DIDN'T NEED TO RUN FOR HIGHER OFFICE TO GET ONE.
ASK ANY *FIREFIGHTER* IF HE'S HAD TROUBLE GETTING LAID IN THIS TOWN RECENTLY.
THEN WHAT'S HIS ANGLE? I MEAN, ARE THERE ANY ISSUES HE EVEN *CARES* ABOUT? I'VE JUST SEEN THAT ONE COMMERCIAL WHERE HE SPOUTS A BUNCH OF LAME PLATITUDES ABOUT BUILDING BRIDGES.
LIKE, HOW PRO-CHOICE IS HE?
I DON'T KNOW, ACTUALLY.
YOU DON'T KNOW WHERE HE STANDS ON *ABORTION?*
I'M NOT A SINGLE-ISSUE VOTER, JANUARY.
YOU WILL BE AFTER THIS CREEP INSEMINATES YOU.

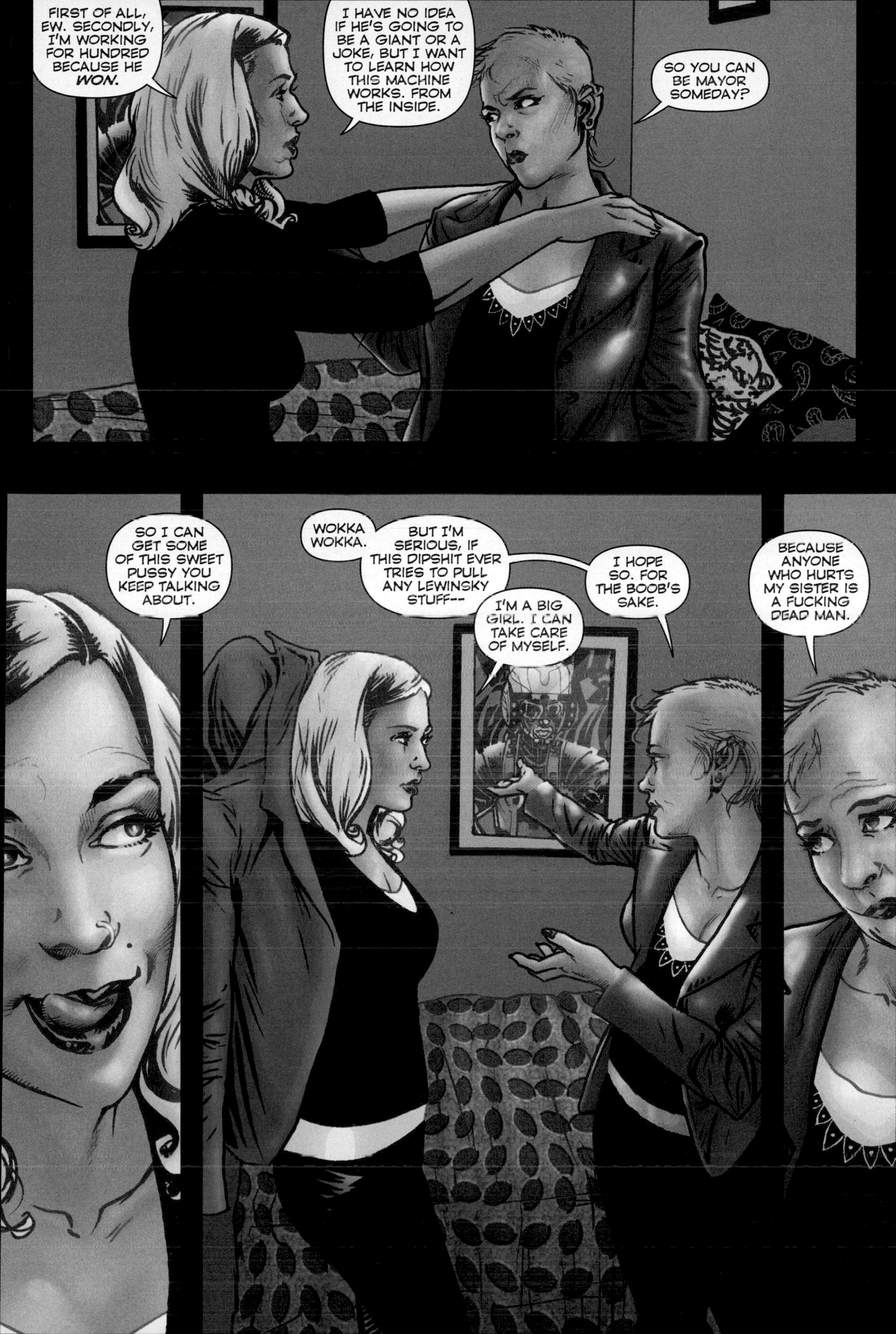
FIRST OF ALL, EW. SECONDLY, I'M WORKING FOR HUNDRED BECAUSE HE *WON*.
I HAVE NO IDEA IF HE'S GOING TO BE A GIANT OR A JOKE, BUT I WANT TO LEARN HOW THIS MACHINE WORKS. FROM THE INSIDE.
SO YOU CAN BE MAYOR SOMEDAY?
SO I CAN GET SOME OF THIS SWEET PUSSY YOU KEEP TALKING ABOUT.
WOKKA WOKKA.
BUT I'M SERIOUS, IF THIS DIPSHIT EVER TRIES TO PULL ANY LEWINSKY STUFF--
I'M A BIG GIRL. I CAN TAKE CARE OF MYSELF.
I HOPE SO. FOR THE BOOB'S SAKE.
BECAUSE ANYONE WHO HURTS MY SISTER IS A FUCKING DEAD MAN.

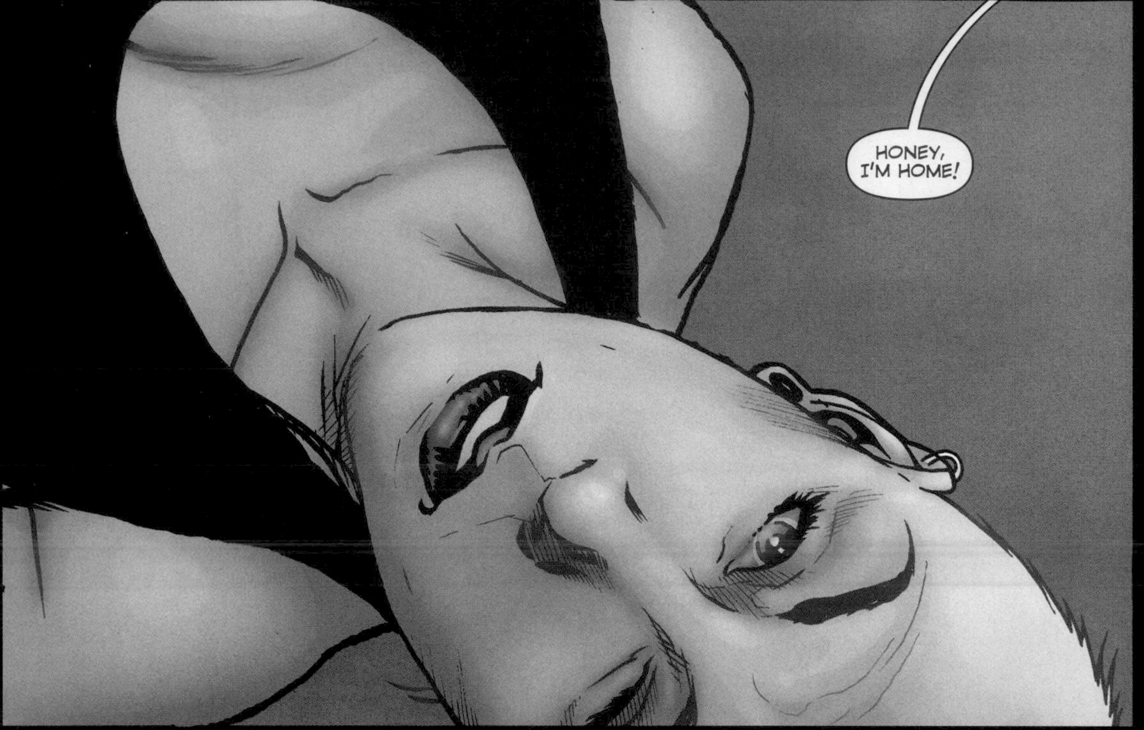
HONEY, I'M HOME!

TUESDAY, APRIL 12, 2005

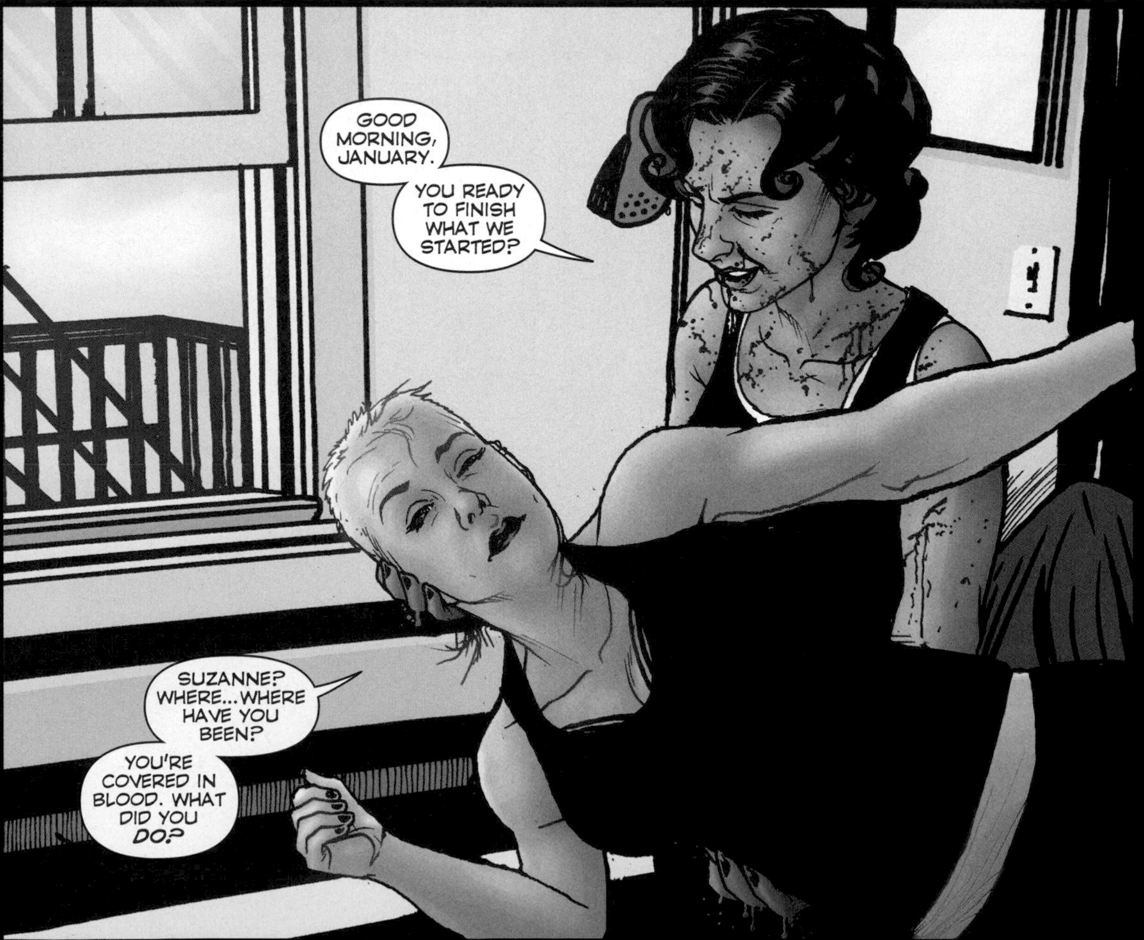
GOOD MORNING, JANUARY.
YOU READY TO FINISH WHAT WE STARTED?
SUZANNE? WHERE...WHERE HAVE YOU BEEN?
YOU'RE COVERED IN BLOOD. WHAT DID YOU DO?

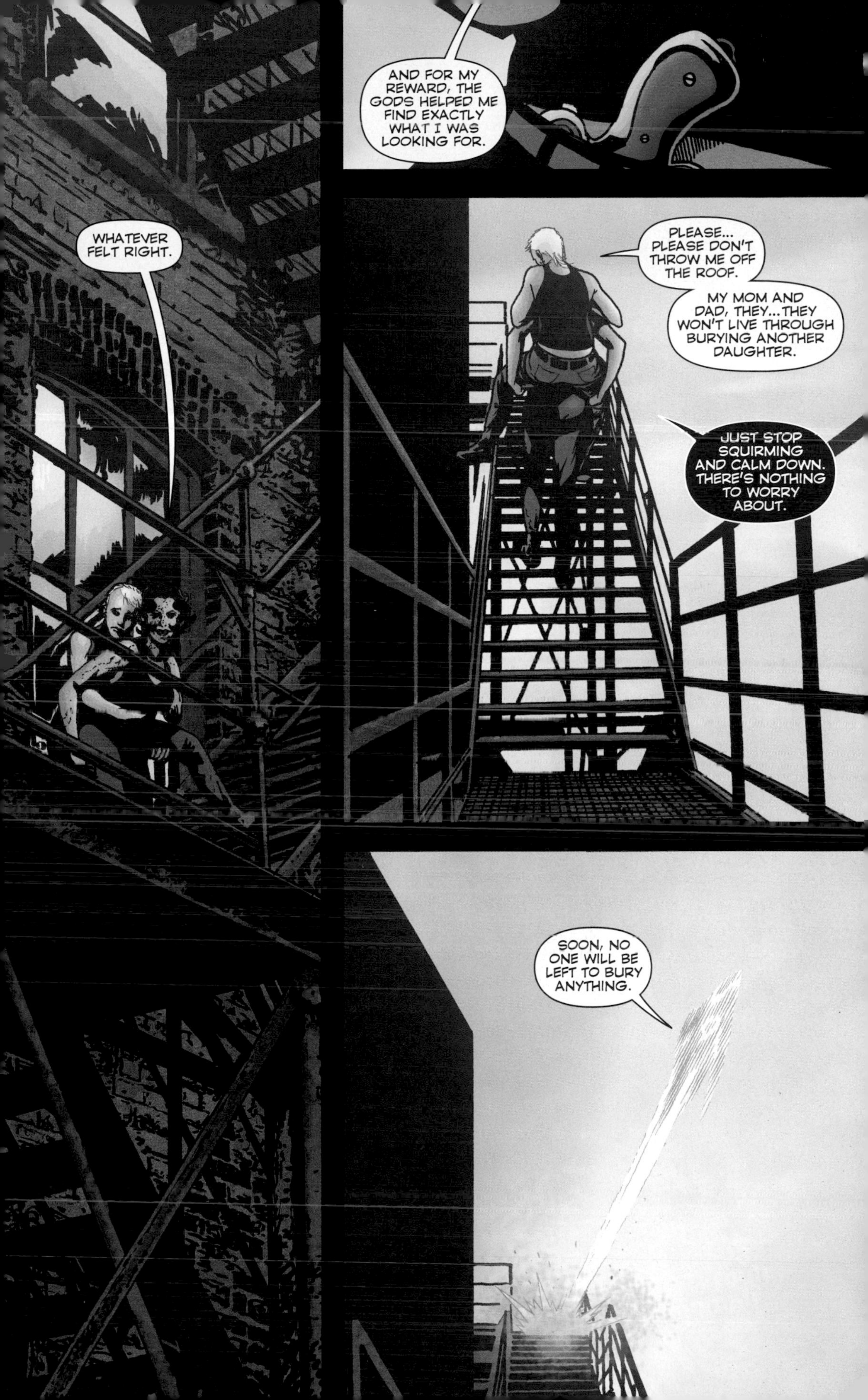
WHATEVER FELT RIGHT.
AND FOR MY REWARD, THE GODS HELPED ME FIND EXACTLY WHAT I WAS LOOKING FOR.
PLEASE... PLEASE DON'T THROW ME OFF THE ROOF.
MY MOM AND DAD, THEY...THEY WON'T LIVE THROUGH BURYING ANOTHER DAUGHTER.
JUST STOP SQUIRMING AND CALM DOWN. THERE'S NOTHING TO WORRY ABOUT.
SOON, NO ONE WILL BE LEFT TO BURY ANYTHING.

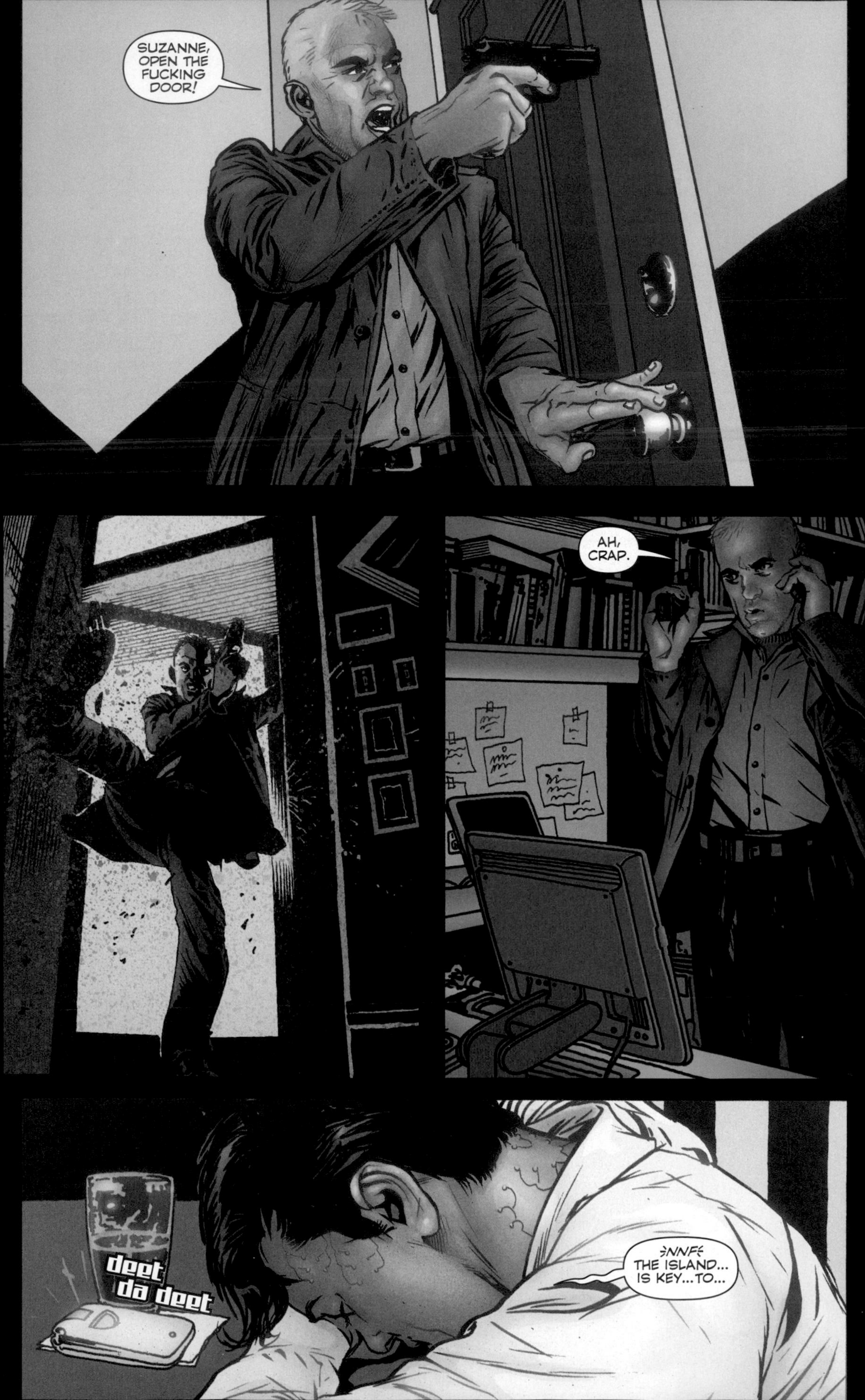
SUZANNE, OPEN THE FUCKING DOOR!
AH, CRAP.
deet da deet
≈NNF≈ THE ISLAND... IS KEY...TO...

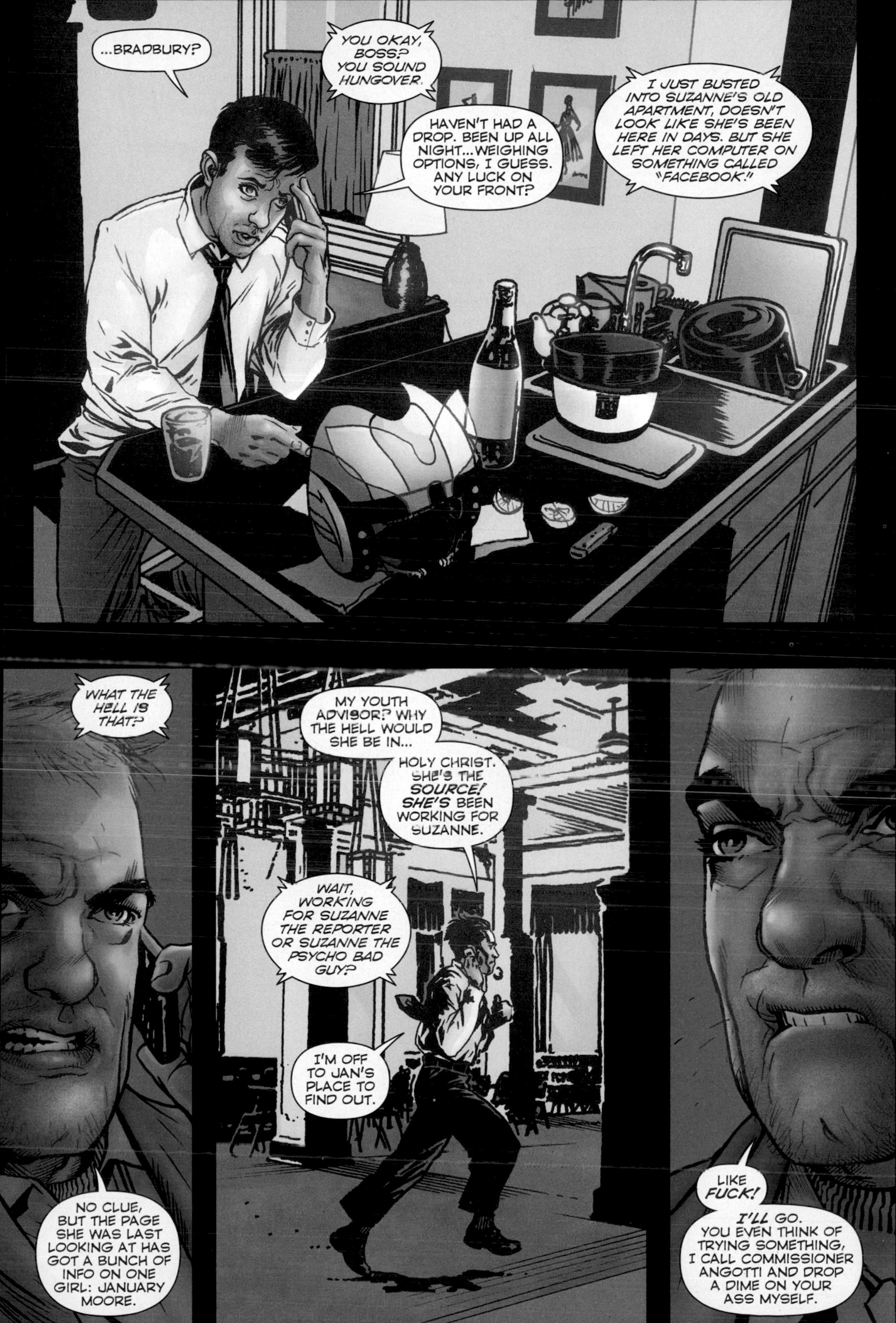
...BRADBURY?
YOU OKAY, BOSS? YOU SOUND HUNGOVER.
HAVEN'T HAD A DROP. BEEN UP ALL NIGHT...WEIGHING OPTIONS, I GUESS. ANY LUCK ON YOUR FRONT?
I JUST BUSTED INTO SUZANNE'S OLD APARTMENT, DOESN'T LOOK LIKE SHE'S BEEN HERE IN DAYS. BUT SHE LEFT HER COMPUTER ON SOMETHING CALLED "FACEBOOK."
WHAT THE HELL IS THAT?
NO CLUE, BUT THE PAGE SHE WAS LAST LOOKING AT HAS GOT A BUNCH OF INFO ON ONE GIRL: JANUARY MOORE.
MY YOUTH ADVISOR? WHY THE HELL WOULD SHE BE IN...
HOLY CHRIST. SHE'S THE ***SOURCE! SHE'S*** BEEN WORKING FOR SUZANNE.
WAIT, WORKING FOR SUZANNE THE REPORTER OR SUZANNE THE PSYCHO BAD GUY?
I'M OFF TO JAN'S PLACE TO FIND OUT.
LIKE ***FUCK!***
I'LL GO. YOU EVEN THINK OF TRYING SOMETHING, I CALL COMMISSIONER ANGOTTI AND DROP A DIME ON YOUR ASS MYSELF.

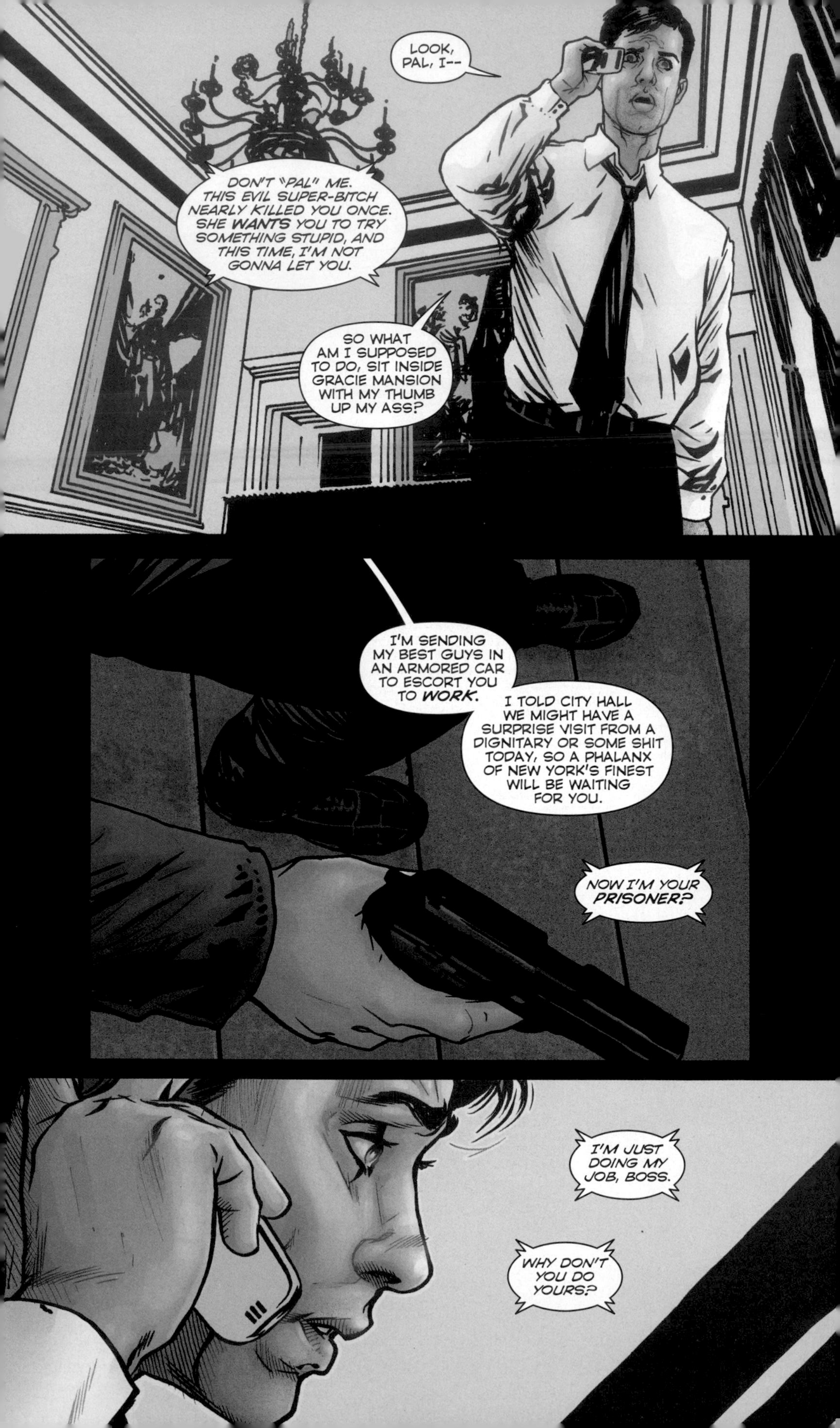
LOOK, PAL, I--
DON'T "PAL" ME. THIS EVIL SUPER-BITCH NEARLY KILLED YOU ONCE. SHE WANTS YOU TO TRY SOMETHING STUPID, AND THIS TIME, I'M NOT GONNA LET YOU.
SO WHAT AM I SUPPOSED TO DO, SIT INSIDE GRACIE MANSION WITH MY THUMB UP MY ASS?
I'M SENDING MY BEST GUYS IN AN ARMORED CAR TO ESCORT YOU TO WORK.
I TOLD CITY HALL WE MIGHT HAVE A SURPRISE VISIT FROM A DIGNITARY OR SOME SHIT TODAY, SO A PHALANX OF NEW YORK'S FINEST WILL BE WAITING FOR YOU.
NOW I'M YOUR PRISONER?
I'M JUST DOING MY JOB, BOSS.
WHY DON'T YOU DO YOURS?

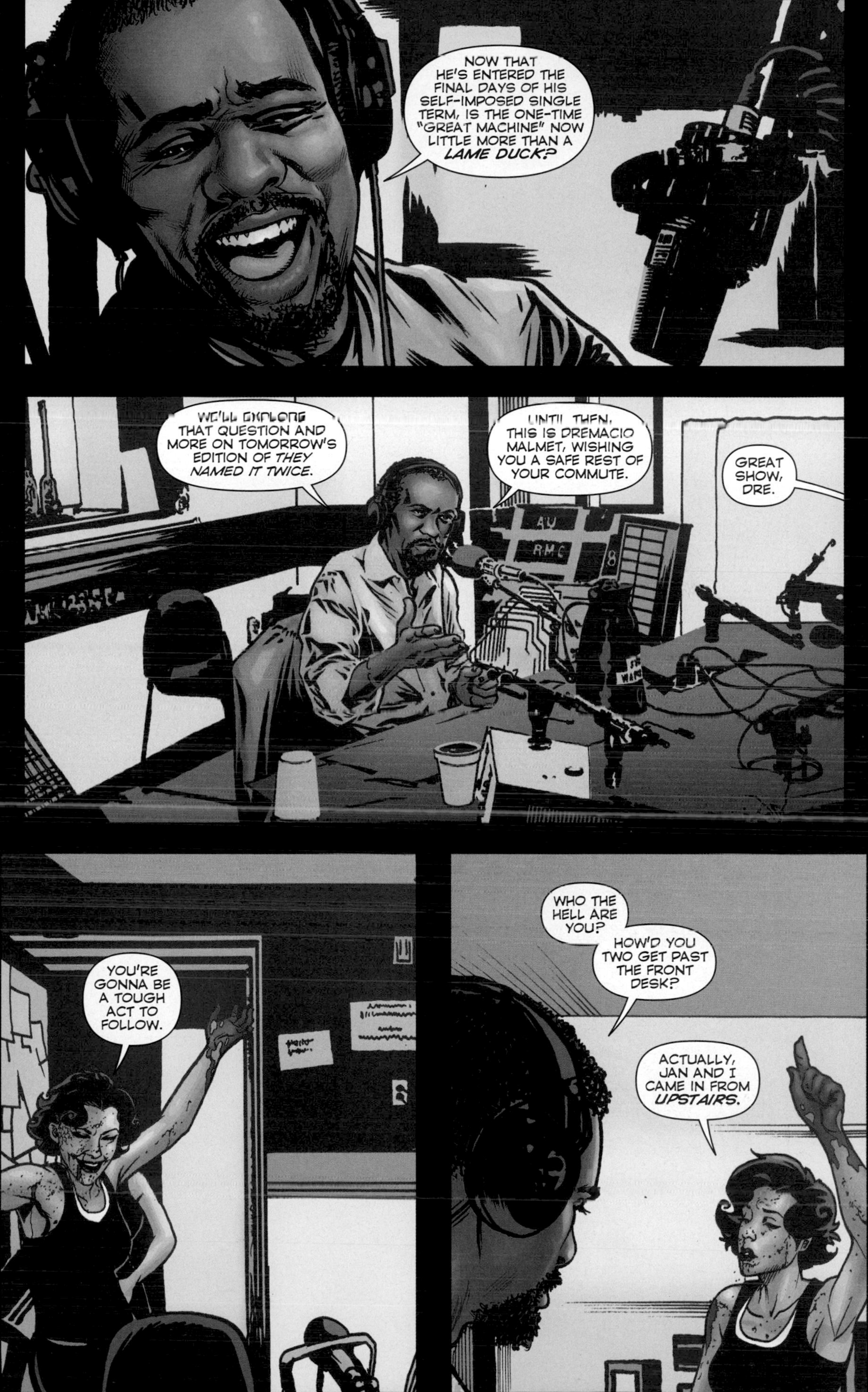
NOW THAT HE'S ENTERED THE FINAL DAYS OF HIS SELF-IMPOSED SINGLE TERM, IS THE ONE-TIME "GREAT MACHINE" NOW LITTLE MORE THAN A *LAME DUCK?*
WE'LL EXPLORE THAT QUESTION AND MORE ON TOMORROW'S EDITION OF *THEY NAMED IT TWICE*.
UNTIL THEN, THIS IS DREMACIO MALMET, WISHING YOU A SAFE REST OF YOUR COMMUTE.
GREAT SHOW, DRE.
YOU'RE GONNA BE A TOUGH ACT TO FOLLOW.
WHO THE HELL ARE YOU?
HOW'D YOU TWO GET PAST THE FRONT DESK?
ACTUALLY, JAN AND I CAME IN FROM *UPSTAIRS*.

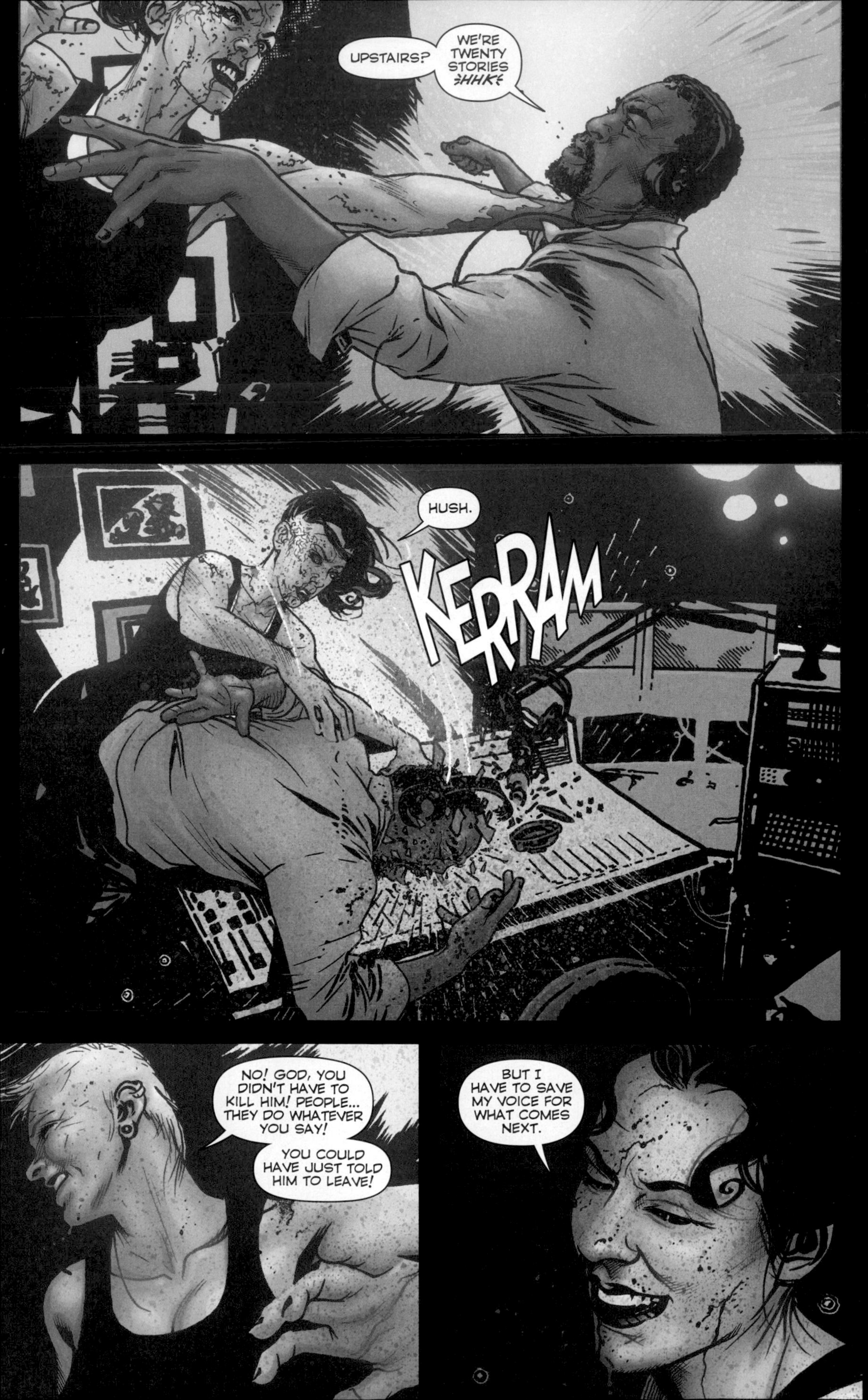
UPSTAIRS?
WE'RE TWENTY STORIES ƎHHKƐ
HUSH.
KERRAM
NO! GOD, YOU DIDN'T HAVE TO KILL HIM! PEOPLE... THEY DO WHATEVER YOU SAY!
YOU COULD HAVE JUST TOLD HIM TO LEAVE!
BUT I HAVE TO SAVE MY VOICE FOR WHAT COMES NEXT.

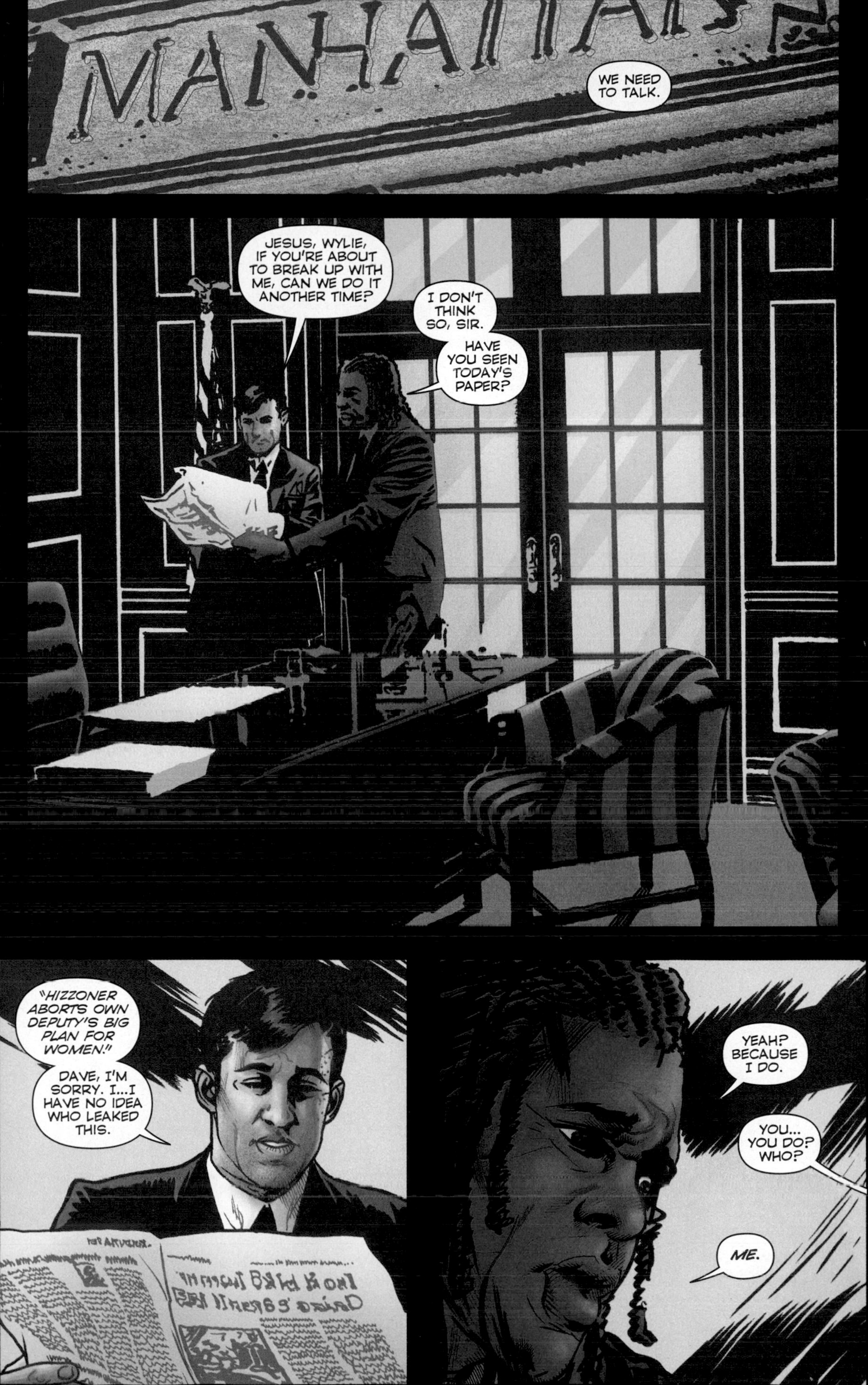
WE NEED TO TALK.
JESUS, WYLIE, IF YOU'RE ABOUT TO BREAK UP WITH ME, CAN WE DO IT ANOTHER TIME?
I DON'T THINK SO, SIR.
HAVE YOU SEEN TODAY'S PAPER?
"HIZZONER ABORTS OWN DEPUTY'S BIG PLAN FOR WOMEN."
DAVE, I'M SORRY. I...I HAVE NO IDEA WHO LEAKED THIS.
YEAH? BECAUSE I DO.
YOU... YOU DO? WHO?
ME.

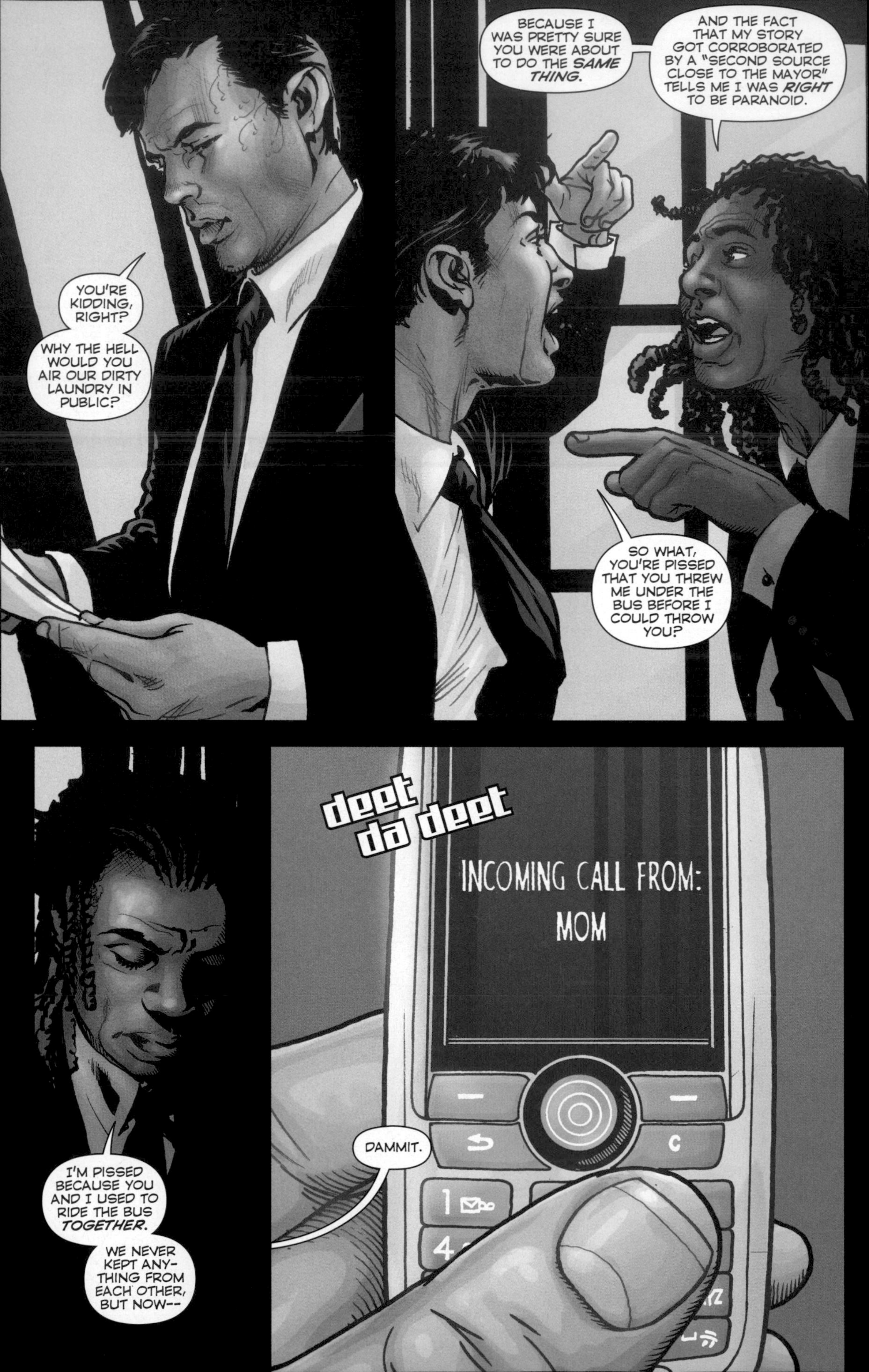
YOU'RE KIDDING, RIGHT?
WHY THE HELL WOULD YOU AIR OUR DIRTY LAUNDRY IN PUBLIC?
BECAUSE I WAS PRETTY SURE YOU WERE ABOUT TO DO THE *SAME THING*.
AND THE FACT THAT MY STORY GOT CORROBORATED BY A "SECOND SOURCE CLOSE TO THE MAYOR" TELLS ME I WAS *RIGHT* TO BE PARANOID.
SO WHAT, YOU'RE PISSED THAT YOU THREW ME UNDER THE BUS BEFORE I COULD THROW YOU?
I'M PISSED BECAUSE YOU AND I USED TO RIDE THE BUS *TOGETHER*.
WE NEVER KEPT ANY-THING FROM EACH OTHER, BUT NOW--
deet da deet
INCOMING CALL FROM:
MOM
DAMMIT.

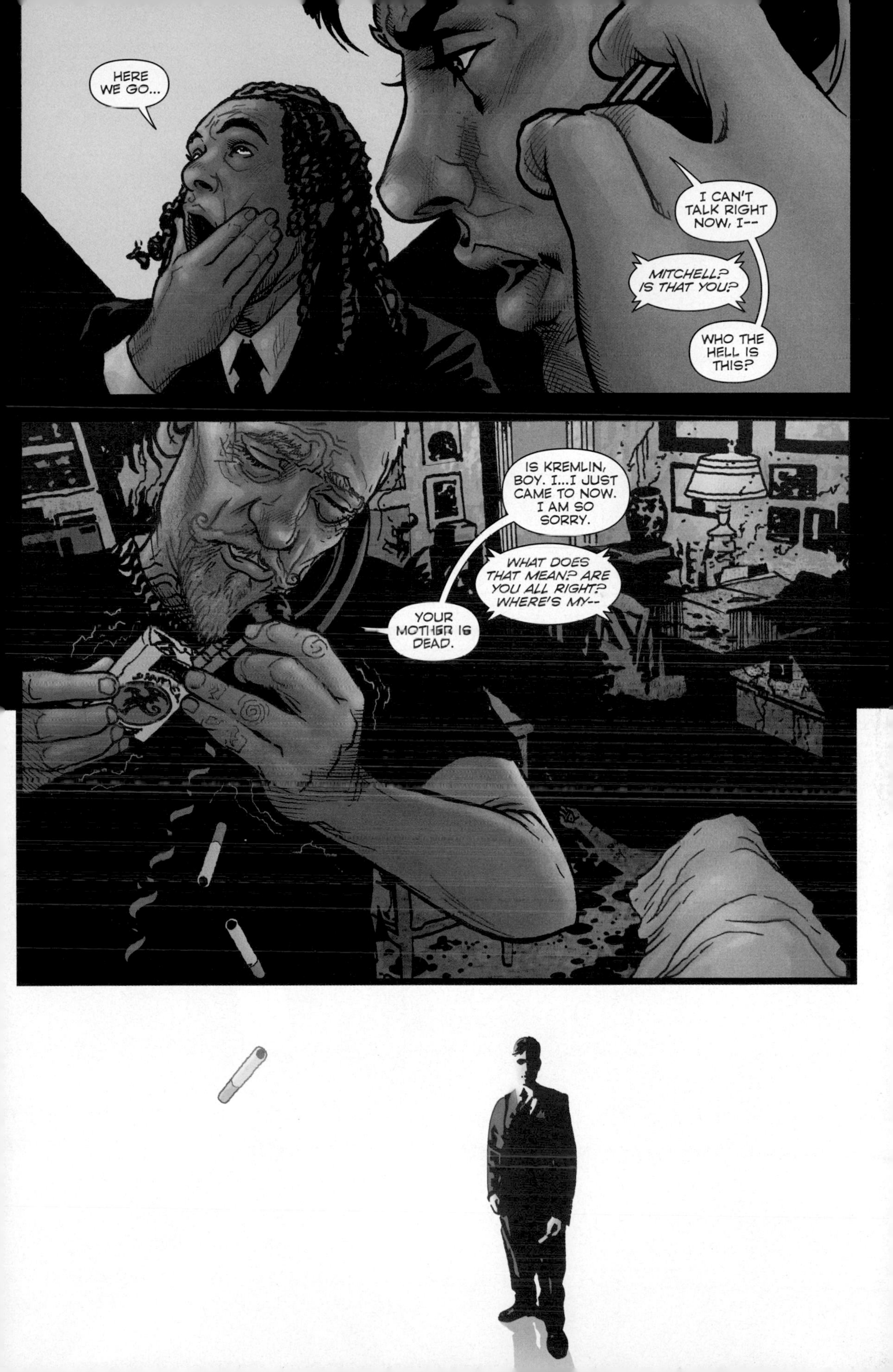
HERE WE GO...
I CAN'T TALK RIGHT NOW, I--
MITCHELL? IS THAT YOU?
WHO THE HELL IS THIS?
IS KREMLIN, BOY. I...I JUST CAME TO NOW. I AM SO SORRY.
WHAT DOES THAT MEAN? ARE YOU ALL RIGHT? WHERE'S MY--
YOUR MOTHER IS DEAD.

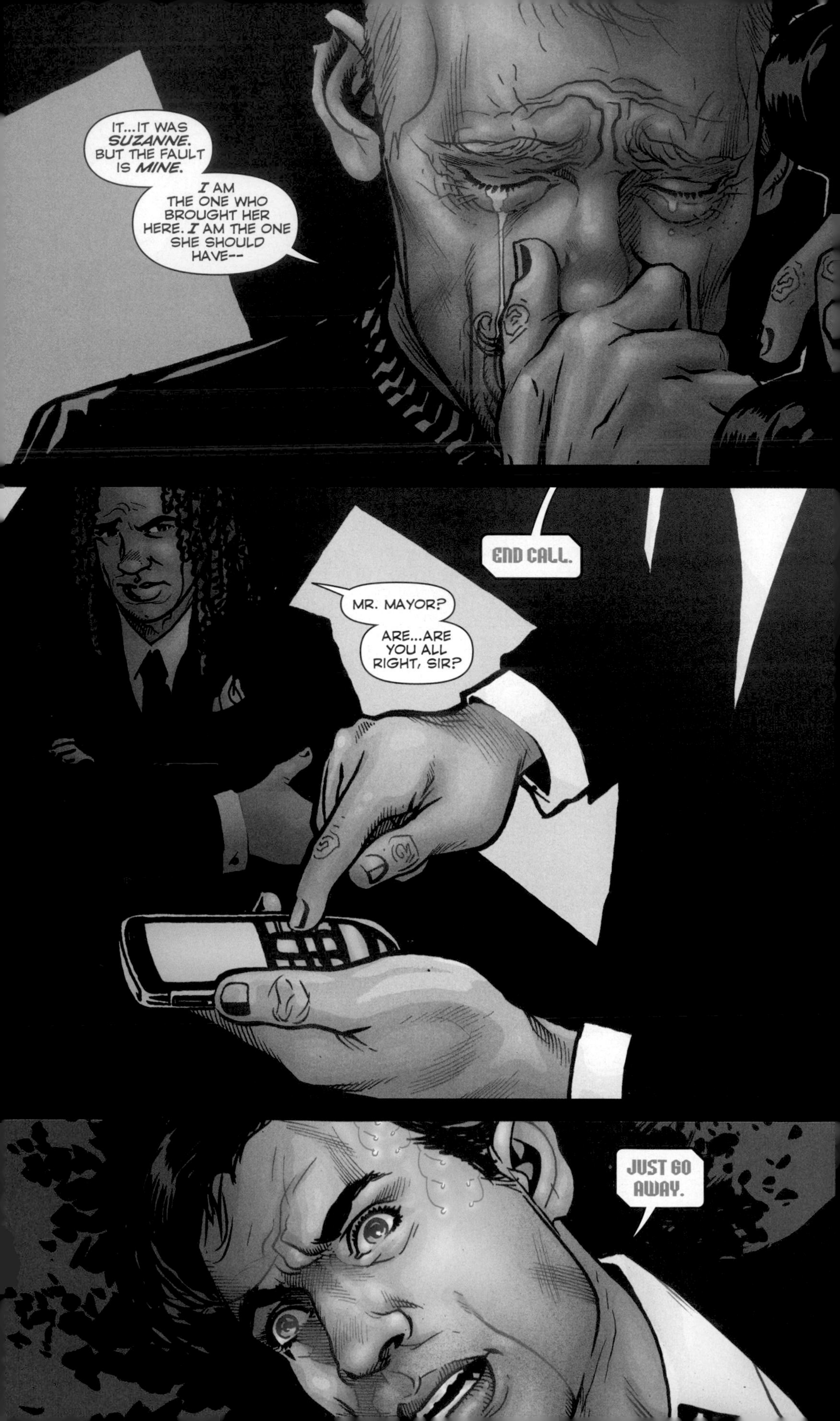
IT...IT WAS SUZANNE. BUT THE FAULT IS MINE.
I AM THE ONE WHO BROUGHT HER HERE. I AM THE ONE SHE SHOULD HAVE--
END CALL.
MR. MAYOR?
ARE...ARE YOU ALL RIGHT, SIR?
JUST GO AWAY.

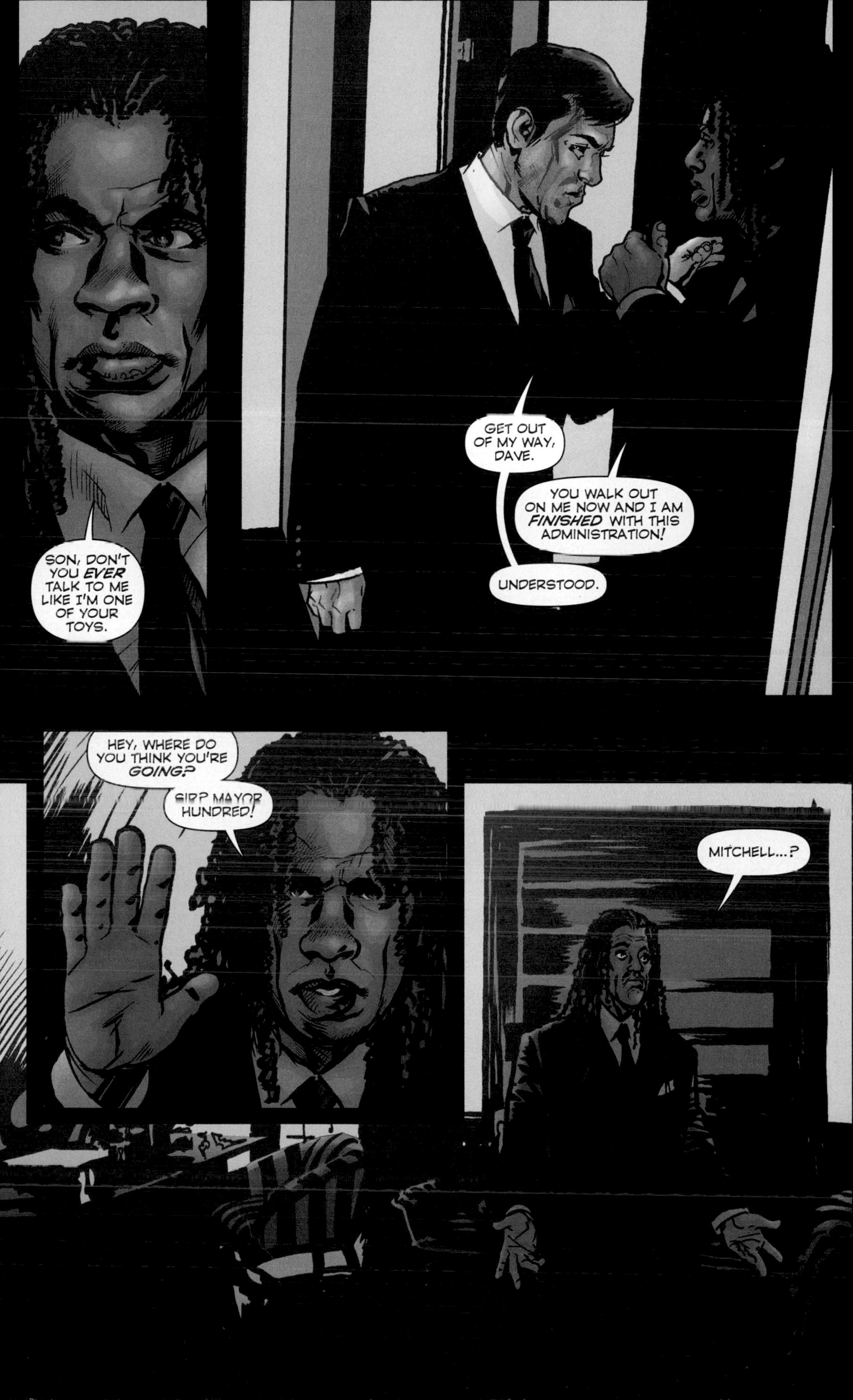
SON, DON'T YOU EVER TALK TO ME LIKE I'M ONE OF YOUR TOYS.
GET OUT OF MY WAY, DAVE.
YOU WALK OUT ON ME NOW AND I AM FINISHED WITH THIS ADMINISTRATION!
UNDERSTOOD.
HEY, WHERE DO YOU THINK YOU'RE GOING?
SIR? MAYOR HUNDRED!
MITCHELL...?

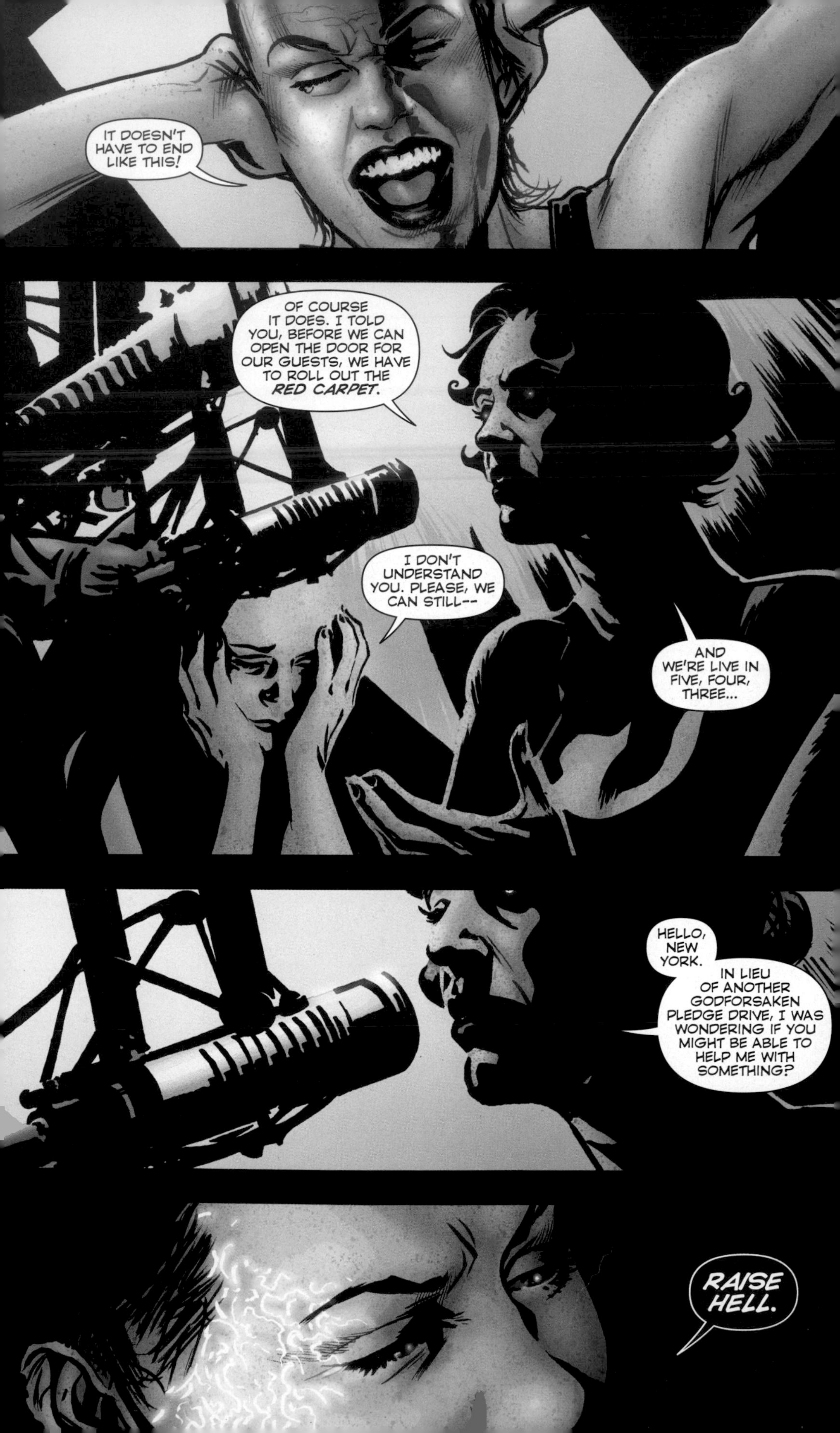
IT DOESN'T HAVE TO END LIKE THIS!
OF COURSE IT DOES. I TOLD YOU, BEFORE WE CAN OPEN THE DOOR FOR OUR GUESTS, WE HAVE TO ROLL OUT THE *RED CARPET*.
I DON'T UNDERSTAND YOU. PLEASE, WE CAN STILL--
AND WE'RE LIVE IN FIVE, FOUR, THREE...
HELLO, NEW YORK.
IN LIEU OF ANOTHER GODFORSAKEN PLEDGE DRIVE, I WAS WONDERING IF YOU MIGHT BE ABLE TO HELP ME WITH SOMETHING?
RAISE HELL.

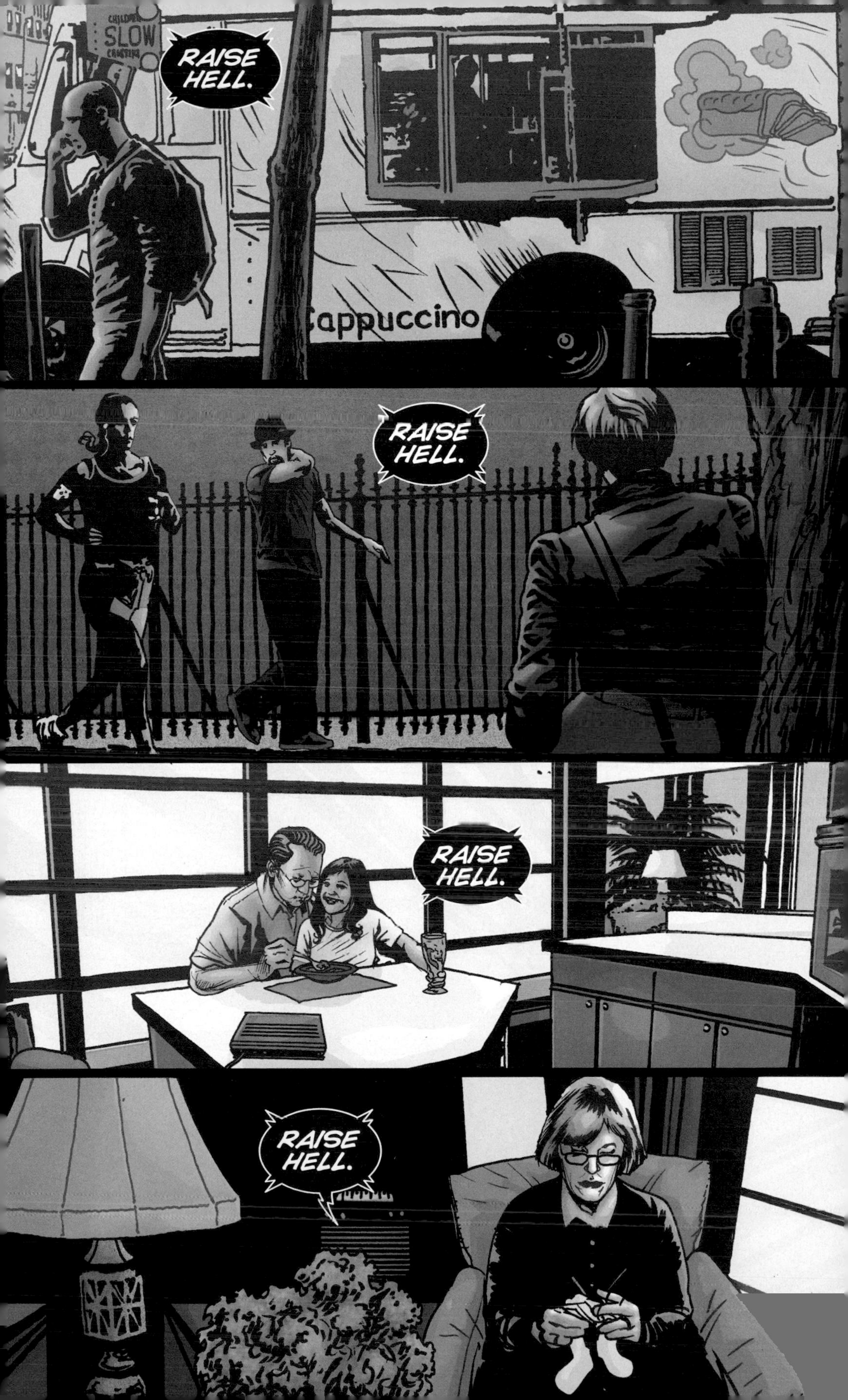
SLOW
RAISE HELL.
Cappuccino
RAISE HELL.
RAISE HELL.
RAISE HELL.

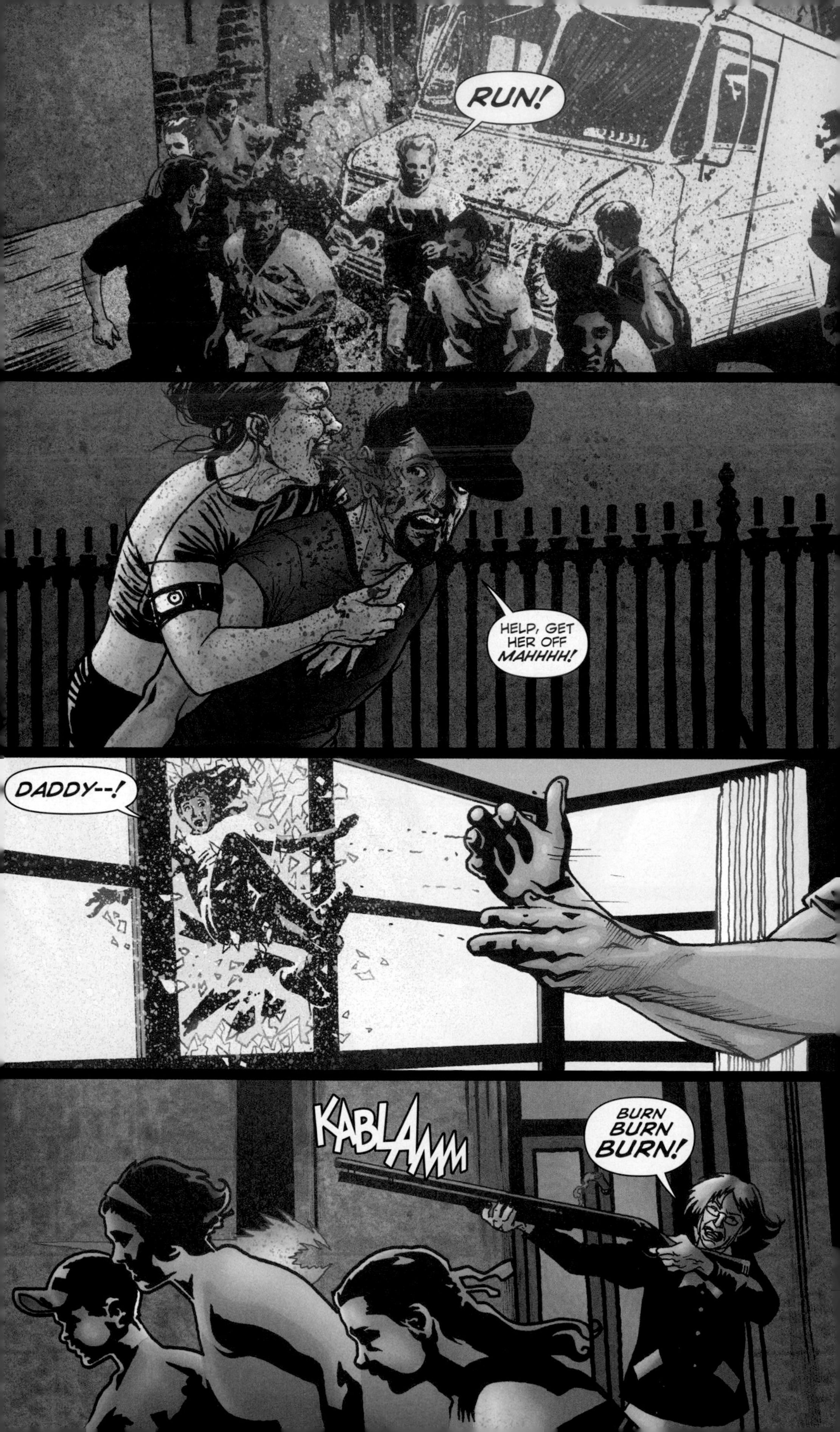
RUN!
HELP, GET HER OFF MAHHHH!
DADDY--!
KABLAMM
BURN BURN BURN!

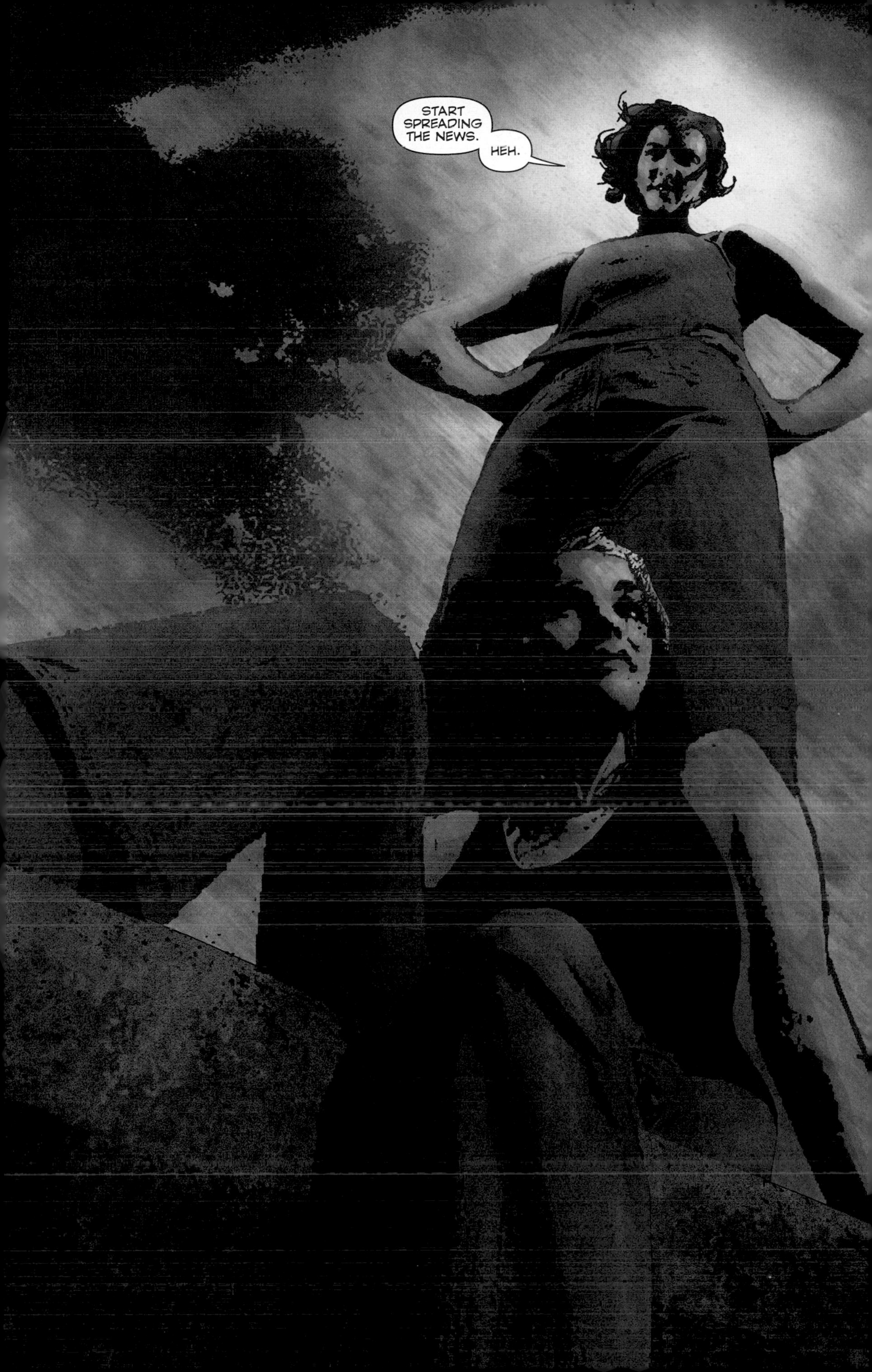
START SPREADING THE NEWS.
HEH.

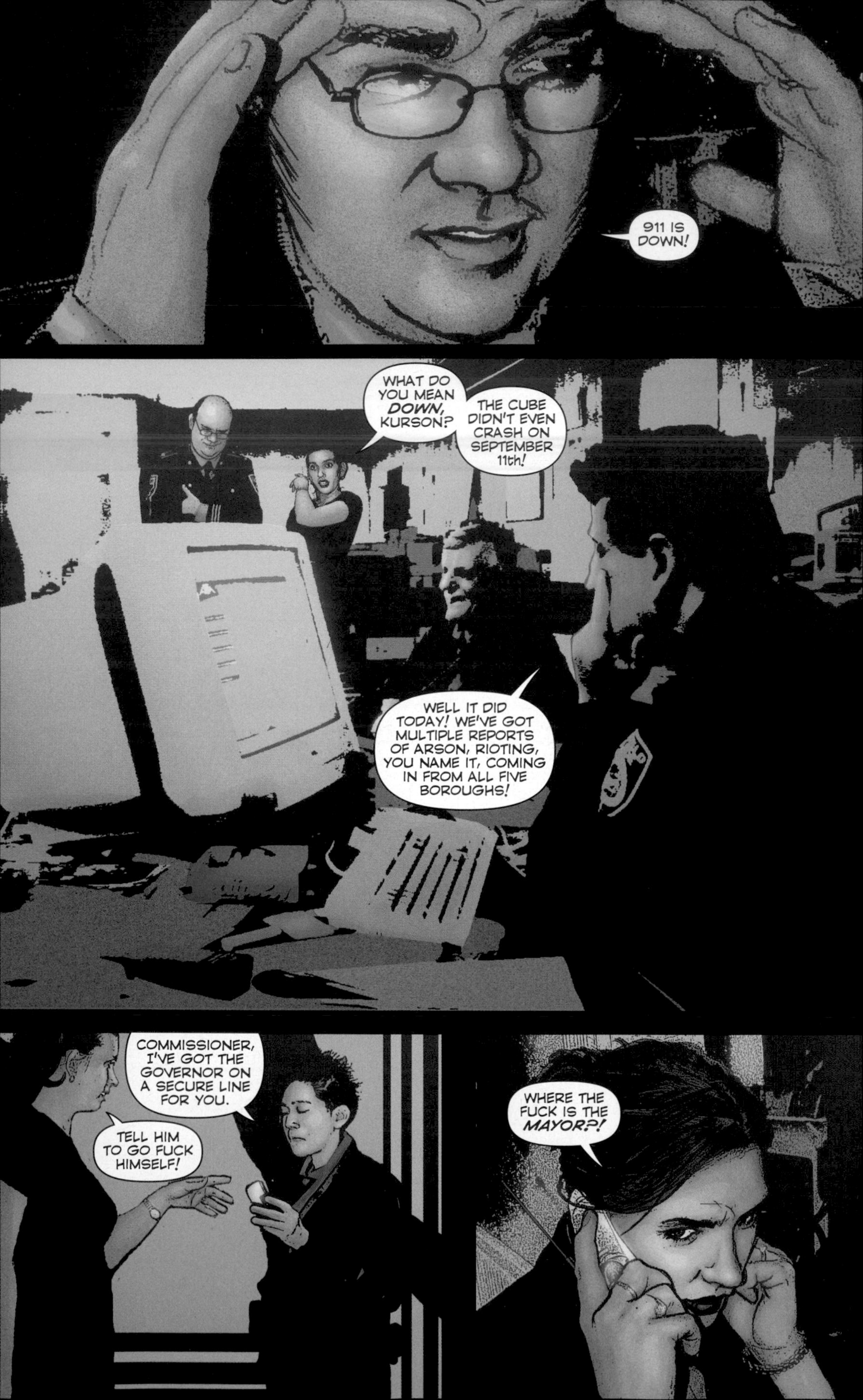
911 IS DOWN!
WHAT DO YOU MEAN *DOWN*, KURSON?
THE CUBE DIDN'T EVEN CRASH ON SEPTEMBER 11th!
WELL IT DID TODAY! WE'VE GOT MULTIPLE REPORTS OF ARSON, RIOTING, YOU NAME IT, COMING IN FROM ALL FIVE BOROUGHS!
COMMISSIONER, I'VE GOT THE GOVERNOR ON A SECURE LINE FOR YOU.
TELL HIM TO GO FUCK HIMSELF!
WHERE THE FUCK IS THE *MAYOR?!*

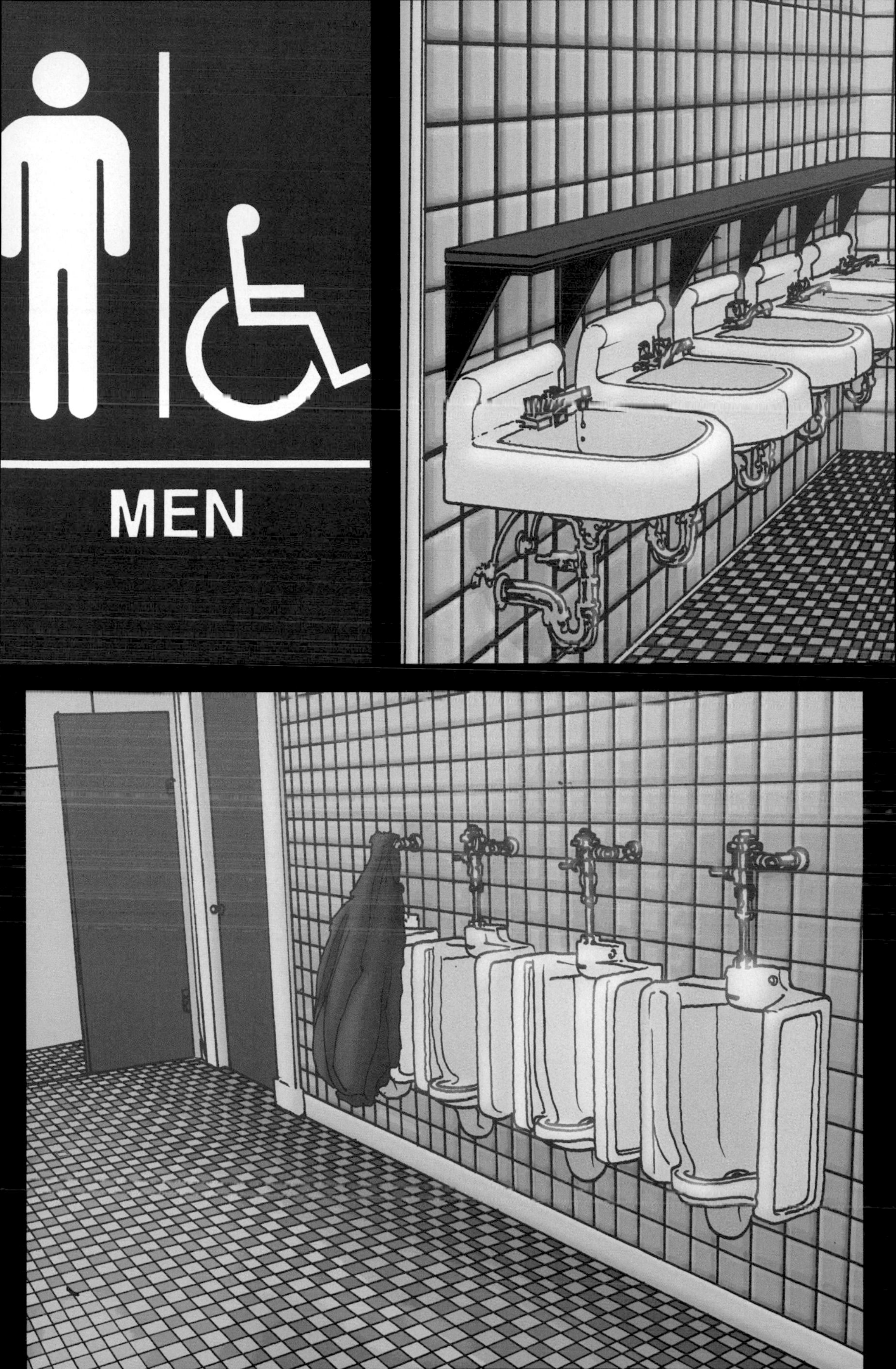
MEN

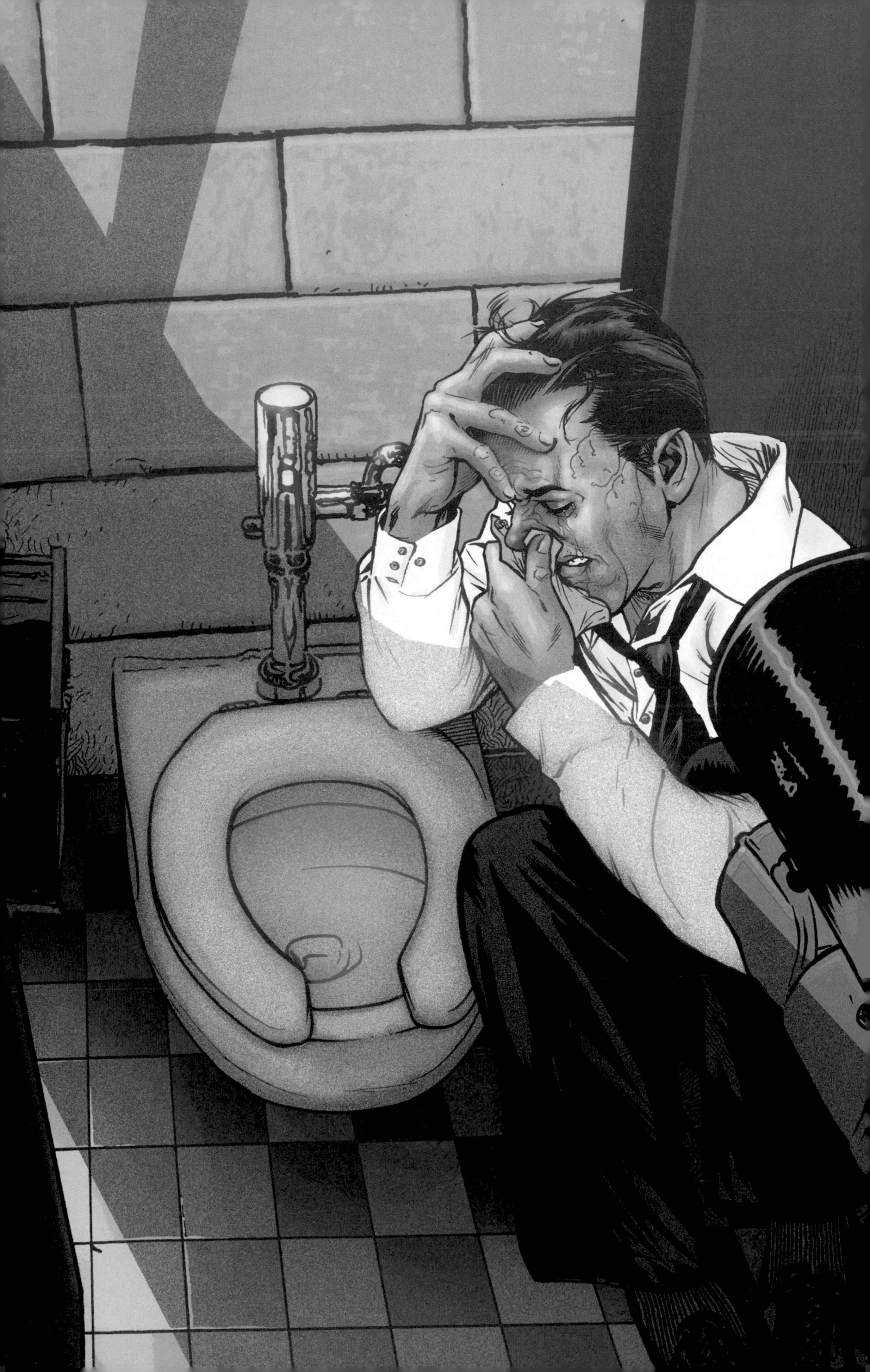

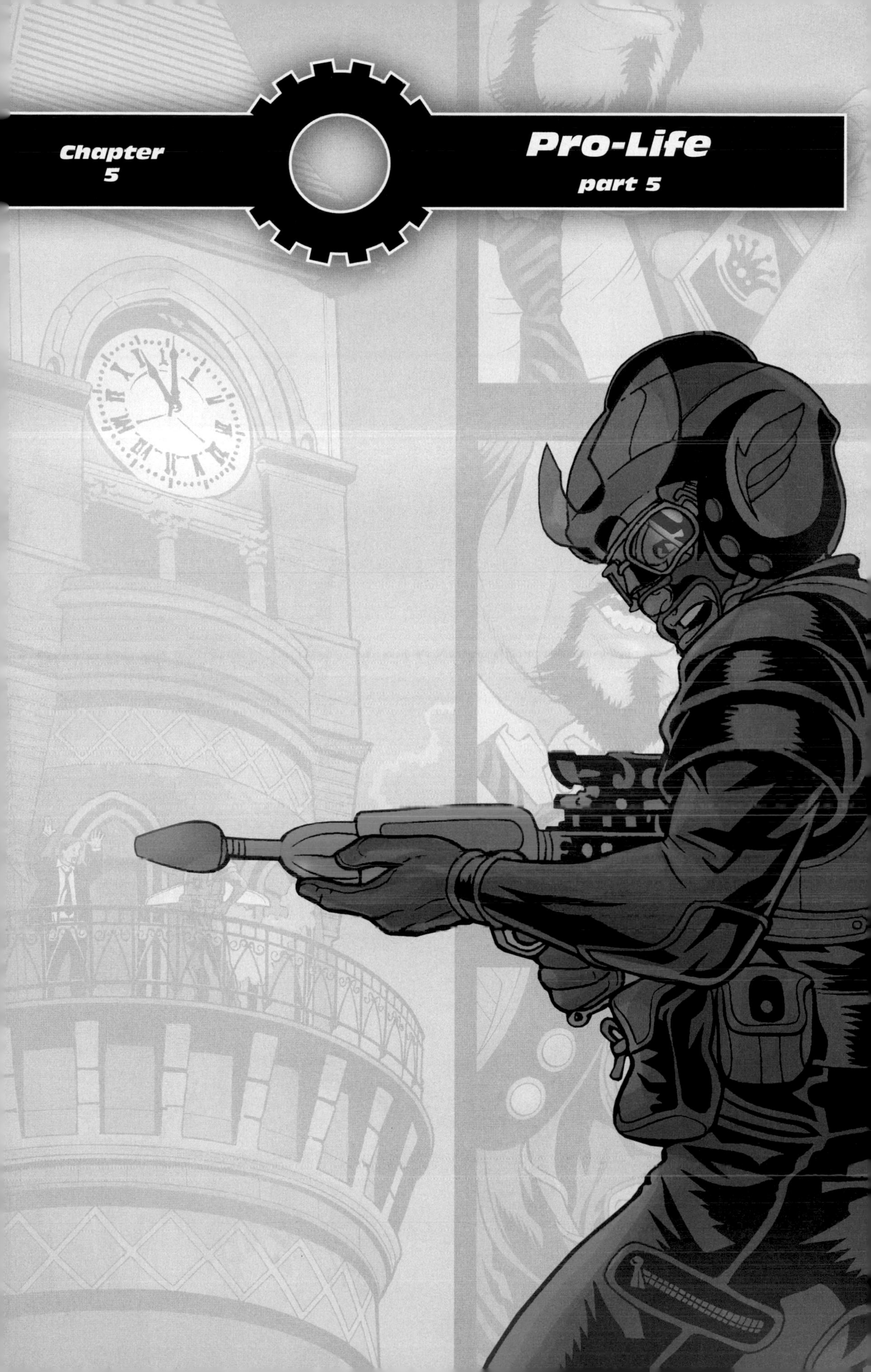
Chapter 5
Pro-Life
part 5

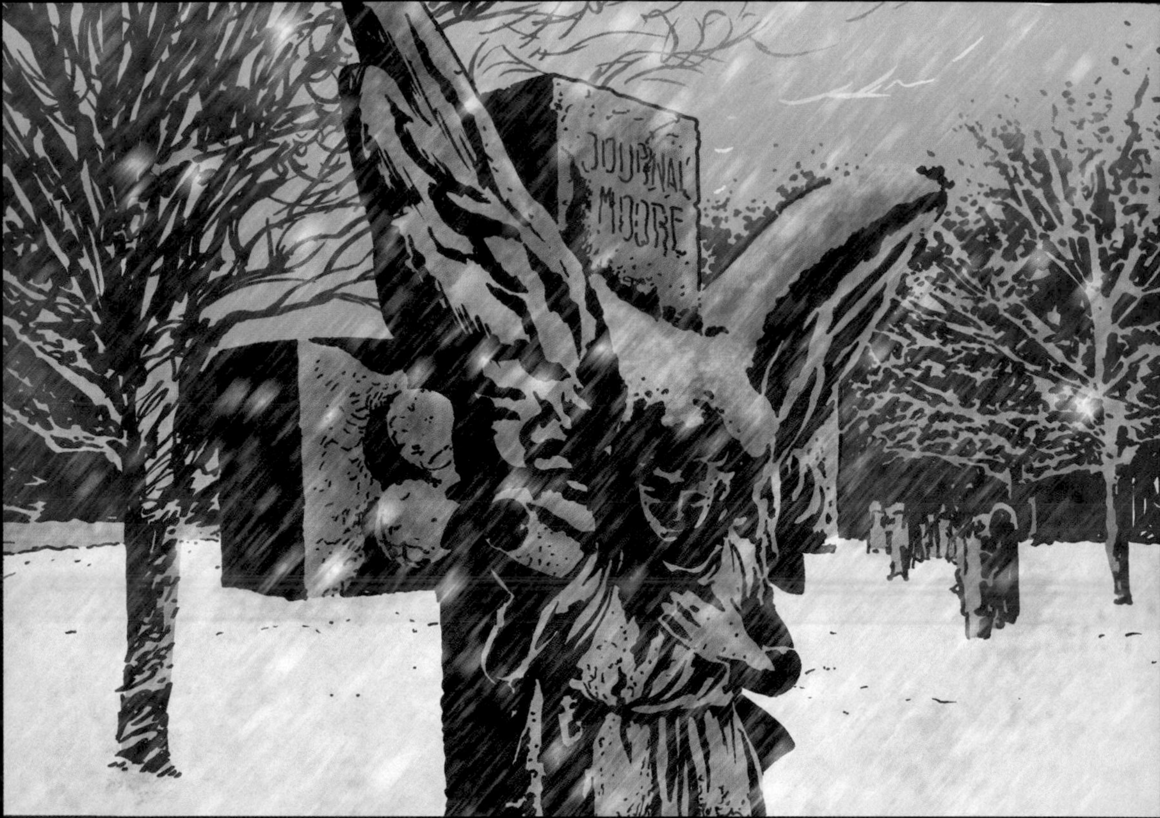
JOURNAL
MOORE

MONDAY, FEBRUARY 24, 2003

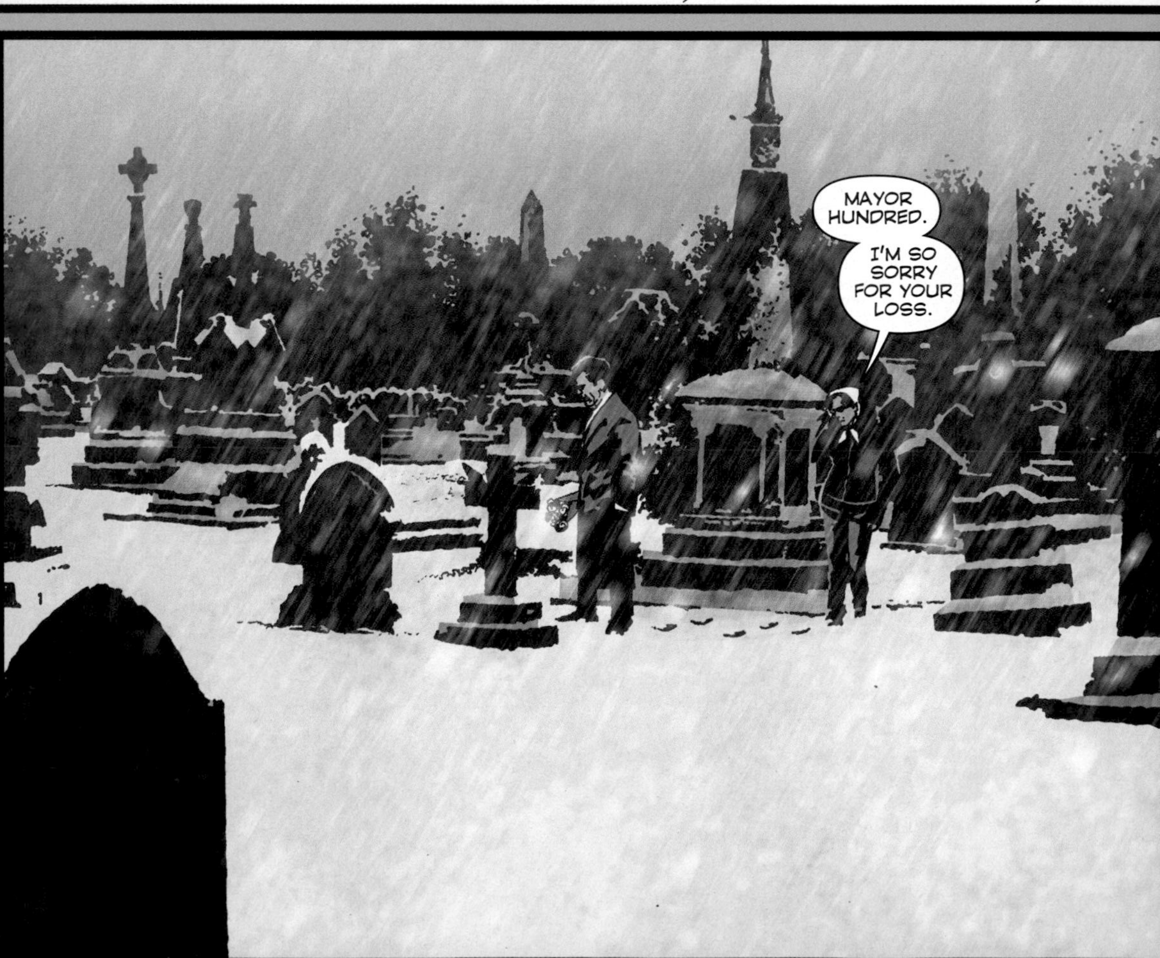
MAYOR HUNDRED.
I'M SO SORRY FOR YOUR LOSS.

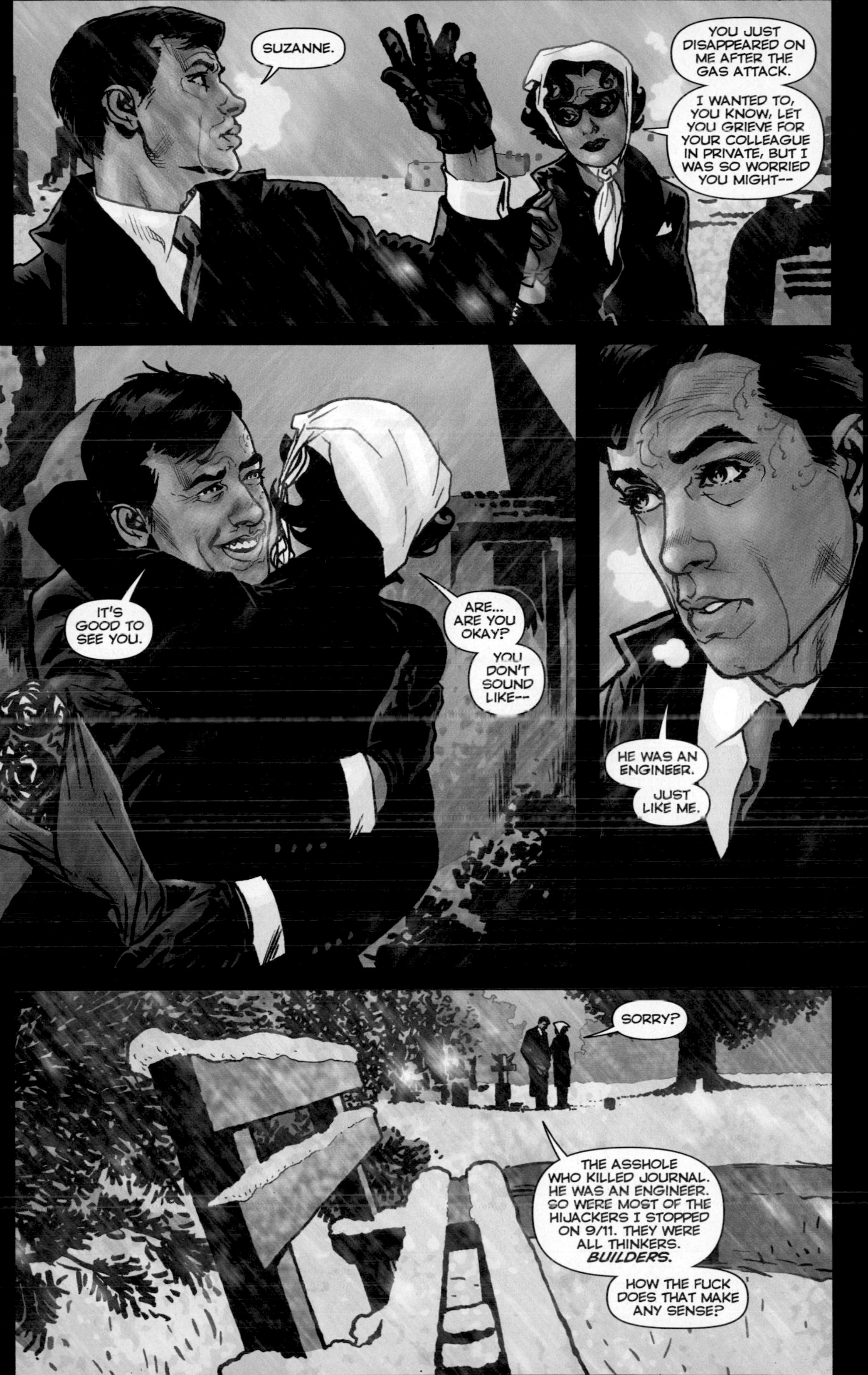
SUZANNE.
YOU JUST DISAPPEARED ON ME AFTER THE GAS ATTACK.
I WANTED TO, YOU KNOW, LET YOU GRIEVE FOR YOUR COLLEAGUE IN PRIVATE, BUT I WAS SO WORRIED YOU MIGHT--
IT'S GOOD TO SEE YOU.
ARE... ARE YOU OKAY?
YOU DON'T SOUND LIKE--
HE WAS AN ENGINEER.
JUST LIKE ME.
SORRY?
THE ASSHOLE WHO KILLED JOURNAL. HE WAS AN ENGINEER. SO WERE MOST OF THE HIJACKERS I STOPPED ON 9/11. THEY WERE ALL THINKERS. *BUILDERS*.
HOW THE FUCK DOES THAT MAKE ANY SENSE?

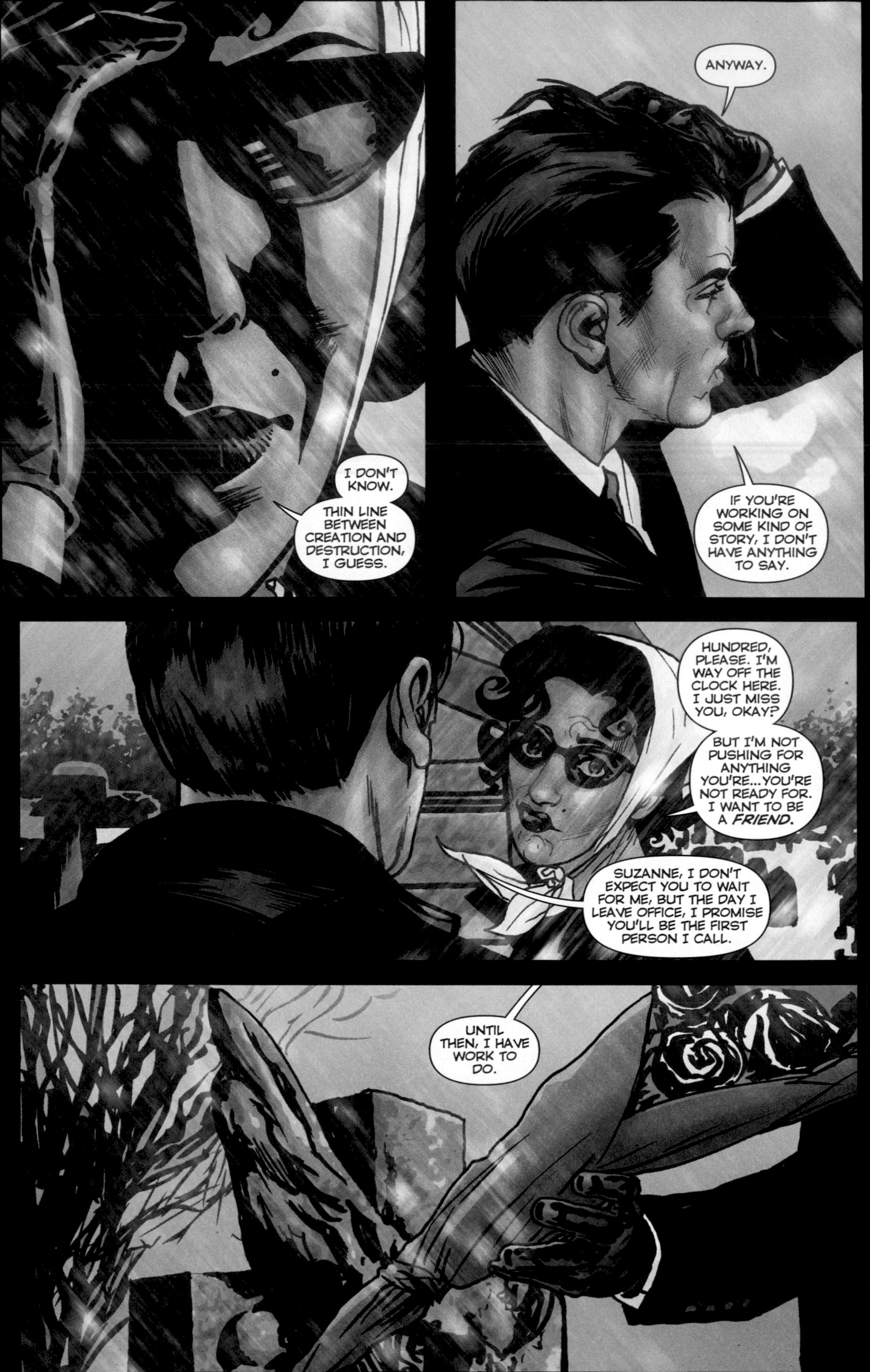
I DON'T KNOW.
THIN LINE BETWEEN CREATION AND DESTRUCTION, I GUESS.
ANYWAY.
IF YOU'RE WORKING ON SOME KIND OF STORY, I DON'T HAVE ANYTHING TO SAY.
HUNDRED, PLEASE. I'M WAY OFF THE CLOCK HERE. I JUST MISS YOU, OKAY?
BUT I'M NOT PUSHING FOR ANYTHING YOU'RE...YOU'RE NOT READY FOR. I WANT TO BE A *FRIEND*.
SUZANNE, I DON'T EXPECT YOU TO WAIT FOR ME, BUT THE DAY I LEAVE OFFICE, I PROMISE YOU'LL BE THE FIRST PERSON I CALL.
UNTIL THEN, I HAVE WORK TO DO.

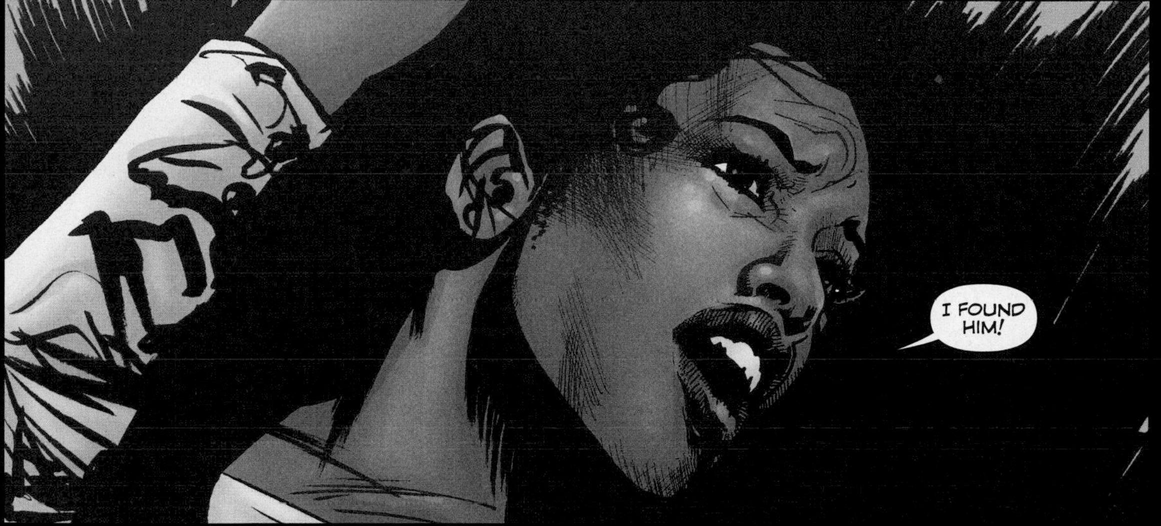
I FOUND HIM!

TUESDAY, APRIL 12, 2005

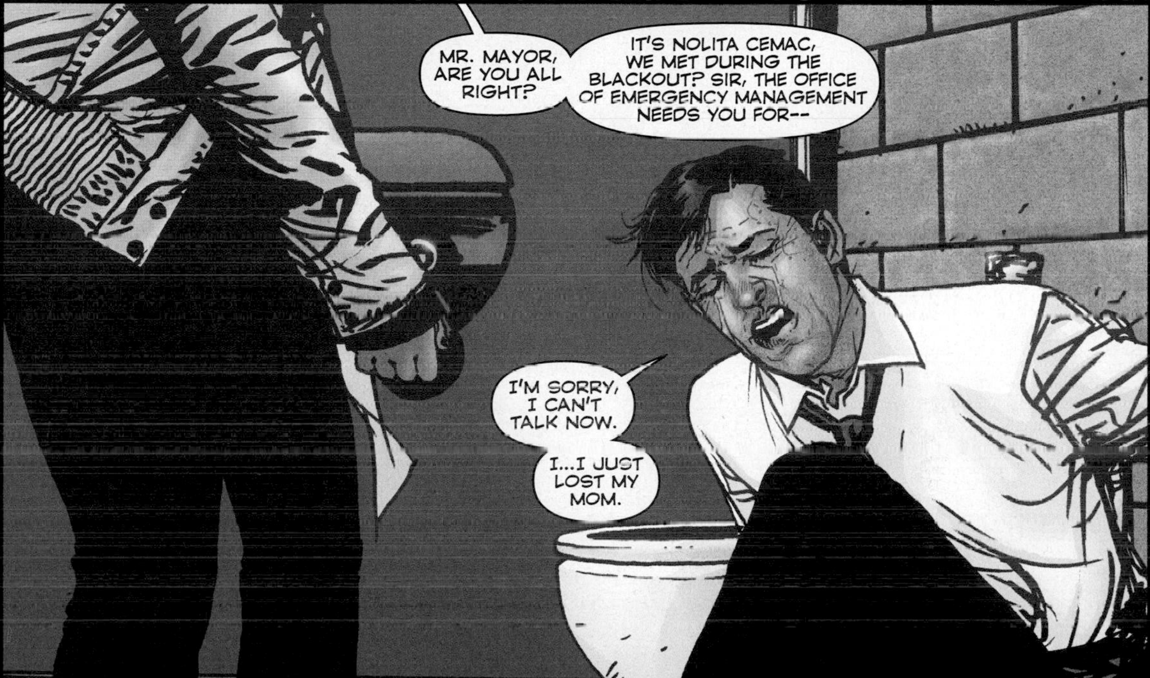
MR. MAYOR, ARE YOU ALL RIGHT?
IT'S NOLITA CEMAC, WE MET DURING THE BLACKOUT? SIR, THE OFFICE OF EMERGENCY MANAGEMENT NEEDS YOU FOR--
I'M SORRY, I CAN'T TALK NOW.
I...I JUST LOST MY MOM.

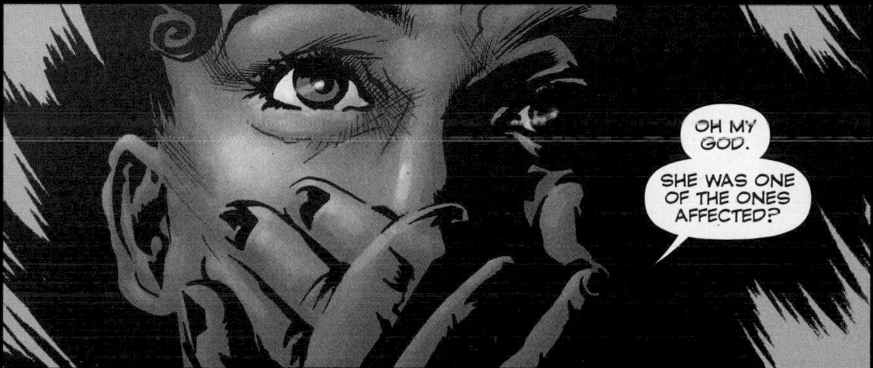
OH MY GOD.
SHE WAS ONE OF THE ONES AFFECTED?

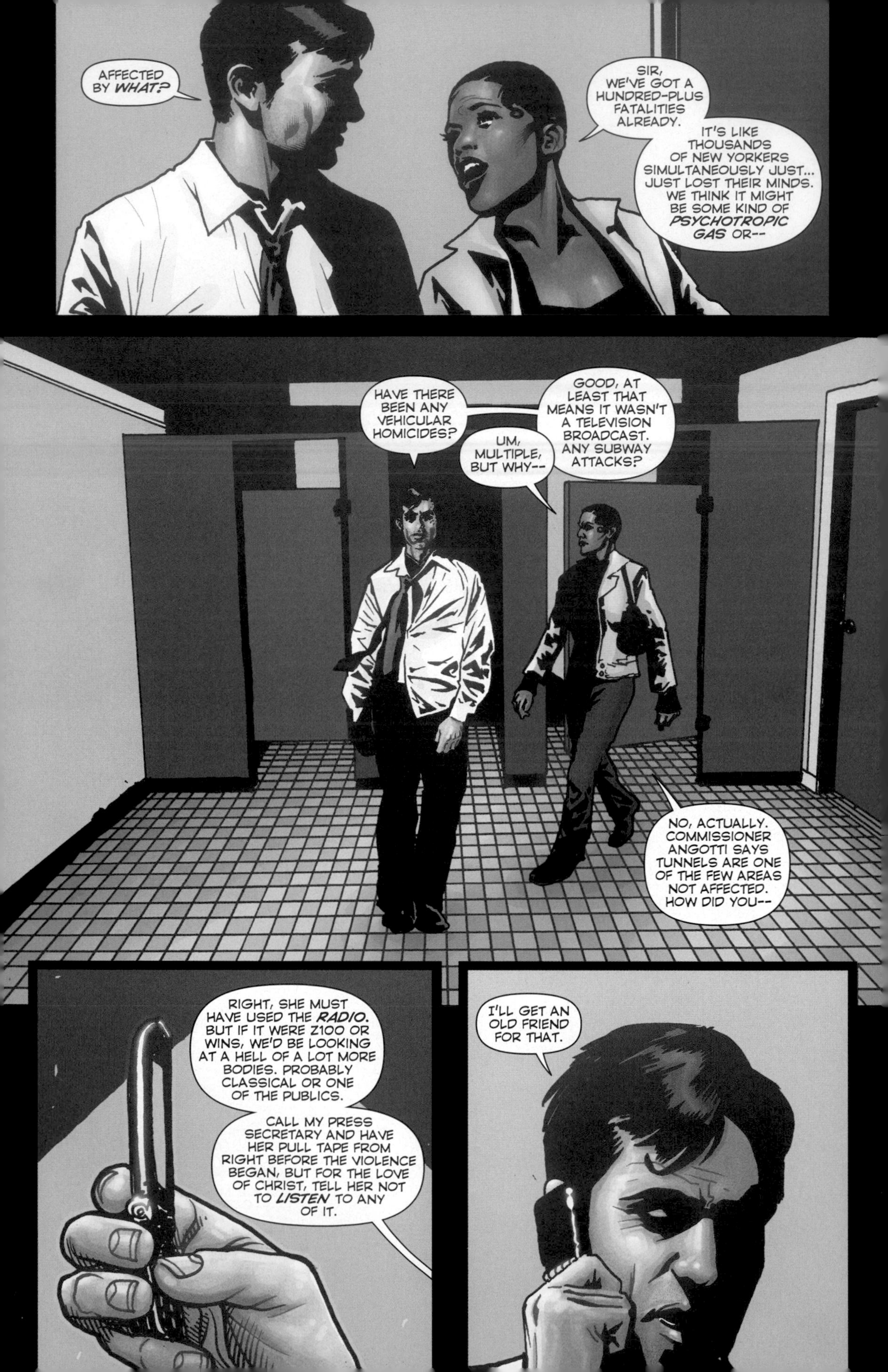
AFFECTED BY WHAT?
SIR, WE'VE GOT A HUNDRED-PLUS FATALITIES ALREADY.
IT'S LIKE THOUSANDS OF NEW YORKERS SIMULTANEOUSLY JUST... JUST LOST THEIR MINDS. WE THINK IT MIGHT BE SOME KIND OF PSYCHOTROPIC GAS OR--
HAVE THERE BEEN ANY VEHICULAR HOMICIDES?
UM, MULTIPLE, BUT WHY--
GOOD, AT LEAST THAT MEANS IT WASN'T A TELEVISION BROADCAST. ANY SUBWAY ATTACKS?
NO, ACTUALLY. COMMISSIONER ANGOTTI SAYS TUNNELS ARE ONE OF THE FEW AREAS NOT AFFECTED. HOW DID YOU--
RIGHT, SHE MUST HAVE USED THE RADIO. BUT IF IT WERE Z100 OR WINS, WE'D BE LOOKING AT A HELL OF A LOT MORE BODIES. PROBABLY CLASSICAL OR ONE OF THE PUBLICS.
CALL MY PRESS SECRETARY AND HAVE HER PULL TAPE FROM RIGHT BEFORE THE VIOLENCE BEGAN, BUT FOR THE LOVE OF CHRIST, TELL HER NOT TO LISTEN TO ANY OF IT.
I'LL GET AN OLD FRIEND FOR THAT.

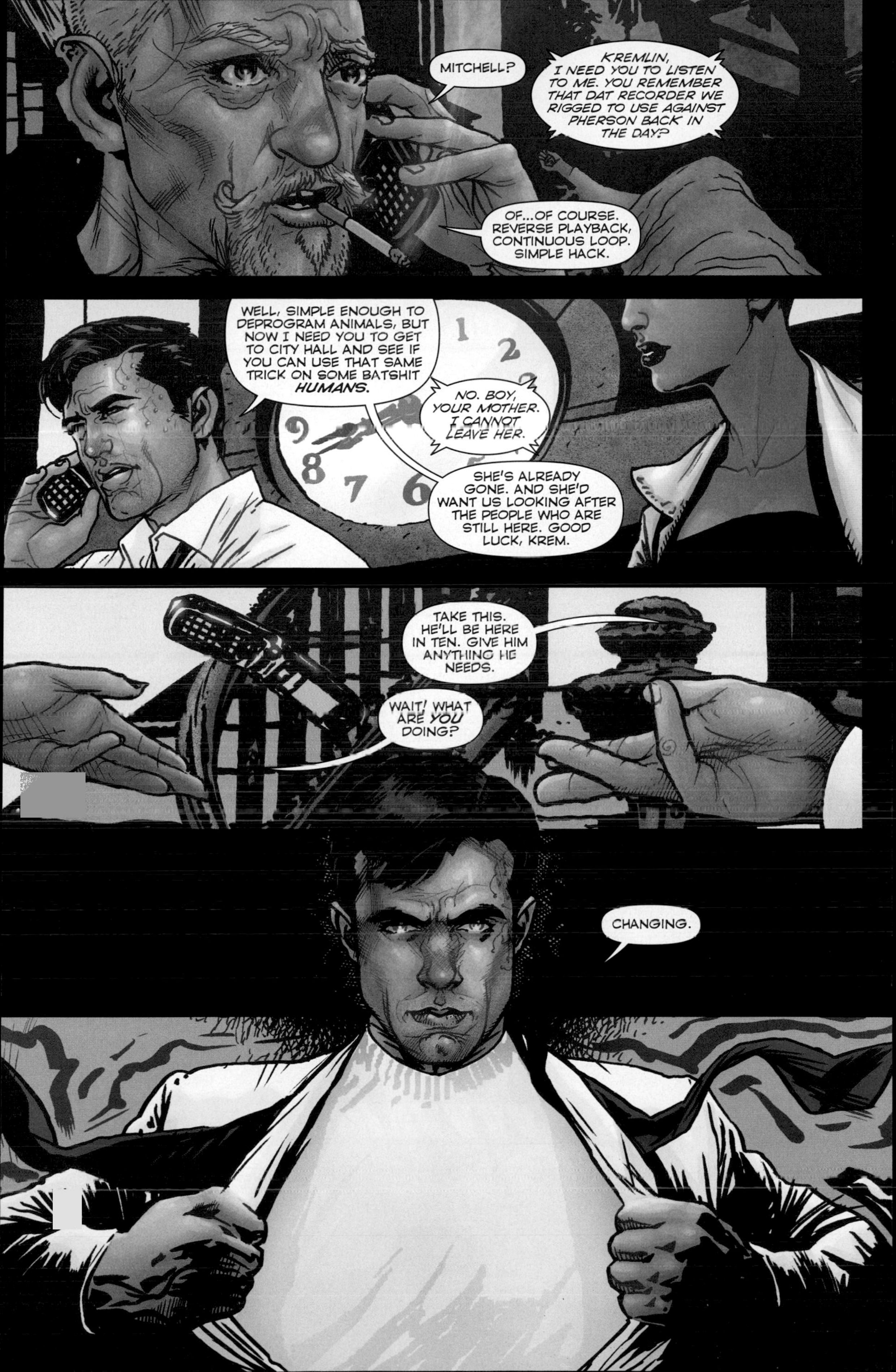
MITCHELL?
KREMLIN, I NEED YOU TO LISTEN TO ME. YOU REMEMBER THAT DAT RECORDER WE RIGGED TO USE AGAINST PHERSON BACK IN THE DAY?
OF...OF COURSE. REVERSE PLAYBACK, CONTINUOUS LOOP. SIMPLE HACK.
WELL, SIMPLE ENOUGH TO DEPROGRAM ANIMALS, BUT NOW I NEED YOU TO GET TO CITY HALL AND SEE IF YOU CAN USE THAT SAME TRICK ON SOME BATSHIT HUMANS.
NO. BOY, YOUR MOTHER. I CANNOT LEAVE HER.
SHE'S ALREADY GONE. AND SHE'D WANT US LOOKING AFTER THE PEOPLE WHO ARE STILL HERE. GOOD LUCK, KREM.
TAKE THIS. HE'LL BE HERE IN TEN. GIVE HIM ANYTHING HE NEEDS.
WAIT! WHAT ARE YOU DOING?
CHANGING.

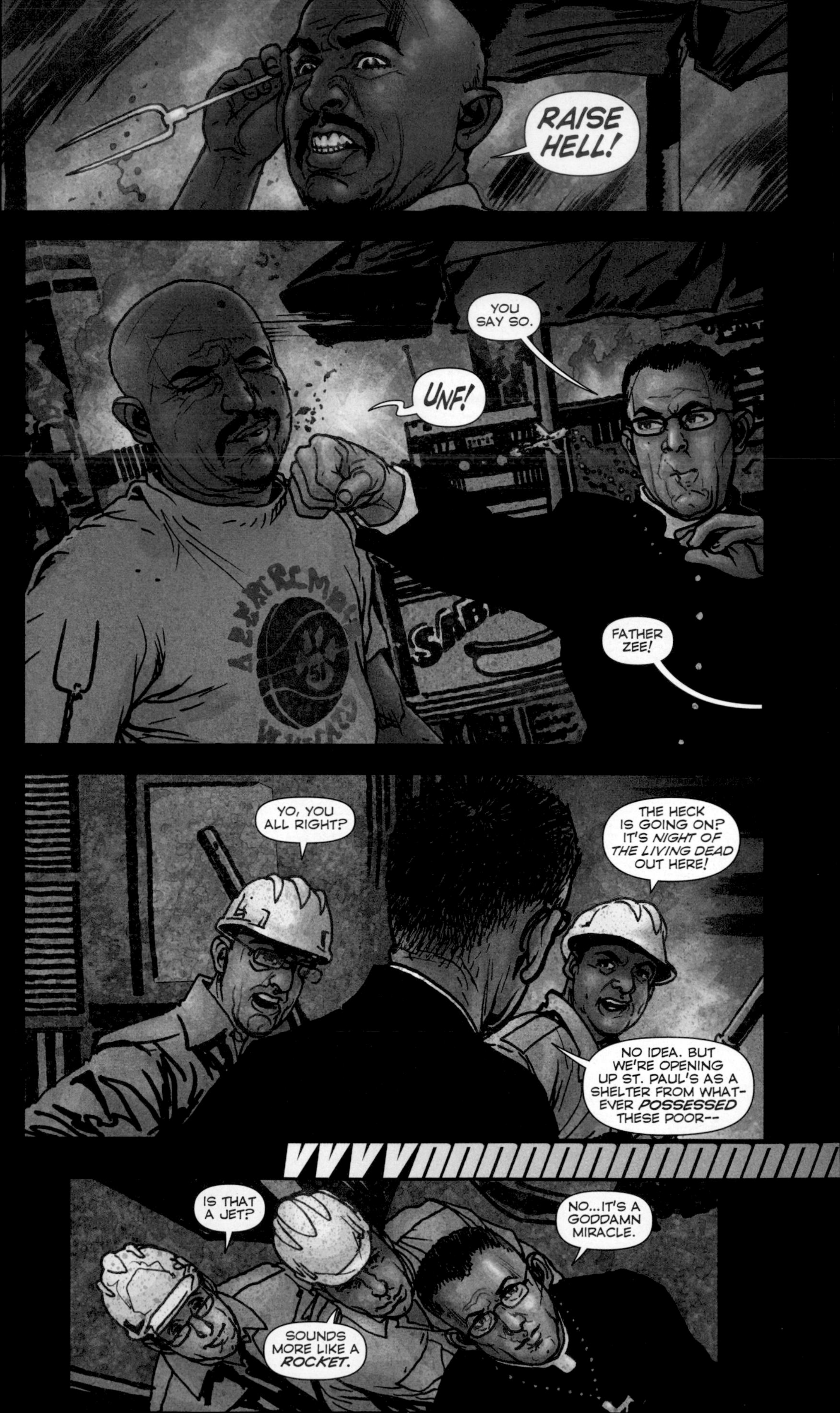
RAISE HELL!
YOU SAY SO.
UNF!
FATHER ZEE!
YO, YOU ALL RIGHT?
THE HECK IS GOING ON? IT'S *NIGHT OF THE LIVING DEAD* OUT HERE!
NO IDEA. BUT WE'RE OPENING UP ST. PAUL'S AS A SHELTER FROM WHATEVER *POSSESSED* THESE POOR--
VVVVNNNNNNNNNNNNNNNN
IS THAT A JET?
SOUNDS MORE LIKE A *ROCKET*.
NO...IT'S A GODDAMN MIRACLE.

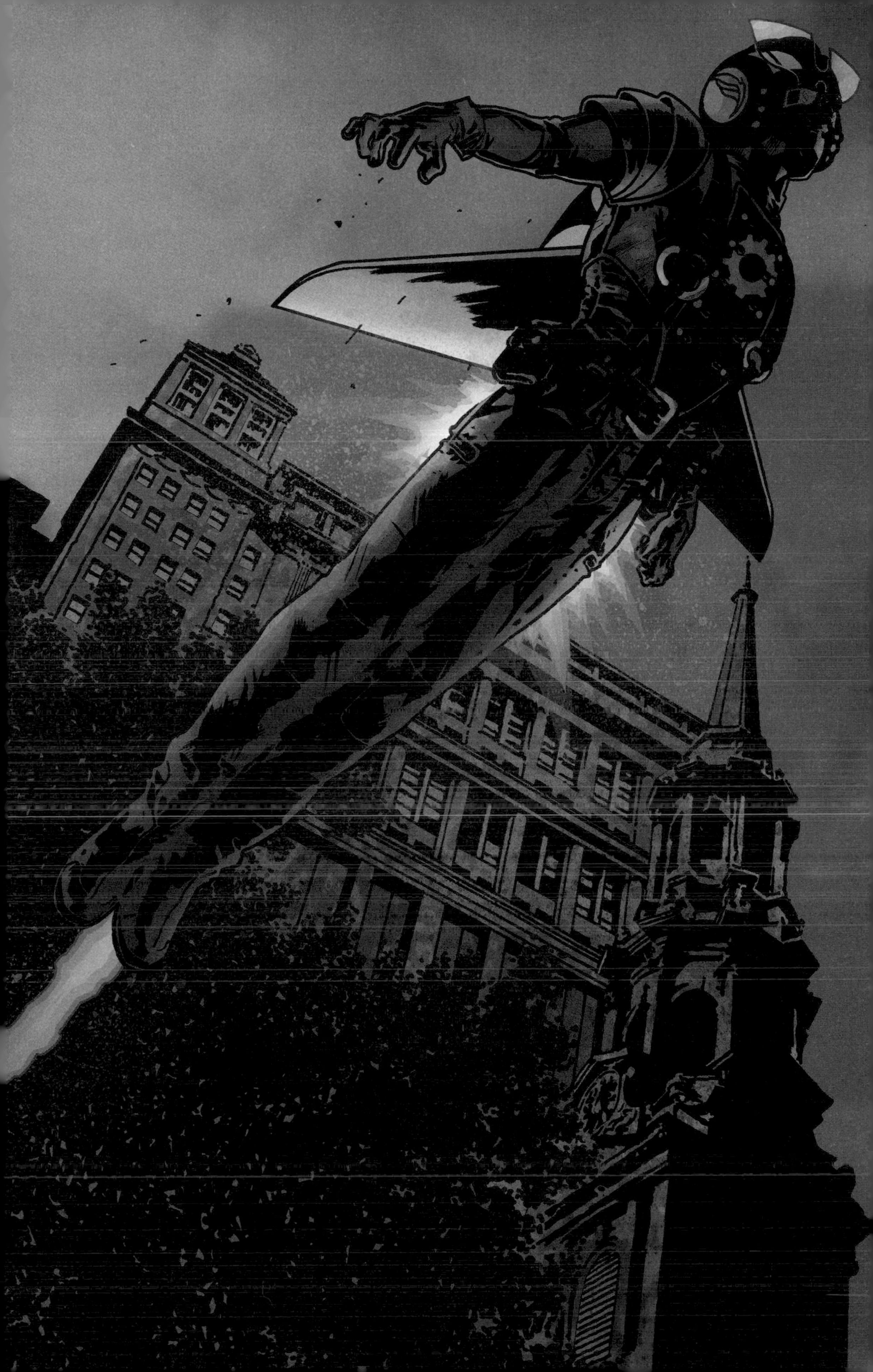

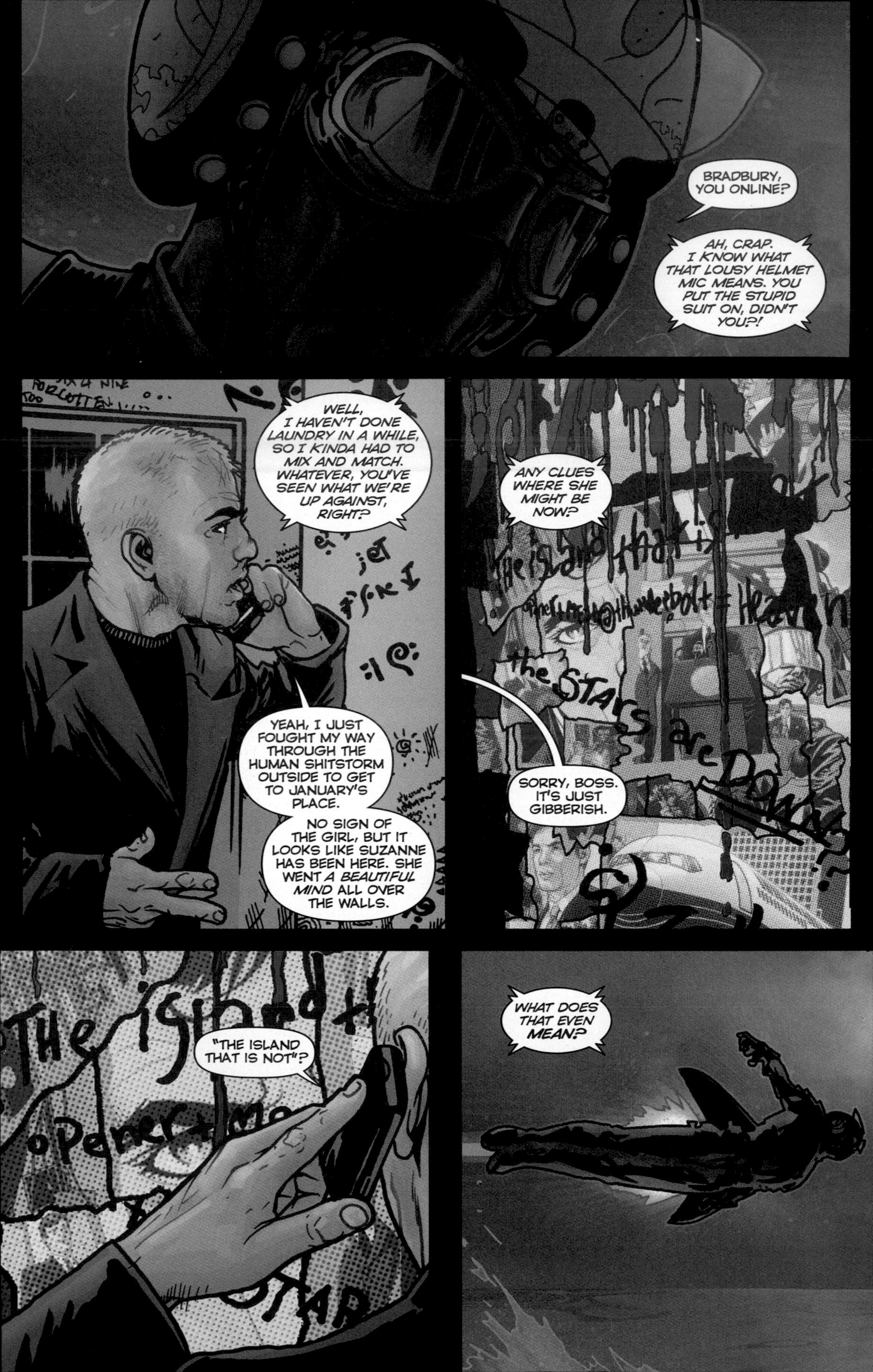
BRADBURY, YOU ONLINE?
AH, CRAP. I KNOW WHAT THAT LOUSY HELMET MIC MEANS. YOU PUT THE STUPID SUIT ON, DIDN'T YOU?!
WELL, I HAVEN'T DONE LAUNDRY IN A WHILE, SO I KINDA HAD TO MIX AND MATCH. WHATEVER, YOU'VE SEEN WHAT WE'RE UP AGAINST, RIGHT?
YEAH, I JUST FOUGHT MY WAY THROUGH THE HUMAN SHITSTORM OUTSIDE TO GET TO JANUARY'S PLACE.
NO SIGN OF THE GIRL, BUT IT LOOKS LIKE SUZANNE HAS BEEN HERE. SHE WENT *A BEAUTIFUL MIND* ALL OVER THE WALLS.
ANY CLUES WHERE SHE MIGHT BE NOW?
the STARS are DOWN
SORRY, BOSS. IT'S JUST GIBBERISH.
"THE ISLAND THAT IS NOT"?
WHAT DOES THAT EVEN *MEAN*?

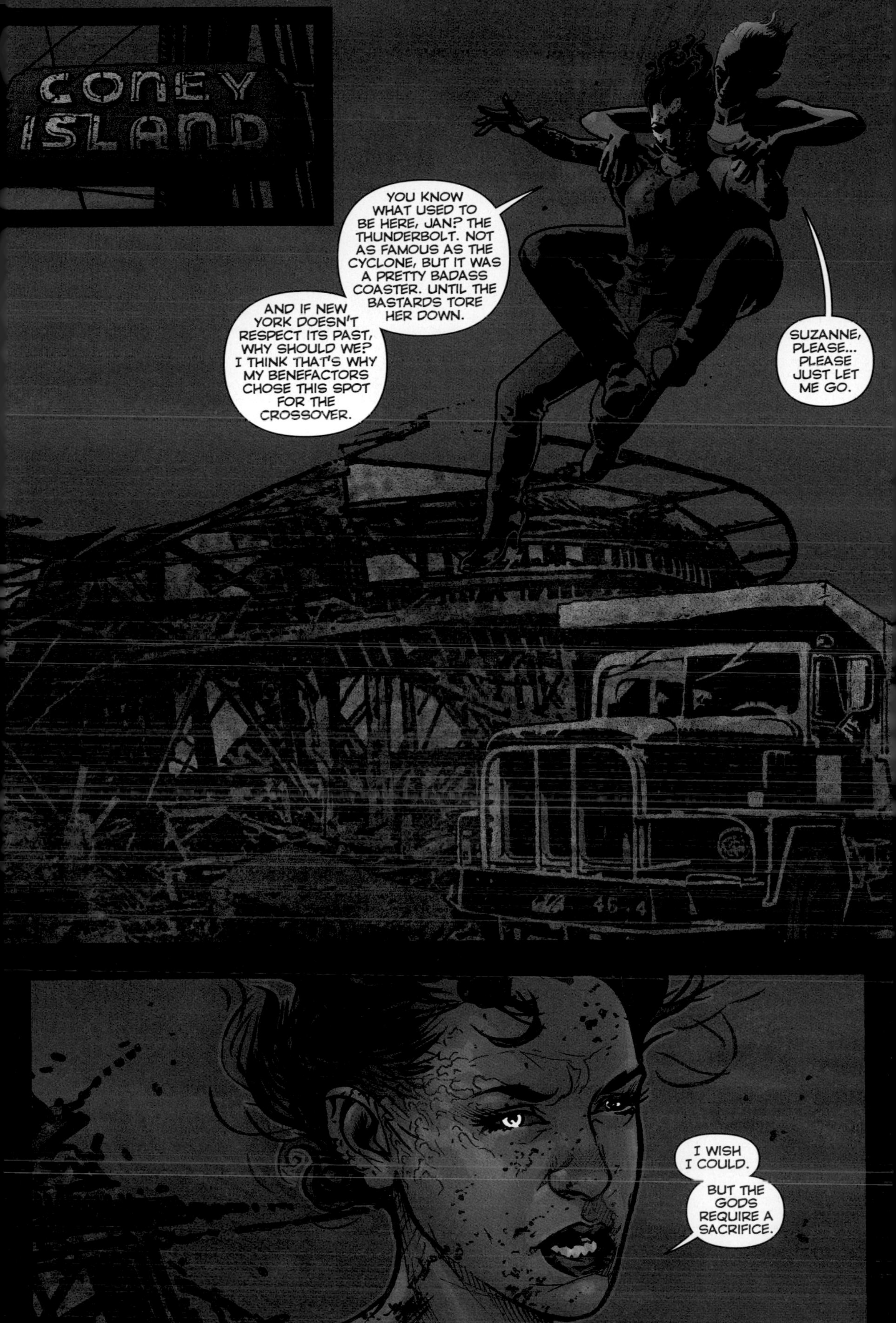
CONEY ISLAND
YOU KNOW WHAT USED TO BE HERE, JAN? THE THUNDERBOLT. NOT AS FAMOUS AS THE CYCLONE, BUT IT WAS A PRETTY BADASS COASTER. UNTIL THE BASTARDS TORE HER DOWN.
AND IF NEW YORK DOESN'T RESPECT ITS PAST, WHY SHOULD WE? I THINK THAT'S WHY MY BENEFACTORS CHOSE THIS SPOT FOR THE CROSSOVER.
SUZANNE, PLEASE... PLEASE JUST LET ME GO.
I WISH I COULD.
BUT THE GODS REQUIRE A SACRIFICE.

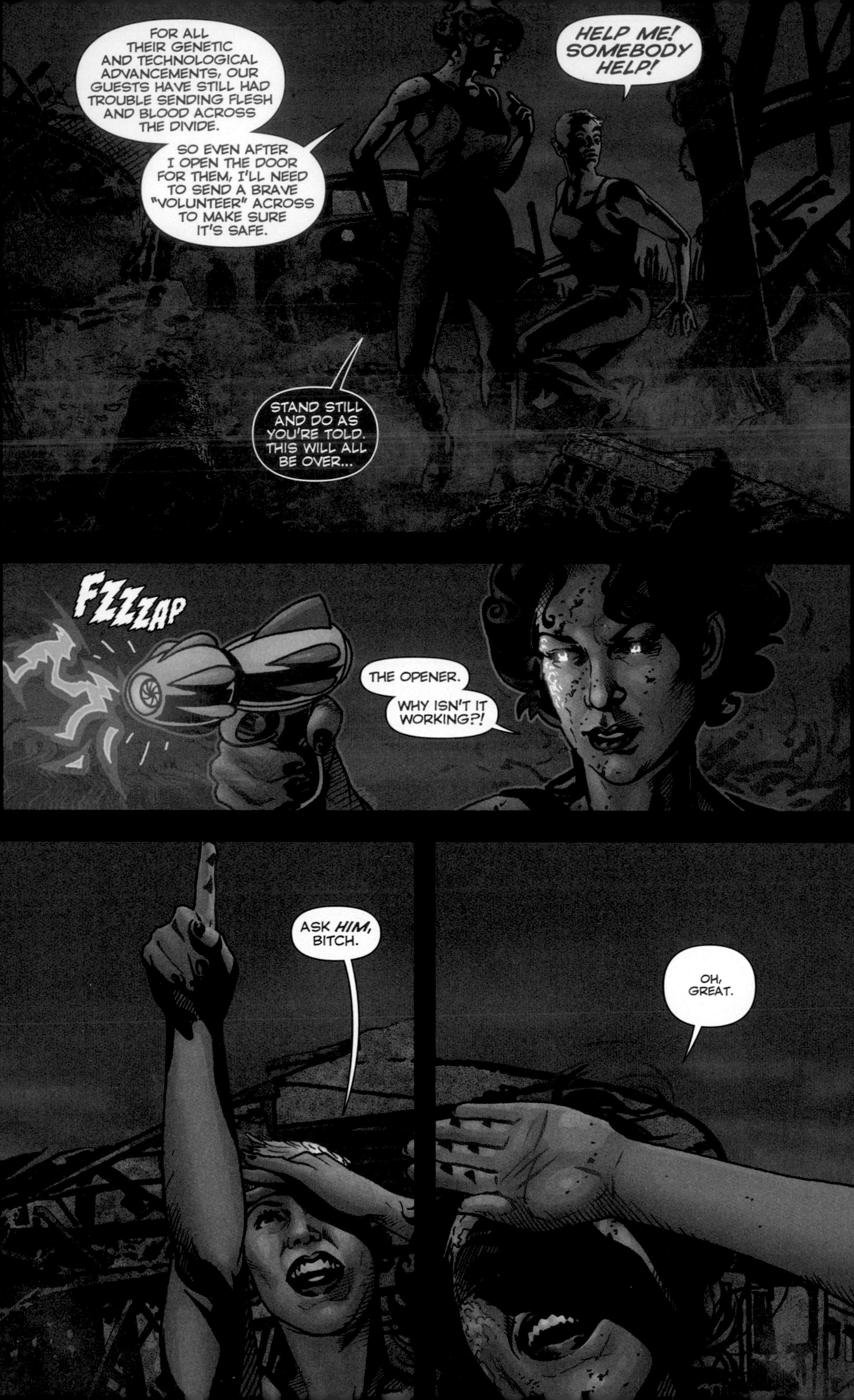
FOR ALL THEIR GENETIC AND TECHNOLOGICAL ADVANCEMENTS, OUR GUESTS HAVE STILL HAD TROUBLE SENDING FLESH AND BLOOD ACROSS THE DIVIDE.
SO EVEN AFTER I OPEN THE DOOR FOR THEM, I'LL NEED TO SEND A BRAVE "VOLUNTEER" ACROSS TO MAKE SURE IT'S SAFE.
HELP ME! SOMEBODY HELP!
STAND STILL AND DO AS YOU'RE TOLD. THIS WILL ALL BE OVER...
FZZZAP
THE OPENER.
WHY ISN'T IT WORKING?!
ASK HIM, BITCH.
OH, GREAT.

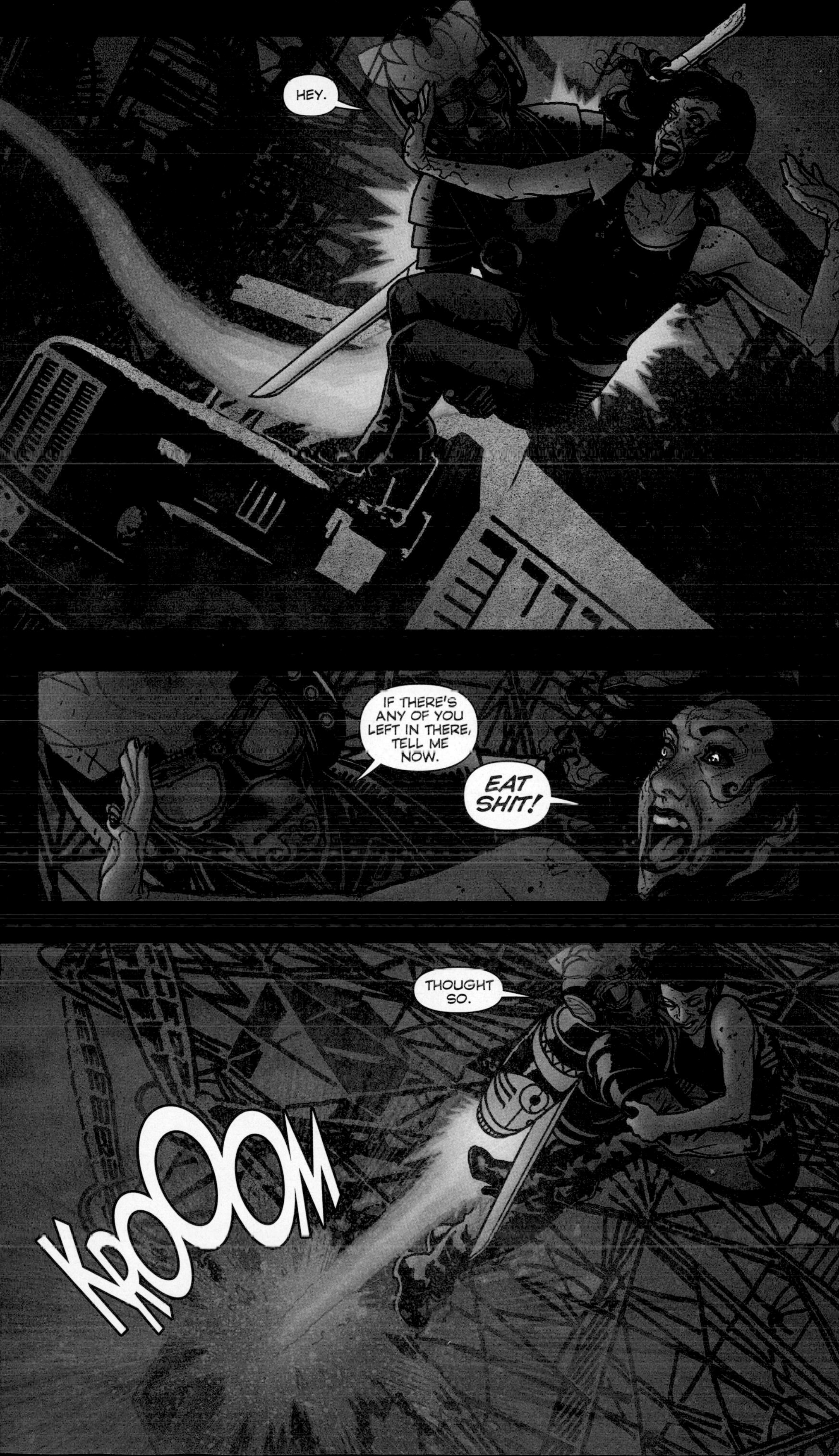
HEY.
IF THERE'S ANY OF YOU LEFT IN THERE, TELL ME NOW.
EAT SHIT!
THOUGHT SO.
KROOOM

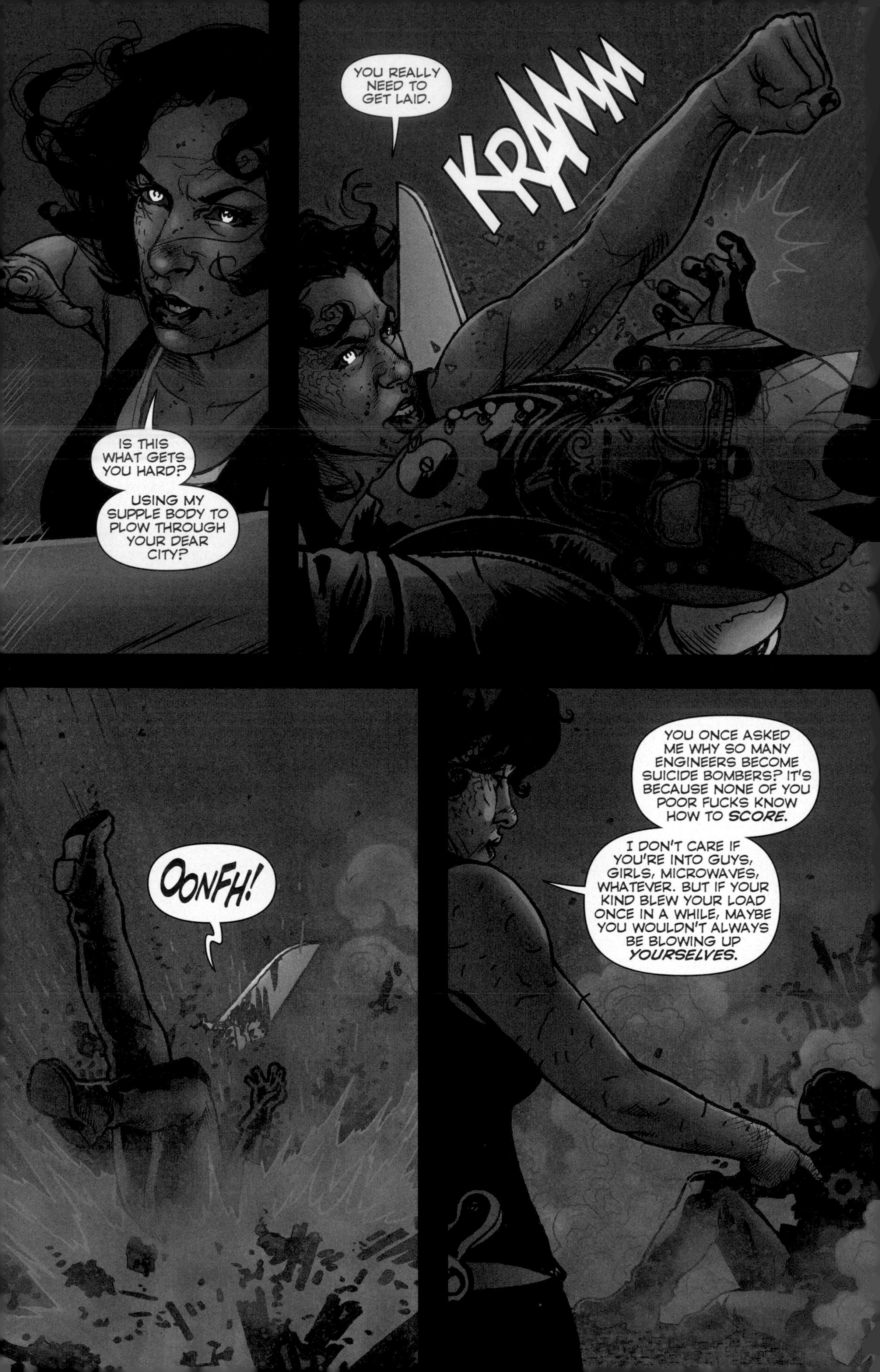
IS THIS WHAT GETS YOU HARD?
USING MY SUPPLE BODY TO PLOW THROUGH YOUR DEAR CITY?
YOU REALLY NEED TO GET LAID.
KRAMM
OONFH!
YOU ONCE ASKED ME WHY SO MANY ENGINEERS BECOME SUICIDE BOMBERS? IT'S BECAUSE NONE OF YOU POOR FUCKS KNOW HOW TO *SCORE*.
I DON'T CARE IF YOU'RE INTO GUYS, GIRLS, MICROWAVES, WHATEVER. BUT IF YOUR KIND BLEW YOUR LOAD ONCE IN A WHILE, MAYBE YOU WOULDN'T ALWAYS BE BLOWING UP *YOURSELVES*.

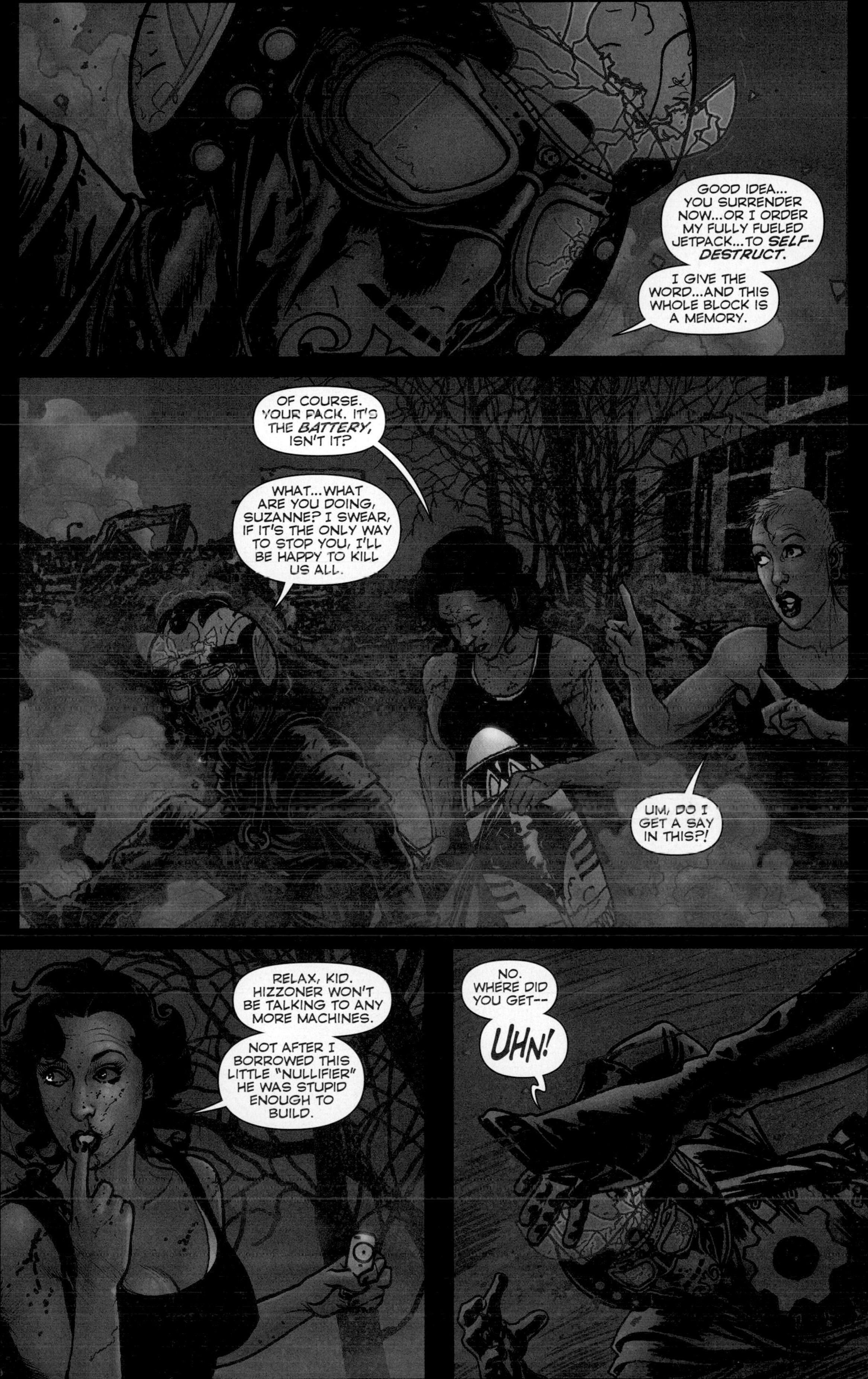
GOOD IDEA... YOU SURRENDER NOW...OR I ORDER MY FULLY FUELED JETPACK...TO SELF-DESTRUCT.
I GIVE THE WORD...AND THIS WHOLE BLOCK IS A MEMORY.
OF COURSE. YOUR PACK. IT'S THE BATTERY, ISN'T IT?
WHAT...WHAT ARE YOU DOING, SUZANNE? I SWEAR, IF IT'S THE ONLY WAY TO STOP YOU, I'LL BE HAPPY TO KILL US ALL.
UM, DO I GET A SAY IN THIS?!
RELAX, KID. HIZZONER WON'T BE TALKING TO ANY MORE MACHINES.
NOT AFTER I BORROWED THIS LITTLE "NULLIFIER" HE WAS STUPID ENOUGH TO BUILD.
NO. WHERE DID YOU GET--
UHN!

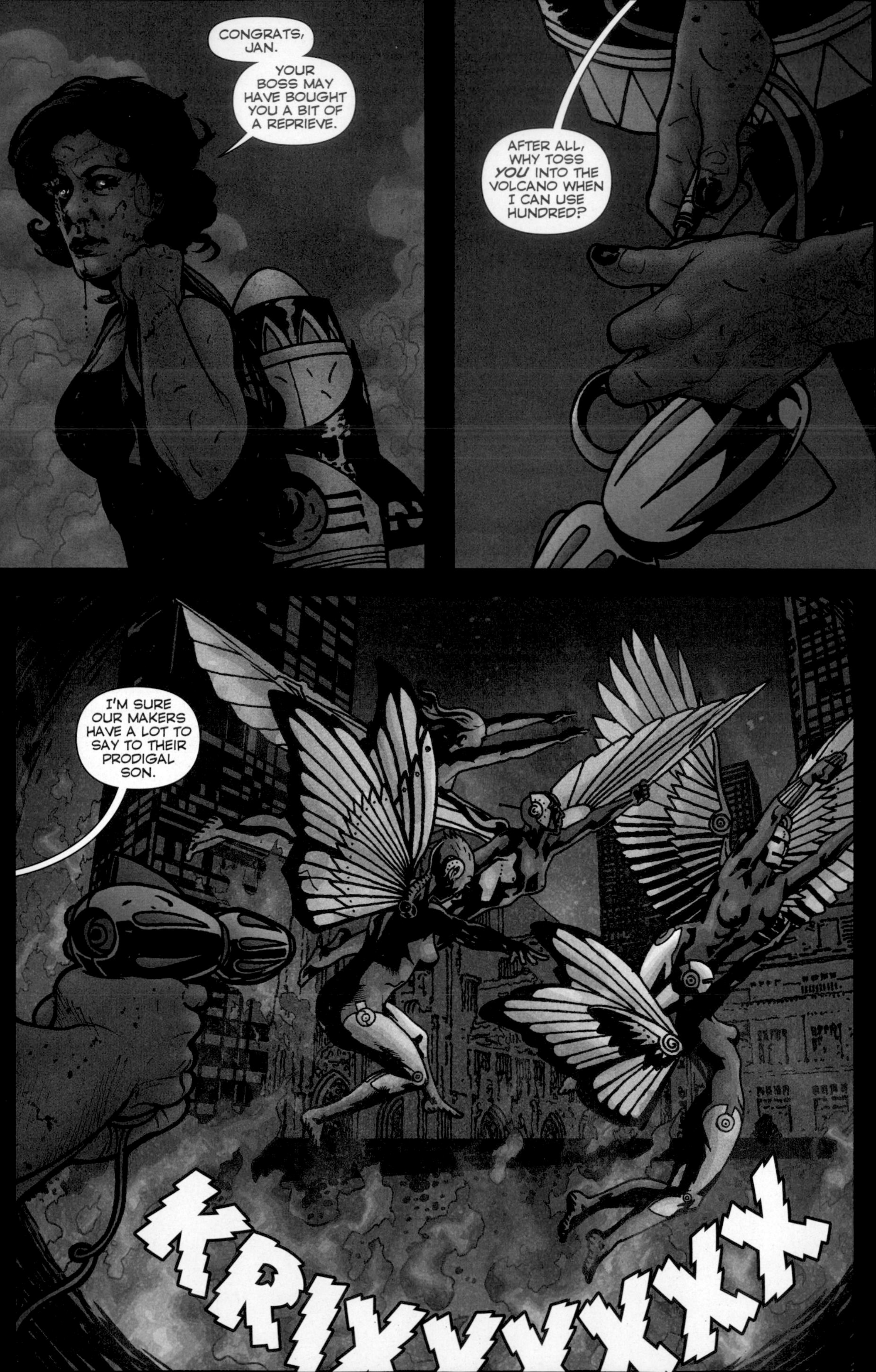

CONGRATS, JAN.
YOUR BOSS MAY HAVE BOUGHT YOU A BIT OF A REPRIEVE.
AFTER ALL, WHY TOSS *YOU* INTO THE VOLCANO WHEN I CAN USE HUNDRED?
I'M SURE OUR MAKERS HAVE A LOT TO SAY TO THEIR PRODIGAL SON.
KRIXXXXXX

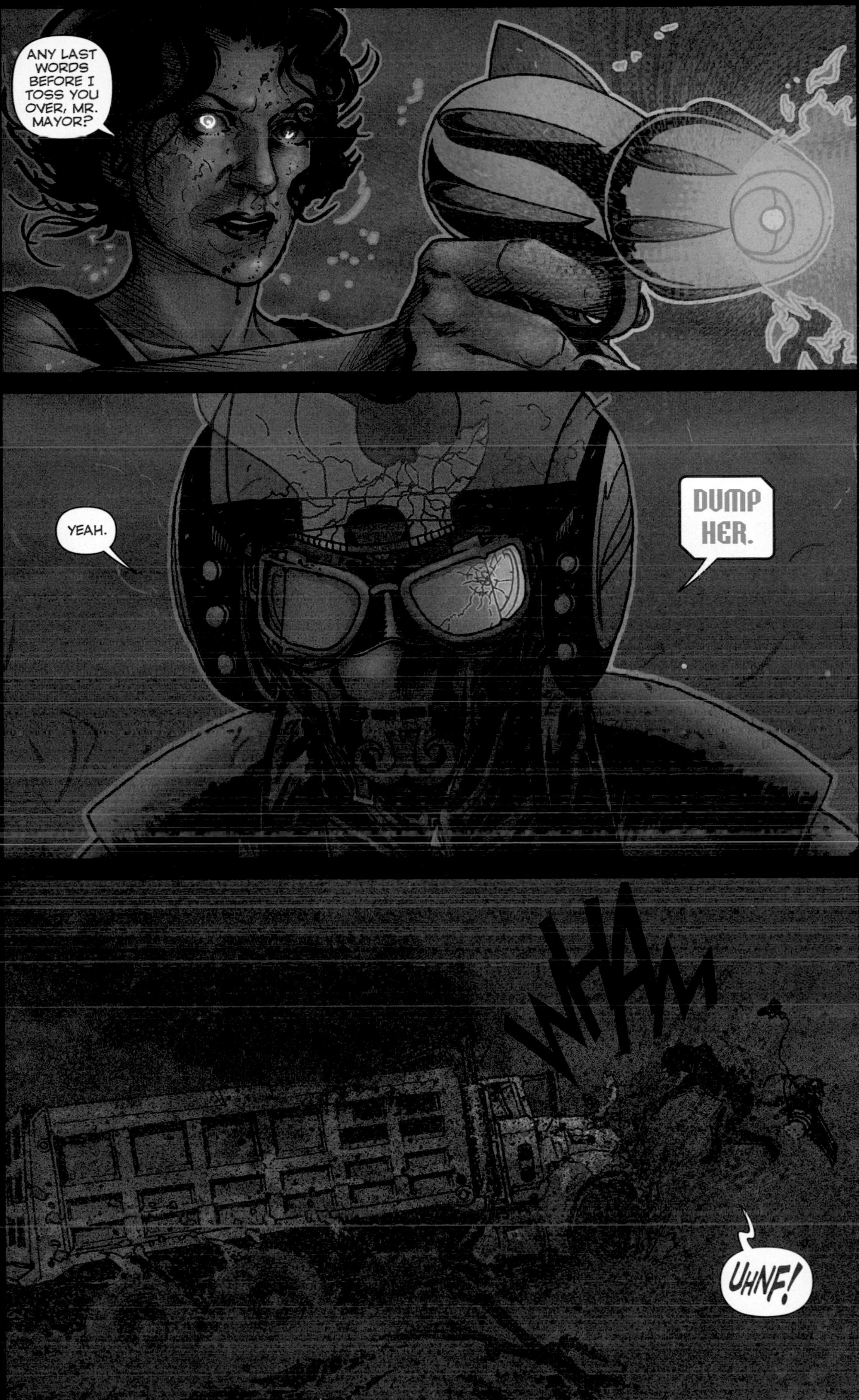
ANY LAST WORDS BEFORE I TOSS YOU OVER, MR. MAYOR?
YEAH.
DUMP HER.
WHAM
UHNF!

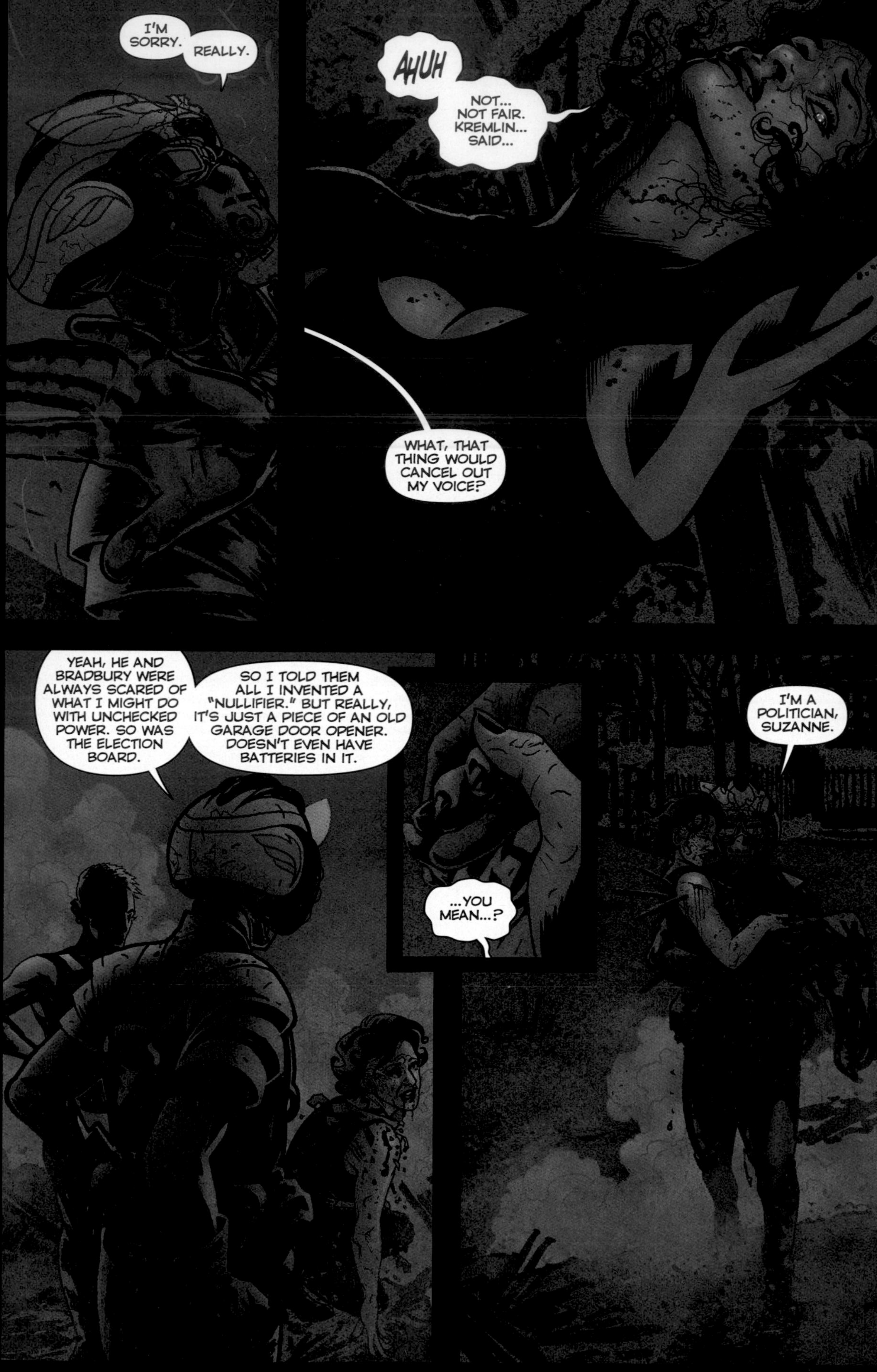
I'M SORRY.
REALLY.
AHUH
NOT... NOT FAIR. KREMLIN... SAID...
WHAT, THAT THING WOULD CANCEL OUT MY VOICE?
YEAH, HE AND BRADBURY WERE ALWAYS SCARED OF WHAT I MIGHT DO WITH UNCHECKED POWER. SO WAS THE ELECTION BOARD.
SO I TOLD THEM ALL I INVENTED A "NULLIFIER." BUT REALLY, IT'S JUST A PIECE OF AN OLD GARAGE DOOR OPENER. DOESN'T EVEN HAVE BATTERIES IN IT.
...YOU MEAN...?
I'M A POLITICIAN, SUZANNE.

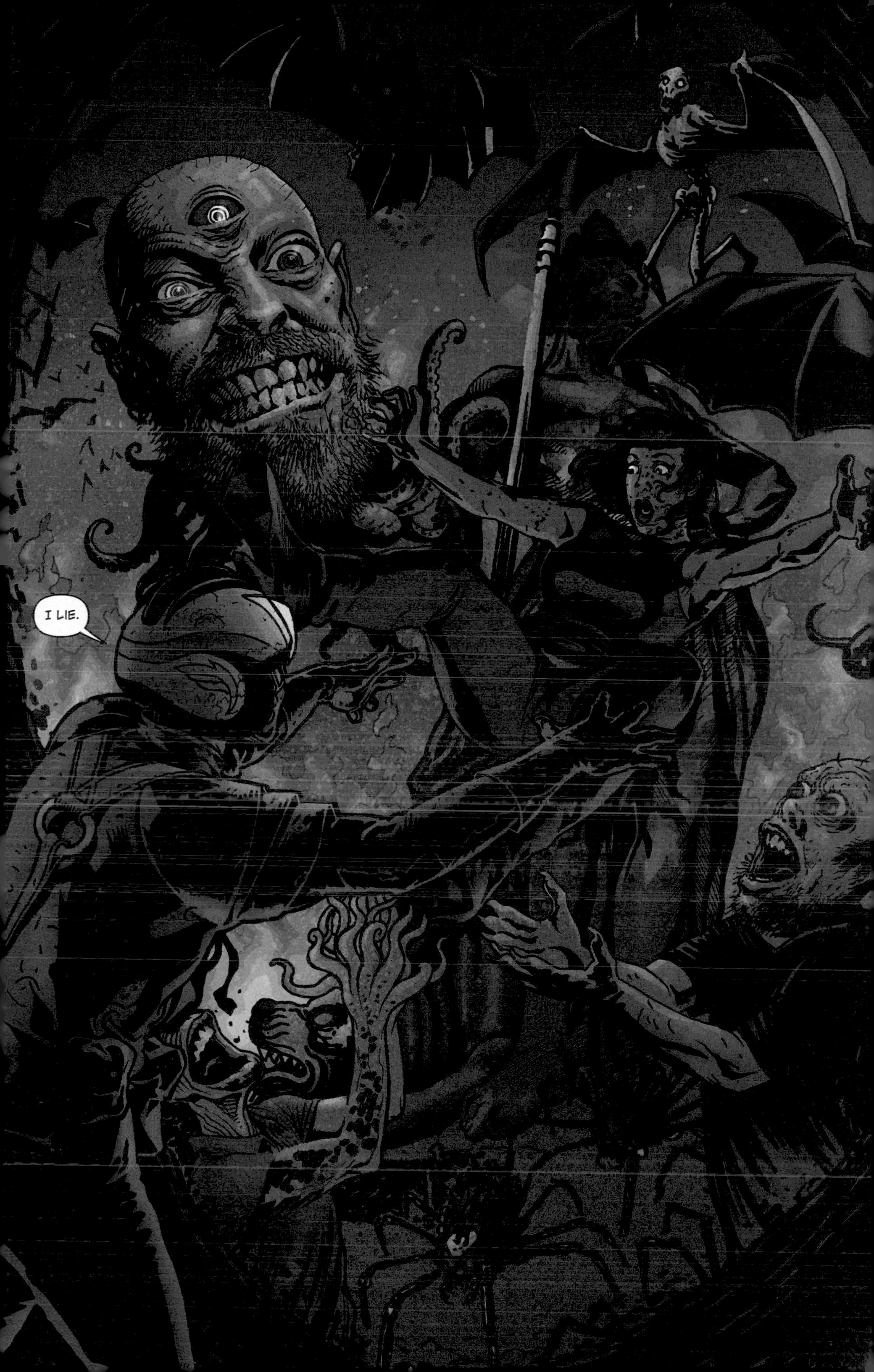
I LIE.

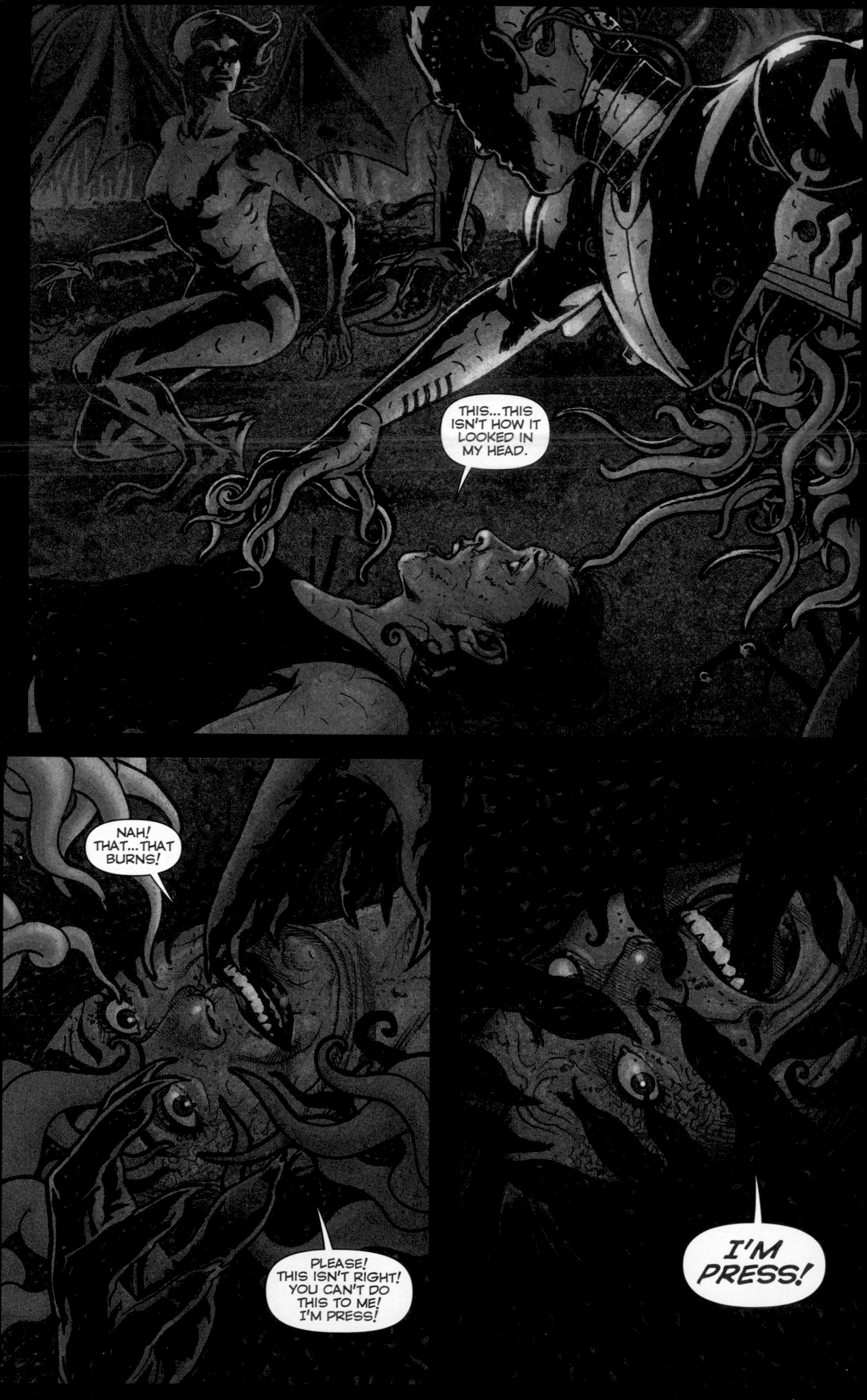
THIS...THIS ISN'T HOW IT LOOKED IN MY HEAD.
NAH! THAT...THAT BURNS!
PLEASE! THIS ISN'T RIGHT! YOU CAN'T DO THIS TO ME! I'M PRESS!
I'M PRESS!

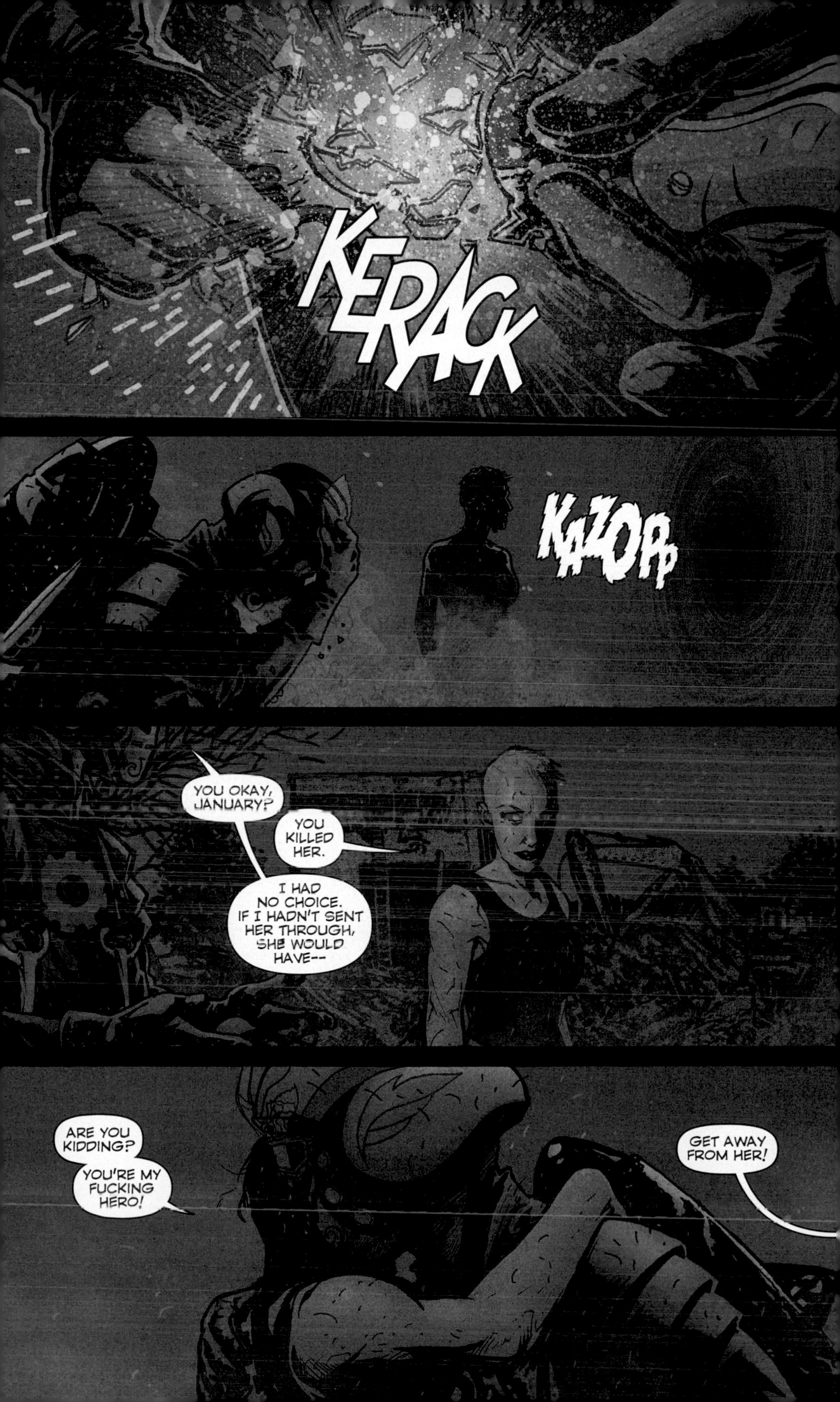
KERACK
KAZOPP
YOU OKAY, JANUARY?
YOU KILLED HER.
I HAD NO CHOICE. IF I HADN'T SENT HER THROUGH, SHE WOULD HAVE--
ARE YOU KIDDING?
YOU'RE MY FUCKING HERO!
GET AWAY FROM HER!

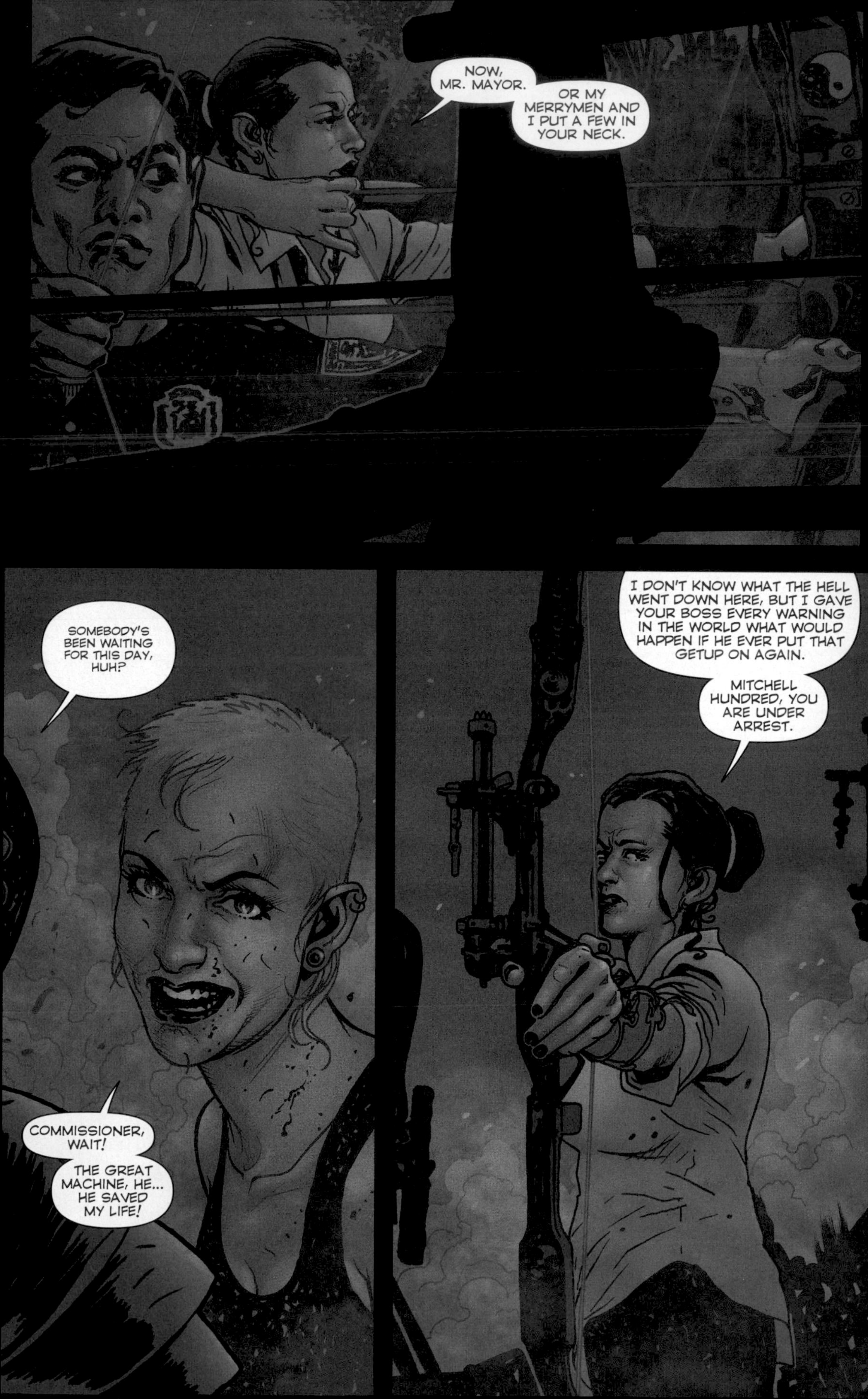
NOW, MR. MAYOR.
OR MY MERRYMEN AND I PUT A FEW IN YOUR NECK.
SOMEBODY'S BEEN WAITING FOR THIS DAY, HUH?
COMMISSIONER, WAIT!
THE GREAT MACHINE, HE... HE SAVED MY LIFE!
I DON'T KNOW WHAT THE HELL WENT DOWN HERE, BUT I GAVE YOUR BOSS EVERY WARNING IN THE WORLD WHAT WOULD HAPPEN IF HE EVER PUT THAT GETUP ON AGAIN.
MITCHELL HUNDRED, YOU ARE UNDER ARREST.

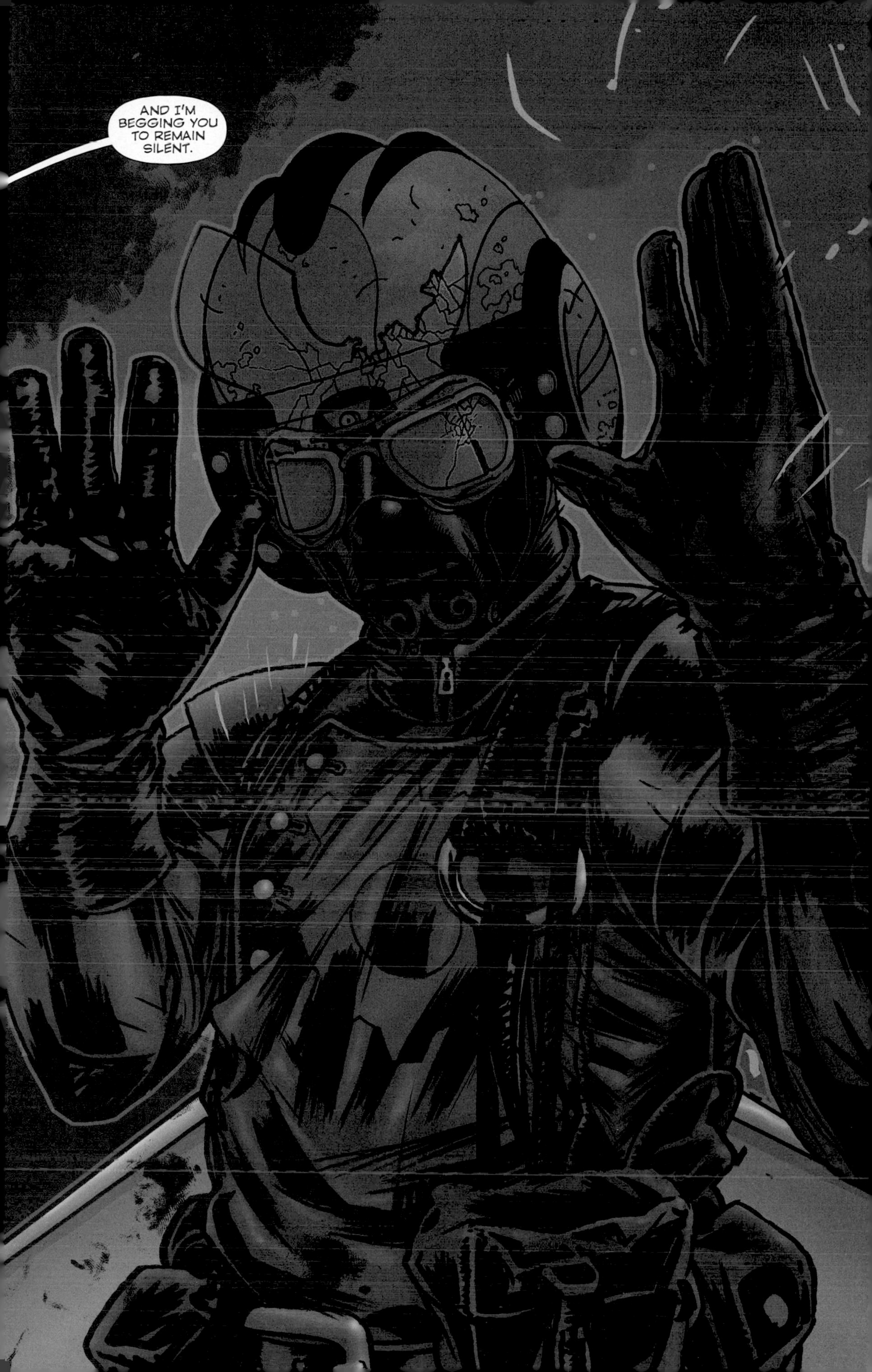
AND I'M BEGGING YOU TO REMAIN SILENT.

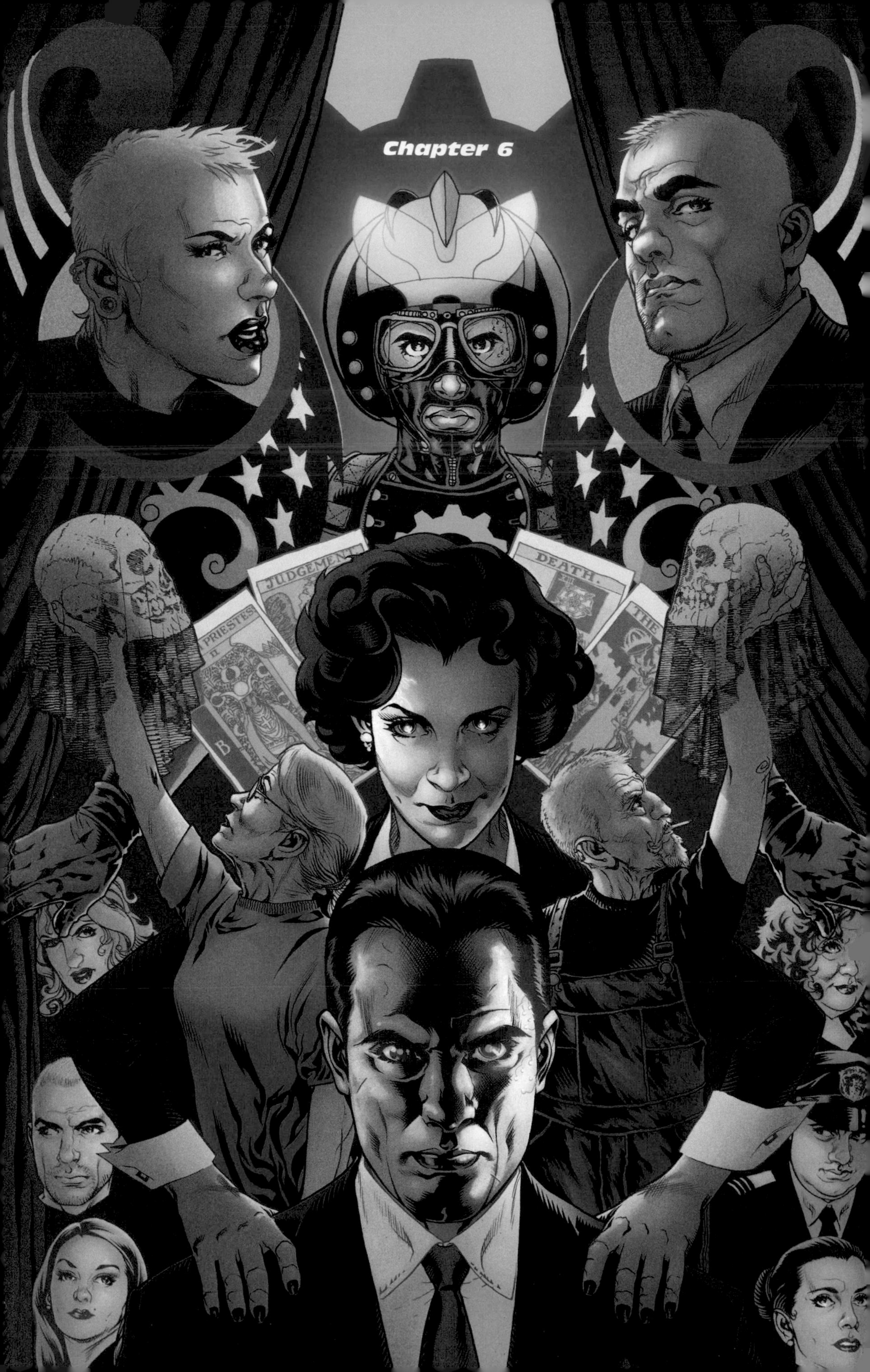
Chapter 6
JUDGEMENT
DEATH.
PRIESTES
THE

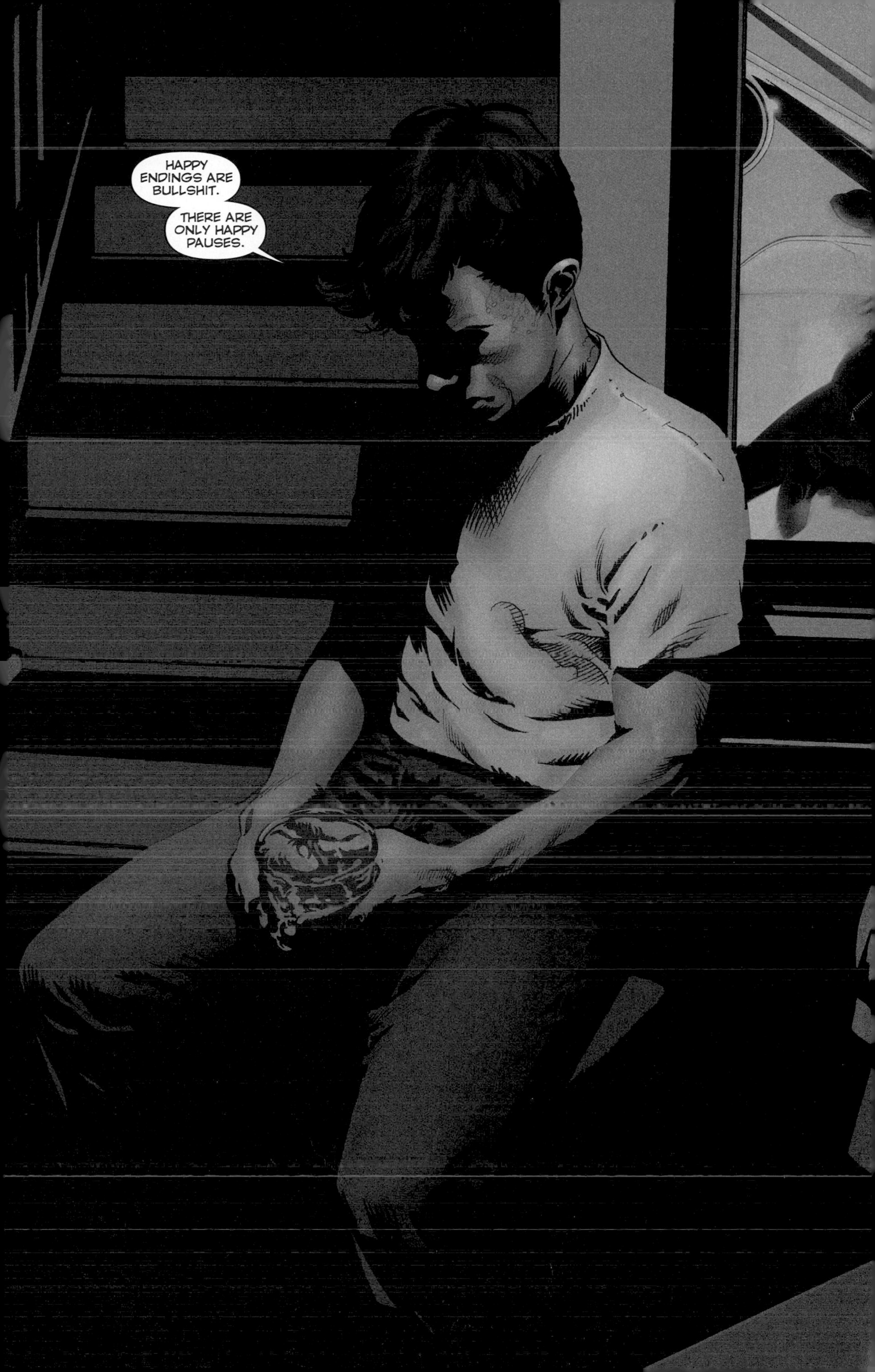
HAPPY ENDINGS ARE BULLSHIT.
THERE ARE ONLY HAPPY PAUSES.

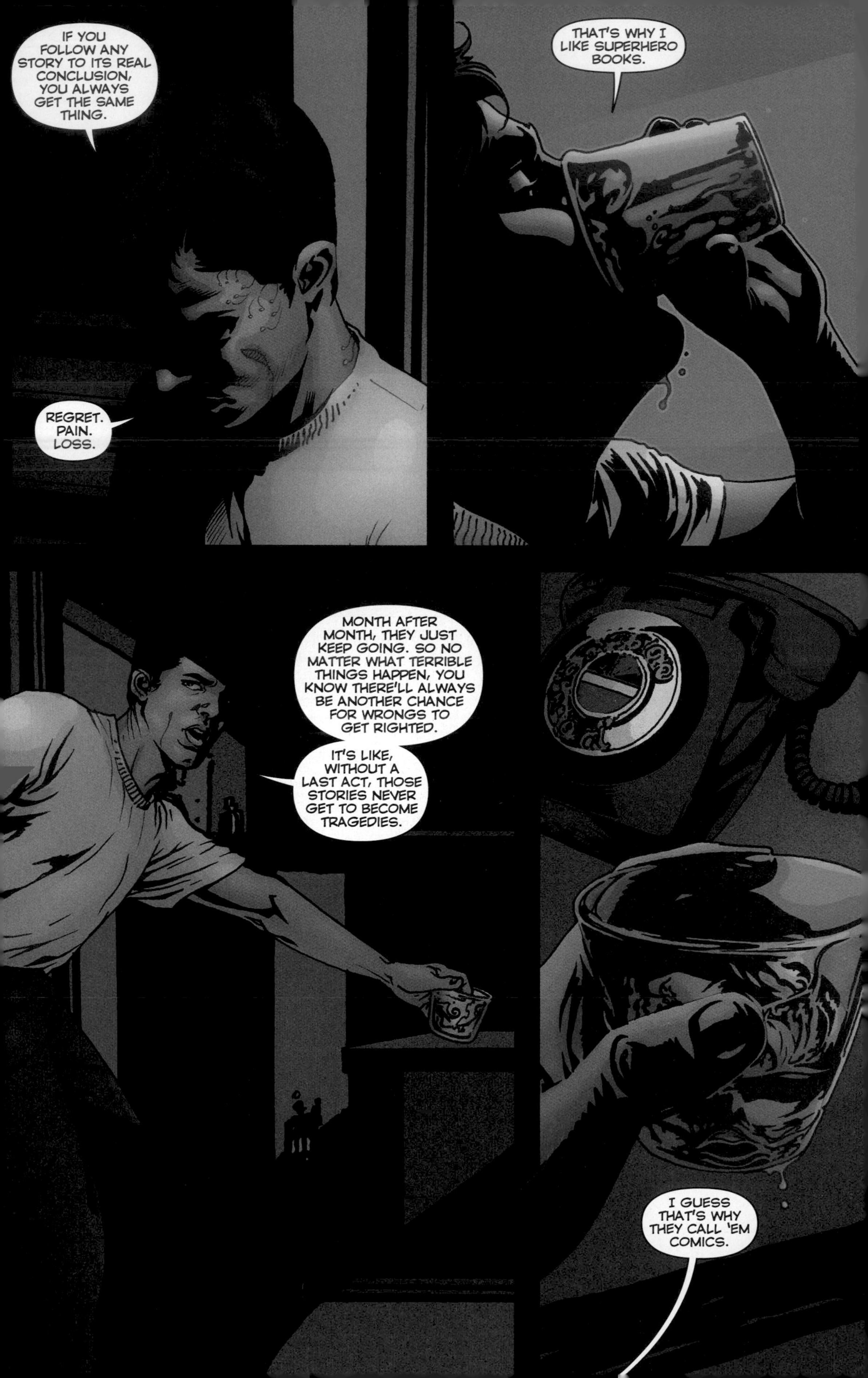
IF YOU FOLLOW ANY STORY TO ITS REAL CONCLUSION, YOU ALWAYS GET THE SAME THING.
REGRET. PAIN. LOSS.
THAT'S WHY I LIKE SUPERHERO BOOKS.
MONTH AFTER MONTH, THEY JUST KEEP GOING. SO NO MATTER WHAT TERRIBLE THINGS HAPPEN, YOU KNOW THERE'LL ALWAYS BE ANOTHER CHANCE FOR WRONGS TO GET RIGHTED.
IT'S LIKE, WITHOUT A LAST ACT, THOSE STORIES NEVER GET TO BECOME TRAGEDIES.
I GUESS THAT'S WHY THEY CALL 'EM COMICS.

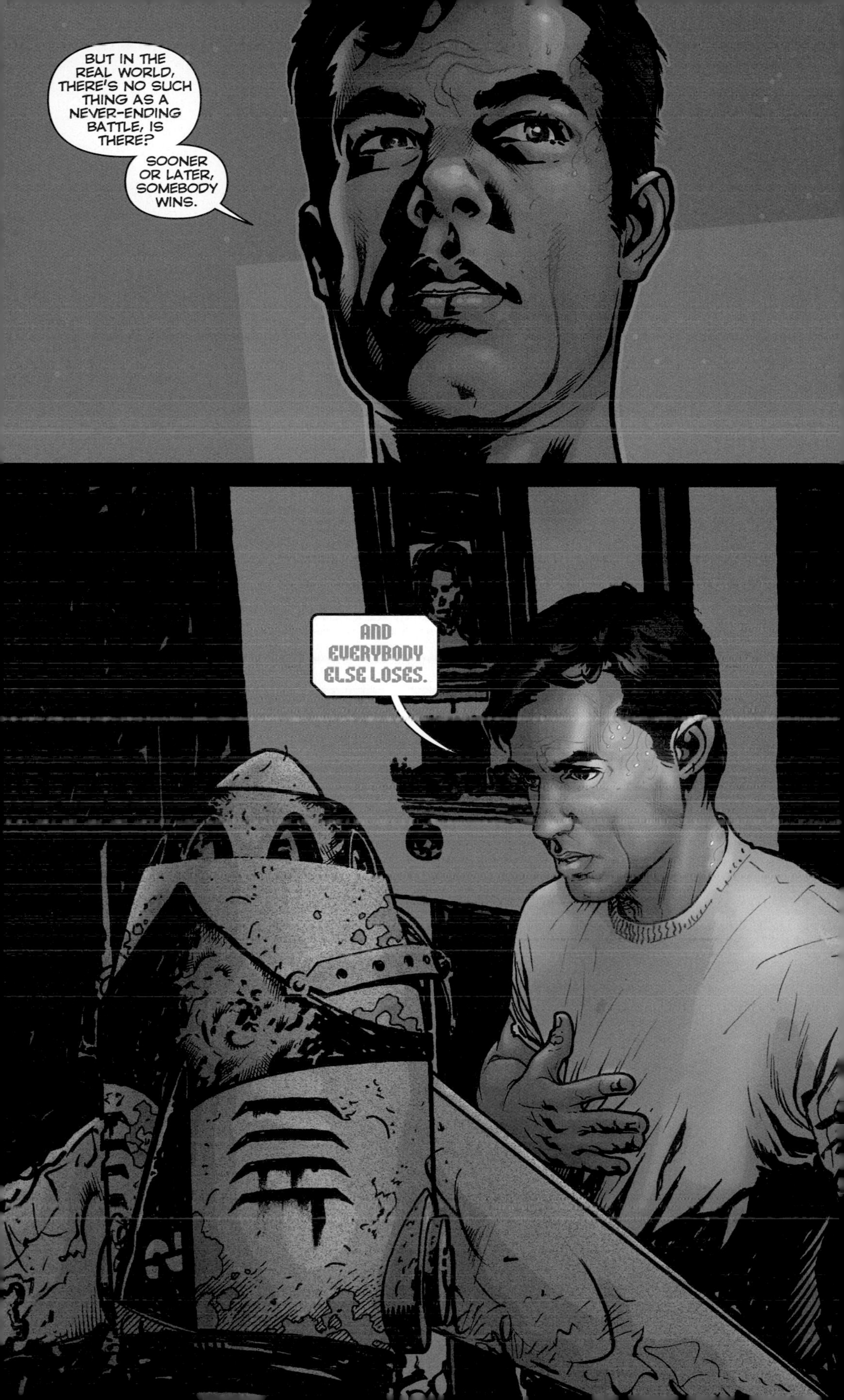
BUT IN THE REAL WORLD, THERE'S NO SUCH THING AS A NEVER-ENDING BATTLE, IS THERE?
SOONER OR LATER, SOMEBODY WINS.
AND EVERYBODY ELSE LOSES.

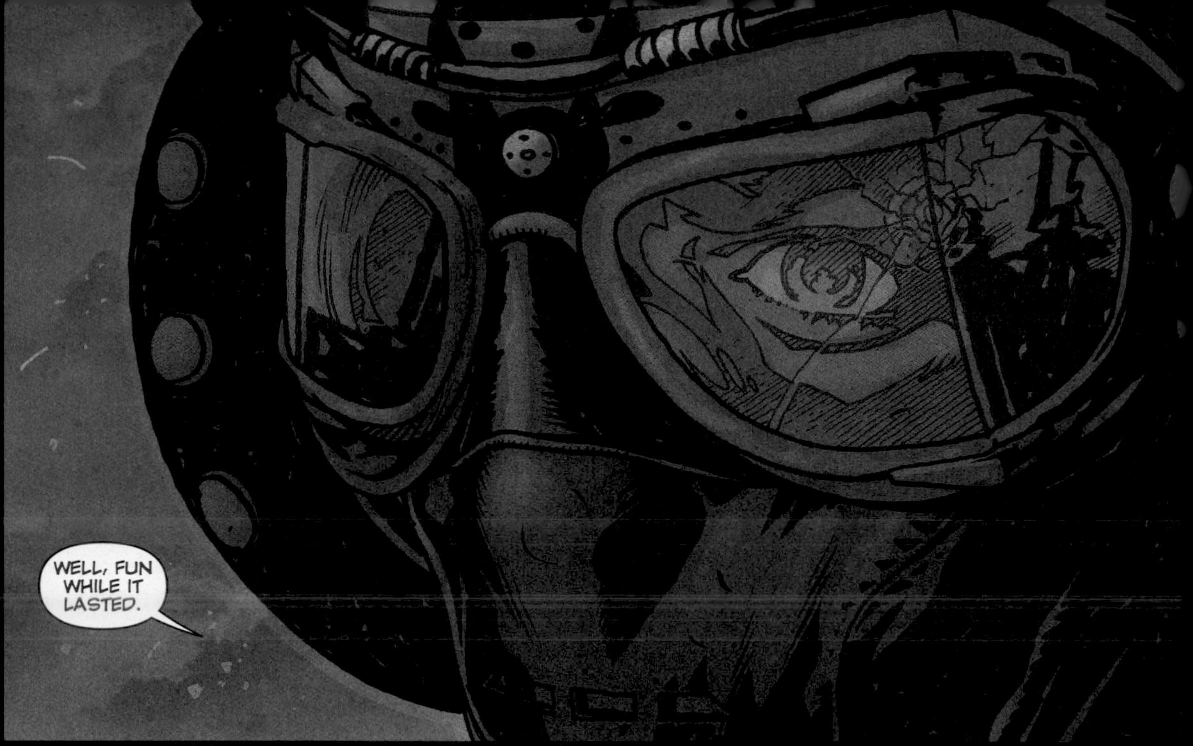
WELL, FUN WHILE IT LASTED.

TUESDAY, APRIL 12, 2005

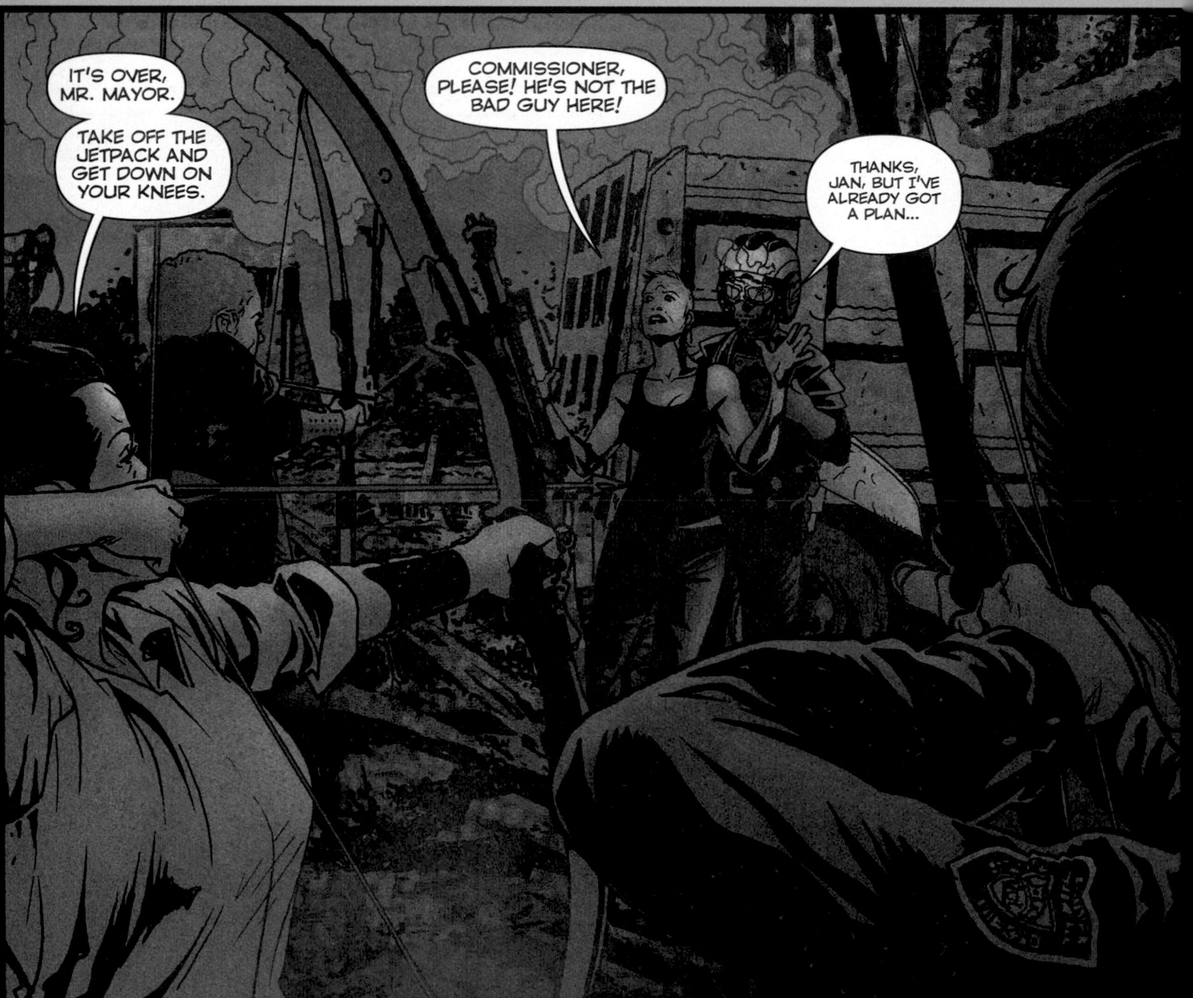
IT'S OVER, MR. MAYOR.
TAKE OFF THE JETPACK AND GET DOWN ON YOUR KNEES.
COMMISSIONER, PLEASE! HE'S NOT THE BAD GUY HERE!
THANKS, JAN, BUT I'VE ALREADY GOT A PLAN...

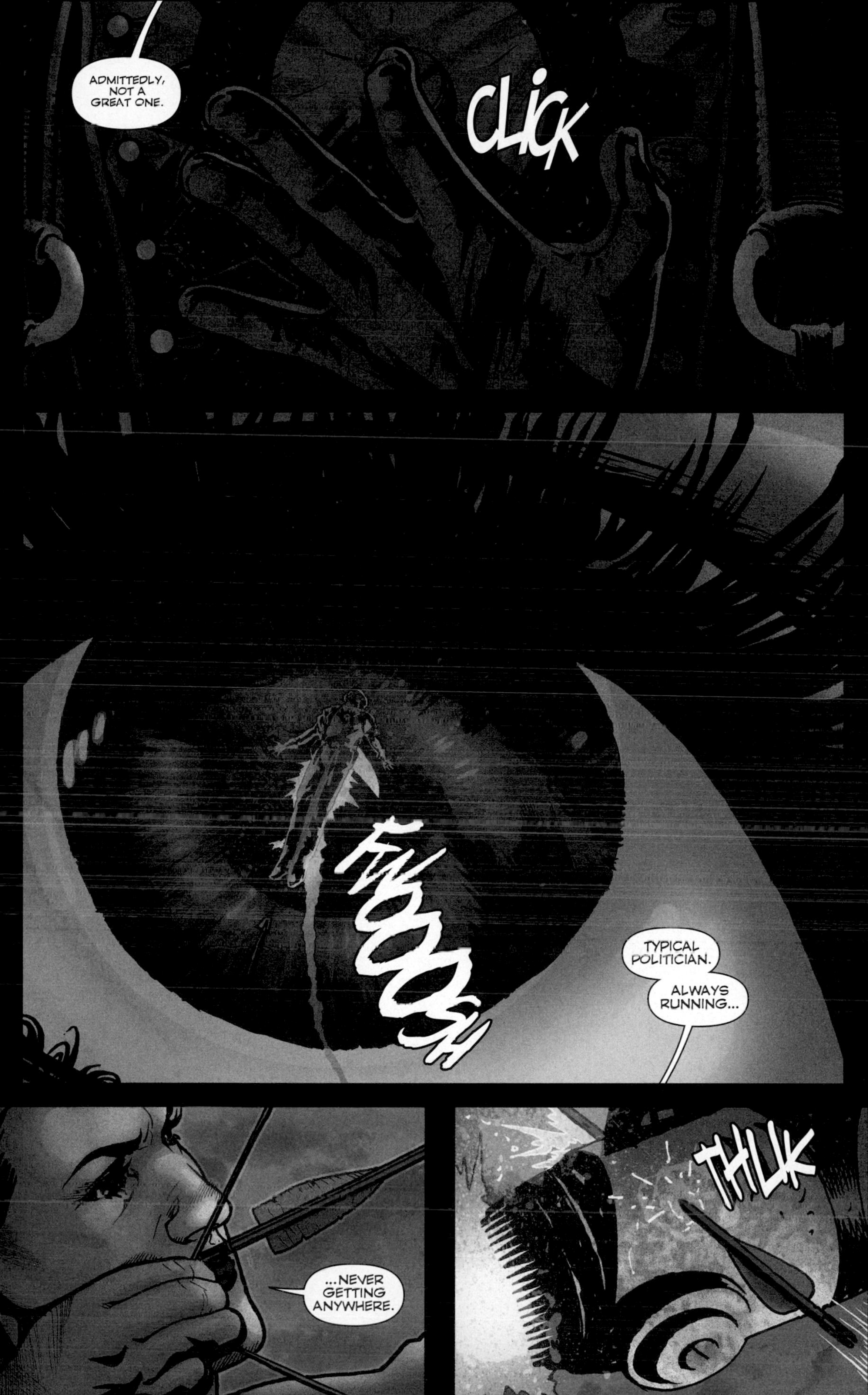
ADMITTEDLY, NOT A GREAT ONE.
CLICK
FWOOOSH
TYPICAL POLITICIAN.
ALWAYS RUNNING...
...NEVER GETTING ANYWHERE.
THUK

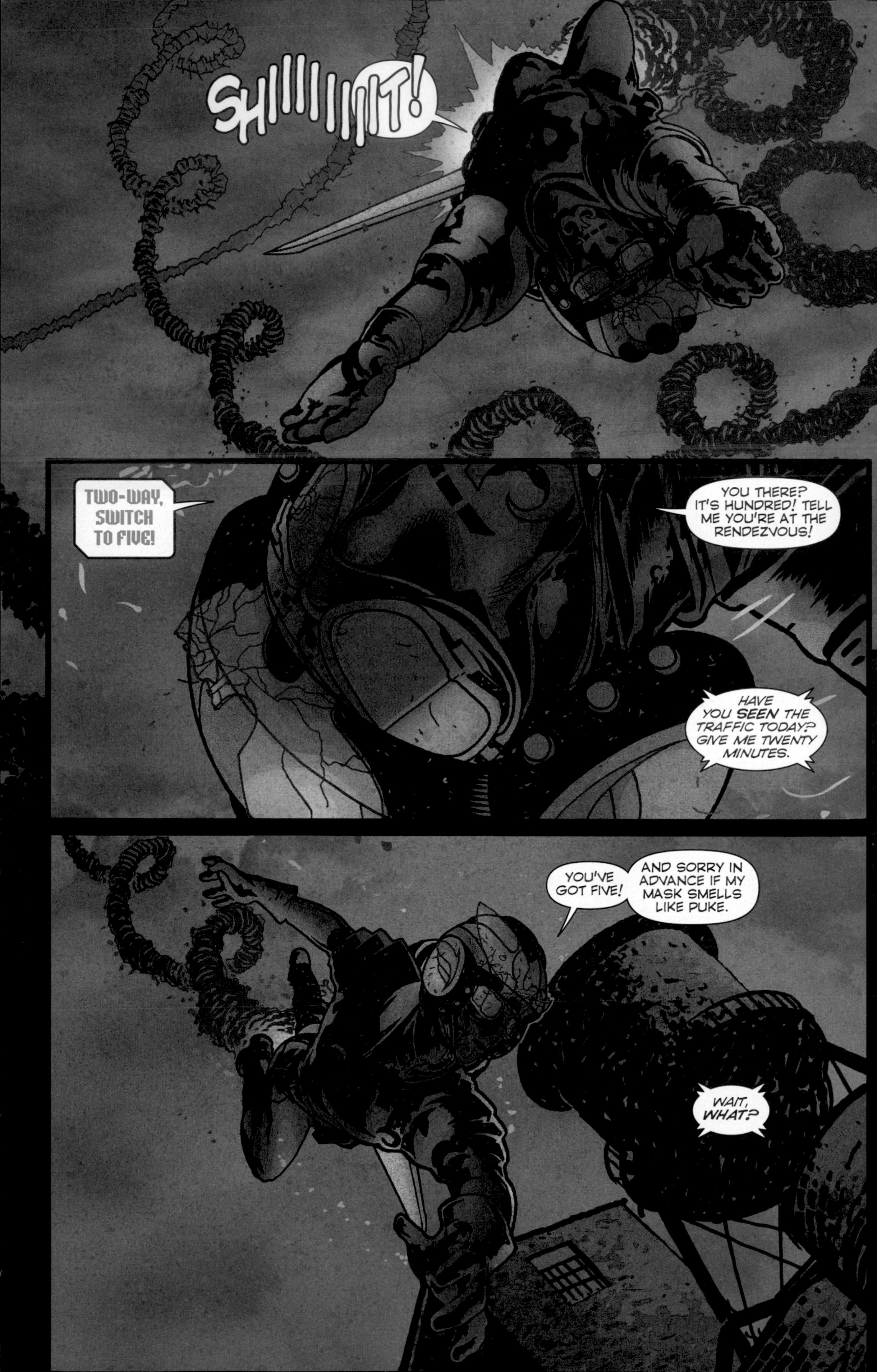
SHIIIIIIIT!
TWO-WAY, SWITCH TO FIVE!
YOU THERE? IT'S HUNDRED! TELL ME YOU'RE AT THE RENDEZVOUS!
HAVE YOU SEEN THE TRAFFIC TODAY? GIVE ME TWENTY MINUTES.
YOU'VE GOT FIVE!
AND SORRY IN ADVANCE IF MY MASK SMELLS LIKE PUKE.
WAIT, WHAT?

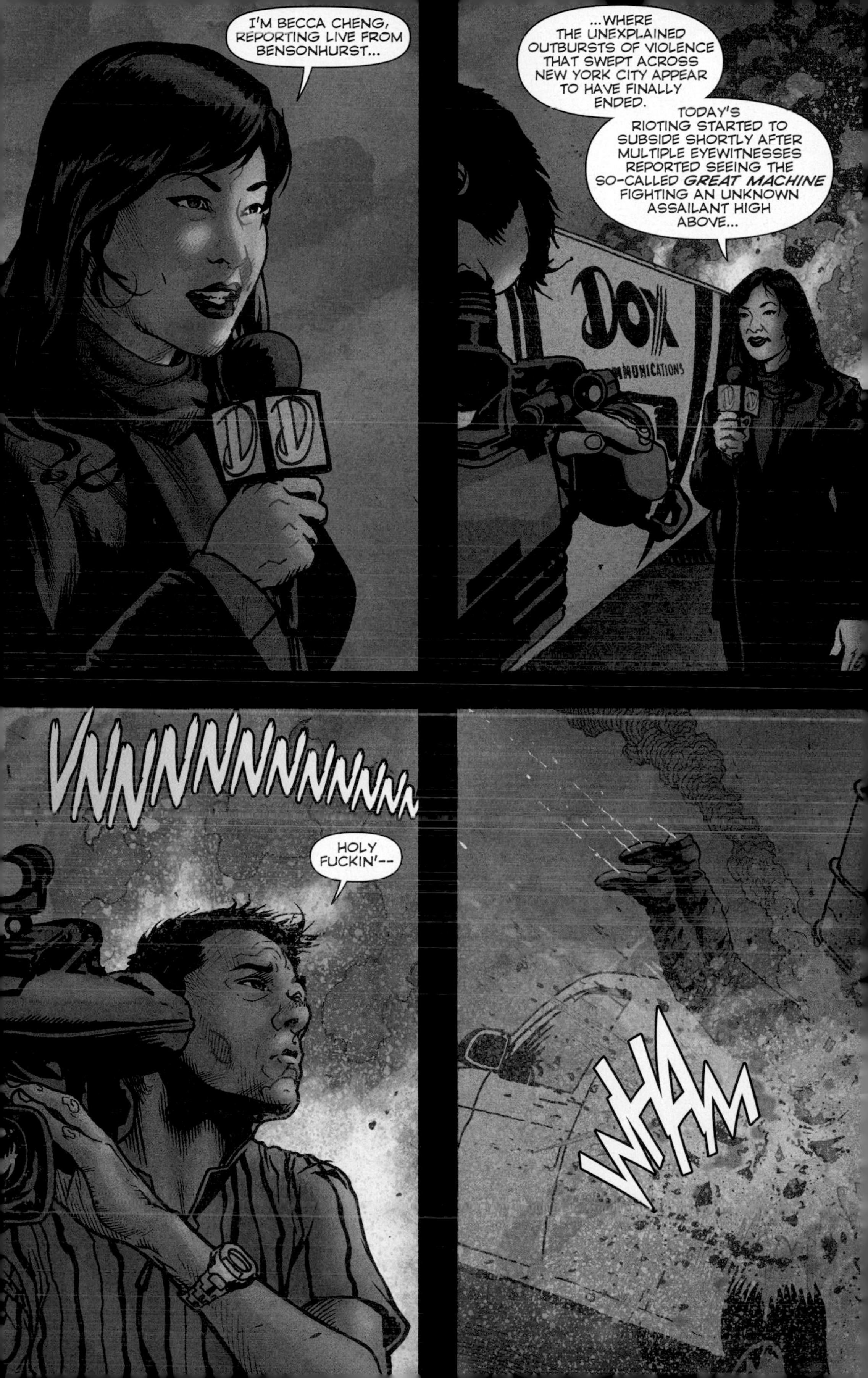

I'M BECCA CHENG, REPORTING LIVE FROM BENSONHURST...
...WHERE THE UNEXPLAINED OUTBURSTS OF VIOLENCE THAT SWEPT ACROSS NEW YORK CITY APPEAR TO HAVE FINALLY ENDED.
TODAY'S RIOTING STARTED TO SUBSIDE SHORTLY AFTER MULTIPLE EYEWITNESSES REPORTED SEEING THE SO-CALLED *GREAT MACHINE* FIGHTING AN UNKNOWN ASSAILANT HIGH ABOVE...
DOX
VNNNNNNNNNNNN
HOLY FUCKIN'--
WHAM

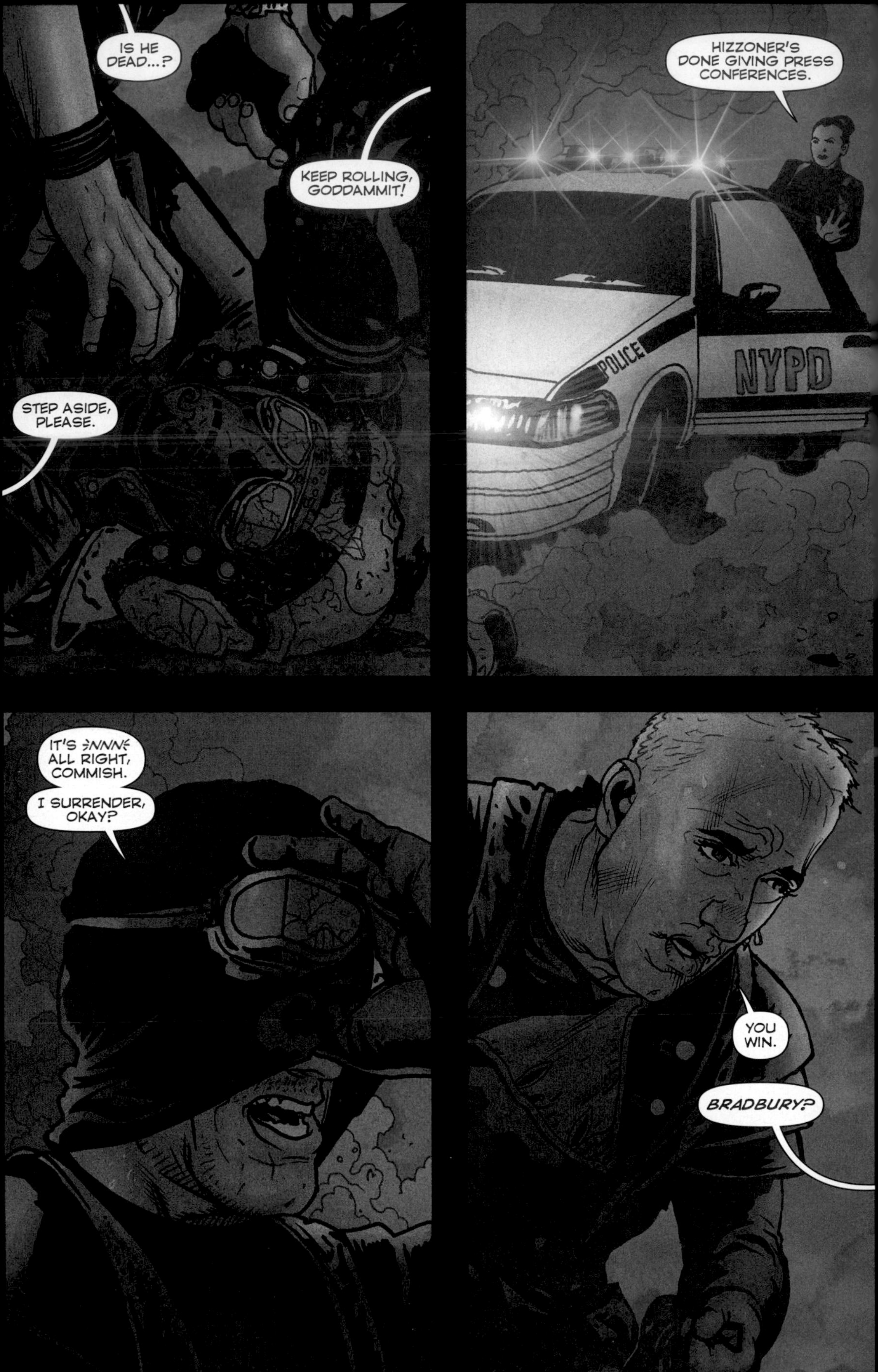
IS HE DEAD...?
KEEP ROLLING, GODDAMMIT!
STEP ASIDE, PLEASE.
HIZZONER'S DONE GIVING PRESS CONFERENCES.
NYPD
POLICE
IT'S ≈NNN≈ ALL RIGHT, COMMISH.
I SURRENDER, OKAY?
YOU WIN.
BRADBURY?

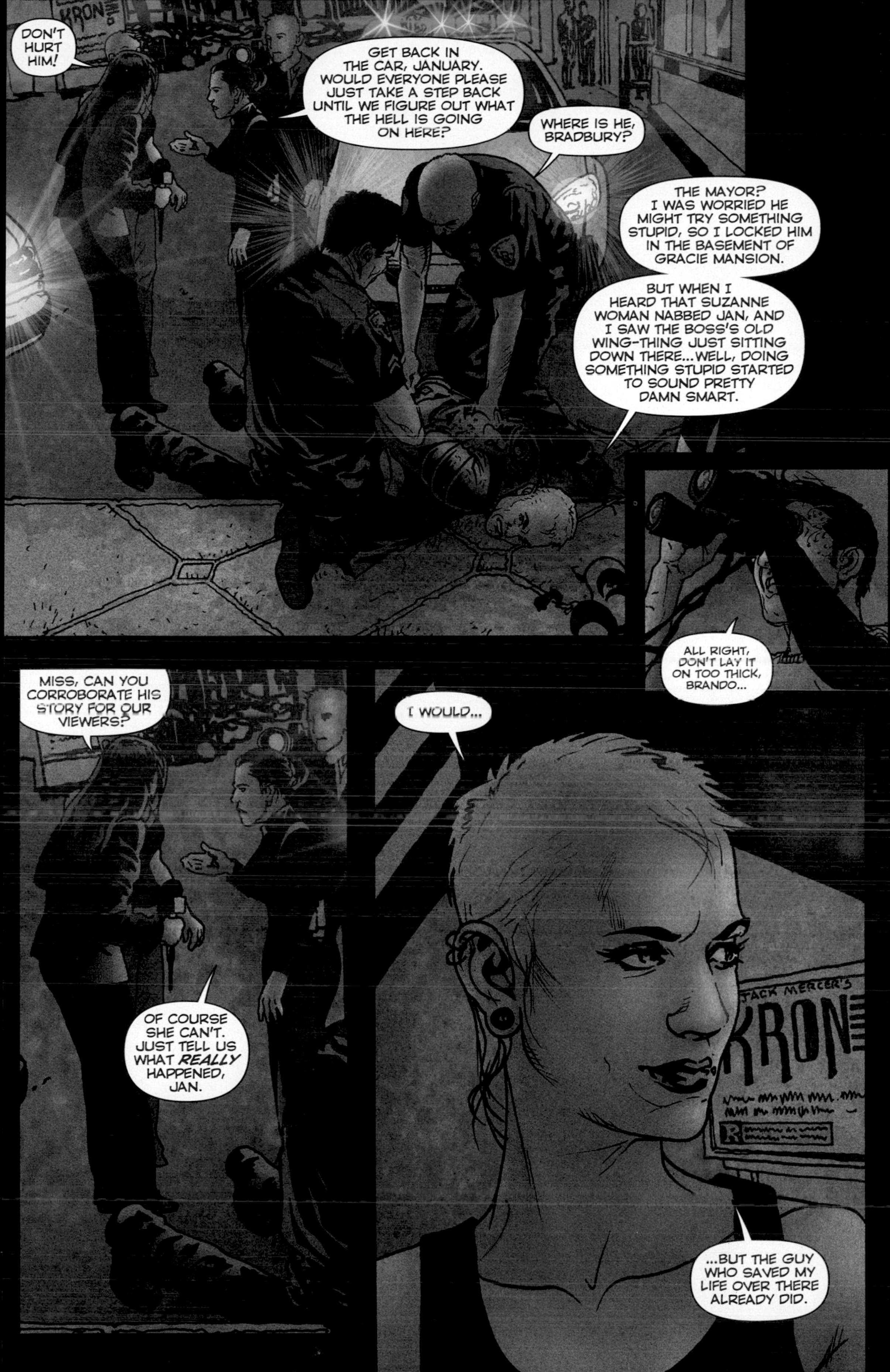
DON'T HURT HIM!
GET BACK IN THE CAR, JANUARY. WOULD EVERYONE PLEASE JUST TAKE A STEP BACK UNTIL WE FIGURE OUT WHAT THE HELL IS GOING ON HERE?
WHERE IS HE, BRADBURY?
THE MAYOR? I WAS WORRIED HE MIGHT TRY SOMETHING STUPID, SO I LOCKED HIM IN THE BASEMENT OF GRACIE MANSION.
BUT WHEN I HEARD THAT SUZANNE WOMAN NABBED JAN, AND I SAW THE BOSS'S OLD WING-THING JUST SITTING DOWN THERE...WELL, DOING SOMETHING STUPID STARTED TO SOUND PRETTY DAMN SMART.
ALL RIGHT, DON'T LAY IT ON TOO THICK, BRANDO...
MISS, CAN YOU CORROBORATE HIS STORY FOR OUR VIEWERS?
OF COURSE SHE CAN'T. JUST TELL US WHAT *REALLY* HAPPENED, JAN.
I WOULD...
JACK MERCER'S
KRON
...BUT THE GUY WHO SAVED MY LIFE OVER THERE ALREADY DID.

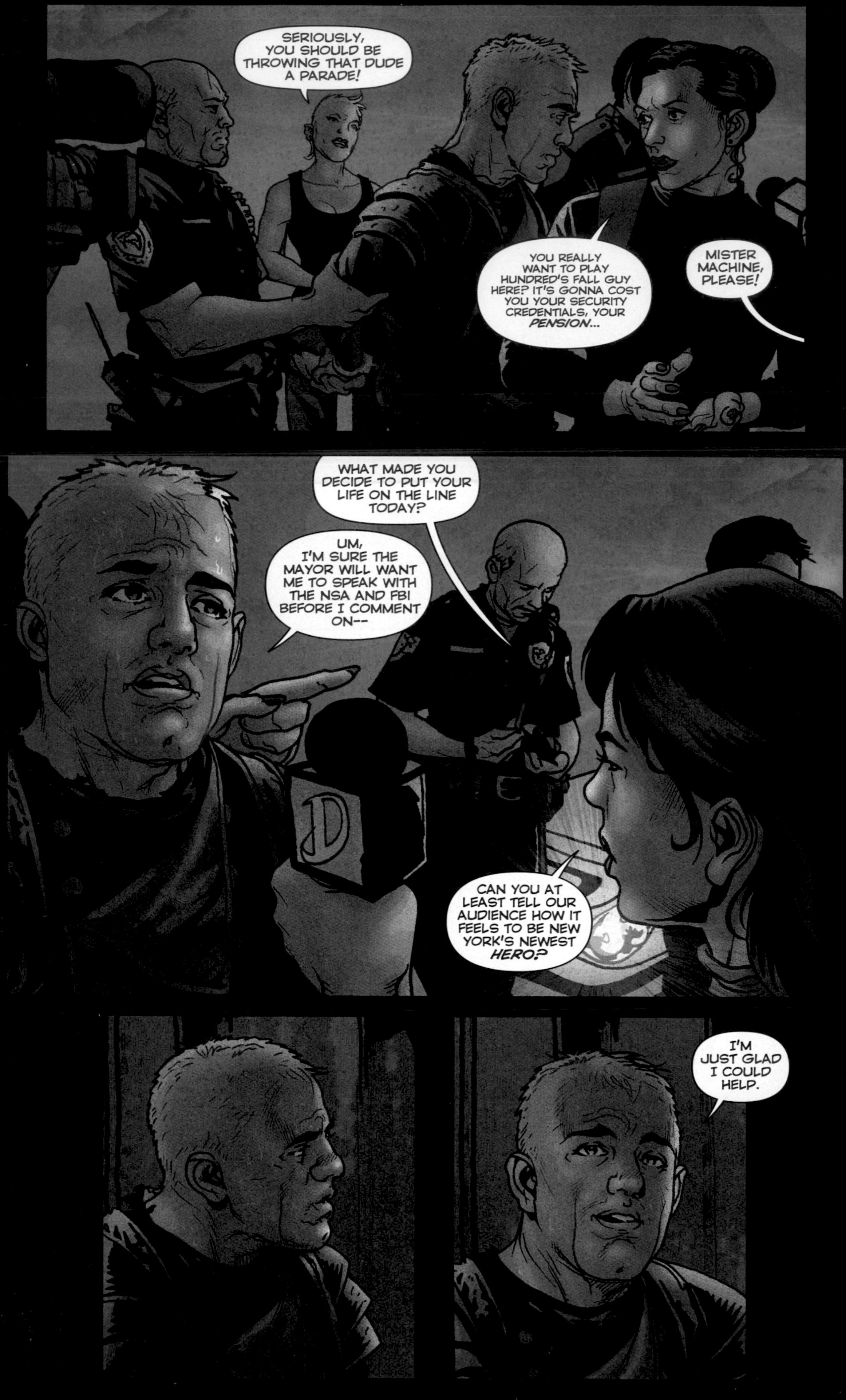
SERIOUSLY, YOU SHOULD BE THROWING THAT DUDE A PARADE!
YOU REALLY WANT TO PLAY HUNDRED'S FALL GUY HERE? IT'S GONNA COST YOU YOUR SECURITY CREDENTIALS, YOUR *PENSION*...
MISTER MACHINE, PLEASE!
WHAT MADE YOU DECIDE TO PUT YOUR LIFE ON THE LINE TODAY?
UM, I'M SURE THE MAYOR WILL WANT ME TO SPEAK WITH THE NSA AND FBI BEFORE I COMMENT ON--
CAN YOU AT LEAST TELL OUR AUDIENCE HOW IT FEELS TO BE NEW YORK'S NEWEST *HERO?*
I'M JUST GLAD I COULD HELP.

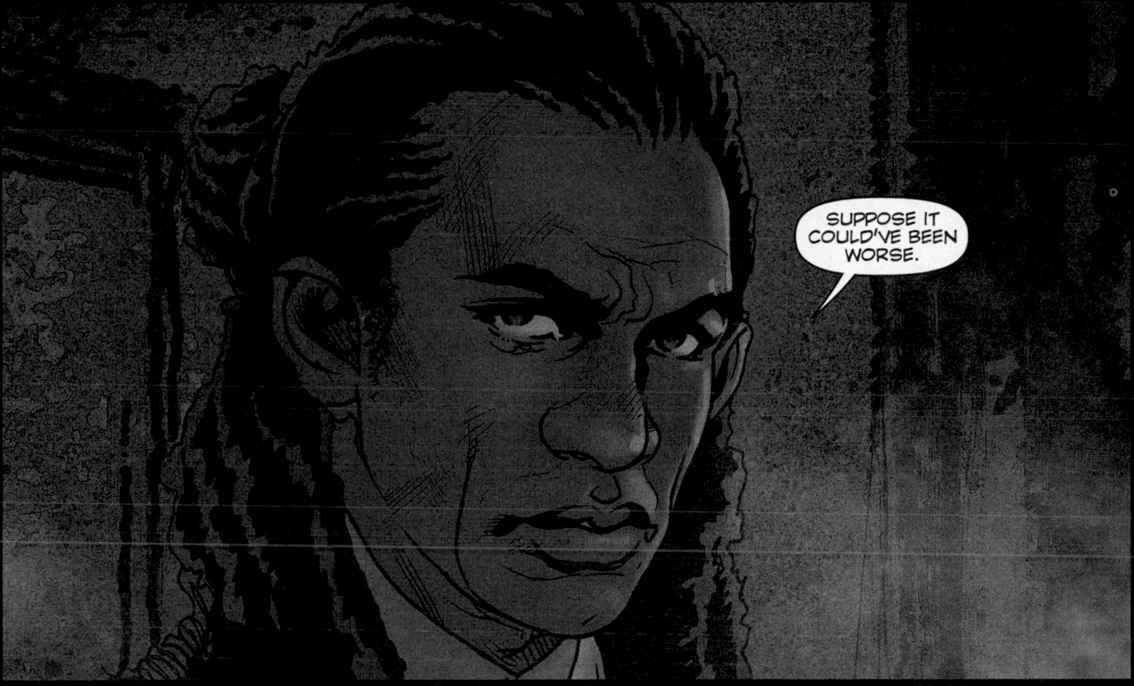
SUPPOSE IT COULD'VE BEEN WORSE.

THURSDAY, APRIL 14, 2005

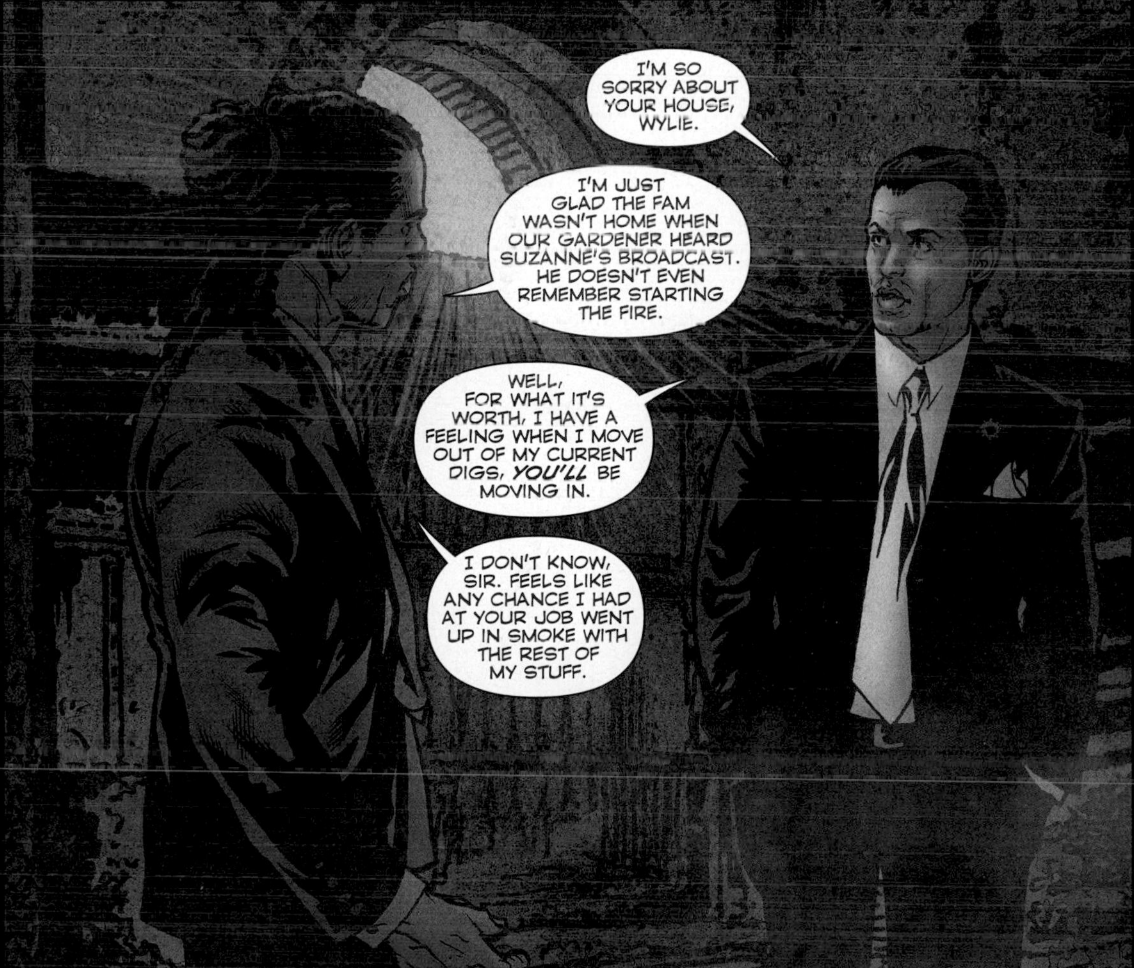
I'M SO SORRY ABOUT YOUR HOUSE, WYLIE.
I'M JUST GLAD THE FAM WASN'T HOME WHEN OUR GARDENER HEARD SUZANNE'S BROADCAST. HE DOESN'T EVEN REMEMBER STARTING THE FIRE.
WELL, FOR WHAT IT'S WORTH, I HAVE A FEELING WHEN I MOVE OUT OF MY CURRENT DIGS, *YOU'LL* BE MOVING IN.
I DON'T KNOW, SIR. FEELS LIKE ANY CHANCE I HAD AT YOUR JOB WENT UP IN SMOKE WITH THE REST OF MY STUFF.

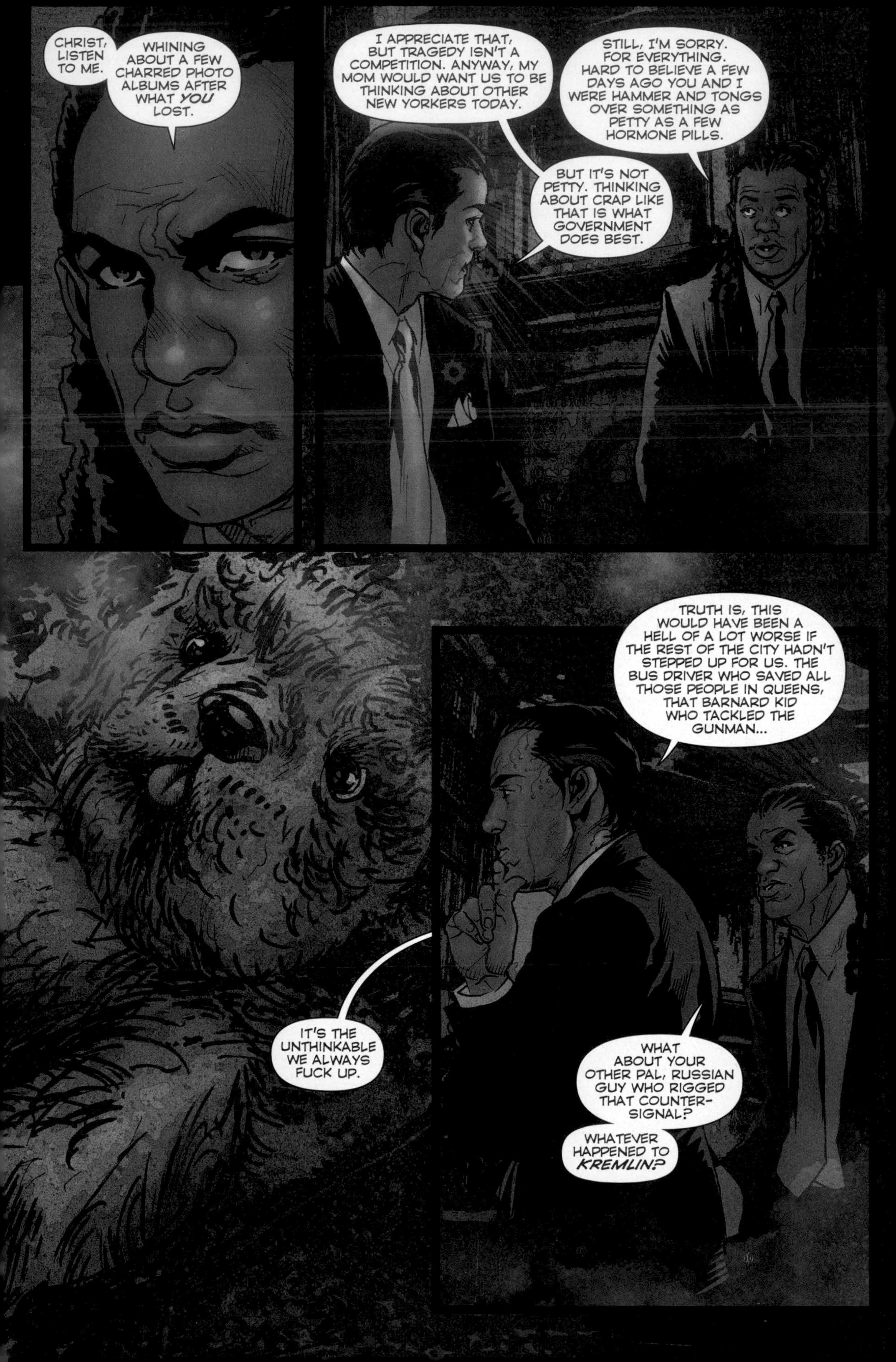
CHRIST, LISTEN TO ME.
WHINING ABOUT A FEW CHARRED PHOTO ALBUMS AFTER WHAT *YOU* LOST.
I APPRECIATE THAT, BUT TRAGEDY ISN'T A COMPETITION. ANYWAY, MY MOM WOULD WANT US TO BE THINKING ABOUT OTHER NEW YORKERS TODAY.
STILL, I'M SORRY. FOR EVERYTHING. HARD TO BELIEVE A FEW DAYS AGO YOU AND I WERE HAMMER AND TONGS OVER SOMETHING AS PETTY AS A FEW HORMONE PILLS.
BUT IT'S NOT PETTY. THINKING ABOUT CRAP LIKE THAT IS WHAT GOVERNMENT DOES BEST.
TRUTH IS, THIS WOULD HAVE BEEN A HELL OF A LOT WORSE IF THE REST OF THE CITY HADN'T STEPPED UP FOR US. THE BUS DRIVER WHO SAVED ALL THOSE PEOPLE IN QUEENS, THAT BARNARD KID WHO TACKLED THE GUNMAN...
IT'S THE UNTHINKABLE WE ALWAYS FUCK UP.
WHAT ABOUT YOUR OTHER PAL, RUSSIAN GUY WHO RIGGED THAT COUNTER-SIGNAL?
WHATEVER HAPPENED TO *KREMLIN?*

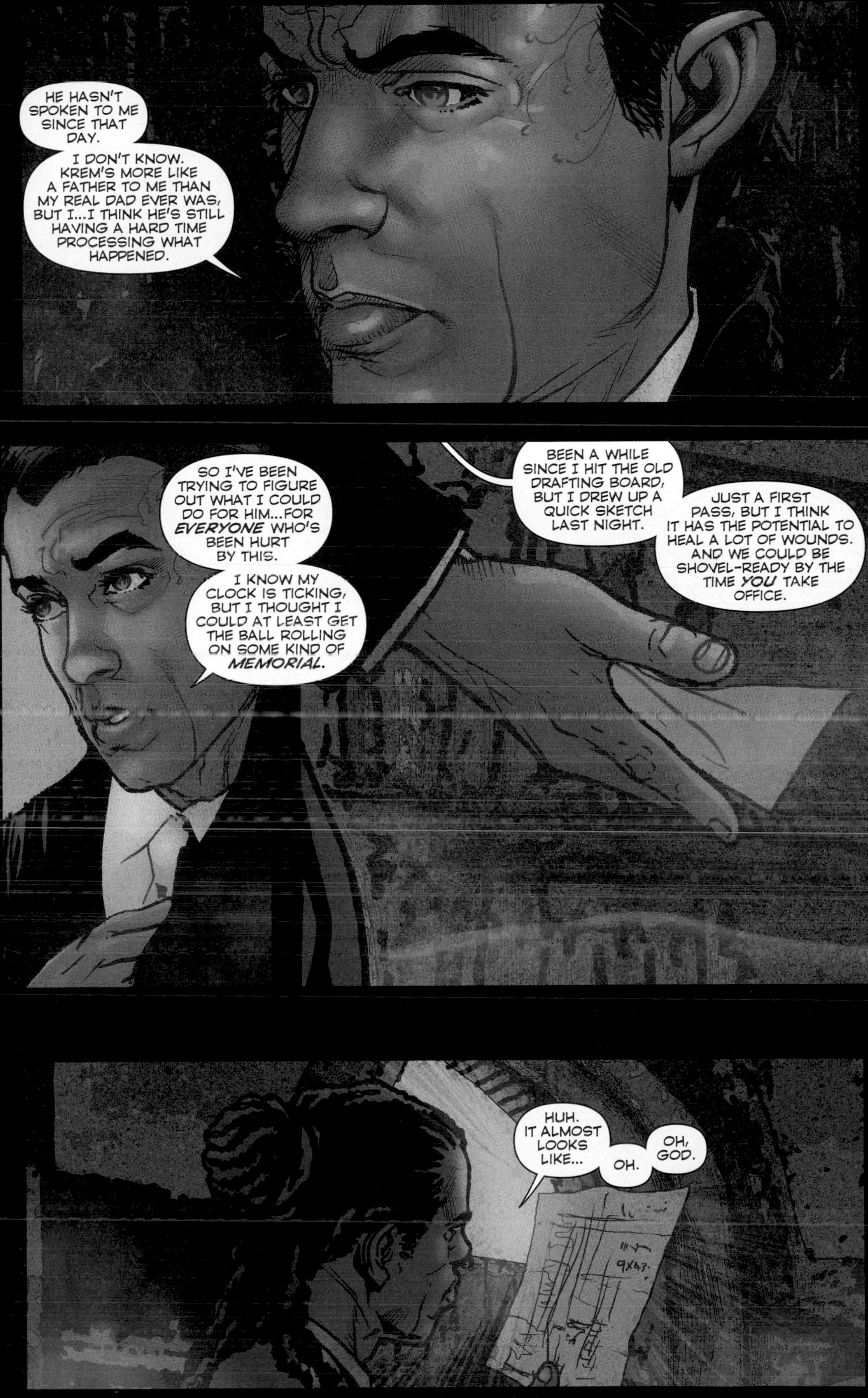
HE HASN'T SPOKEN TO ME SINCE THAT DAY.
I DON'T KNOW. KREM'S MORE LIKE A FATHER TO ME THAN MY REAL DAD EVER WAS, BUT I...I THINK HE'S STILL HAVING A HARD TIME PROCESSING WHAT HAPPENED.
SO I'VE BEEN TRYING TO FIGURE OUT WHAT I COULD DO FOR HIM...FOR EVERYONE WHO'S BEEN HURT BY THIS.
I KNOW MY CLOCK IS TICKING, BUT I THOUGHT I COULD AT LEAST GET THE BALL ROLLING ON SOME KIND OF MEMORIAL.
BEEN A WHILE SINCE I HIT THE OLD DRAFTING BOARD, BUT I DREW UP A QUICK SKETCH LAST NIGHT.
JUST A FIRST PASS, BUT I THINK IT HAS THE POTENTIAL TO HEAL A LOT OF WOUNDS. AND WE COULD BE SHOVEL-READY BY THE TIME YOU TAKE OFFICE.
HUH. IT ALMOST LOOKS LIKE...
OH.
OH, GOD.

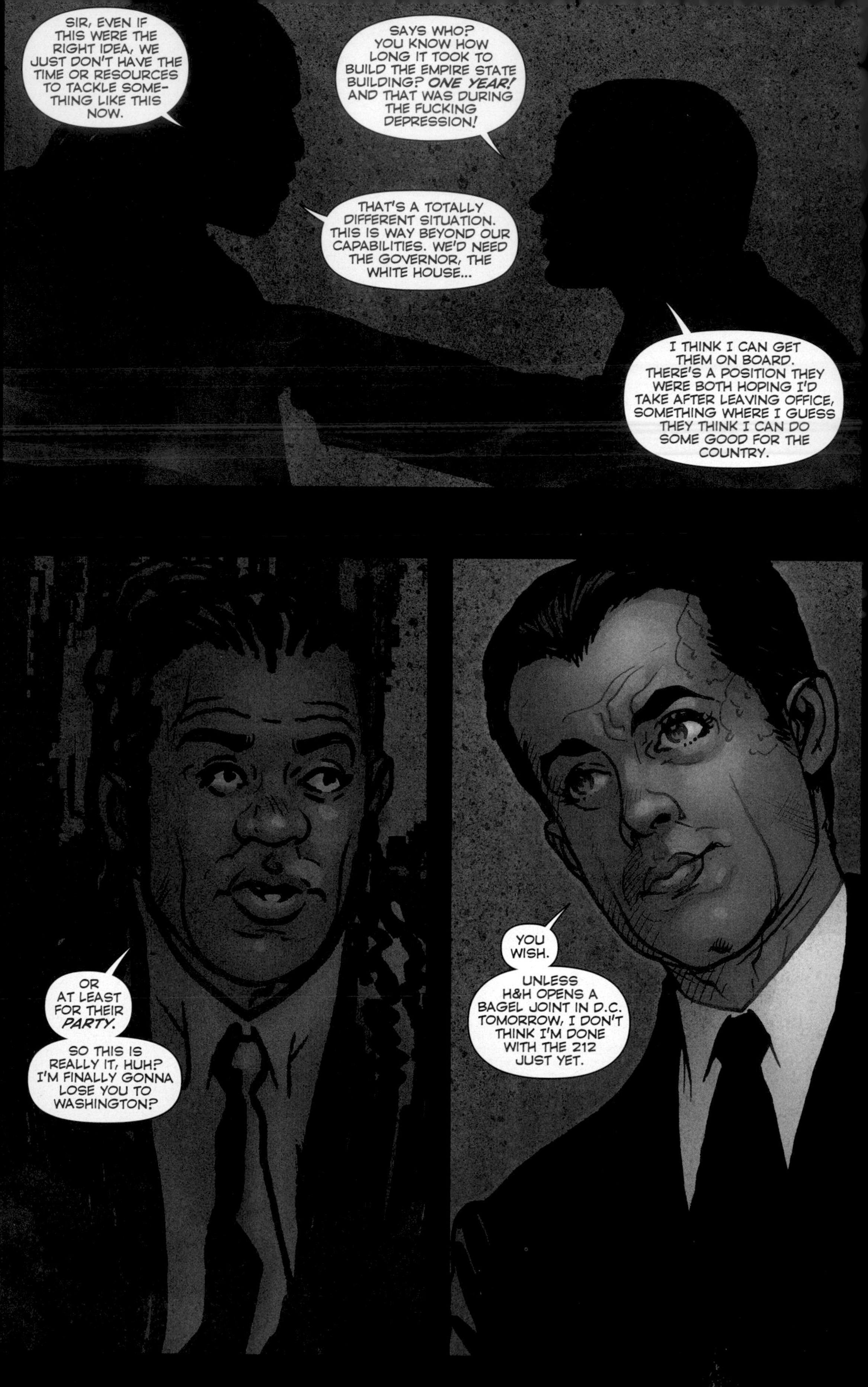
SIR, EVEN IF THIS WERE THE RIGHT IDEA, WE JUST DON'T HAVE THE TIME OR RESOURCES TO TACKLE SOME-THING LIKE THIS NOW.
SAYS WHO? YOU KNOW HOW LONG IT TOOK TO BUILD THE EMPIRE STATE BUILDING? ONE YEAR! AND THAT WAS DURING THE FUCKING DEPRESSION!
THAT'S A TOTALLY DIFFERENT SITUATION. THIS IS WAY BEYOND OUR CAPABILITIES. WE'D NEED THE GOVERNOR, THE WHITE HOUSE...
I THINK I CAN GET THEM ON BOARD. THERE'S A POSITION THEY WERE BOTH HOPING I'D TAKE AFTER LEAVING OFFICE, SOMETHING WHERE I GUESS THEY THINK I CAN DO SOME GOOD FOR THE COUNTRY.
OR AT LEAST FOR THEIR PARTY.
SO THIS IS REALLY IT, HUH? I'M FINALLY GONNA LOSE YOU TO WASHINGTON?
YOU WISH.
UNLESS H&H OPENS A BAGEL JOINT IN D.C. TOMORROW, I DON'T THINK I'M DONE WITH THE 212 JUST YET.

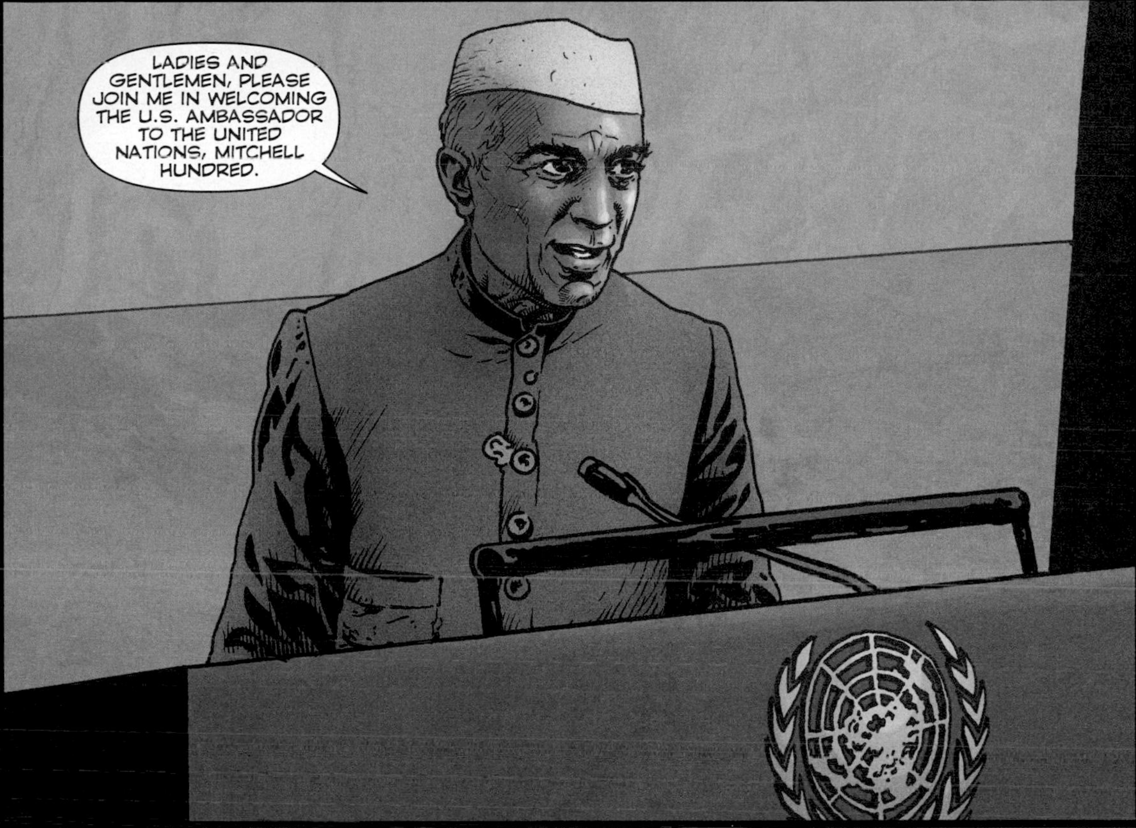
LADIES AND GENTLEMEN, PLEASE JOIN ME IN WELCOMING THE U.S. AMBASSADOR TO THE UNITED NATIONS, MITCHELL HUNDRED.

FRIDAY, SEPTEMBER 1, 2006

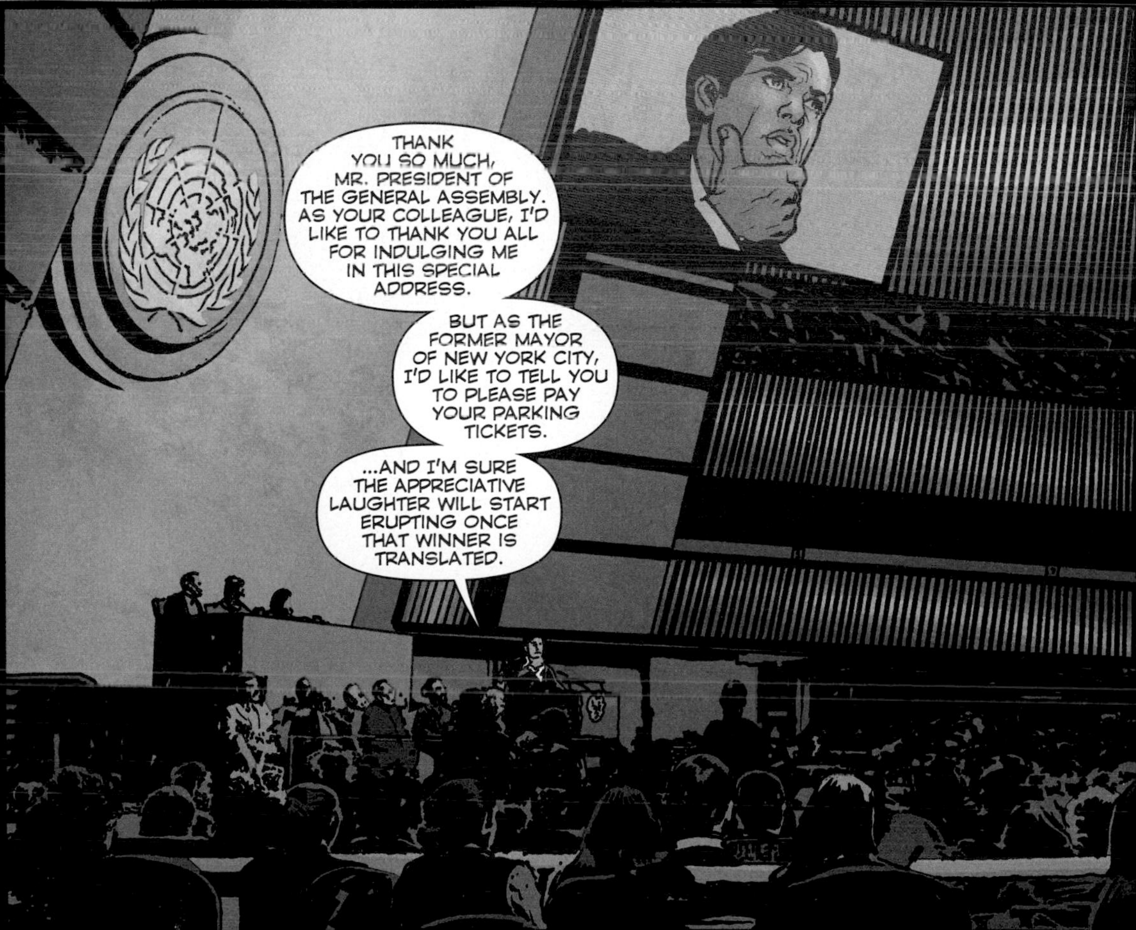
THANK YOU SO MUCH, MR. PRESIDENT OF THE GENERAL ASSEMBLY. AS YOUR COLLEAGUE, I'D LIKE TO THANK YOU ALL FOR INDULGING ME IN THIS SPECIAL ADDRESS.
BUT AS THE FORMER MAYOR OF NEW YORK CITY, I'D LIKE TO TELL YOU TO PLEASE PAY YOUR PARKING TICKETS.
...AND I'M SURE THE APPRECIATIVE LAUGHTER WILL START ERUPTING ONCE THAT WINNER IS TRANSLATED.

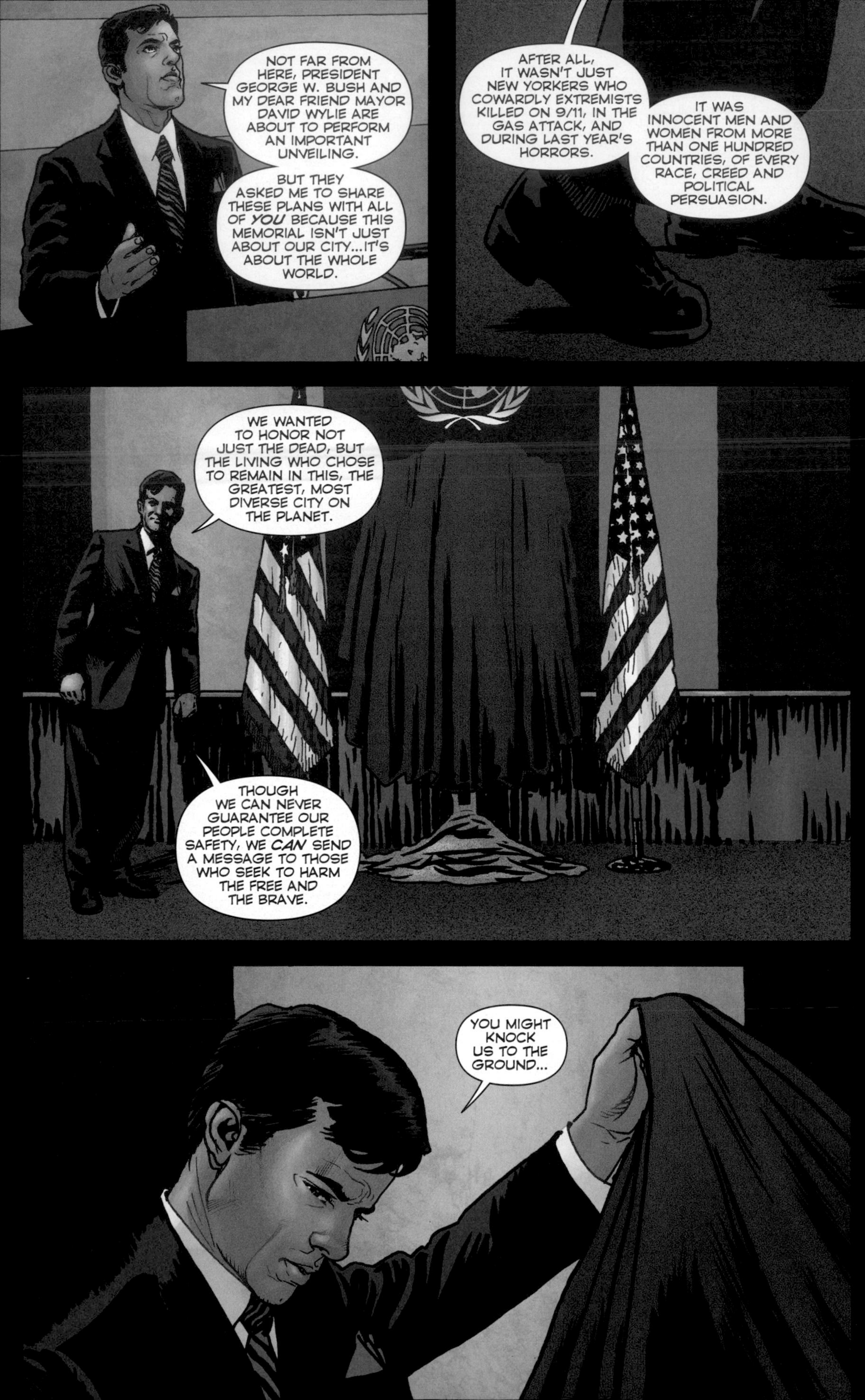
NOT FAR FROM HERE, PRESIDENT GEORGE W. BUSH AND MY DEAR FRIEND MAYOR DAVID WYLIE ARE ABOUT TO PERFORM AN IMPORTANT UNVEILING.
BUT THEY ASKED ME TO SHARE THESE PLANS WITH ALL OF YOU BECAUSE THIS MEMORIAL ISN'T JUST ABOUT OUR CITY...IT'S ABOUT THE WHOLE WORLD.
AFTER ALL, IT WASN'T JUST NEW YORKERS WHO COWARDLY EXTREMISTS KILLED ON 9/11, IN THE GAS ATTACK, AND DURING LAST YEAR'S HORRORS.
IT WAS INNOCENT MEN AND WOMEN FROM MORE THAN ONE HUNDRED COUNTRIES, OF EVERY RACE, CREED AND POLITICAL PERSUASION.
WE WANTED TO HONOR NOT JUST THE DEAD, BUT THE LIVING WHO CHOSE TO REMAIN IN THIS, THE GREATEST, MOST DIVERSE CITY ON THE PLANET.
THOUGH WE CAN NEVER GUARANTEE OUR PEOPLE COMPLETE SAFETY, WE CAN SEND A MESSAGE TO THOSE WHO SEEK TO HARM THE FREE AND THE BRAVE.
YOU MIGHT KNOCK US TO THE GROUND...

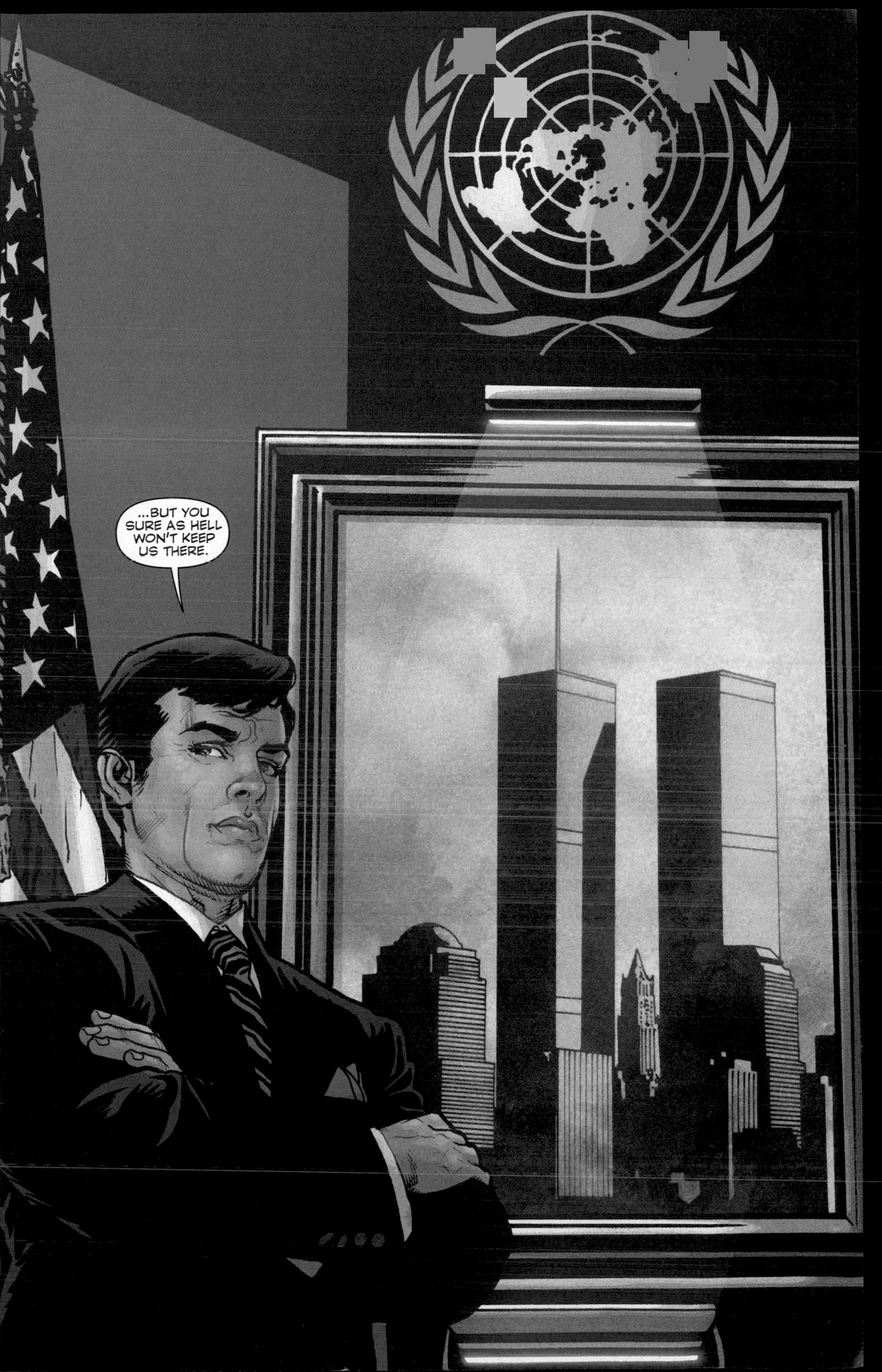
...BUT YOU SURE AS HELL WON'T KEEP US THERE.

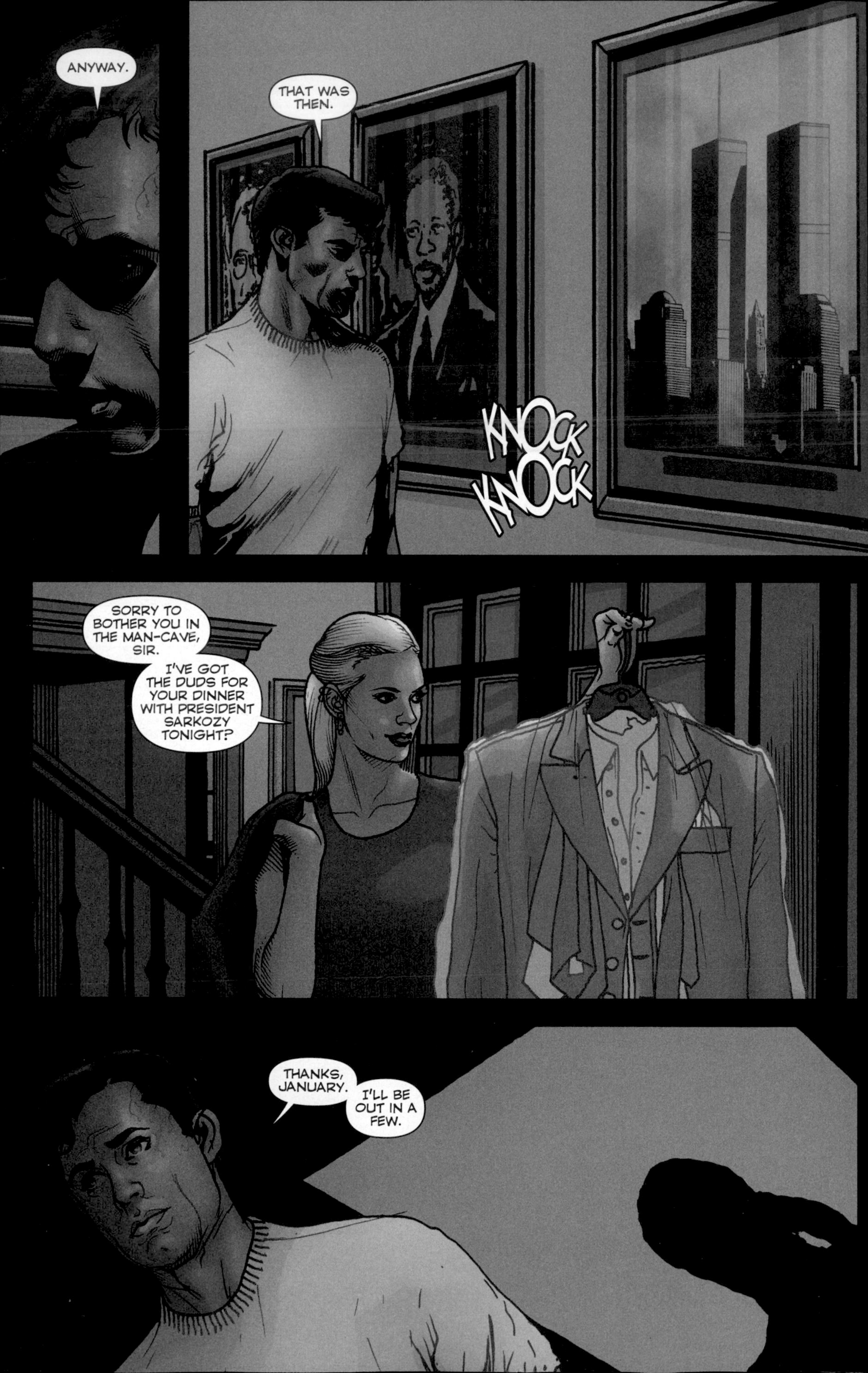
ANYWAY.
THAT WAS THEN.
KNOCK KNOCK
SORRY TO BOTHER YOU IN THE MAN-CAVE, SIR.
I'VE GOT THE DUDS FOR YOUR DINNER WITH PRESIDENT SARKOZY TONIGHT?
THANKS, JANUARY.
I'LL BE OUT IN A FEW.

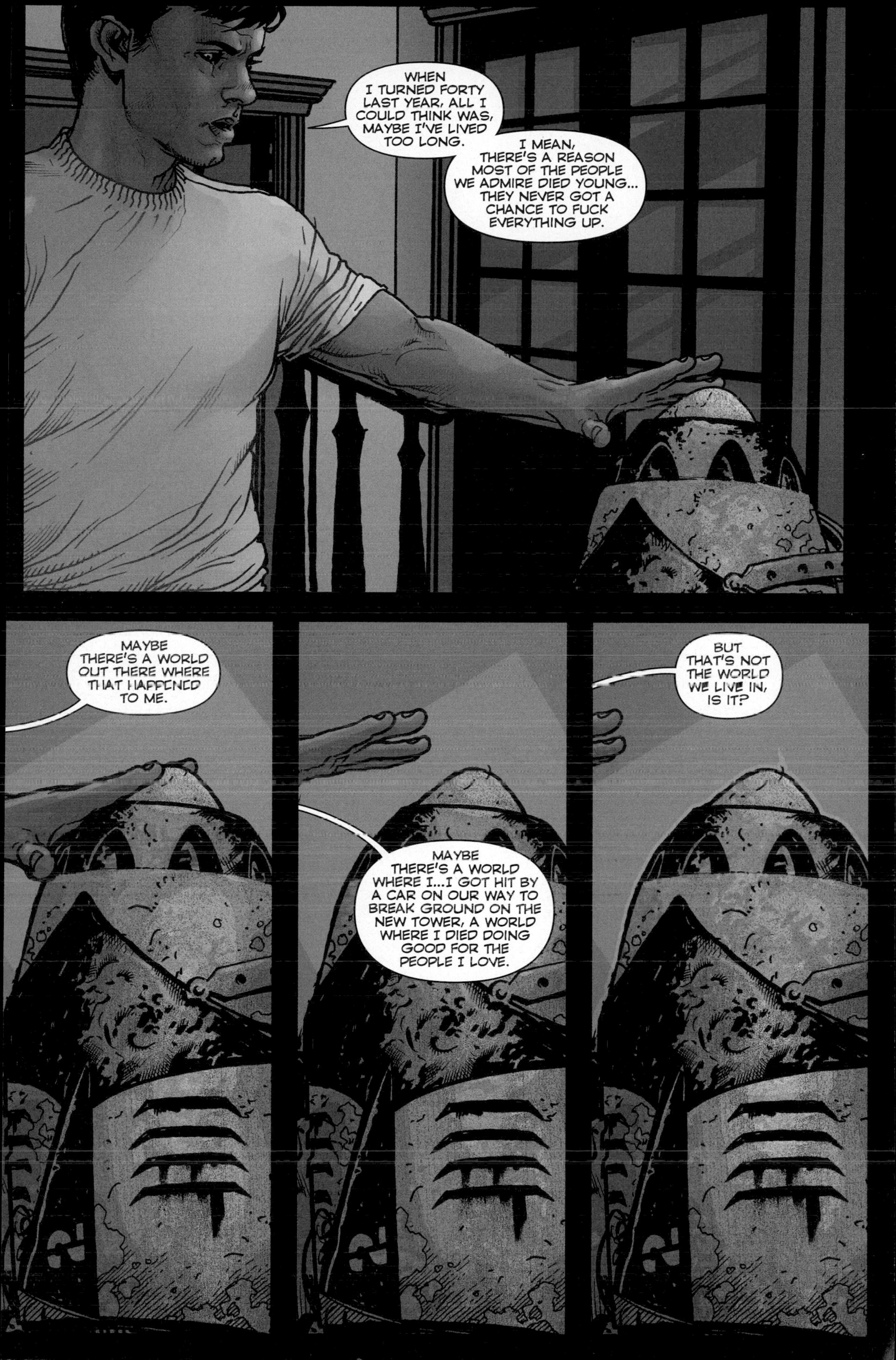
WHEN I TURNED FORTY LAST YEAR, ALL I COULD THINK WAS, MAYBE I'VE LIVED TOO LONG.
I MEAN, THERE'S A REASON MOST OF THE PEOPLE WE ADMIRE DIED YOUNG... THEY NEVER GOT A CHANCE TO FUCK EVERYTHING UP.
MAYBE THERE'S A WORLD OUT THERE WHERE THAT HAPPENED TO ME.
MAYBE THERE'S A WORLD WHERE I...I GOT HIT BY A CAR ON OUR WAY TO BREAK GROUND ON THE NEW TOWER, A WORLD WHERE I DIED DOING GOOD FOR THE PEOPLE I LOVE.
BUT THAT'S NOT THE WORLD WE LIVE IN, IS IT?

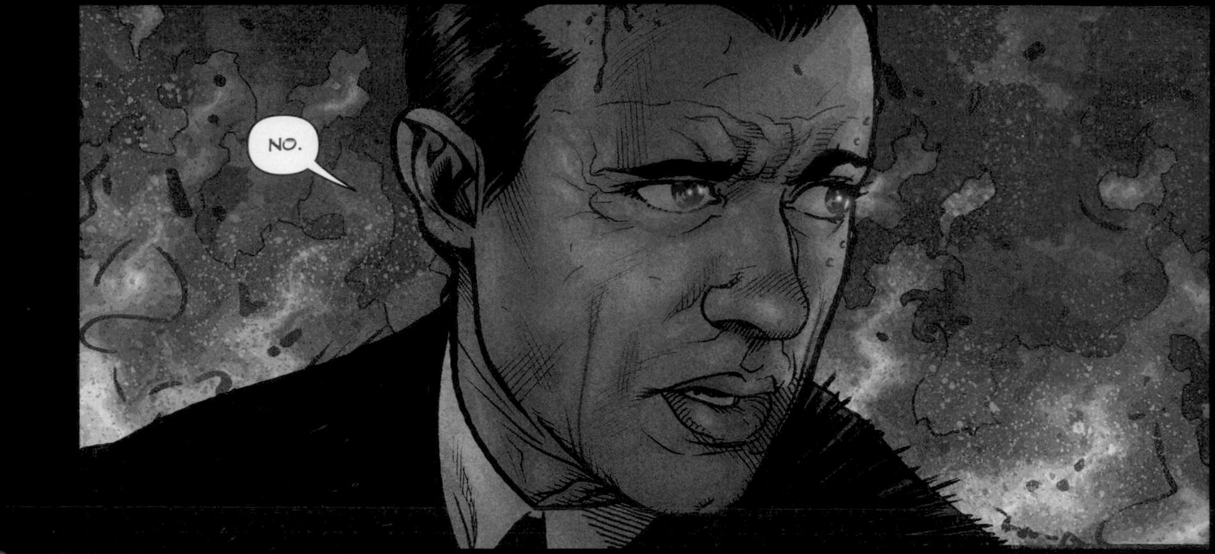
NO.

SUNDAY, MARCH 4, 2007

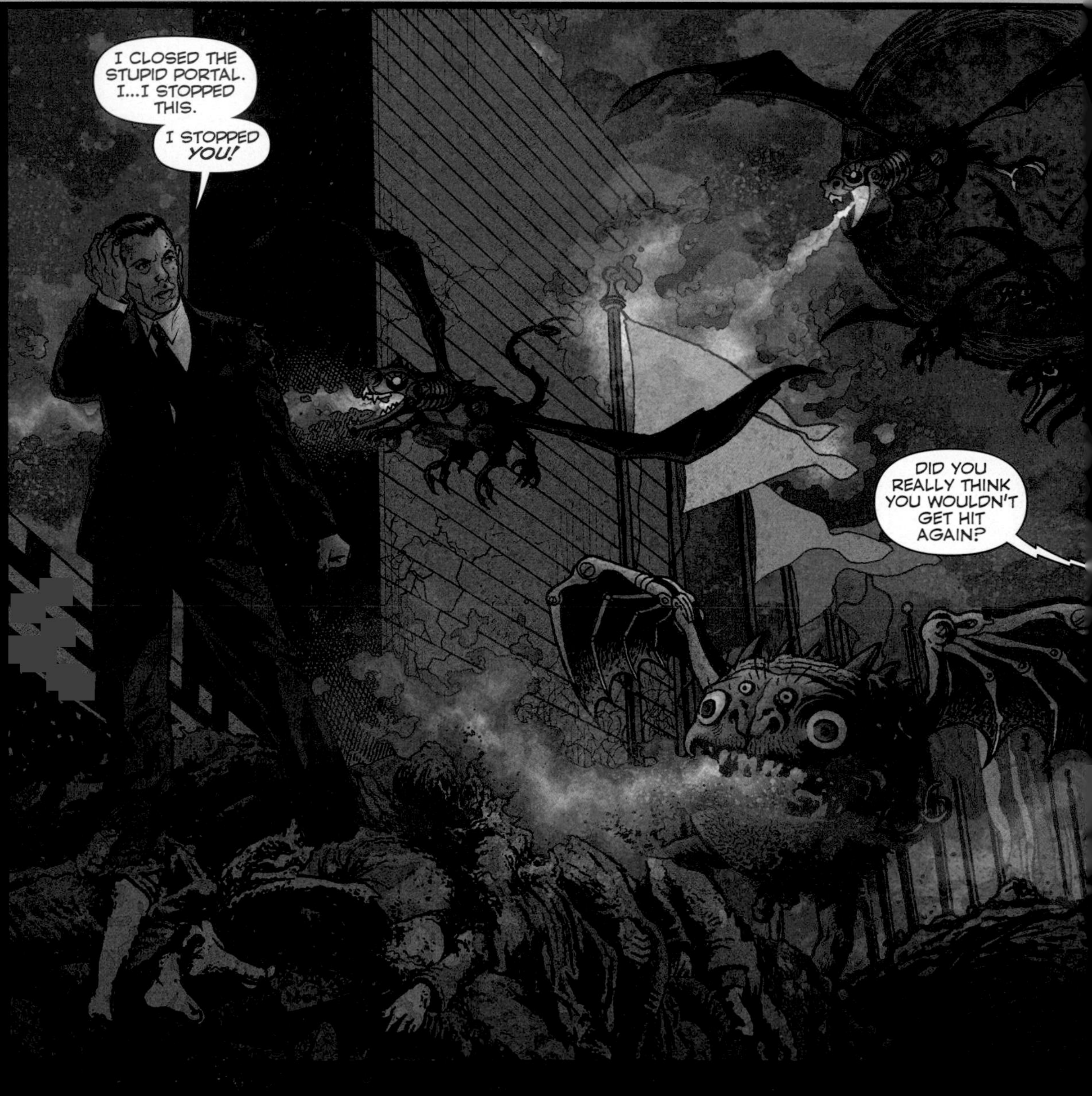
I CLOSED THE STUPID PORTAL. I...I STOPPED THIS.
I STOPPED *YOU!*
DID YOU REALLY THINK YOU WOULDN'T GET HIT AGAIN?

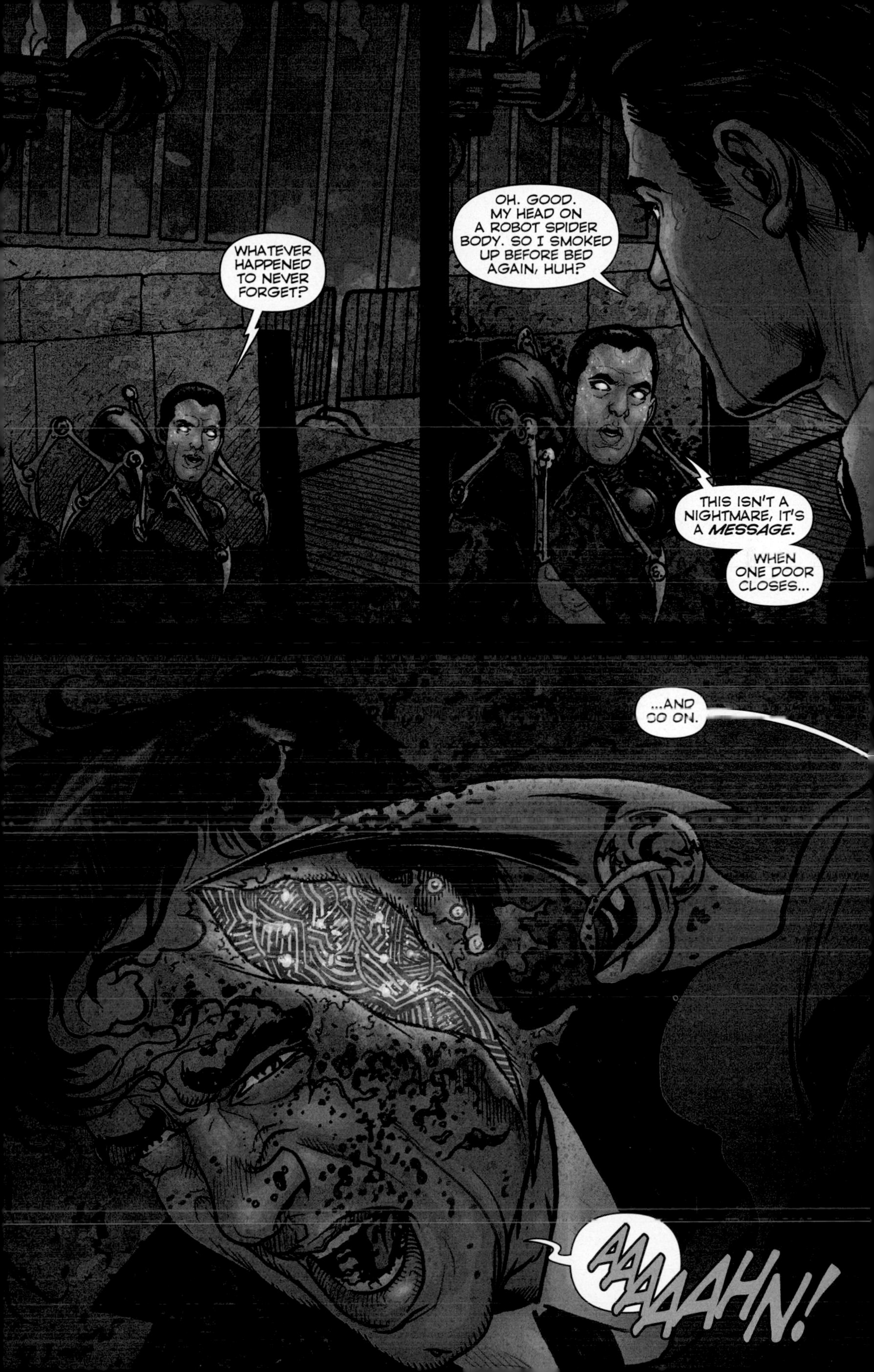
WHATEVER HAPPENED TO NEVER FORGET?
OH. GOOD. MY HEAD ON A ROBOT SPIDER BODY. SO I SMOKED UP BEFORE BED AGAIN, HUH?
THIS ISN'T A NIGHTMARE, IT'S A *MESSAGE*.
WHEN ONE DOOR CLOSES...
...AND SO ON.
AAAAAAHN!

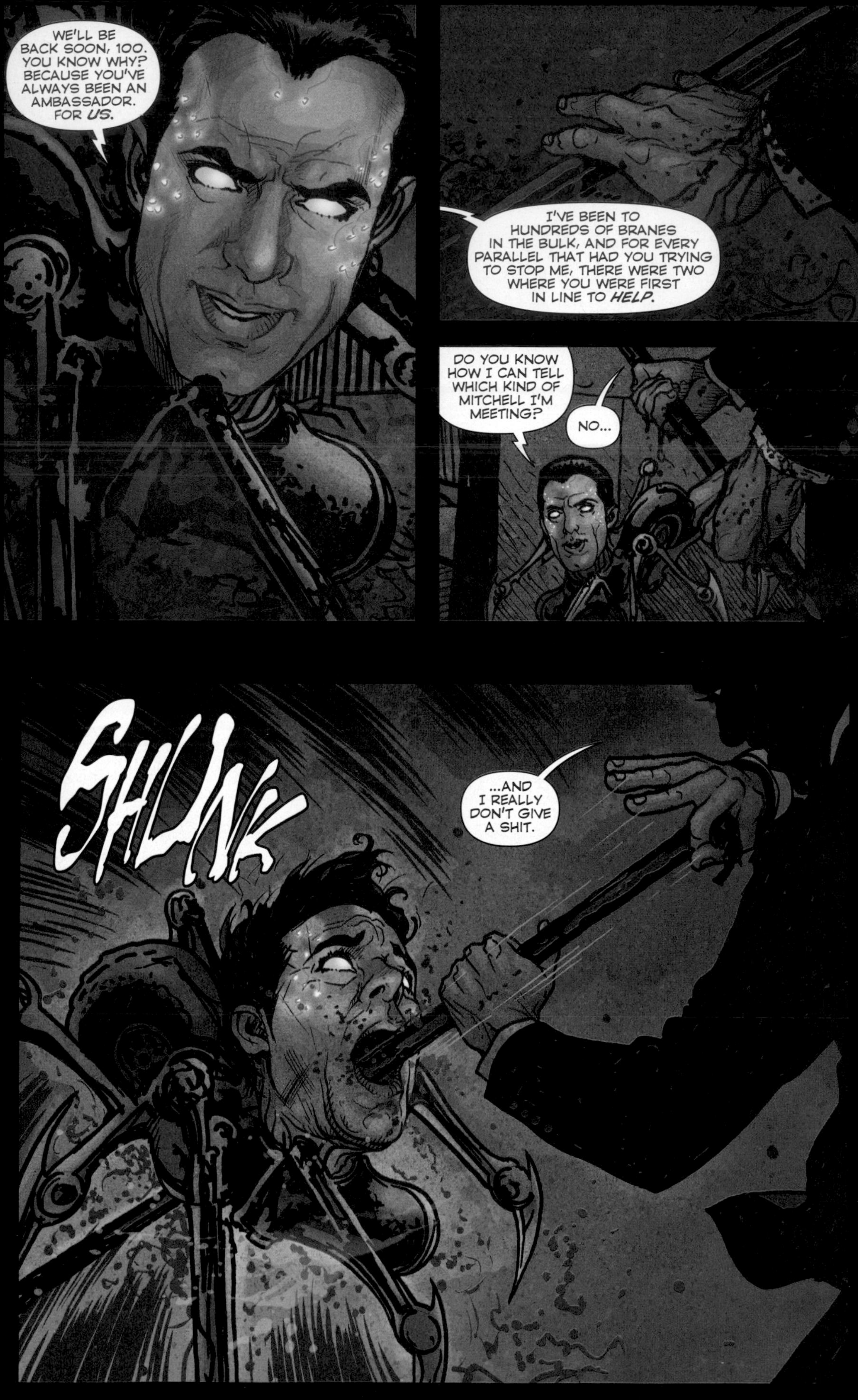
WE'LL BE BACK SOON, 100. YOU KNOW WHY? BECAUSE YOU'VE ALWAYS BEEN AN AMBASSADOR. FOR US.
I'VE BEEN TO HUNDREDS OF BRANES IN THE BULK, AND FOR EVERY PARALLEL THAT HAD YOU TRYING TO STOP ME, THERE WERE TWO WHERE YOU WERE FIRST IN LINE TO HELP.
DO YOU KNOW HOW I CAN TELL WHICH KIND OF MITCHELL I'M MEETING?
NO...
SHUNK
...AND I REALLY DON'T GIVE A SHIT.

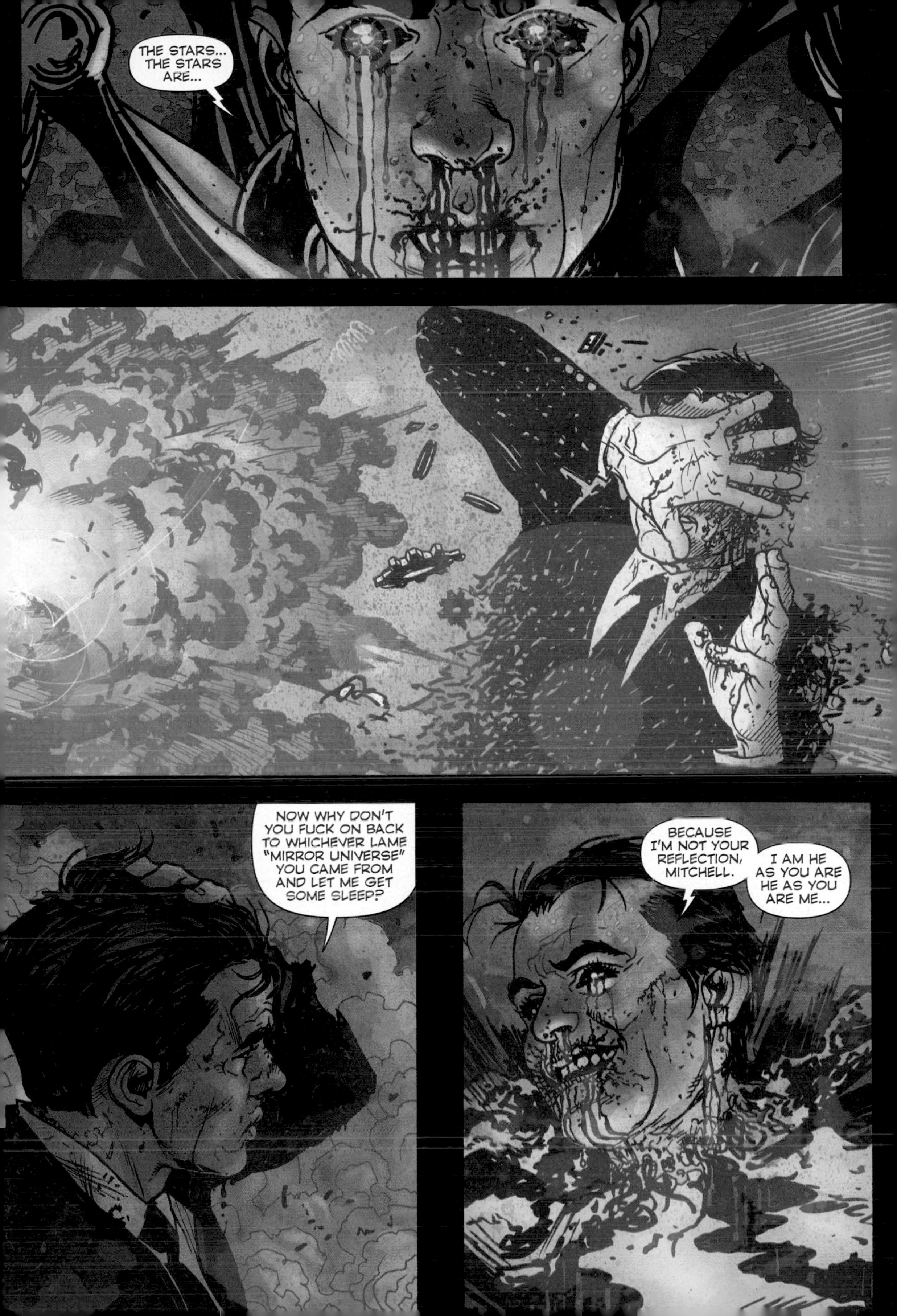
THE STARS... THE STARS ARE...
NOW WHY DON'T YOU FUCK ON BACK TO WHICHEVER LAME "MIRROR UNIVERSE" YOU CAME FROM AND LET ME GET SOME SLEEP?
BECAUSE I'M NOT YOUR REFLECTION, MITCHELL.
I AM HE AS YOU ARE HE AS YOU ARE ME...

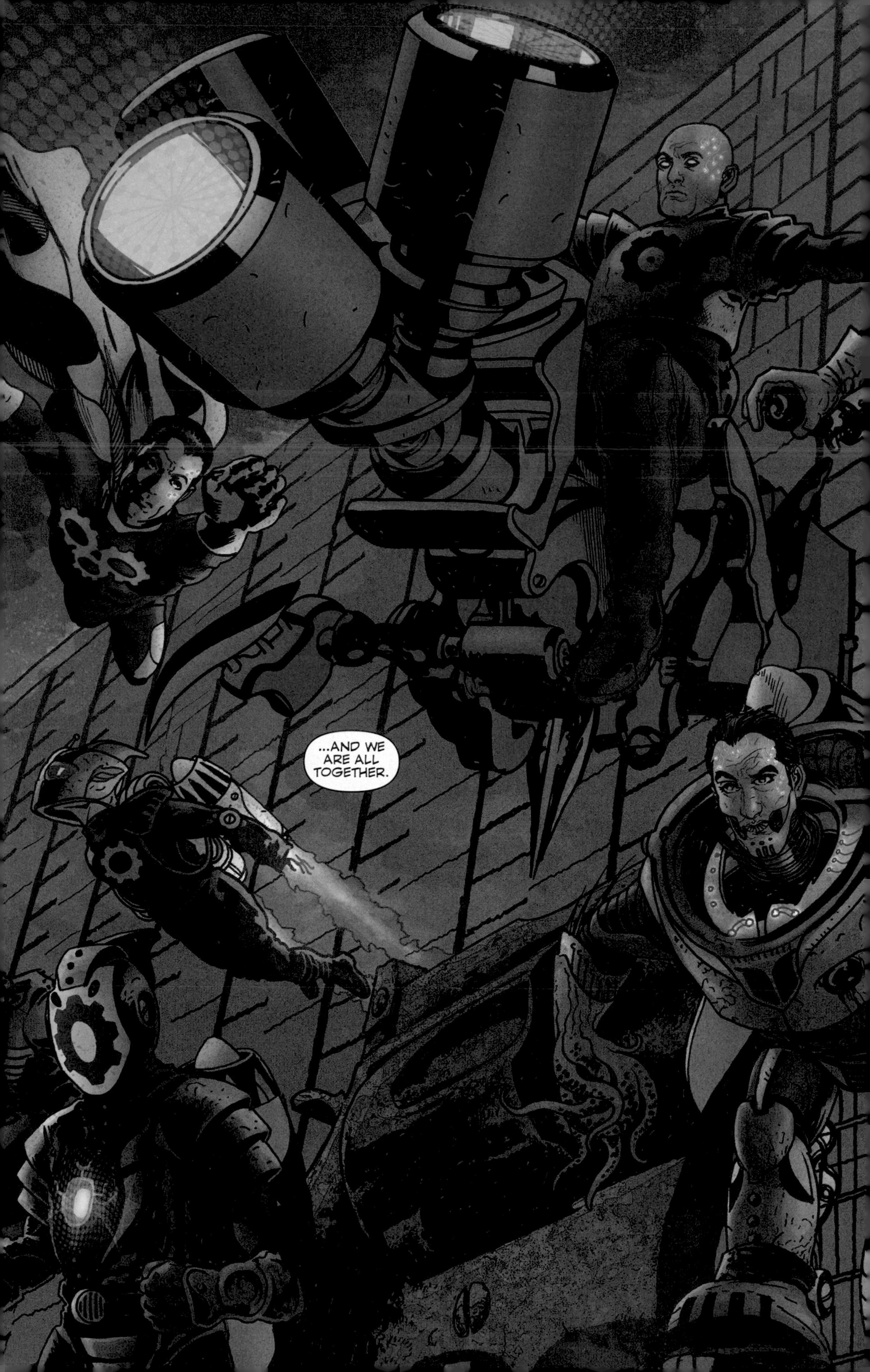
...AND WE ARE ALL TOGETHER.

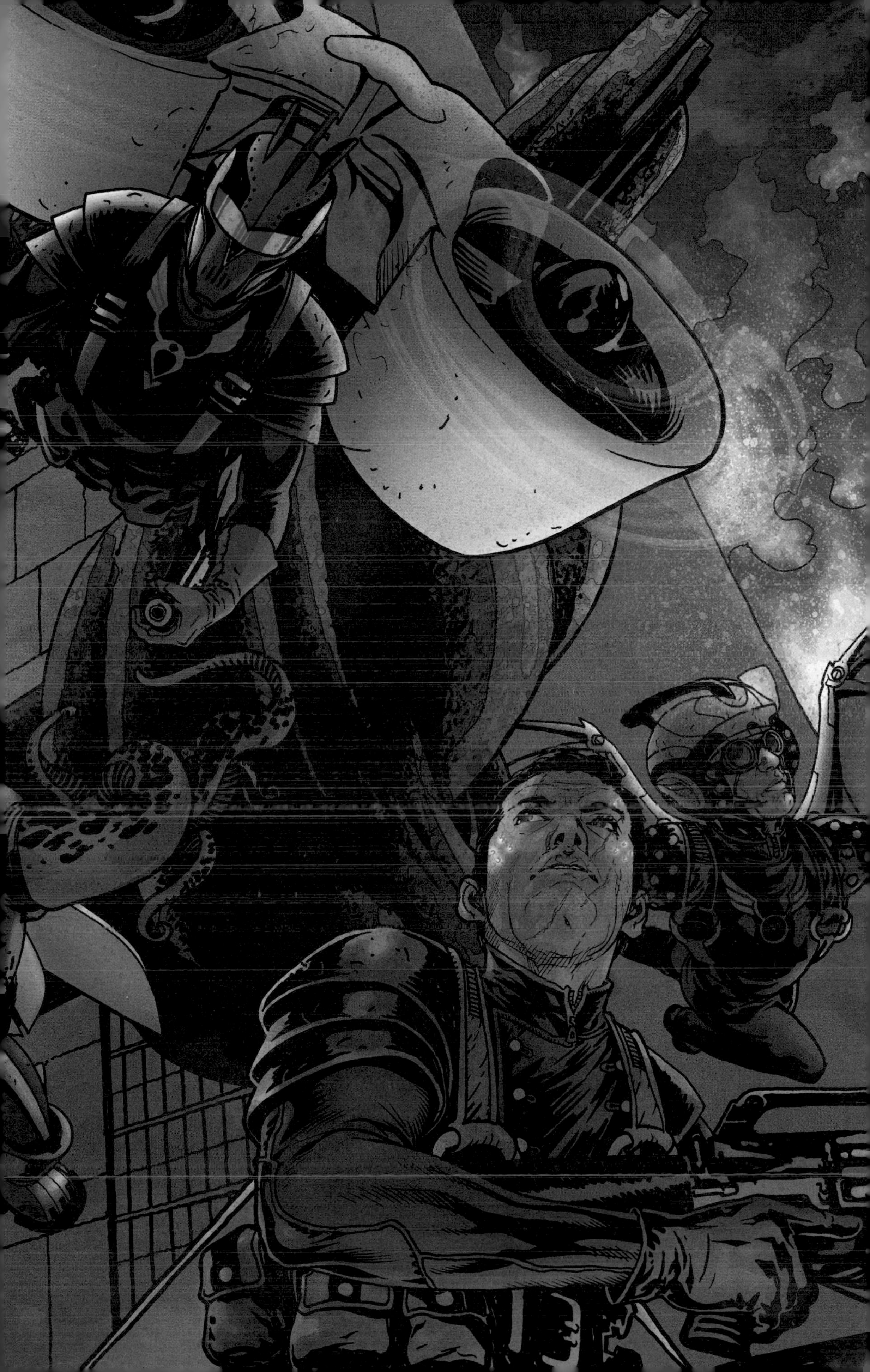

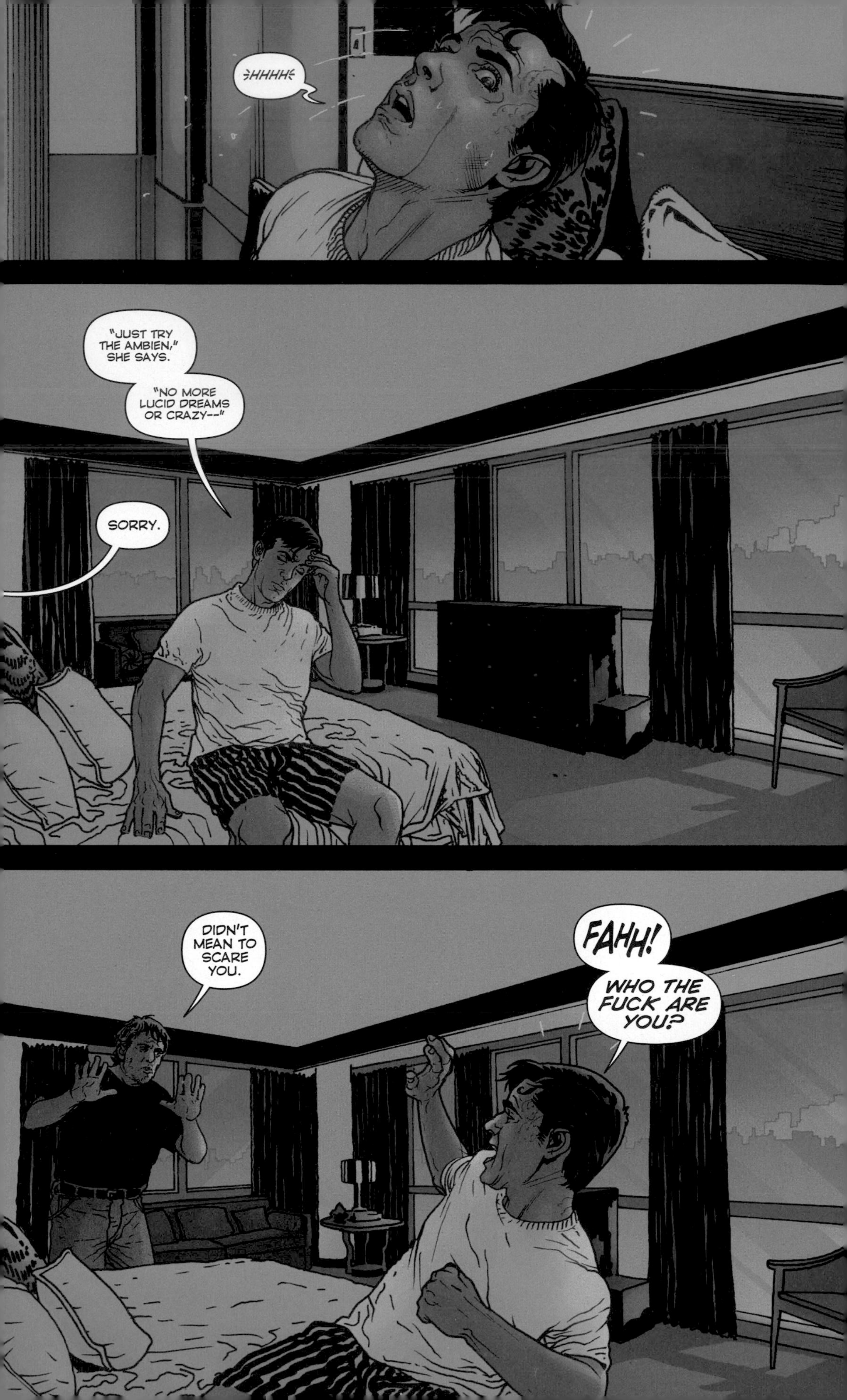
HHHH
"JUST TRY THE AMBIEN," SHE SAYS.
"NO MORE LUCID DREAMS OR CRAZY--"
SORRY.
DIDN'T MEAN TO SCARE YOU.
FAHH!
WHO THE FUCK ARE YOU?

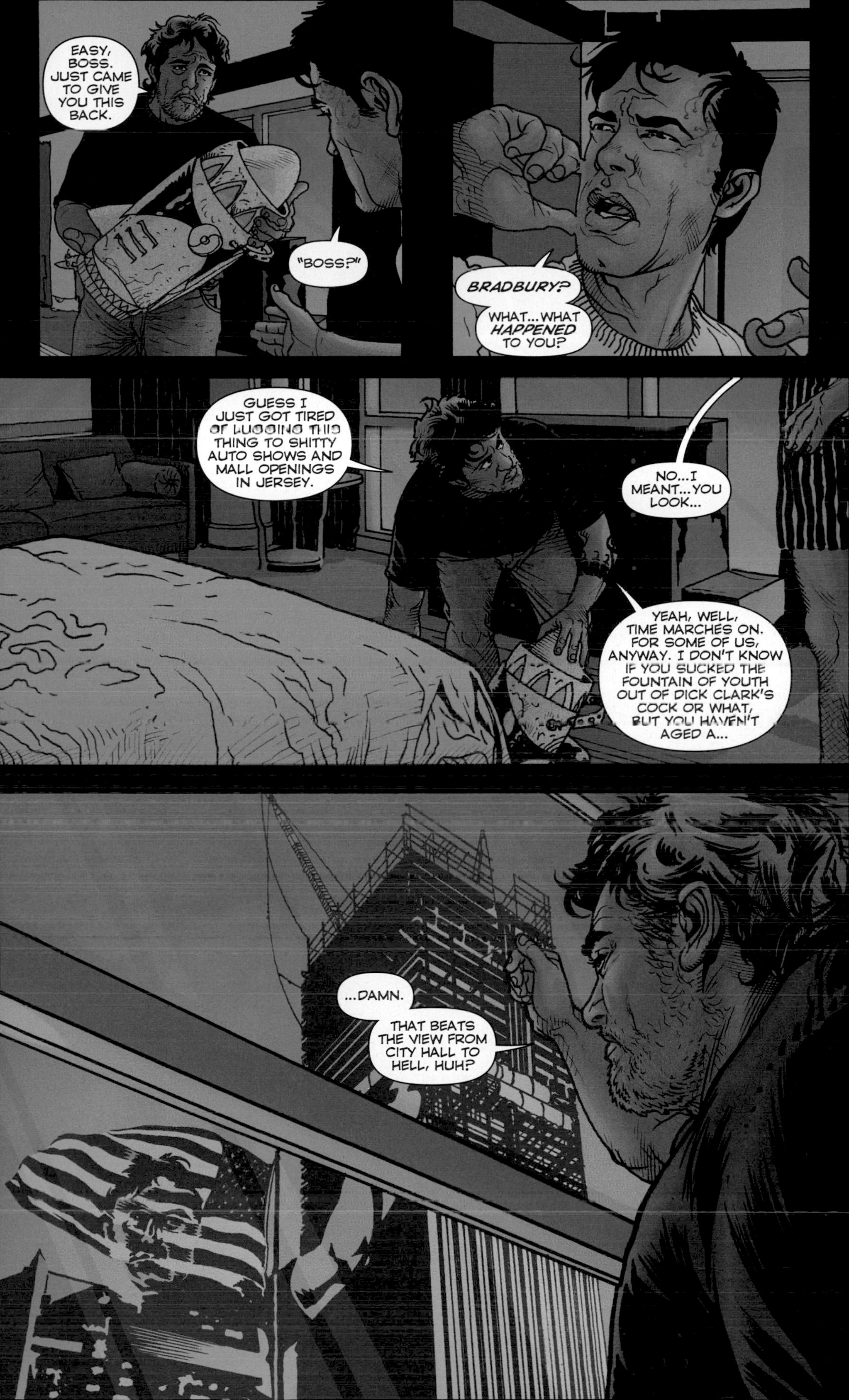
EASY, BOSS. JUST CAME TO GIVE YOU THIS BACK.
"BOSS?"
BRADBURY?
WHAT...WHAT HAPPENED TO YOU?
GUESS I JUST GOT TIRED OF LUGGING THIS THING TO SHITTY AUTO SHOWS AND MALL OPENINGS IN JERSEY.
NO...I MEANT...YOU LOOK...
YEAH, WELL, TIME MARCHES ON. FOR SOME OF US, ANYWAY. I DON'T KNOW IF YOU SUCKED THE FOUNTAIN OF YOUTH OUT OF DICK CLARK'S COCK OR WHAT, BUT YOU HAVEN'T AGED A...
...DAMN.
THAT BEATS THE VIEW FROM CITY HALL TO HELL, HUH?

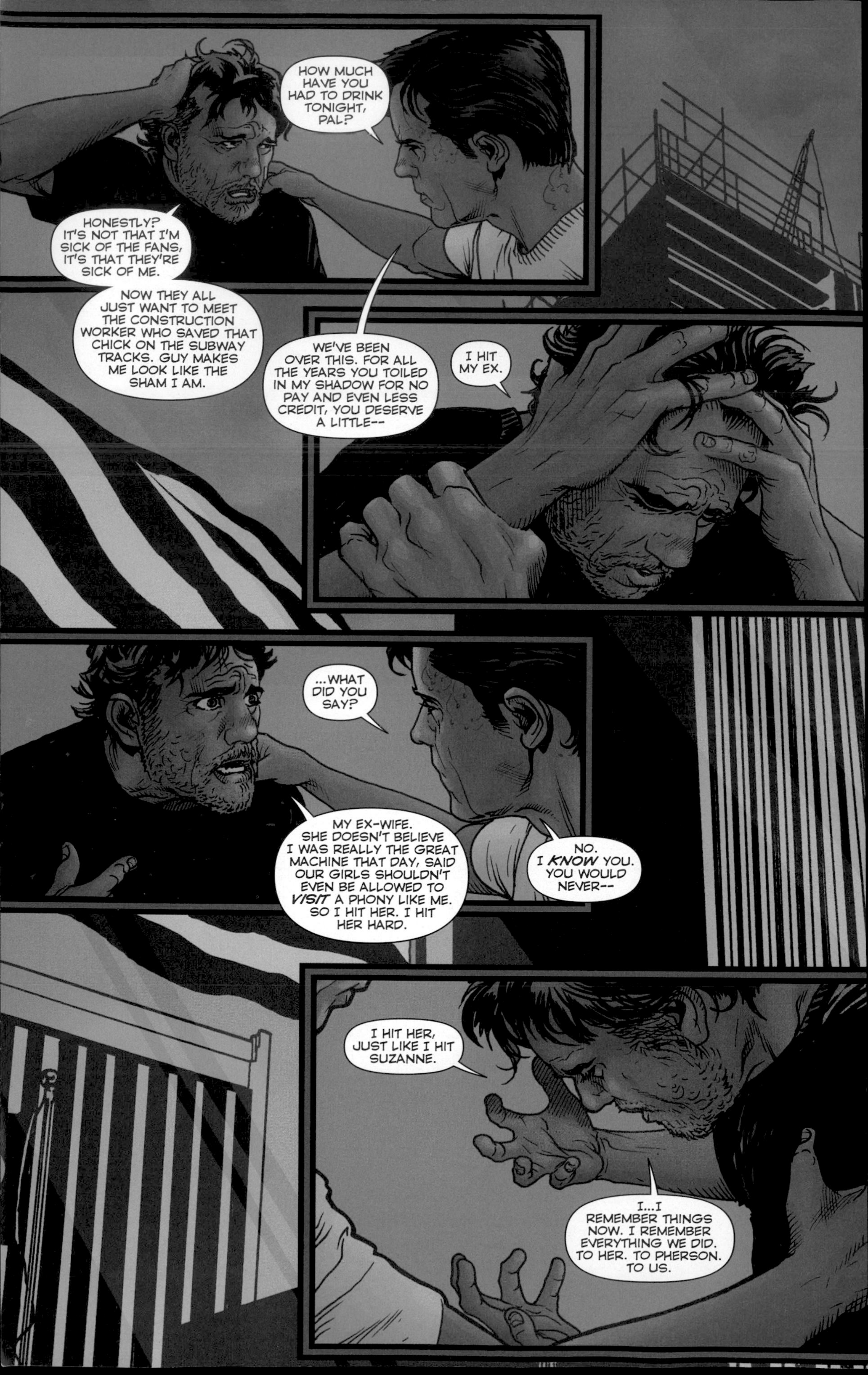
HOW MUCH HAVE YOU HAD TO DRINK TONIGHT, PAL?
HONESTLY? IT'S NOT THAT I'M SICK OF THE FANS, IT'S THAT THEY'RE SICK OF ME.
NOW THEY ALL JUST WANT TO MEET THE CONSTRUCTION WORKER WHO SAVED THAT CHICK ON THE SUBWAY TRACKS. GUY MAKES ME LOOK LIKE THE SHAM I AM.
WE'VE BEEN OVER THIS. FOR ALL THE YEARS YOU TOILED IN MY SHADOW FOR NO PAY AND EVEN LESS CREDIT, YOU DESERVE A LITTLE--
I HIT MY EX.
...WHAT DID YOU SAY?
MY EX-WIFE. SHE DOESN'T BELIEVE I WAS REALLY THE GREAT MACHINE THAT DAY, SAID OUR GIRLS SHOULDN'T EVEN BE ALLOWED TO VISIT A PHONY LIKE ME. SO I HIT HER. I HIT HER HARD.
NO. I KNOW YOU. YOU WOULD NEVER--
I HIT HER, JUST LIKE I HIT SUZANNE.
I...I REMEMBER THINGS NOW. I REMEMBER EVERYTHING WE DID. TO HER. TO PHERSON. TO US.

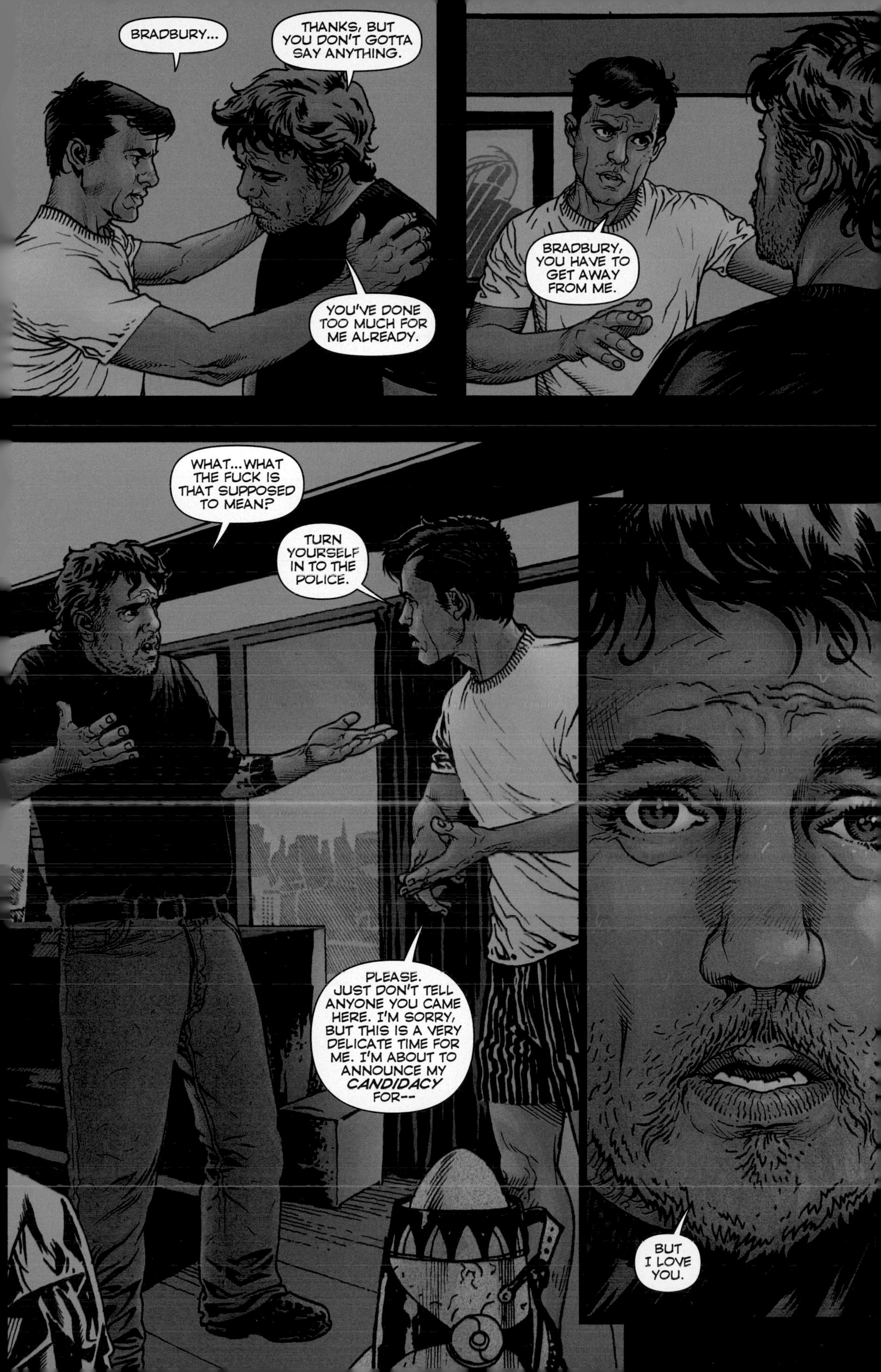
BRADBURY...
THANKS, BUT YOU DON'T GOTTA SAY ANYTHING.
YOU'VE DONE TOO MUCH FOR ME ALREADY.
BRADBURY, YOU HAVE TO GET AWAY FROM ME.
WHAT...WHAT THE FUCK IS THAT SUPPOSED TO MEAN?
TURN YOURSELF IN TO THE POLICE.
PLEASE. JUST DON'T TELL ANYONE YOU CAME HERE. I'M SORRY, BUT THIS IS A VERY DELICATE TIME FOR ME. I'M ABOUT TO ANNOUNCE MY CANDIDACY FOR--
BUT I LOVE YOU.

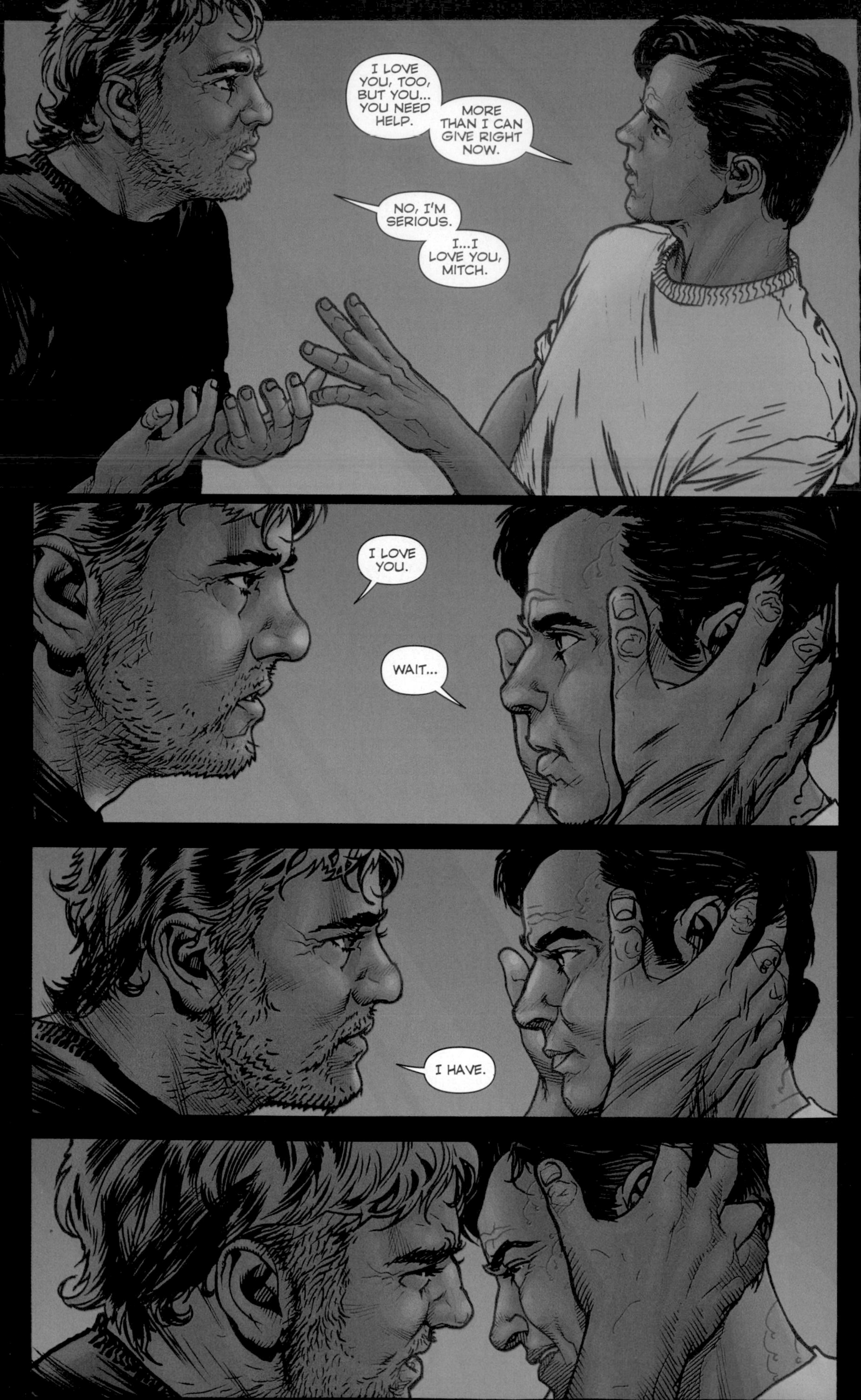
I LOVE YOU, TOO, BUT YOU... YOU NEED HELP.
MORE THAN I CAN GIVE RIGHT NOW.
NO, I'M SERIOUS.
I...I LOVE YOU, MITCH.
I LOVE YOU.
WAIT...
I HAVE.

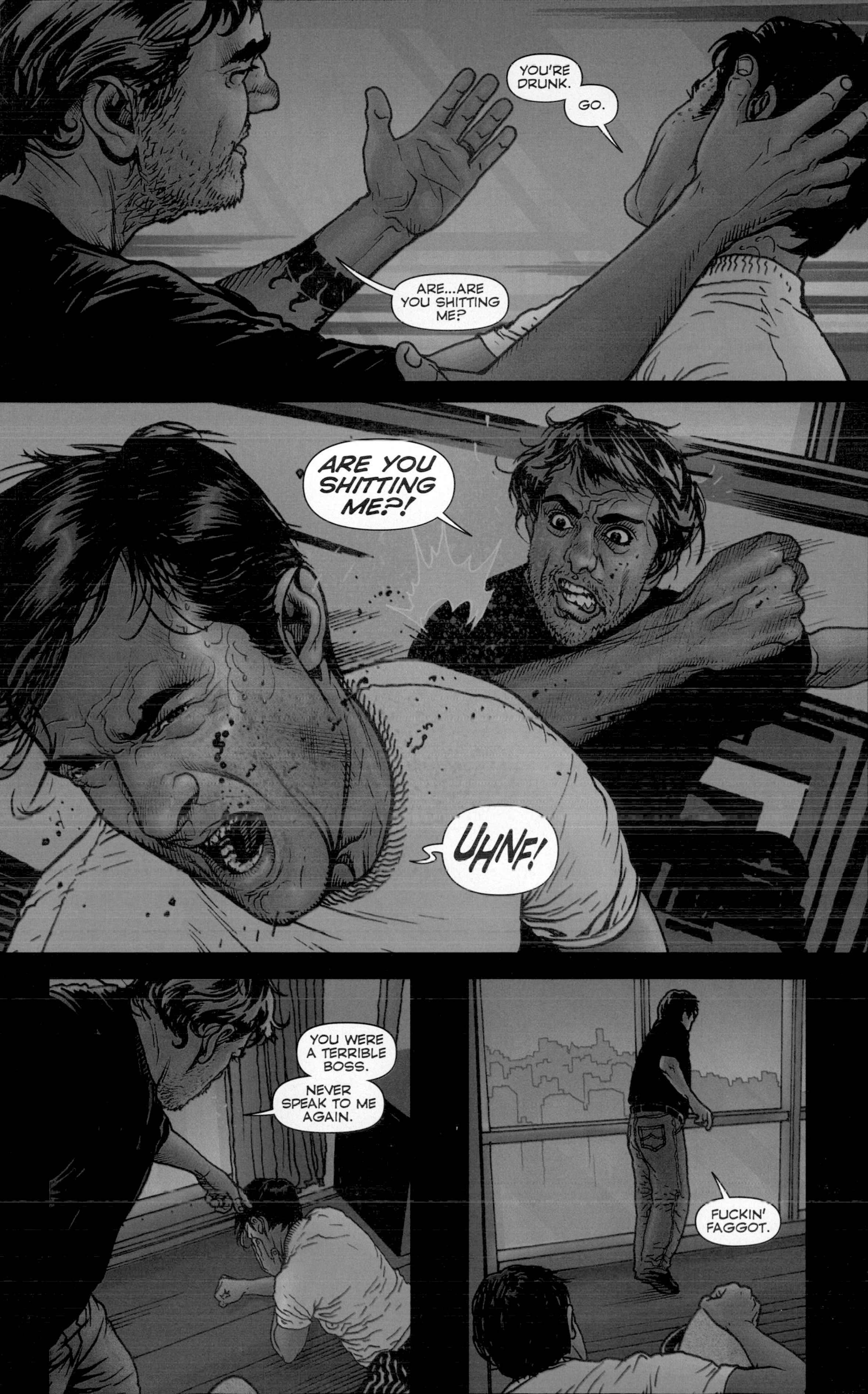
YOU'RE DRUNK.
GO.
ARE...ARE YOU SHITTING ME?
ARE YOU SHITTING ME?!
UHNF!
YOU WERE A TERRIBLE BOSS.
NEVER SPEAK TO ME AGAIN.
FUCKIN' FAGGOT.

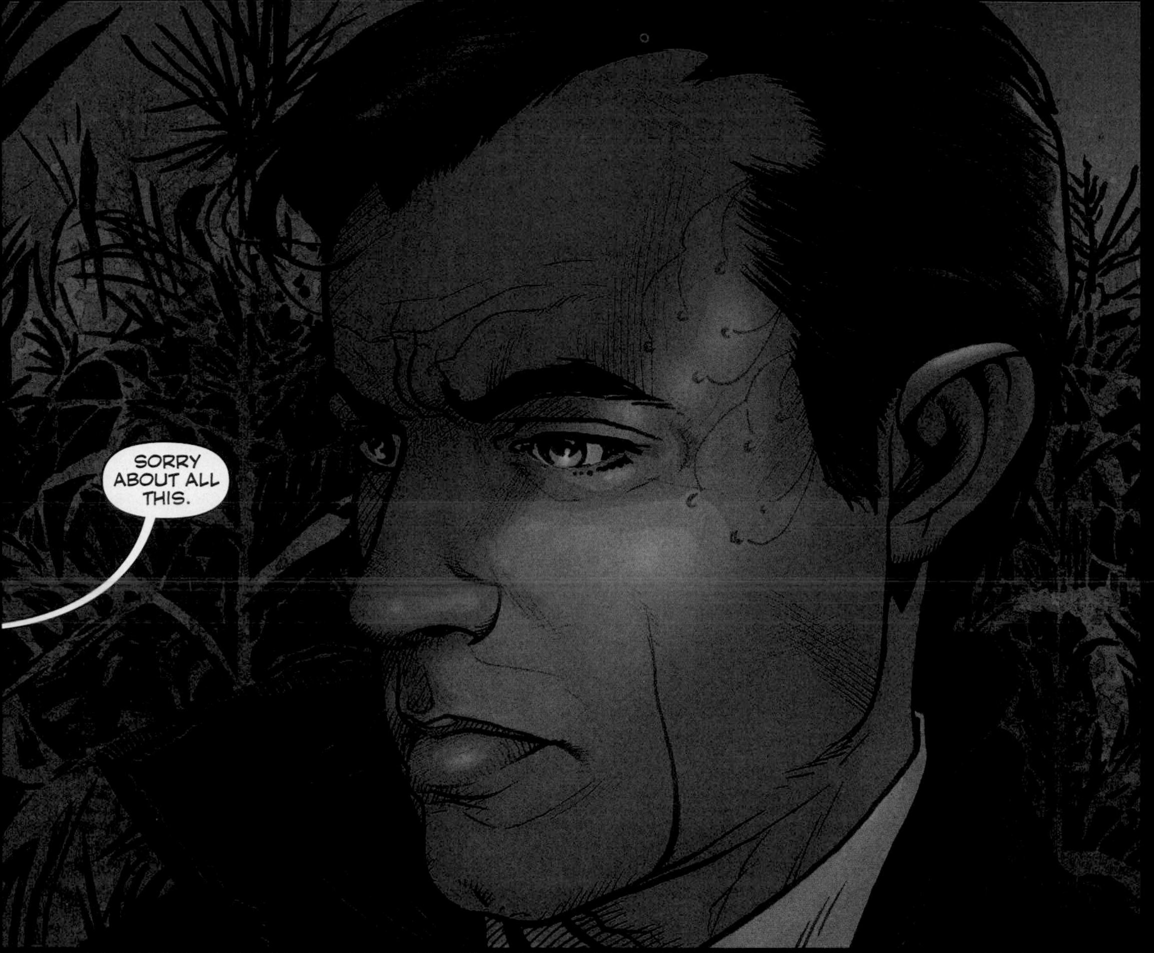
SORRY ABOUT ALL THIS.

WEDNESDAY, OCTOBER 31, 2007

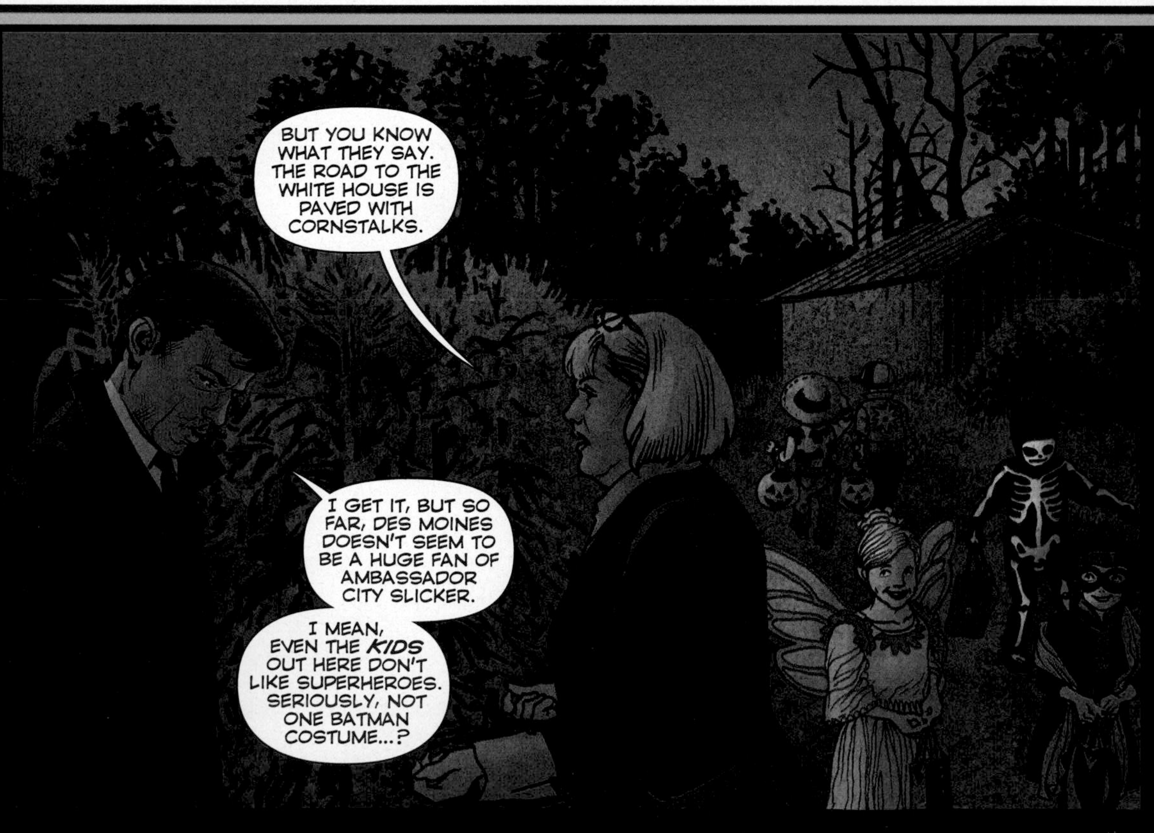
BUT YOU KNOW WHAT THEY SAY. THE ROAD TO THE WHITE HOUSE IS PAVED WITH CORNSTALKS.
I GET IT, BUT SO FAR, DES MOINES DOESN'T SEEM TO BE A HUGE FAN OF AMBASSADOR CITY SLICKER.
I MEAN, EVEN THE *KIDS* OUT HERE DON'T LIKE SUPERHEROES. SERIOUSLY, NOT ONE BATMAN COSTUME...?

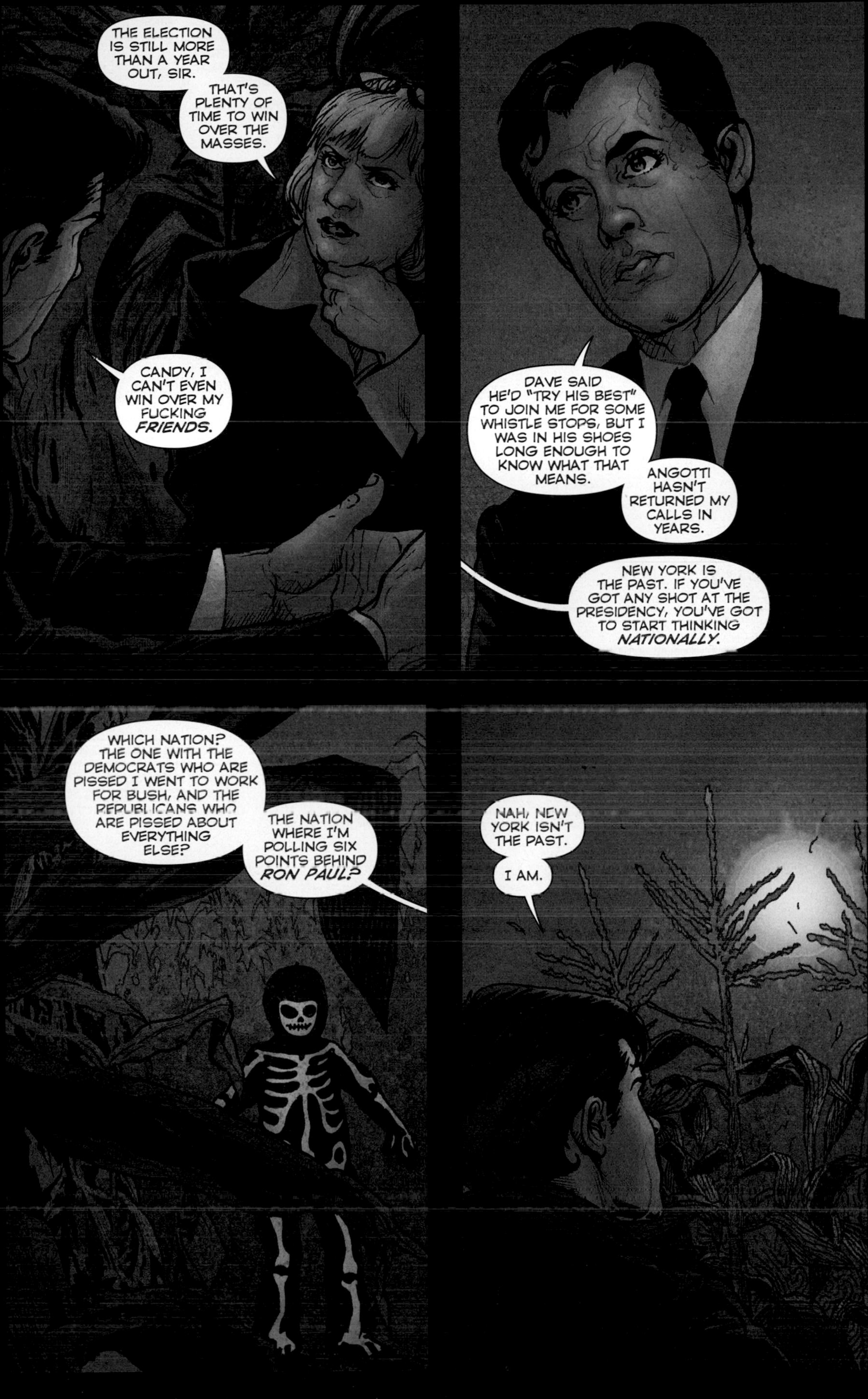
THE ELECTION IS STILL MORE THAN A YEAR OUT, SIR.
THAT'S PLENTY OF TIME TO WIN OVER THE MASSES.
CANDY, I CAN'T EVEN WIN OVER MY FUCKING *FRIENDS*.
DAVE SAID HE'D "TRY HIS BEST" TO JOIN ME FOR SOME WHISTLE STOPS, BUT I WAS IN HIS SHOES LONG ENOUGH TO KNOW WHAT THAT MEANS.
ANGOTTI HASN'T RETURNED MY CALLS IN YEARS.
NEW YORK IS THE PAST. IF YOU'VE GOT ANY SHOT AT THE PRESIDENCY, YOU'VE GOT TO START THINKING *NATIONALLY*.
WHICH NATION? THE ONE WITH THE DEMOCRATS WHO ARE PISSED I WENT TO WORK FOR BUSH, AND THE REPUBLICANS WHO ARE PISSED ABOUT EVERYTHING ELSE?
THE NATION WHERE I'M POLLING SIX POINTS BEHIND *RON PAUL?*
NAH, NEW YORK ISN'T THE PAST.
I AM.

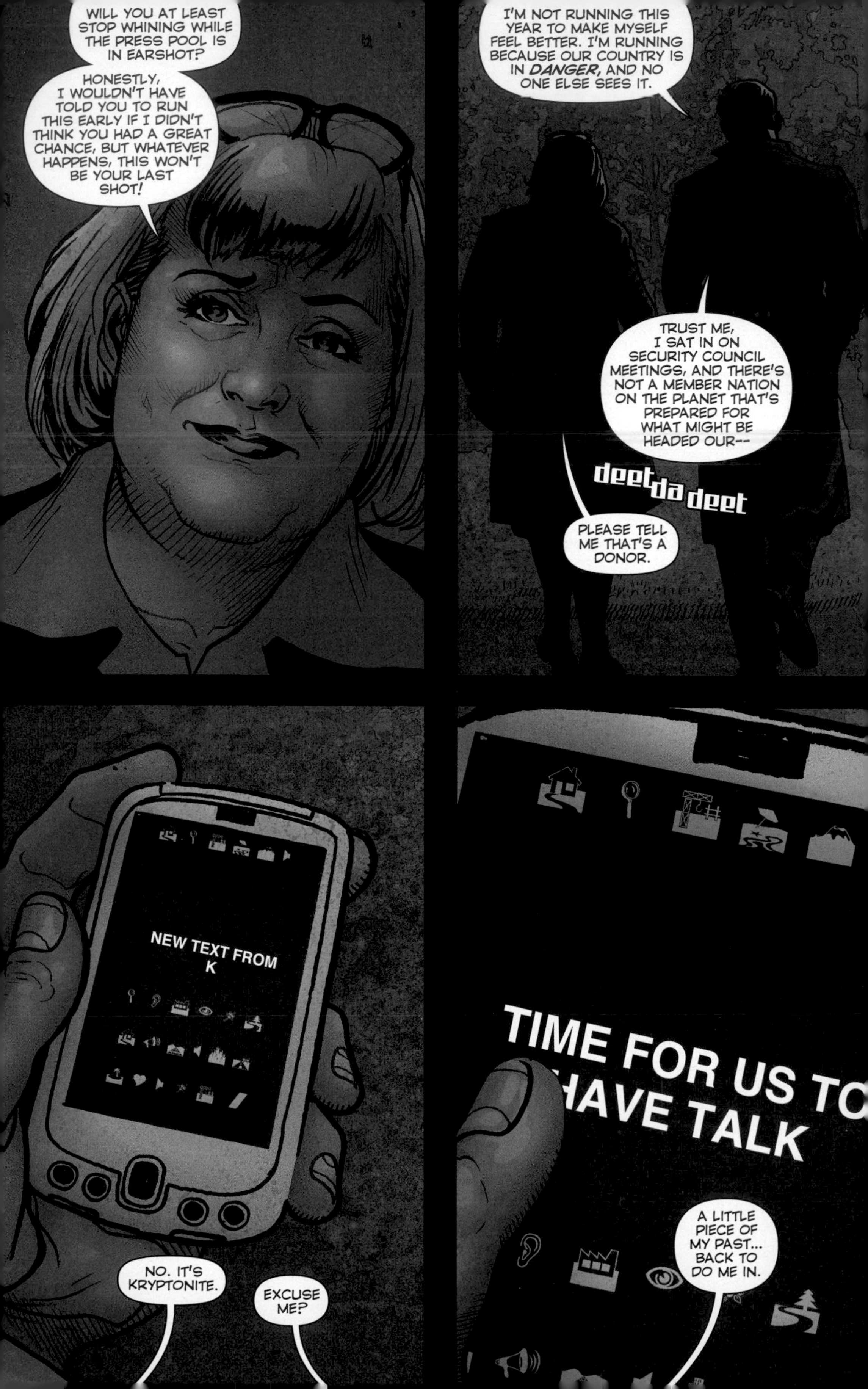
WILL YOU AT LEAST STOP WHINING WHILE THE PRESS POOL IS IN EARSHOT?
HONESTLY, I WOULDN'T HAVE TOLD YOU TO RUN THIS EARLY IF I DIDN'T THINK YOU HAD A GREAT CHANCE, BUT WHATEVER HAPPENS, THIS WON'T BE YOUR LAST SHOT!
I'M NOT RUNNING THIS YEAR TO MAKE MYSELF FEEL BETTER. I'M RUNNING BECAUSE OUR COUNTRY IS IN DANGER, AND NO ONE ELSE SEES IT.
TRUST ME, I SAT IN ON SECURITY COUNCIL MEETINGS, AND THERE'S NOT A MEMBER NATION ON THE PLANET THAT'S PREPARED FOR WHAT MIGHT BE HEADED OUR--
deet da deet
PLEASE TELL ME THAT'S A DONOR.
NEW TEXT FROM K
NO. IT'S KRYPTONITE.
EXCUSE ME?
TIME FOR US TO HAVE TALK
A LITTLE PIECE OF MY PAST... BACK TO DO ME IN.

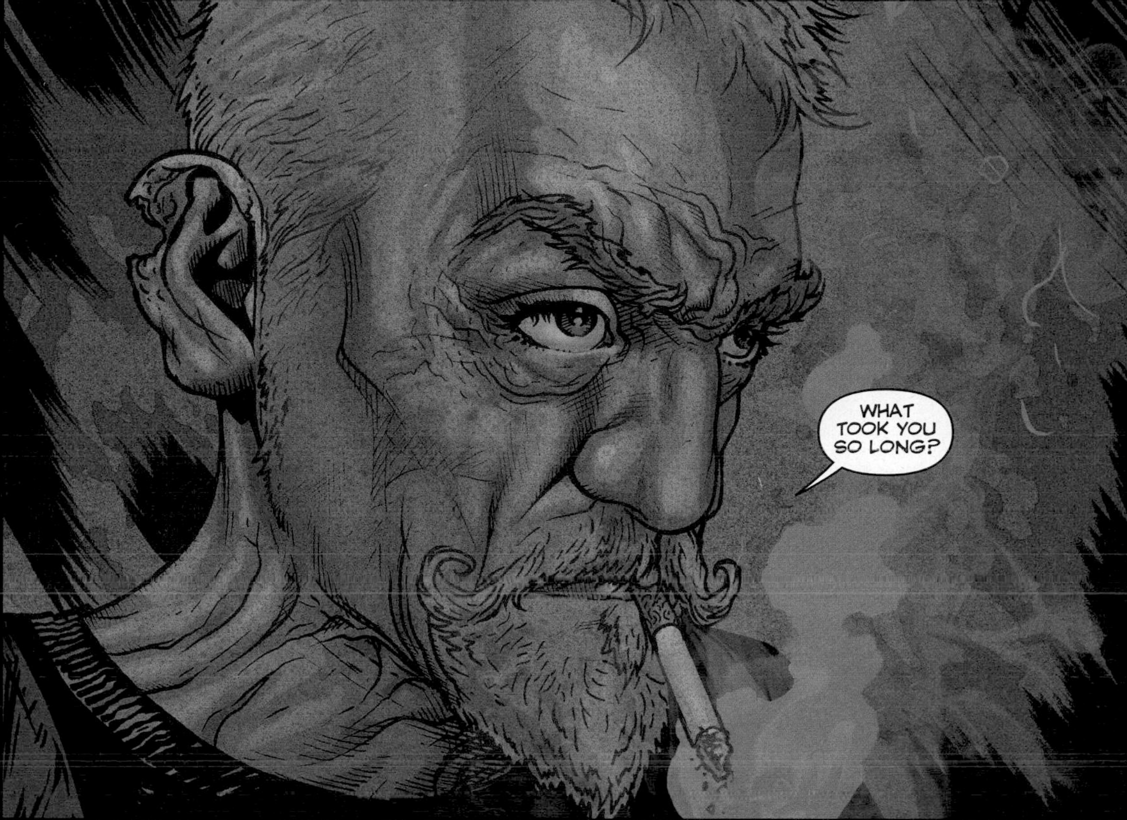
WHAT TOOK YOU SO LONG?

THURSDAY, JANUARY 17, 2008

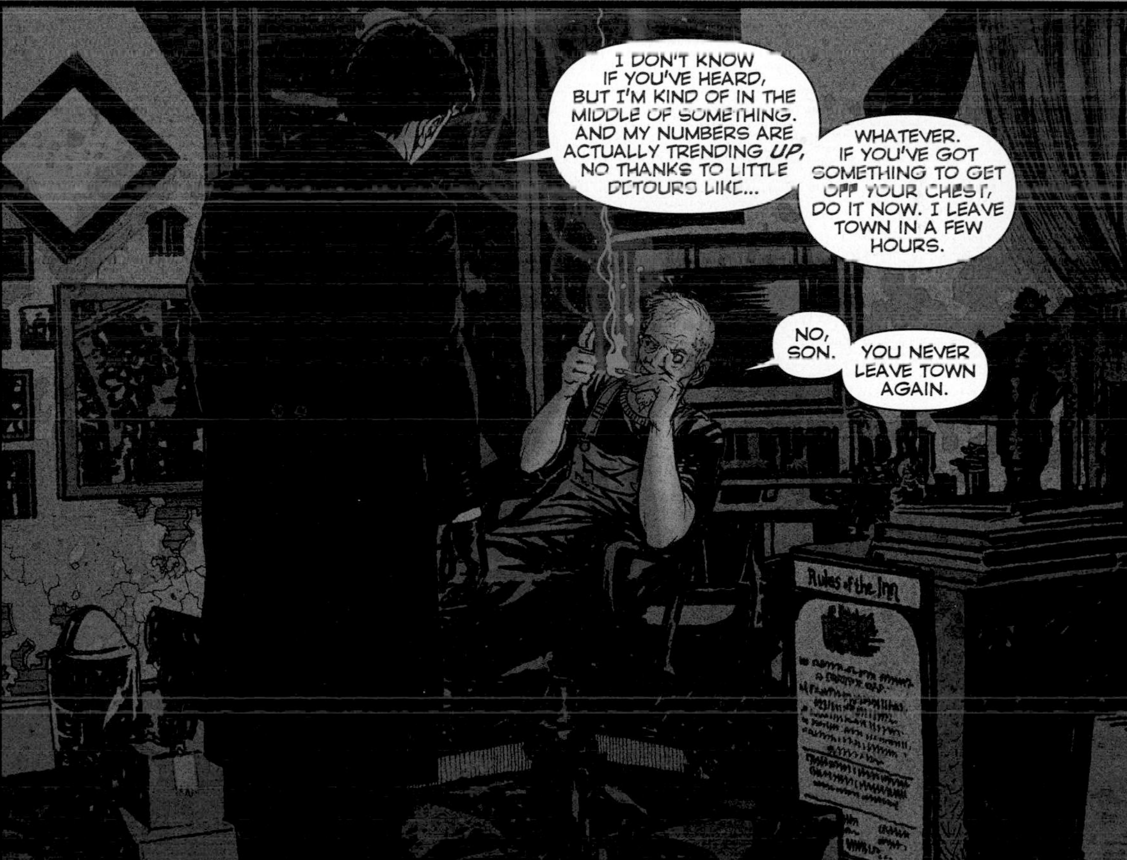
I DON'T KNOW IF YOU'VE HEARD, BUT I'M KIND OF IN THE MIDDLE OF SOMETHING. AND MY NUMBERS ARE ACTUALLY TRENDING *UP*, NO THANKS TO LITTLE DETOURS LIKE...
WHATEVER. IF YOU'VE GOT SOMETHING TO GET OFF YOUR CHEST, DO IT NOW. I LEAVE TOWN IN A FEW HOURS.
NO, SON.
YOU NEVER LEAVE TOWN AGAIN.
Rules of the Inn

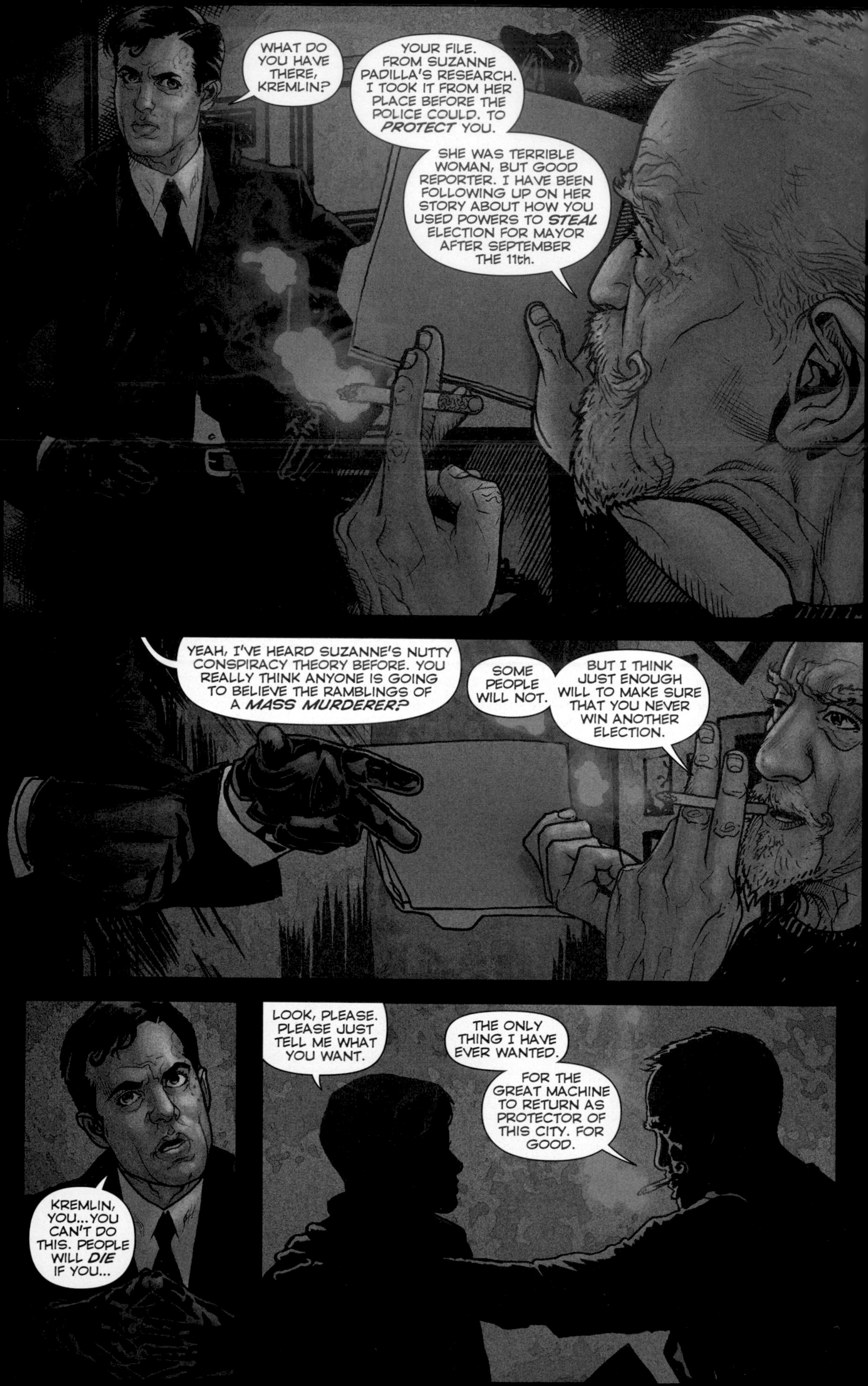
WHAT DO YOU HAVE THERE, KREMLIN?
YOUR FILE. FROM SUZANNE PADILLA'S RESEARCH. I TOOK IT FROM HER PLACE BEFORE THE POLICE COULD. TO PROTECT YOU.
SHE WAS TERRIBLE WOMAN, BUT GOOD REPORTER. I HAVE BEEN FOLLOWING UP ON HER STORY ABOUT HOW YOU USED POWERS TO STEAL ELECTION FOR MAYOR AFTER SEPTEMBER THE 11th.
YEAH, I'VE HEARD SUZANNE'S NUTTY CONSPIRACY THEORY BEFORE. YOU REALLY THINK ANYONE IS GOING TO BELIEVE THE RAMBLINGS OF A MASS MURDERER?
SOME PEOPLE WILL NOT.
BUT I THINK JUST ENOUGH WILL TO MAKE SURE THAT YOU NEVER WIN ANOTHER ELECTION.
KREMLIN, YOU...YOU CAN'T DO THIS. PEOPLE WILL DIE IF YOU...
LOOK, PLEASE. PLEASE JUST TELL ME WHAT YOU WANT.
THE ONLY THING I HAVE EVER WANTED.
FOR THE GREAT MACHINE TO RETURN AS PROTECTOR OF THIS CITY. FOR GOOD.

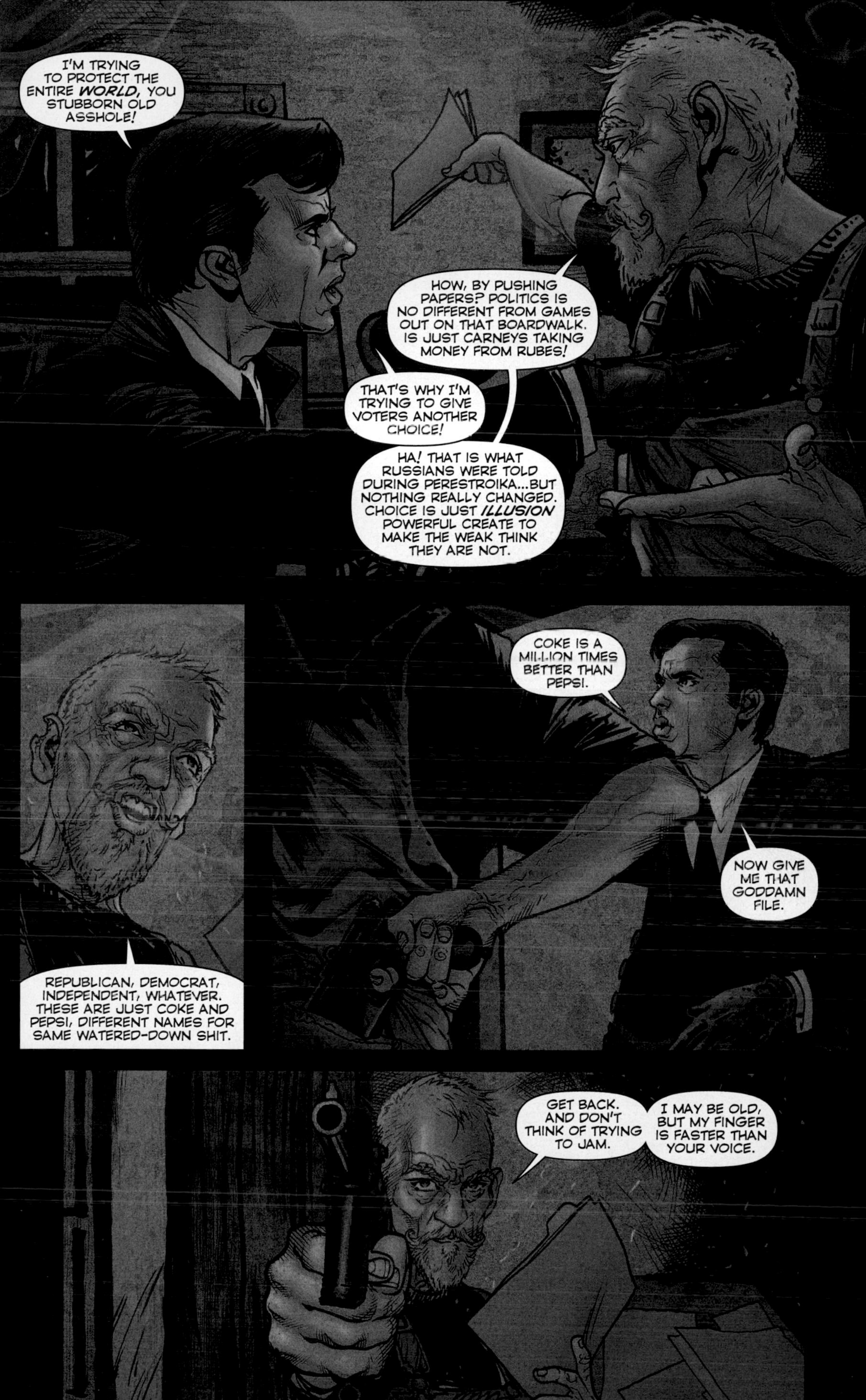

I'M TRYING TO PROTECT THE ENTIRE *WORLD*, YOU STUBBORN OLD ASSHOLE!
HOW, BY PUSHING PAPERS? POLITICS IS NO DIFFERENT FROM GAMES OUT ON THAT BOARDWALK. IS JUST CARNEYS TAKING MONEY FROM RUBES!
THAT'S WHY I'M TRYING TO GIVE VOTERS ANOTHER CHOICE!
HA! THAT IS WHAT RUSSIANS WERE TOLD DURING PERESTROIKA...BUT NOTHING REALLY CHANGED. CHOICE IS JUST *ILLUSION* POWERFUL CREATE TO MAKE THE WEAK THINK THEY ARE NOT.
REPUBLICAN, DEMOCRAT, INDEPENDENT, WHATEVER. THESE ARE JUST COKE AND PEPSI, DIFFERENT NAMES FOR SAME WATERED-DOWN SHIT.
COKE IS A MILLION TIMES BETTER THAN PEPSI.
NOW GIVE ME THAT GODDAMN FILE.
GET BACK. AND DON'T THINK OF TRYING TO JAM.
I MAY BE OLD, BUT MY FINGER IS FASTER THAN YOUR VOICE.

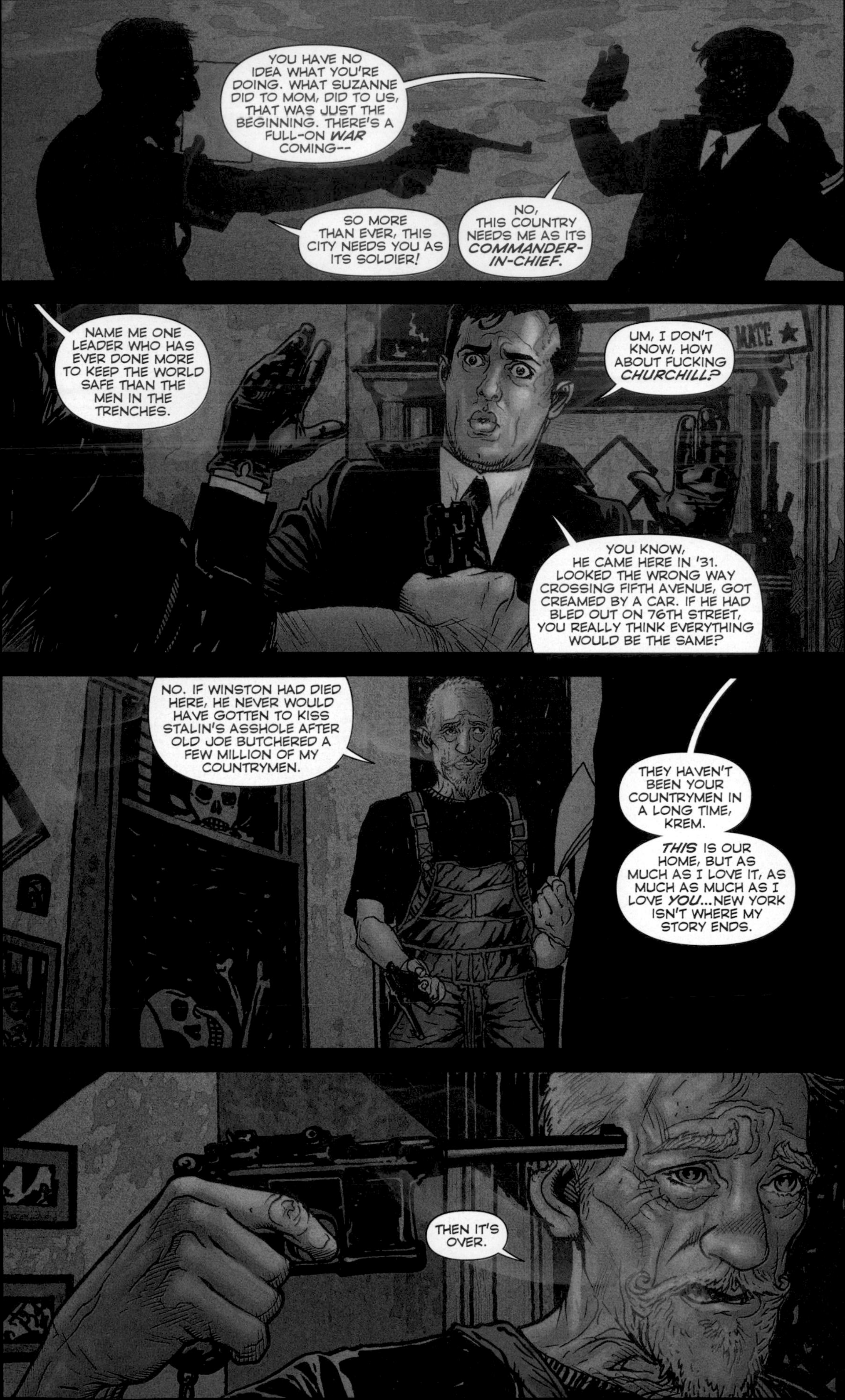
YOU HAVE NO IDEA WHAT YOU'RE DOING. WHAT SUZANNE DID TO MOM, DID TO US, THAT WAS JUST THE BEGINNING. THERE'S A FULL-ON *WAR* COMING--
SO MORE THAN EVER, THIS CITY NEEDS YOU AS ITS SOLDIER!
NO, THIS COUNTRY NEEDS ME AS ITS ***COMMANDER-IN-CHIEF.***
NAME ME ONE LEADER WHO HAS EVER DONE MORE TO KEEP THE WORLD SAFE THAN THE MEN IN THE TRENCHES.
UM, I DON'T KNOW, HOW ABOUT FUCKING ***CHURCHILL?***
YOU KNOW, HE CAME HERE IN '31. LOOKED THE WRONG WAY CROSSING FIFTH AVENUE, GOT CREAMED BY A CAR. IF HE HAD BLED OUT ON 76TH STREET, YOU REALLY THINK EVERYTHING WOULD BE THE SAME?
NO. IF WINSTON HAD DIED HERE, HE NEVER WOULD HAVE GOTTEN TO KISS STALIN'S ASSHOLE AFTER OLD JOE BUTCHERED A FEW MILLION OF MY COUNTRYMEN.
THEY HAVEN'T BEEN YOUR COUNTRYMEN IN A LONG TIME, KREM.
THIS IS OUR HOME, BUT AS MUCH AS I LOVE IT, AS MUCH AS MUCH AS I LOVE *YOU*...NEW YORK ISN'T WHERE MY STORY ENDS.
THEN IT'S OVER.

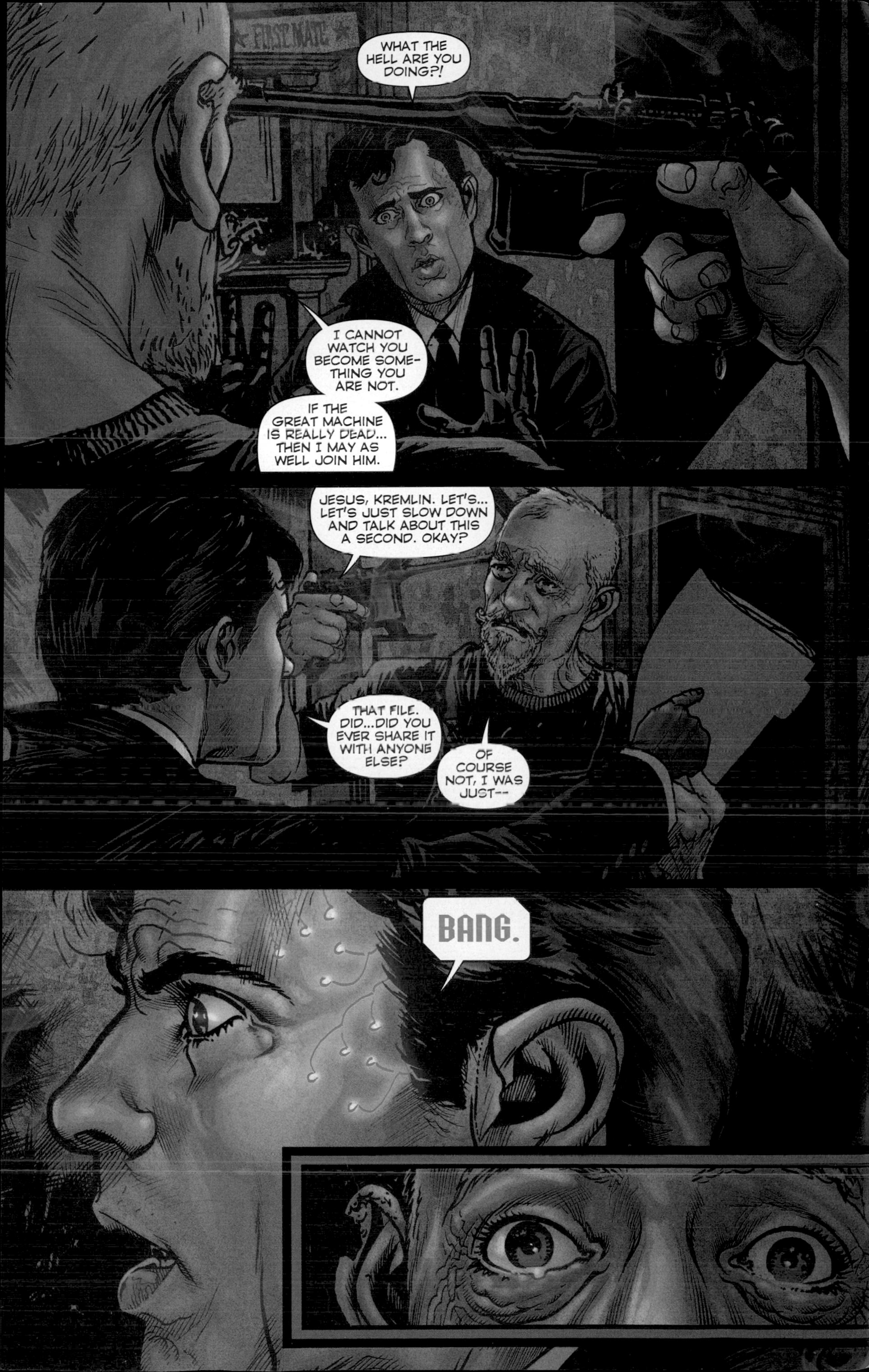
WHAT THE HELL ARE YOU DOING?!
I CANNOT WATCH YOU BECOME SOMETHING YOU ARE NOT.
IF THE GREAT MACHINE IS REALLY DEAD... THEN I MAY AS WELL JOIN HIM.
JESUS, KREMLIN. LET'S... LET'S JUST SLOW DOWN AND TALK ABOUT THIS A SECOND. OKAY?
THAT FILE. DID...DID YOU EVER SHARE IT WITH ANYONE ELSE?
OF COURSE NOT, I WAS JUST--
BANG.

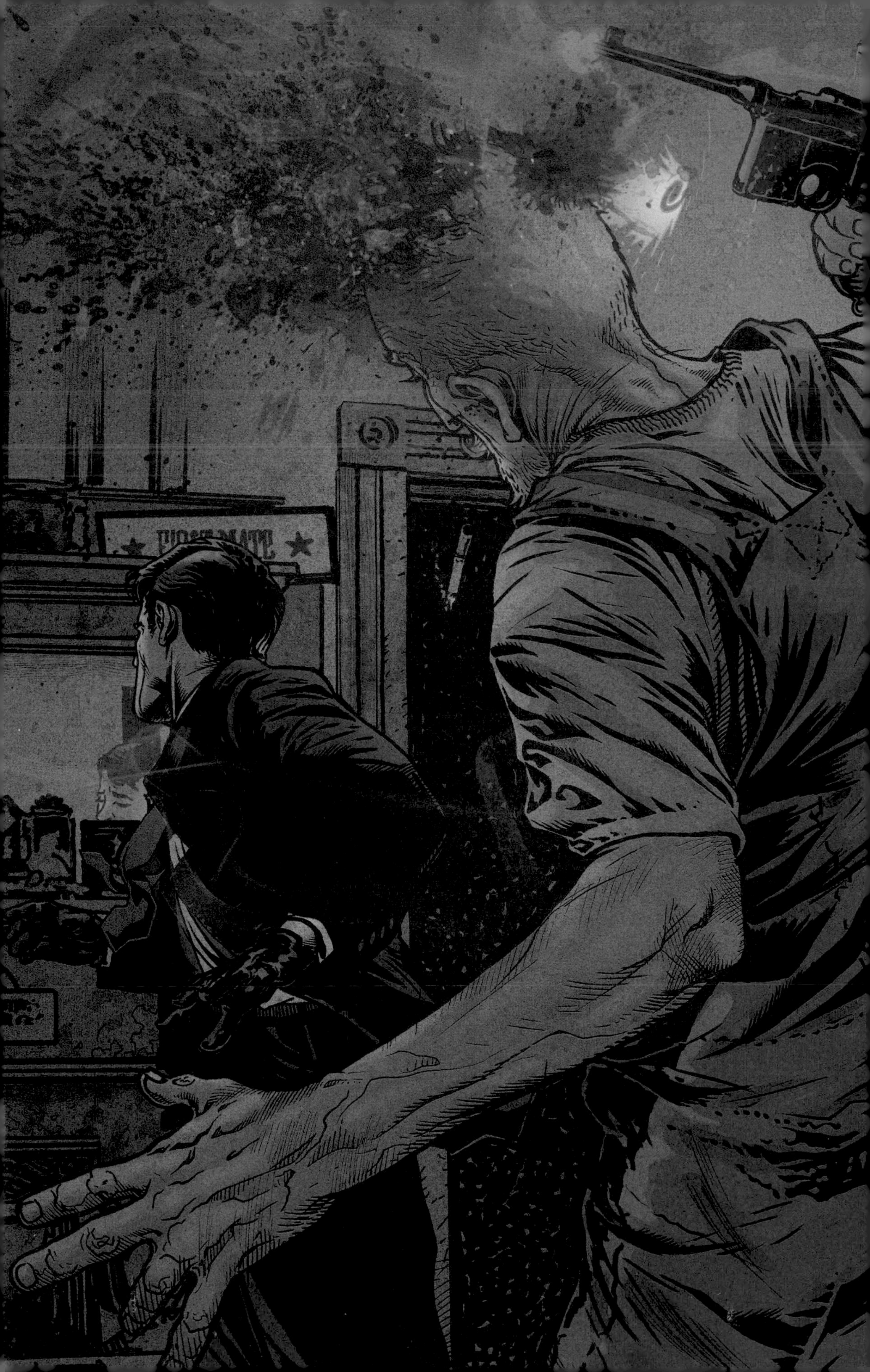

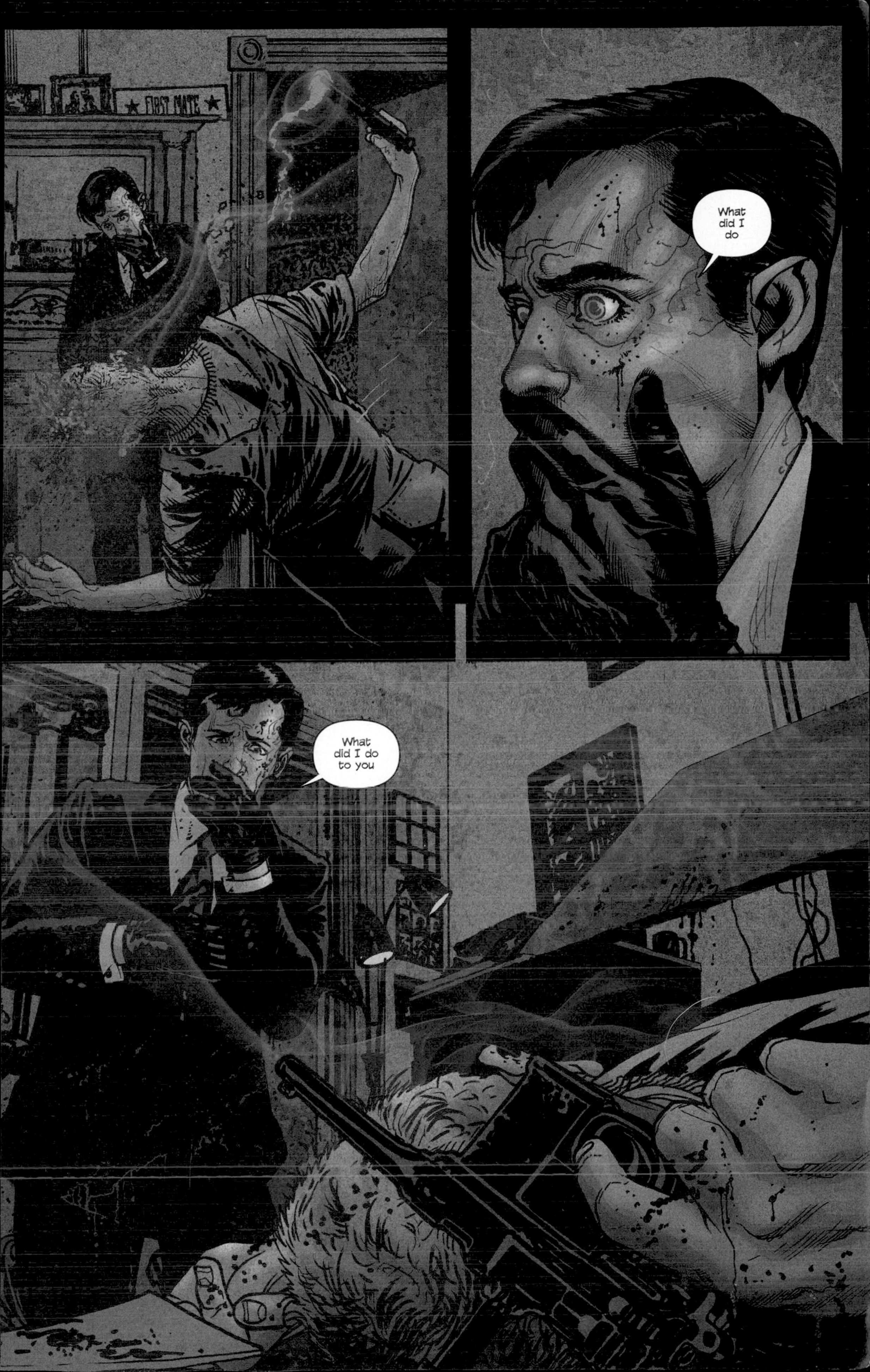
FIRST MATE
What did I do
What did I do to you

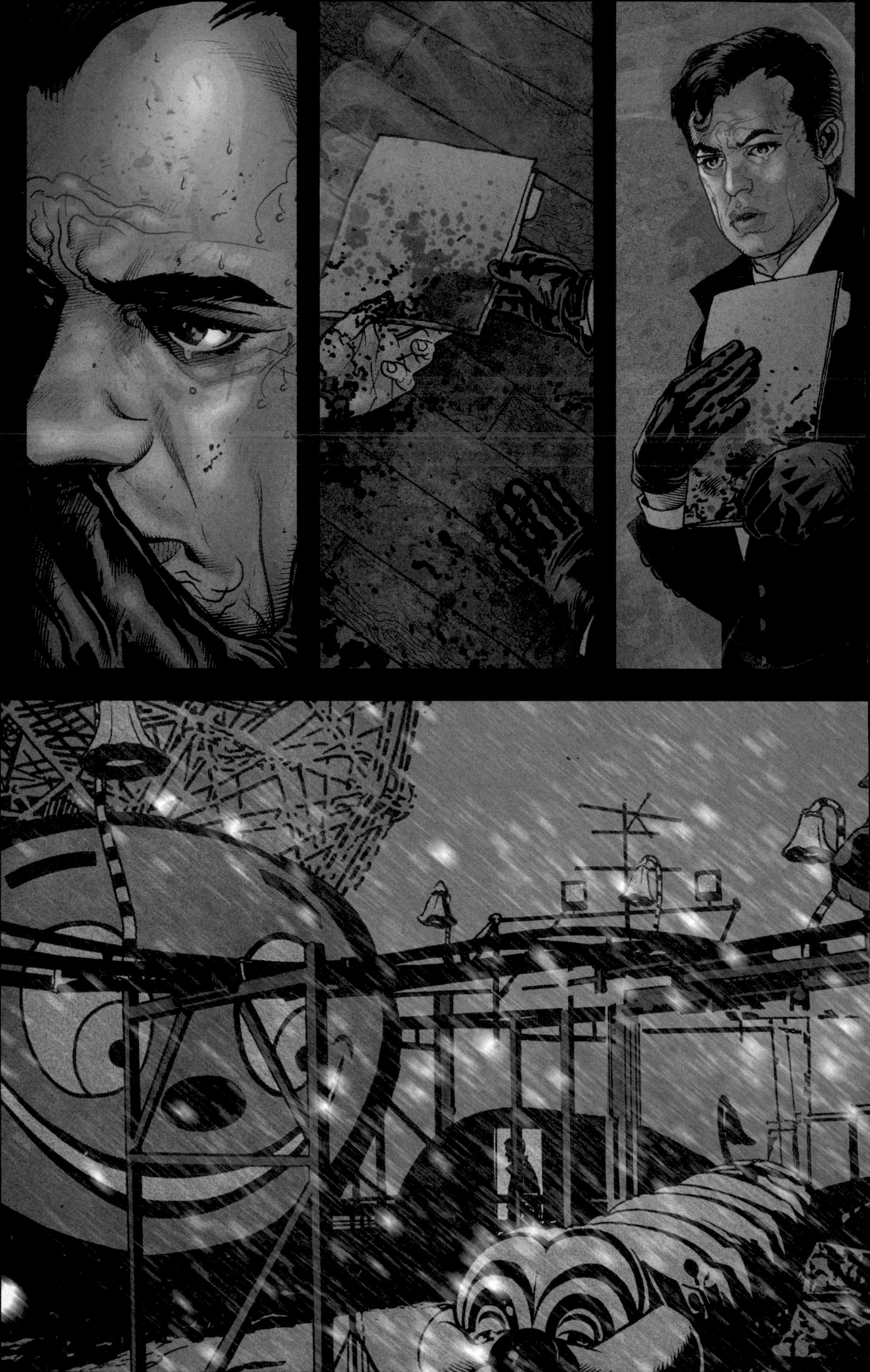

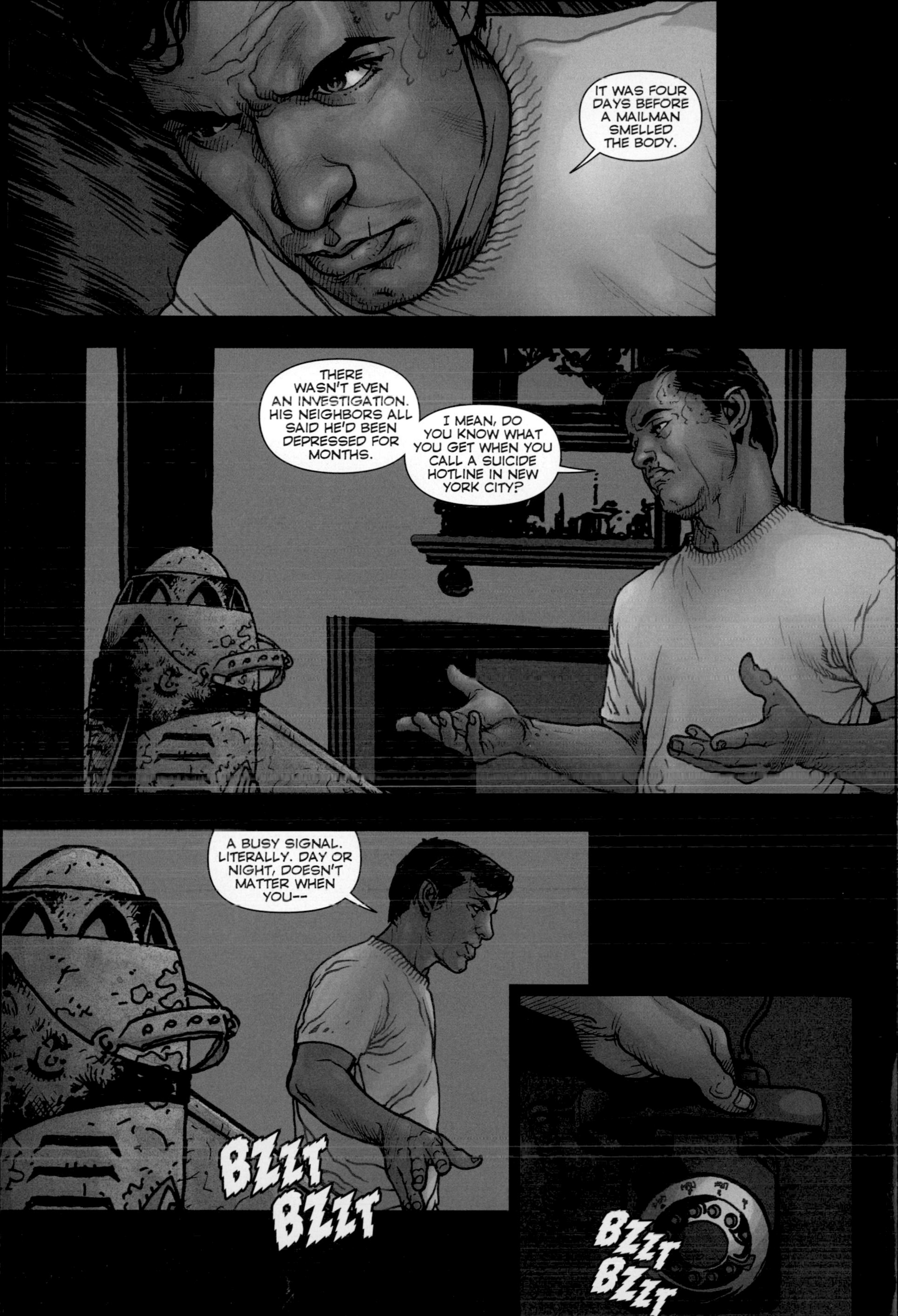
IT WAS FOUR DAYS BEFORE A MAILMAN SMELLED THE BODY.
THERE WASN'T EVEN AN INVESTIGATION. HIS NEIGHBORS ALL SAID HE'D BEEN DEPRESSED FOR MONTHS.
I MEAN, DO YOU KNOW WHAT YOU GET WHEN YOU CALL A SUICIDE HOTLINE IN NEW YORK CITY?
A BUSY SIGNAL. LITERALLY. DAY OR NIGHT, DOESN'T MATTER WHEN YOU--
BZZT BZZT
BZZT BZZT

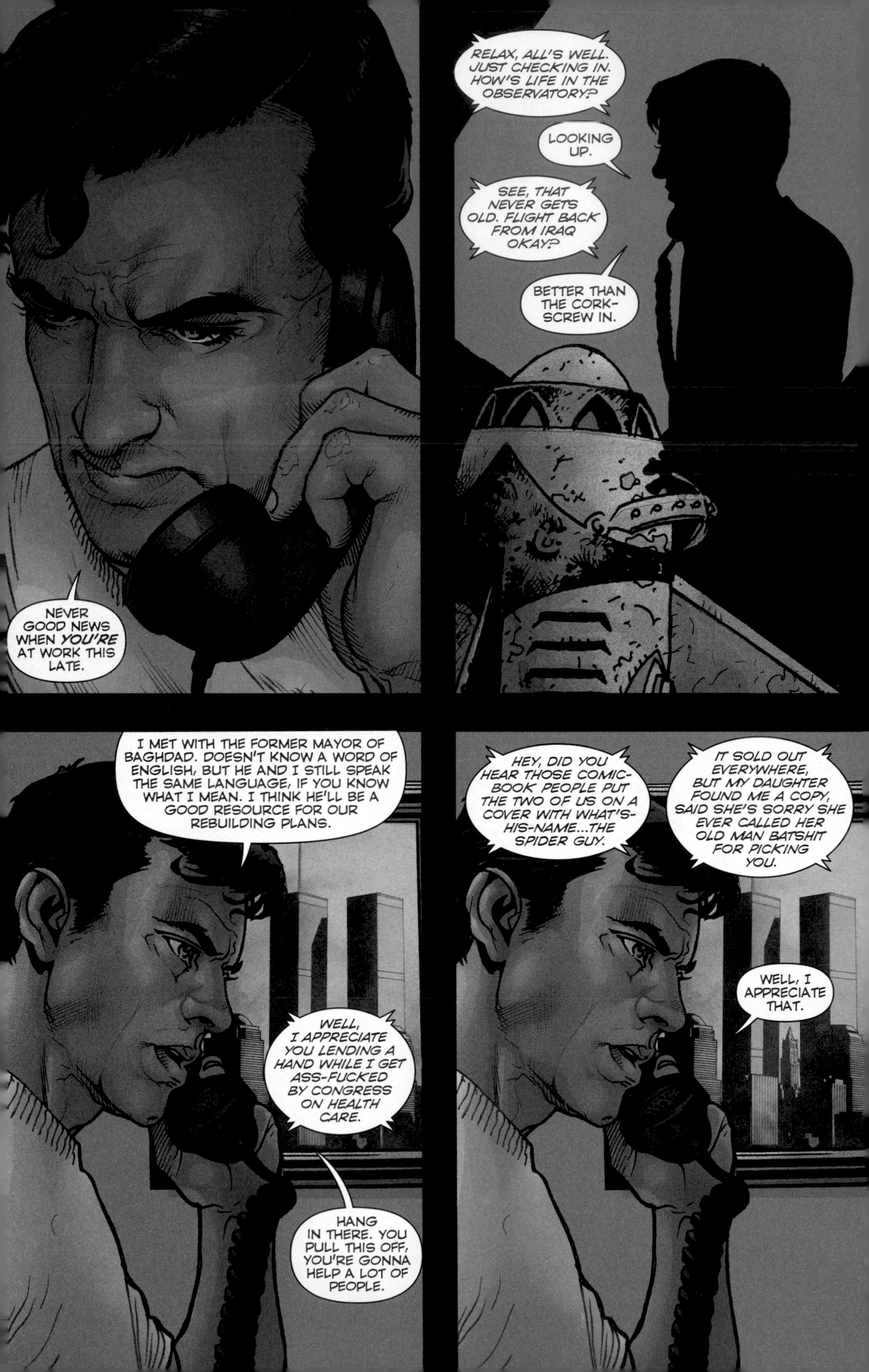
NEVER GOOD NEWS WHEN *YOU'RE* AT WORK THIS LATE.
RELAX, ALL'S WELL. JUST CHECKING IN. HOW'S LIFE IN THE OBSERVATORY?
LOOKING UP.
SEE, THAT NEVER GETS OLD. FLIGHT BACK FROM IRAQ OKAY?
BETTER THAN THE CORK-SCREW IN.
I MET WITH THE FORMER MAYOR OF BAGHDAD. DOESN'T KNOW A WORD OF ENGLISH, BUT HE AND I STILL SPEAK THE SAME LANGUAGE, IF YOU KNOW WHAT I MEAN. I THINK HE'LL BE A GOOD RESOURCE FOR OUR REBUILDING PLANS.
WELL, I APPRECIATE YOU LENDING A HAND WHILE I GET ASS-FUCKED BY CONGRESS ON HEALTH CARE.
HANG IN THERE. YOU PULL THIS OFF, YOU'RE GONNA HELP A LOT OF PEOPLE.
HEY, DID YOU HEAR THOSE COMIC-BOOK PEOPLE PUT THE TWO OF US ON A COVER WITH WHAT'S-HIS-NAME...THE SPIDER GUY.
IT SOLD OUT EVERYWHERE, BUT MY DAUGHTER FOUND ME A COPY, SAID SHE'S SORRY SHE EVER CALLED HER OLD MAN BATSHIT FOR PICKING YOU.
WELL, I APPRECIATE THAT.

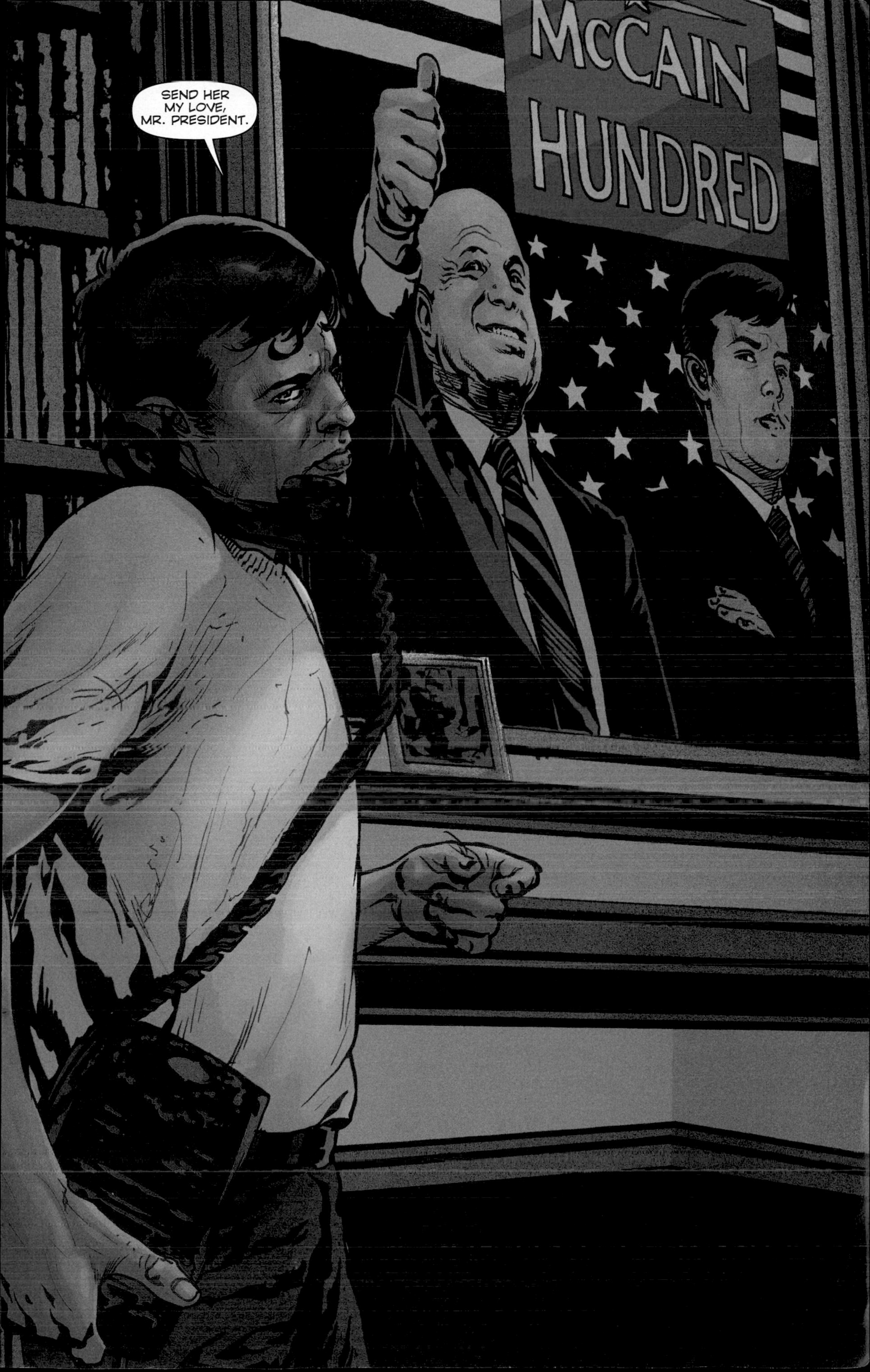
SEND HER MY LOVE, MR. PRESIDENT.
McCAIN HUNDRED

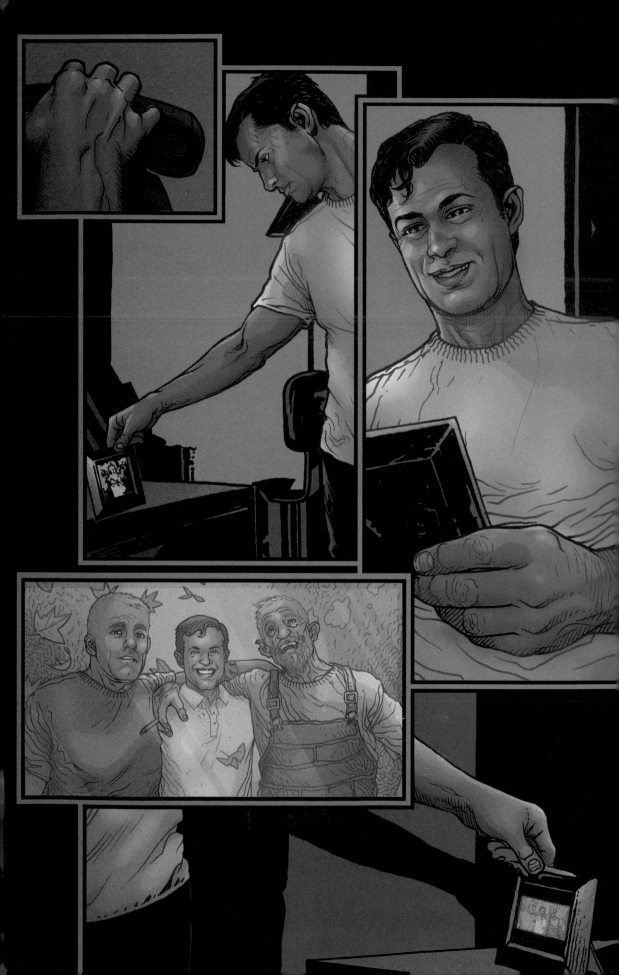

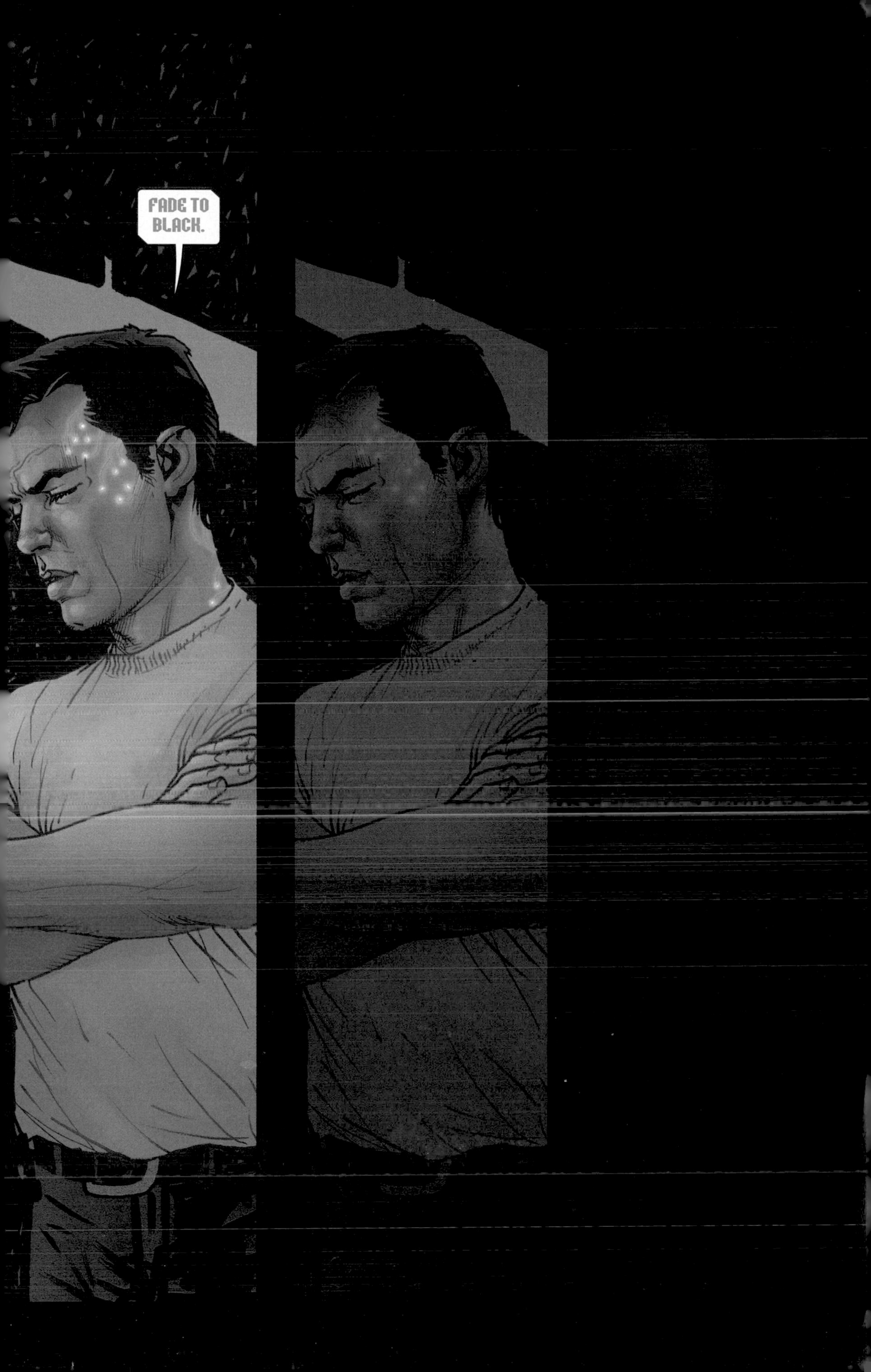
FADE TO BLACK.

VICE

BRIAN K. VAUGHAN *writer* **TONY HARRIS** *artist*

JD METTLER *colorist* **JARED K. FLETCHER** *letters*

KRISTY QUINN *assistant editor* **BEN ABERNATHY** *editor*

JIM LEE *variant cover*

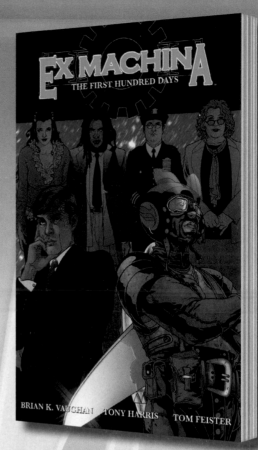